Library of
Davidson College

THE AUSTRALIAN NATIONAL ELECTIONS OF 1977

AEI's AT THE POLLS STUDIES

The American Enterprise Institute
has initiated this series in order to promote
an understanding of the electoral process as it functions in
democracies around the world. The series will include studies
of at least two national elections in each of nineteen countries
on five continents, by scholars from the United States and
abroad who are recognized as experts in their field.
More information on the titles in this series can
be found at the back of this book.

THE AUSTRALIAN NATIONAL ELECTIONS OF 1977

Edited by Howard R. Penniman

American Enterprise Institute for Public Policy Research
Washington, D.C.

Library of Congress Cataloging in Publication Data

Main entry under title:
The Australian national elections of 1977.

   (AEI studies ; 254)
   Includes index.
   1. Australia. Parliament—Elections—Addresses, essays, lectures.
2. Elections—Australia—Addresses, essays, lectures. 3. Australia—
Politics and government–1945-   —Addresses, essays, lectures.
I. Penniman, Howard Rae, 1916–   II. Series: American
Enterprise Institute for Public Policy Research.
AEI studies ; 254.
JQ4094.A82   329'.023'9406   79-22627
ISBN 0-8447-3357-1

AEI Studies 254

© 1979 by American Enterprise Institute for Public Policy Research,
Washington, D.C. All rights reserved. No part of this publication may
be used or reproduced in any manner whatsoever without permission
in writing from the American Enterprise Institute except in the case of
brief quotations embodied in news articles, critical articles, or reviews.

The views expressed in the publications of the American Enterprise Institute
are those of the authors and do not necessarily reflect the views of the staff,
advisory panels, officers, or trustees of AEI.

"American Enterprise Institute" is the registered service mark of the
American Enterprise Institute for Public Policy Research.

Printed in the United States of America

CONTENTS

PREFACE *Howard R. Penniman*

1 INTRODUCTION *David Butler* — 1
The Circumstances of the Election 3
A Dull Election—and a Surprising Outcome 7
The Issues 12
Conclusion 16

2 THE AUSTRALIAN ELECTORATE *David A. Kemp* — 19
The Distribution of Political Resources 20
A National Electorate 26
Changing Patterns of Electoral Loyalties 28
Social Structure and Partisan Loyalties 34
Partisanship and the Vote in 1977 44
Values, Beliefs, and Attitudes of the Australian Electorate 48
Conclusion 63

3 THE LABOR PARTY AND ITS 1977 CAMPAIGN *Patrick Weller* — 65
The Australian Labor Party: Theory and Practice 67
Labor, the Leadership, and Whitlam 69
The Perth Conference and the Labor Platform 74
The Prelude to the Campaign 77
Organizing the Campaign 78
The Policy Speech 80

The Campaign 82
  The New Leadership 85
  The End of Labor? 86
  Prospects for the Hayden Labor Party 88

4 THE LIBERAL-NATIONAL COUNTRY PARTY COALITION *Jean Holmes* 92

  Introduction 92
  The Coalition in Action 104
  The 1977 Election 110
  Australian Democracy and the 1977 Election Outcome 118

5 THE AUSTRALIAN DEMOCRATS *Paul Reynolds* 125

  The Emergence of the Australian Democrats 127
  The Democrats in the State Elections 129
  The National Elections 134

6 THE POLLS, THE PUBLIC, AND THE REELECTION OF THE FRASER GOVERNMENT *Murray Goot and Terence W. Beed* 141

  The Pre-Campaign Period, 1976–1977 142
  The Campaign Period 152
  The Issues and the Outcome 167

7 MONITORING THE PUBLIC, MARKETING THE PARTIES *Murray Goot* 185

  The Liberal Party 187
  The Labor Party 202
  The National Country Party 220
  The Minor Parties 223
  Final Observations 229

8 A LEAN CAMPAIGN FOR THE MEDIA *C. J. Lloyd* 231

  The Electoral Context 231
  The Media and the Issues 234
  Party Strategies 251
  Campaign Patterns 261
  Conclusion 264

9 THE ECONOMIC PROGRAM OF THE LIBERAL PARTY *Ainsley Jolley* 226

The Economic Policy of the Labor Government:
December 1975 to December 1977   266
The State of the Australian Economy, November 1977   272
The 1977 Election Campaign   275
Main Influences on the Fraser Government's Economic
Policy   278
Conclusions   287

10 THE ECONOMIC PROGRAM OF THE LABOR PARTY *Duncan Ironmonger* 288

The Platform   288
The Campaign   291
Labor and Economic Management   296

11 THE CASE OF THE ARRESTED PENDULUM *Colin A. Hughes* 299

The 1977 Redistribution   305
Competitiveness   310
Fairness   313
Preferential Voting   316
The Senate Count   322
The "Informal" Vote   327
Campaign Expenditures   327
Results   330

APPENDIX A   The Vote and the Count   333

APPENDIX B   How-to-Vote Cards   347

APPENDIX C   Australian National Election Results, 1977
Compiled by Richard M. Scammon   352

CONTRIBUTORS   357

INDEX   359

PREFACE

The Australian National Elections of 1977 is the second of two studies of Australian elections published by the American Enterprise Institute (AEI). It completes the first pair of volumes in the At the Polls series, which will eventually describe two national elections in each of nineteen countries on five continents.[1]

The series began with books on the 1974 parliamentary elections in Britain, Canada, and Japan and the presidential election in France the same year. Since that time AEI has published analyses of national elections in Scandinavia (Denmark, Norway, and Sweden), Italy, Ireland, India, Israel, and Germany as well as the first Australian book, on the national elections of 1975. Volumes are in progress on elections in Spain, Greece, New Zealand, Venezuela, and Colombia and on the election of representatives from nine countries to the European Parliament in 1979; a study of the 1979 Swiss elections is planned, and second volumes are under way for Japan, Britain, France, Italy, and the three Scandinavian countries.

The assumptions and goals underlying the series were outlined in the preface to the first volume, *Britain at the Polls*, published in 1974:

> Every political system is unique. Even very similar electoral institutions may produce different results when operating in countries with differing historical and cultural traditions.

---

[1] The democracies included in the series constitute 66 percent of the twenty-nine countries with populations of at least 3 million that were classified as "free nations" by the 1979 Freedom House annual "Survey of Freedom." Raymond D. Gastil, "The Comparative Survey of Freedom—IX," *Freedom at Issue*, no. 49 (January-February 1979), pp. 1-14. The list of free nations appears on page 14. This annual study, which rates all nations and dependent territories for the level of both political rights and civil liberties enjoyed by their people, is widely recognized as the most authoritative available comparative ranking. The list of free nations is based on the rankings for both political rights and civil liberties.

PREFACE

> Nonetheless, democratic electoral systems have enough in common that an understanding of the laws and practices of one democracy makes possible a more sophisticated analysis of the political institutions of others. By publishing descriptions of elections in a number of sometimes quite dissimilar democratic societies AEI hopes that it will provide its readers a better sense of democratic institutions at work and help to inform those working to improve existing electoral institutions and processes in many countries.

In practice, the project has indeed drawn attention to the great variety of electoral arrangements, political party systems, campaign styles, campaign financing laws, and so on, as well as to the electoral problems that are common to all or most democratic societies. And it has described experiences in other countries that are certainly relevant to the debates going on in the United States about proposed changes in American campaign rules and practices.

Candidate selection—a subject that has concerned American reformers for many years—is just one case in point. Everywhere but in the United States the nominating systems are governed primarily by internal party rules, not by public law, and in most parties participation in the nominating process is restricted either to a handful of leaders or to caucuses of dues-paying members. In Israel in 1977 a new "party of principle," the Democratic Movement for Change (DMC), rebelled against this state of affairs and vowed that, in order to ensure a more representative slate, its candidates would be chosen by a vote of all party members. They were, but the innovation backfired, embarrassing the party's leadership: not a single direct representative of the disadvantaged groups for whom the DMC aspired to speak was elected to a place on the ticket that carried any chance of winning.

Overall, an analysis of candidate selection in democracies other than the United States suggests that the greater the numbers involved in the process the weaker the influence of party leaders, not only over candidate selection but also over public policy. This finding, of course, fits with American experience in the use of the direct primary to select candidates for Congress and state offices and more recently in the decentralization of the process of selecting delegates to the presidential nominating conventions. If national and state party leaders are to control or even much influence the votes of members of Congress or state legislatures, the number of people participating in the nominating process must be restricted.

Aside from structural aspects of electoral systems, there are other strands connecting the experience of the democracies studied in the series. Inflation, often at a very high rate, faced virtually every one of them in the mid-1970s, sometimes accompanied by a serious increase in unemployment. In some countries unique local issues have had little effect on the electoral outcome, while in others they have dominated campaign debates. In 1975 the Australian candidates, for example, spent an enormous amount of time discussing the scandals of the Gough Whitlam government and the constitutional issues involved in its dismissal by the governor general. In Israel scandals and the ever-present foreign policy problems were important campaign issues and factors in the 1977 outcome, and India's parliamentary elections the same year were fought on the single issue of restoring democracy.

In all of the countries studied, except Britain and Canada in their 1974 elections, the voters elected, reelected, or strengthened relatively conservative political leaders and parties, and in 1979 both Britain and Canada chose distinctly more conservative governments. Opinion survey data suggest that middle-income voters, frightened by inflation with its threat to savings and standard of living, led the shift to more conservative governments. Despite inflation, conservatives were reelected, apparently because the voters feared that liberal or left solutions would make matters worse.

The Australian House and Senate elections of December 1977, which are discussed in this book, marked the fourth time in five years that Australian voters had been called upon to choose a national government. The prime minister was not forced to call the elections, as his predecessor had been in 1974 and 1975, but chose to do so a year early to preserve his advantage in the Senate for at least three more years and, perhaps equally important, to take his case to the voters before inflation, already high, became any worse. As David Butler notes in the introductory chapter, he also wished to hold the elections before the Labor party had rid itself of "what Malcolm Fraser saw as [its] greatest electoral handicap—the leadership of Gough Whitlam."

The reelection of the Liberal-National Country party coalition with virtually no loss of seats was, in Butler's view, the result of the voters' eagerness to defeat the tax program Labor had proposed and of their preference for Fraser over Whitlam. It was, he notes, "the smallest turnover in membership the House has known."

In spite of the very limited change in legislative membership and the voters' strong preference for Fraser over Whitlam, there were some voters who wished a plague on both major parties and threw their support instead to the newly created Australian Democrats

PREFACE

led by Don Chipp. According to Paul Reynolds in Chapter 5, the Australian Democrats "gave a focus to those who were increasingly dissatisfied with the course Australian politics had taken in the past five years." These voters liked some of the reforms pressed by the Labor party in the social, moral, and political arenas but doubted that party's ability to handle the basic economic difficulties of the day. On the other hand they felt that the Fraser government might handle the economic problems reasonably well but objected to its positions in other areas. The Australian Democrats received 9.4 percent of the votes in the House elections. Each of the major parties lost more than three percentage points from its share of the vote two years earlier.

In the concluding chapter Colin A. Hughes writes, the "two most remarkable features of the 1977 election—the performance of the Australian Democrats . . . and the unexpected absence of any real swing to the ALP—are both difficult to explain." The Australian Democrats drew votes from both major parties, unlike earlier large third parties, which, Hughes points out, drew their support primarily from one end of the political spectrum. What this means for the future of the Australian Democrats is uncertain. Equally uncertain, says Hughes, is whether new Labor leadership "will combine with a further deterioration in the economy to start the tide flowing again" in the direction of Labor candidates.

With the exception of Butler, who is at Oxford, the authors of these chapters are Australian scholars working at Australian universities. In addition to the three already mentioned, David A. Kemp analyzes the underlying character of the Australian electorate; Patrick Weller and Jean Holmes describe the campaigns of the Labor party and the Liberal-National Country party coalition; Terence Beed and Murray Goot discuss the role of opinion polls and marketing techniques in the election; Ainsley Jolley and Duncan Ironmonger assess the major parties' handling of the economic issues; and C. J. Lloyd looks at the campaign in the media. In the appendix Australia's complicated procedures for counting the votes are described in detail, and Richard M. Scammon provides a complete breakdown of the 1977 election returns.

HOWARD R. PENNIMAN

1
INTRODUCTION
David Butler

To students of comparative government, Australia is a country of quite exceptional interest. It offers one of the few textbook examples of a federal system that really works. For almost eighty years, six states have engaged in a civilized tug of war with the federal government—a government to which, as six independent colonies, they originally delegated some of their sovereignty. The central government has grown but there has never been any question of the states' losing their identity: Canberra does not loom as large in the thinking of most Australians as does their state capital (and over two-thirds of Australians actually live in a capital city).

Australia also offers a classic example of the Westminster model of government at work (or rather seven examples, if one allows for each of the states). All over the world democratic governments seem to derive primarily from Westminster or from Washington. Every country that Britain once ruled started out in independence with some variant of the Westminster model. Most lacked the infrastructure and the tradition needed to maintain one of its essential prerequisites—a competitive party system. But in Australia, as in Canada and New Zealand, the basic governmental arrangements that evolved over the centuries in Britain found fertile soil. With the passage of time, the plant has developed differently in different climates, but it is still recognizably the same species. A British political scientist asking British questions about the Australian system finds that almost all of his questions are relevant, even if the answers are often not British answers. Between Britain and the United States detailed comparisons seldom throw light on either system; the basic differences are too great. Between Britain (or Canada) and Australia, detailed comparisons are extraordinarily rewarding.

INTRODUCTION

The Australian electoral system has three characteristics that make it of peculiar interest to the student of government. It is the larger of the two democracies that enforce compulsory voting (Belgium is the other). It is the larger of the two democracies that employ the single-transferable-vote system of proportional representation (Ireland is the other). And it is the only democracy to use the alternative vote in single-member constituencies. The Australian experience with each of these devices knocks on the head many simplistic generalizations offered about them in discussions elsewhere.

Compulsory voting does not have much effect on the party balance but it does mean that election campaigns are designed to convert waverers; they are not primarily attempts to get the faithful to go and record their votes, as they so often are in other countries.

The single transferable vote,[1] which is used in Australian Senate elections, does not in fact break down a predominantly two-party system, nor does it mean that the power of party machines is threatened because electors can discriminate between the candidates of their own party: not once in the twelve elections since proportional representation was introduced in 1949 have voters in any state changed the order of candidates recommended by their party.

The alternative vote,[2] used for the Lower House since 1919, has basically left the two-party system and the relationship between votes and seats very much as they are in the first-past-the-post system of Britain, New Zealand, and Canada (not to mention the United States, India, and many other countries). Its main importance is that it has

---

[1] The single transferable vote (STV) requires the voter to rank all of the candidates in the multimember constituency in order of preference; each candidate who gets a quota of votes necessary to election has his surplus votes transferred to the candidates who come second on his ballot; then, if necessary, the candidates at the bottom of the poll are eliminated one by one and their votes are transferred to the designated second preferences, and so on. The single transferable vote has been favored by almost all English-speaking analysts of proportional representation—although Ireland has been the only country in the Northern Hemisphere to adopt it. It allows voters to choose candidates within parties as well as to choose between parties, and is supposed to give the parties representation in the legislature proportional to their strength in the country. It has not been used in the countries of Western Europe, which, though almost all addicted to proportional representation, have favored systems based on party lists. For a detailed description of the working of the single transferable vote in Australian Senate elections, see Appendix A.

[2] The alternative vote is a device intended to prevent votes from being wasted in a single-member-constituency system. The voters are required to rank the candidates in order of preference; if none gets a clear majority, the bottom candidate is eliminated and his votes are redistributed among the remaining candidates on the basis of second preferences; if there are several candidates this process will be continued until one candidate gets a clear majority. For further details see Appendix A.

occasionally allowed voters to settle disputes between Liberal and Country party coalition partners over who owns a constituency. Only once in the last thirty years has it allowed a minor party candidate (a Labor rebel) to get into the federal Parliament.

But Australian politics is interesting not just as an exhibition of electoral machinery. It also illustrates how some basic economic and democratic arguments are presented and reacted to within a substantial and prosperous Western society that is to a remarkable degree isolated from neighboring influences.

Australia today is less part of a world political system than it has ever been. It has complex trade relationships with an increasing number of countries and its prosperity is tied to world conditions. But having belatedly cut the apron strings that tied it to Britain, and having since 1972 distanced itself from the United States, Australia is to a unique degree isolated. Ten years ago Britain was part of its frame of reference; one could follow the British political scene in the Australian press. That is no longer true; Australian newspapers carry plenty of foreign stories, but no country, not even the United States, is covered fully or systematically enough for an Australian to know what is going on without referring to overseas journals. New Zealand is humiliatingly ignored, while Japan, Indonesia, and other Pacific countries are not reported on or empathized with. Australia simply does not follow the affairs of its neighbors in the way that the major European countries do.

All this is quite natural. Australia is a long way from other countries and particularly from countries with a Western cultural background. It is not, in the short or medium run, under any possible military threat. It is now, perhaps more than ever, a lucky country, rich in primary products needed by the rest of the world, moderately self-sufficient, secure, and, by any past standards, prosperous. If any country can afford to be inward-turning, Australia can.

The Circumstances of the Election

In December 1977 Australia faced its fourth federal election in five years. Two Parliaments had been brought abruptly to an end after eighteen-month terms and now one was dissolved after two years.[3] Americans with their biennial elections might not consider this exceptional—yet there is no doubt that Australians felt in 1977 that they had suffered from a surfeit of politics. They voted for the outcome that gave most prospect of relative quiescence.

---

[3] Within the same period most Australians had had to vote in two state elections as well.

INTRODUCTION

The Shadow of 1975. The 1977 election can only be understood against the background of the recent past. The 1975 crisis had been the most spectacular confrontation in Australian political history. In December 1972 the Labor party, led by Gough Whitlam, came to office after twenty-three years in the wilderness. But it lacked a majority in the Senate. In April 1974 the Liberal party used its Senate strength to challenge the Labor government and force it to appeal to the voters halfway through the normal three-year term. But Labor won reelection. In October 1975, in a much more unfavorable economic climate, when the Labor party was under serious challenge for its handling of a projected foreign loan, the opposition struck again. The Senate refused to consider the routine granting of "supply," the appropriations necessary for everyday government operations, until the government promised an election. Whitlam decided to "tough it out" and proposed various unconventional means of financing the public service (civil service). On November 11, 1975, the governor general, Sir John Kerr, resolved the crisis by dismissing Gough Whitlam and asking Malcolm Fraser, the new Liberal leader, to form a caretaker administration while an election was held. On December 13, the Australian voters gave an overwhelming majority to the Liberal-Country party coalition in both House and Senate.

The 1975 crisis was an affair of extraordinary constitutional and political complexity. It represented a challenge to the idea that the House of Representatives was the sole body to which an Australian government is responsible. Whether the Senate was within its rights in refusing supply and whether the governor general was within his rights in dismissing a government were questioned, not just by partisans but by respected constitutional authorities. All kinds of procedural issues, such as the filling of Senate vacancies, the interpretation of the Audit Act, and the position of the speaker, assumed a significant place in the argument. And above all these was a wider political issue: was the whole saga to be seen as an establishment conspiracy designed to frustrate a left-wing government in its mission of reform?

The events of 1975 have produced a great quantity of academic and polemic literature, and there is no need to go into the arguments here. But it is important to realize that what happened on Remembrance Day, 1975, had had a shattering impact.[4] The governor

---

[4] Remembrance Day is the Australian name for Armistice Day, November 11—the date of the governor general's dismissal of Prime Minister Whitlam. For fuller discussion of the crisis see Howard R. Penniman, ed., *Australia at the Polls: The National Elections of 1975* (Washington, D.C.: American Enterprise Institute,

general was shunned by the whole Labor party and could not appear in public without provoking violent demonstrations. Fraser and his government were seen by many as lacking true legitimacy, having come to office by an illegal trick. On the other side, Whitlam and his colleagues were remembered by many as an incompetent government which had had to be dismissed and which had then, in a thoroughly unsporting way, refused to accept the umpire's decision.

Yet it was not the events of Remembrance Day but the management of the economy that had dominated the Liberals' 1975 campaign. They had asked for a mandate to set things right after the spendthrift Whitlam era. What happened in 1976 and 1977 did not, however, give them much to boast about. Unemployment rose and inflation continued at a record rate; despite a devaluation of the currency, the country's trading position deteriorated. The opinion polls, which throughout 1976 had confirmed the resounding verdict against Labor of December 1975, by October 1977 showed Labor neck and neck with the government.

Synchronizing House and Senate Elections. Under the Constitution the maximum term of the House of Representatives is three years. Moreover, Fraser had also to face an election for half the seats in the Senate by June 1978.[5] All through the 1960s, House and Senate elections had been out of phase with each other; the half-Senate elections had turned into anti-government plebiscites, and in 1977 Fraser was plainly reluctant to face a rebuff from the voters a few months before the real test was due. He tried to escape from the dilemma by putting to a nationwide referendum a proposal that half-Senate elections be automatically synchronized with House elections, but, despite a 62 percent "yes" vote, he failed to get a majority in a majority of states: the smaller states were afraid of anything that could reduce their blocking power

---

1977); G. Sawer, *Federation Under Strain* (Melbourne: Melbourne University Press, 1977); Gareth J. Evans, ed., *Labor and the Constitution* (Melbourne and London: Heineman, 1977); Laurie Oakes, *Crash Through or Crash: The Unmaking of an Australian Prime Minister* (Melbourne: Drummond, 1975); and Paul Kelly, *The Unmaking of Gough* (Sydney: Angus & Robertson, 1975). See also the accounts by the principal actors themselves: Sir John Kerr, *A Matter of Judgment* (Melbourne: Macmillan, 1978) and Gough Whitlam, *The Truth of the Matter* (Melbourne: Penguin, 1979).

[5] Under Article 13 of the Constitution half the Senate has to stand for election every three years, and those who are elected take up their seats on July 1. Over most of this century, Senate elections have coincided with the end of House terms and Australians have voted simultaneously for all the M.P.s and half of the senators. In December 1975 (for only the fourth time in Australian history) there was a double dissolution and the whole Senate came up for election. Each state elected ten senators; the five who got fewest votes had to come up for reelection before three years elapsed, that is, by July 1, 1978.

INTRODUCTION

in the Senate (where they were so heavily overrepresented).[6] After this disappointment, Fraser found the attractions of holding the House elections at least before the middle of 1978 great.

But he had two other inducements to break the strong Australian tradition of allowing Parliament to serve its full three-year term. On the one hand, the economic situation might get still worse. Even if inflation slowed down, it would still be very high, while employment and trade figures were unlikely to improve. On the other hand, the Labor party might get rid of what Malcolm Fraser saw as their greatest electoral handicap—the leadership of Gough Whitlam.

Gough Whitlam and Malcolm Fraser happen to be the two tallest men in the Australian Parliament. They have also dwarfed their colleagues in political terms. Whitlam, a lawyer from a lawyer's family, quickly rose to the top in the Australian Labor party after entering Parliament at the age of thirty in 1952; he became its deputy leader in 1959 and its leader in 1967. Under him the party recovered from the total disarray of the 1966 election to the clear victory in 1972. He was an orator of style and skill and a man of vision and large ideas. But in office, he showed no special skill in administration or in the handling of his party caucus. His arrogant approach was held partly to blame for the disasters that befell his government.

Malcolm Fraser, the son of a wealthy grazier, entered Parliament at twenty-five in 1955. By 1966 he had been given a position in the government and in 1968 he received rapid promotion from the new prime minister, John Gorton. But he quarrelled with Gorton and led the coup that drove him from office. Early in 1975, at a second attempt, he snatched the leadership of the Liberal party from Bill Snedden. The great Sir Robert Menzies who retired in 1966 had headed the party for twenty-one years: in the next nine years four

---

[6] The results of the referendum on simultaneous elections held May 21, 1977, were as follows:

State	Votes Cast	"Yes"
"Yes" Majority		
New South Wales	3,008,000	71
Victoria	2,253,000	65
South Australia	799,000	66
"No" Majority		
Queensland	1,241,000	48
Western Australia	682,000	48
Tasmania	259,000	34
Australia	8,242,000	62

A referendum must be approved by four of the six states to pass. The two territories (the Northern Territory and the Australian Capital Territory) have never voted in referendums. However in another referendum on May 21, 1977, all six states voted in favor of their doing so in the future (77 percent "yes").

men tried and failed to establish their authority. It was left to Malcolm Fraser to show that it could be done. Fraser had all the arrogance of Whitlam but none of his eloquence or humor. His cool handling of the 1975 crisis that brought him and his party back to power, as well as his assiduity, his ruthlessness, and his administrative talents, quickly made him a dominant if not a popular figure.

As 1977 advanced, Fraser was well aware that he might not long have Gough Whitlam to kick about. In a vote in the Labor caucus in May Whitlam had only defeated a challenge from Bill Hayden, the quiet, respected former treasurer, by thirty-two votes to thirty. In the new year Hayden might well displace his old leader.

Hayden, although a senior member of the 1972–1975 government, was notably free from association with its failures. Whitlam, still a giant-sized figure, symbolized the reckless exuberance of those Labor years which had coincided with the coming of the worldwide slump. Fraser, who had no great reserves of personal popularity to draw on, shrank from the possibility of a contest with a likable Hayden in the honeymoon period usually given to a new leader.

So on October 24, 1977, Fraser called an election, citing as a reason only the desirability of getting House and Senate contests into phase.

A Dull Election—and a Surprising Outcome

A "no change" election looks dull in the history books, but it may still be a major landmark. The outcome on December 10 confirmed some basic facts about the Australian scene, facts that had been in doubt as little as two weeks before when the polls seemed for a moment to indicate a cliffhanger or even a Labor victory.

The campaign was not held in crisis circumstances. It was not, by Australian standards, conducted too unfairly; the arguments for both sides were reported reasonably fully in the media. And the people's verdict in favor of the status quo was as clear cut as any that they have ever given. Even though the economy was in a trough and there were scandals around, the existing government was asked to continue with its policies. The votes could be represented as a triumph of national conservatism. Yet the choice offered to Australians was not a radical one. They were spurning not a set of revolutionary nostrums but a Labor tax program that might have been designed for the stern monitors of the International Monetary Fund. They were saying simply that Malcolm Fraser and his men were a better risk than Gough Whitlam and his. Images from the past dominated the public mood more than proposals for the future.

INTRODUCTION

Certainly the election gave a new legitimacy to Malcolm Fraser. Constitutional controversy had clouded his coming to office, and some could not accept the coalition's 1975 election triumph as the outcome of a fair fight. But by 1977 he had been in power for two years, and he had been exposed, warts and all, for everyone to see. No one could now challenge the democratic authority by which he ruled. Perhaps prematurely, people could look to a Fraser era in the way that there had once been a Menzies era. Fraser was only forty-five in 1975, while Robert Menzies had been fifty-five in 1949 when his seventeen-year run had begun. Like Menzies, Fraser seemed to dominate, even to intimidate, his cabinet. And unlike Menzies he did not even depend upon the Country party to command a majority in the House of Representatives.[7] He had demonstrated the toughness needed to get and to retain power; what he had still to demonstrate was the larger vision needed to keep his allies loyal in rough times and to build up a positive consensus about the virtues of his rule—to win by his own merits rather than by the defects of his opponents.

Yet it is wrong to suggest that the 1977 election was wholly a "no change" affair. Its most immediate consequence was the withdrawal from the scene, even before the results were all in, of Gough Whitlam, that towering, flawed figure who had left such a mark on the decade.

It also saw the arrival of a significant new party—and a total of minor party votes that was greater than at any election since the war. The Australian Democrat party, a mere six months old, jumped from nothing to 10 percent of the national vote. Its leader, Don Chipp, was a former Liberal minister with considerable talent for publicity. He offered a promise of open, honest, libertarian government, a trendy social policy, and a moderate, middle-of-the-road economic policy, well designed to appeal to voters disillusioned with either of the main parties. He built up enough of an organization to field candidates throughout Australia, and they polled unexpectedly well everywhere except in Tasmania. Twenty years earlier the Democratic Labor party had won similar support, but that had flowed from a party split. Chipp drew his following fairly evenly from both sides, in what was surely a general expression of no-confidence in both the established parties.

---

[7] In the period from 1949 to 1972 the Liberal party never had a clear lead over all the other parties put together. It held between 45 and 62 seats and needed its reliable coalition partner, the Country party, with its 17 to 20 seats, to form a majority government. But in 1975 the Liberals won 68 of the 127 seats, and in 1977, 67 of the 124 seats, in the House of Representatives.

Labor's Dilemma. The 1977 election left the Labor party with a basic dilemma. The failure to make any headway from its 1975 position was devastating. The Fraser government, after all, had made plenty of mistakes: it had had two years in office while unemployment shot up and inflation stayed high. It had not produced any notable new talents, and Phillip Lynch, the treasurer, its most publicized figure after the prime minister, had had to resign under a cloud at the beginning of the campaign. At the state level, too, the omens had been encouraging for Labor. In New South Wales the Labor party had returned to power in 1976 and its new premier had been well received by the public. In Victoria a protracted scandal seemed to besmirch the state Liberal government. In the Queensland elections in November, there had been a sizable swing to Labor and the partners in the coalition led by Premier Jo Bjelke-Petersen were having a very public quarrel. In South Australia, Don Dunstan's Labor government seemed more popular and assured than ever.

Moreover, Labor had shed some of the handicaps that it was carrying in 1975. The events of Remembrance Day which had cast such a cloud over the party's 1975 campaign were now seen in a somewhat different light: the general judgment on Sir John Kerr had not become more favorable with the passage of time, and in the most unexpected quarters misgivings were expressed about his actions.

In sponsoring the Senate Vacancies Amendment the Fraser government had recognized one of Labor's grievances from 1975.[8] Memories of the "loans affair" and of all the lesser mishaps of the Whitlam government had dimmed, and most of those associated with the worst fiascos had passed from the scene. In the 1977 campaign the party was putting forward men and measures that should have caused no alarm to anyone in middle Australia; its program was one of mild reformism and fiscal responsibility.

Why then did Labor make no headway? Must it be assumed that Australia is so basically conservative that a party associated with trade unions and a radical past can never succeed? Is a fairly prosperous, not very political people fond of a quiet life bound always to suspect that Labor rule must threaten their peace and their pocket book? Is a house-owning, consumer-oriented, petite bourgeoisie ever

---

[8] On May 21, 1977, Australians approved, with a 73 percent "yes" vote, a constitutional amendment which provided that, in the event of a Senate vacancy, the replacement appointed by the state premier should be from the same party as his predecessor. The violation of the convention in Queensland in September 1975 had played an essential role in the crisis that brought Whitlam down, for it had deprived Labor of the one extra senator needed to bring the budget issue to a vote in the Senate.

INTRODUCTION

going to believe that their mainly capitalist society can be run better by skeptics than by capitalists? Such questions can drive the intelligent apparatchiks of the Labor party to despair. But their pessimism may be carried too far. Australia did elect a Labor government in 1972 and, seeing what it had got, still reelected it in 1974. Three of the six states voted for Labor governments in the two years after the 1975 debacle. The 1977 election left Labor better off than in 1966, when it dropped to 43 percent of the two-party-preferred vote.[9] It was still within six percentage points of victory—and between 1966 and 1969 the swing to Labor had been 7.5 percentage points.[10]

Furthermore, time is on Labor's side, if it does not drive away those who are still faithful to it. The young people joining the electoral rolls show a twenty percentage point majority for Labor, while the old cohorts who are struck off by death are evenly divided. Such a balance promises a one percentage point swing to Labor every five years without anyone's actually changing his mind.

The Shape of the Outcome. It is important to realize that the actual outcome of the 1977 election was perhaps the most surprising in Australian history, as far as the margin of victory was concerned. By the end of the campaign everyone expected the government to win—but everyone expected it to lose a lot of seats. To underpredict the majority by thirty or more seats, as most prophets did, was to move into a range of error never before achieved in Australia, even in the shock result of 1961.

The uniformity of the results was their most remarkable feature. Australia is a far-flung federal society. News is purveyed on a state and community basis by local newspapers and local radio stations. Economic problems vary from area to area. There is every reason why regional diversity should manifest itself in voting. Yet in each state the movement—or non-movement—of votes between the main parties was almost identical. The state-wide swing to Labor in the preferred vote was within 1.5 percentage points of the national average (1.1 percentage points) in four of the six states: in South Australia it was

---

[9] "Two-party-preferred vote" (counting the coalition as one party) or simply "preferred vote" is a term used for the percentage share of the vote a party would have if all the votes cast for third and fourth parties were in fact reallocated to the major parties according to estimates of how second preferences would have been distributed. Since the Labor party and the Liberal or Country party provide the dominant two candidates in every constituency, the preferred vote of Labor and that of the government parties add up to 100 percent.

[10] See Malcolm Mackerras, "No Change: An Analysis of the 1977 Election," *Politics* (1978).

3.8 percentage points to Labor, while in Tasmania and Western Australia there was a very slight movement toward the government (0.3 and 1.3 percentage points, respectively). Of the 124 individual seats there were only 9 where the swing either way exceeded 5 percentage points and only 26 where it exceeded 3 percentage points. In 1975 the nationwide swing against Labor had been a dramatic 7 percentage points and every mainland state had moved by within 2 percentage points of that. In 1977 there was an equally surprising and even more standardized absence of swing.

The result was the smallest turnover in membership the House has known. Despite the accidents of redistribution (redistricting), hardly any new blood was brought in; the Labor caucus in particular would feel the absence of the unusually talented younger men who had stood poised to gain marginal seats.

But the uniformity was not complete. The Democratic Labor party only fought in its heartland of Victoria, but there it still secured 6.2 percent of the Senate vote, almost exactly the same as in 1975. And the Australian Democrats in their remarkable debut ranged from 5.9 percent of the vote in Tasmania to 16.2 percent in Victoria. In the House the Democrat preferences split so evenly that they had a negligible effect on the outcome, nowhere upsetting the first-preference leader. In the Senate, they demonstrated the paradoxes of preferential voting, gaining a seat with 8.3 percent of the New South Wales vote, but failing to gain one with 12.5 percent of the Western Australian vote.

The achievement of the Democrats is considerable, and an omen for the future. It is hard to see Don Chipp as a very heroic figure, but he had the genius to discover a vacuum in Australian politics and to fill it. He showed that a large number of voters were dissatisfied with the established alternatives and ready to plunge for an untried but patently unrevolutionary escape. Just as the disillusioned British suddenly flocked to the Liberal party in 1974, so Australian electors, increasingly detached from their traditional party loyalties, chose to thumb their noses at Fraser and Whitlam. Unlike the British they could, of course, do so with the assurance that the preferential system would still leave them with a say in the fundamental choice between the main parties.

Whether Chipp has the skill or the staying power to build on his 1977 achievements has yet to be seen. But even if his party falls apart or discredits itself, Chipp has opened a door through which others will follow; he has shown that there is a significant and growing minority of Australians who want to escape from the two-party

INTRODUCTION

straitjacket. As the Fraser government hits rough going in the years ahead, those who desert it may increasingly prefer the middle ground to the Labor alternative. In the political marketplace there will always be eager entrepreneurs to supply a need, once it has been demonstrated.

The Issues

The reporting of every election in every democratic country is bedevilled by a search for *the* issues. In Australia politicians and journalists are obsessed by this quest to an exceptional degree. But are the themes that dominate the headlines really the subjects that have the power to switch the balance of votes during the campaign?

For a party to benefit by dwelling on an issue, each of three basic conditions must be met. First, the matter must be one that arouses strong feelings in the voters. Second, the strong feelings must be disproportionately in one direction (for if opinion is equally divided, as many people will be repelled by a firm stand as are attracted). Third, the issue must be one on which the voters perceive a clear difference between the positions taken up by the two sides. Time and again, in Australian (and in British) elections, the issues on which politicians have focused have been ones that could hardly affect the outcome, sometimes because too few voters cared about them, sometimes because as many were annoyed as were pleased, and most often because the alternative policies were not understood and differentiated in the public mind.

Unemployment, Taxation, and Leadership. In the 1977 elections, Labor tried to establish unemployment as the preeminent issue. Everybody is opposed to unemployment in theory, and a record number of Australians were unemployed or in fear of losing their jobs. But a very large proportion of the voters were not touched by the employment problem except as a symbol of national prosperity.

Moreover, those who did see unemployment as the first priority must have found it hard to differentiate between the parties' remedies. The government favored a gentle reflation, stimulated by personal tax cuts. Labor wanted to encourage employers to take on more men by ending the payroll tax routinely assessed on salaries and wages. But even professional economists were divided on the likely efficacy of either of these measures in cutting down joblessness.

The government tried to establish taxation as the preeminent issue. Did the voters want to safeguard the tax indexation and the tax cuts that had been promised in the August budget? The Liberals took firm steps to crush the initial expressions of enthusiasm with which the employers' organizations greeted Labor's payroll proposals. Sir Henry Bolte, the outspoken ex-premier of Victoria, in one staggering—and quite unofficial—radio commercial, boasted that his friends on the boards of big companies were laughing all the way to the bank at this handout which would have to be paid for by ordinary folk.

Of course, for every voter the tax he has to pay is a matter for concern. But, though he would like to pay less, he would not necessarily like others to pay less. If the total tax burden stays the same, a reallocation must hurt some as well as help some. If the total tax burden is reduced for everyone, it must almost certainly mean the reduction of some services that people want from government. But perhaps the ordinary voter was not so rational in his reaction to promised tax cuts.

In some ways the parties' stands on taxation were obscure and shifting. Even expert economists found it hard to explain the complexities of indexation, and responsible administrators could be excused a Gladstonian horror as the parties wrote and rewrote their budgets in the course of the campaign.

Probably the tax issue did hit home. Labor clearly fumbled in presenting its policy, with Gough Whitlam, Bill Hayden, and Chris Hurford appearing to take different attitudes to repealing the August budget cuts. The Liberal message that there would be less tax to pay when February came, provided that the government were reelected, may have got through to a significant number of voters. The "hip-pocket nerve"[11] was touched.

One unexpected issue seemed for a moment likely to disrupt the campaign when, three weeks before polling day, Lynch, the Liberal party treasurer, resigned while his private dealings in land were sorted out. Lynch was conveniently, but genuinely, confined to hospital throughout the campaign, which made it difficult to press him on the propriety of his actions and to keep the issue alive. Obviously the resignation dismayed the Liberals at a time when the polls were indicating a dip in their fortunes; the suggestion of a scandal of their own may have inhibited their planned trips down memory lane into the more public scandals of 1974–1975. But the Lynch affair seems to have done them no harm, perhaps because it was not understood, perhaps because Australians are in any case cynical about their politicians, and perhaps because Lynch had little personal appeal, positive or negative.

---

[11] This famous phrase was used by Ben Chifley, the Labor premier, to explain his party's defeat in 1949.

INTRODUCTION

The real issues seem to have been more impalpable ones. On the government side was the appeal to be allowed "to finish the job"; they had only been in office for two years—too short a time for judgment. Just as in May 1974, after eighteen months in power, Labor had been given a second chance, with only a slight diminution in its majority, so in December 1977 the Liberals may have benefited from a charity that would not be there after three or four years of government.

But more important than that was the question of leadership. The two and a half years of Fraser versus Whitlam saw a confrontation of giants that had not been matched in Australia at least since Menzies faced H. V. Evatt in the 1950s. It is true that by 1977 neither Fraser nor Whitlam was popular—on both sides, the fiercest partisans seemed to slip into an apologetic tone when speaking of their leaders. Yet each man dominated his party's campaign.

Malcolm Fraser was patently a more impressive figure than Bill Snedden, or Sir William MacMahon or Sir John Gorton or Harold Holt, although his abrasiveness and his lack of humor or human contact made it hard to set him up as a lovable leader. His poll ratings were low, yet, partly for want of competition, he appeared to be a strong prime minister, firmly in command of his own side.

Gough Whitlam had not lost the wit or the eloquence that had made him so much the most outstanding politician of his generation. But something was missing in him or in his rapport with his audiences. His poll ratings were even lower than Fraser's, and the Labor party made embarrassingly publicized, and not very successful, efforts to play down his role in the campaign and to elevate Hayden's. The Liberals may well have rushed the election to ensure that Whitlam was their opponent; they were confident enough of his unpopularity to flout the traditional wisdom against publicizing one's adversary and splashed full-page photographs of him in the press with the implied message, "Do you want Gough back?" The message was partly a personal one; Australians found the arrogance of the Whitlam style acceptable only so long as it was associated with success. But, even more, the message was political. In an economically depressed but still affluent Australia, a quiet life was attractive; Gough Whitlam symbolized the now unacceptable excitement and disturbance of the over-political past. That, if anything, was *the* issue. The three conditions for it to have an effect were met. People had strong views on Whitlam; these views, at least among floating voters, were predominantly hostile; and there was certainly no confusion about which party he was associated with.

Missing or Latent Themes. The non-issues of the campaign may, in retrospect, seem as significant as the issues. Foreign affairs were notably absent from the debate. A Rip van Winkle from 1966, or even 1972, would have been astonished at the silence on the Indian Ocean, on Vietnam, on ANZUS, on relations with the United States or China or Europe. One development during November, the arrival of shiploads of forlorn Vietnamese refugees at Darwin, was prevented, by a virtuous bipartisanship, from becoming a source of controversy. An exchange or two about the relative priority of frigates and patrol boats seemed to make up the whole of the defense argument. The Australia of 1977 was, for all electoral purposes, isolationist.

Yet an internationalist conscience lay behind one notable sleeper in the campaign—the uranium issue. Whether Australia should exploit its mineral riches to meet the nuclear needs of an energy-hungry world raised enormously complex moral and technical questions. Some had forecast that there would be the first genuinely environmental or ecological campaign in a major democracy. But to a large extent both sides shied away from the question. Opinion was clearly divided in both parties and was becoming, particularly among women, less favorable to uranium exports. And both sides knew that in the end the trade might become inevitable. The government decided not to stir up the law-and-order issue, which anti-uranium demonstrations could provoke. The opposition, with a cautious, wait-for-safeguards policy, only belatedly raised the temperature three days before the poll, with an emotional television commercial about "our children's future." Uranium cannot have changed many votes in 1977 but it showed its potential as an issue of the future.

One other almost silent issue had international implications. It was arguable that to follow one party's promised economic policies rather than the other's would make little measurable difference over the next three years to the key indicators for inflation and unemployment and growth. But the Australian economy depends on foreign investment. A strike of overseas capital could have devastating effects on the most sensible of domestic economic management. Yet neither the Liberals nor the Labor party thought it prudent to raise the question of whether a Labor victory would lead to a balance of payments crisis. The Liberals did not want to stress their connection with big business; the Labor party did not want to frighten voters with what might happen.

Perhaps the most surprising of the non-issues was Remembrance Day 1975. During the election Sir John Kerr slipped away from the governor generalship, inconspicuous and unregretted. But except on

INTRODUCTION

the question whether a Liberal-controlled Senate would again block supply for a Labor government, the events of 1975 were passed by. Two years after the most dramatic day in Australian constitutional history, no one wanted the electorate to dwell on what had happened. Labor offered no serious remedies against a repetition of the events. The government offered no justification for them. One was reminded of British reactions to the Suez affair. In October 1956 the most dramatic confrontation of British postwar politics occurred. But well before the next election, a tacit conspiracy of silence on the whole issue developed between the Conservative and Labour parties. The Labour party in a burst of righteous indignation had cried out to the British people to follow them in protest—and had then found that the mass of the public did not share their views. The Conservatives knew they had been engaged in a mismanaged fiasco. So neither side wanted to talk about it. Suez taught Britain that the days of Empire were numbered. Remembrance Day taught Australia the imperfections of its Constitution. In each case a basic change in national thinking took place in an area too deep and too divisive to be made a routine issue of electoral controversy.

But the Australian experience of 1975 raised too many continuing problems to be altogether ignored. Even if Labor had won a majority in the House in 1977, it would still not have controlled the Senate. But if the Liberal vote had been just two percentage points lower in Tasmania and South Australia, the government would have lost its Senate majority. Despite the protestations of Chipp and even of the larger parties, the possibility of a confrontation between the two houses hung over the 1977 election—and hangs over the future of Australia. For a generation of Australian politicians, Remembrance Day 1975 will remain the most influential and traumatic of political experiences, even if they discuss it as little in the future as they did during the 1977 campaign.

Conclusion

As it was, that campaign proved a lackluster affair. The fire had gone out of Gough Whitlam, the one potentially great orator in the battle, and no new talent had arrived to draw the crowds on either side. But the fault lay also with the opinion polls, with the traditions of campaigning, and with the issues of 1977.

The polls, one week into the campaign, seemed to be infusing it with some excitement: they suggested that Fraser's lead was slipping away and that he might even be going to lose the election that he had so gratuitously called. But after that moment every survey reported an improvement for the government, and by the last week the four nationwide polls agreed in showing Labor behind by from two to eight percentage points in the preferred vote. The polls were widely read and the campaign seemed to have died even before the broadcast blackout of the last three days. Certainly some Labor supporters appeared to give up psychologically, well before the final whistle. It is sad for democracy if polls have such an effect, demoralizing participants and making voters see the whole affair as a bore. Election analysts have a lot to answer for if they encourage the public to abandon interest at the mere suggestion of a foregone conclusion.

But the public lack of enthusiasm had other causes too. In this election, far more than in any of the previous three, the contest often seemed reduced to a rather petty auction of promises, an exchange of point-scoring. The journalists and the politicians made press conferences sound rather like questions without notice in Parliament. Hostile interrogators tried to trip up each spokesman on some detail of fact or policy while crudely planted questions provided opportunities for restatements of the party's plus points. And the spokesmen reacted like ministers at question time, their machismo staked on their never seeming at a loss for a precise but partisan answer. Through the press conferences, through letters to the papers, and even more through the increasing use of broadcast phone-in programs, the party leaders were engaged in an ever faster debate on small issues. The various new arguments could be batted to and fro between the two sides several times within a day—and speedily exhausted. The media's quest for novelty meant that most fresh lines of controversy became worn out in a very short time. Hardly any issues stayed in the headlines throughout the campaign.

In the way the campaign was conducted and reported one seemed to detect in politicians and journalists alike a vision of the voter as a small-minded, logical accountant balancing his political books, totting up the specific promises made by each side to see the advantages for him personally, and then voting for the one that offered most. When the politicians moved away from detail, they tended not to raise wider issues about the future of Australia but to attack the credibility of the other side, usually by pointing out trifling inconsistencies. It was not a particularly dirty campaign and personal attacks were kept within very moderate bounds. What was missing was any vision of a larger future, any ideology.

Happy the nation that has no politics? Perhaps. It is comfortable to live in a place where the result of an election makes so

INTRODUCTION

little difference to everyday life that there is no likelihood of anyone's refusing to accept the result. But there must be some wistfulness about living in a lucky country so contented that there are no great issues, no public challenges, and no outstanding leaders to stir the imagination of the bulk of voters.

2
The Australian Electorate

David A. Kemp

The Australian electorate encompasses some 60 percent of the Australian population—in 1977 8.5 million enrolled voters out of a population of 14 million. The Constitution provides that senators and members of the House of Representatives shall be "directly chosen by the people," though Parliament itself largely has control over who constitute "the people" and over the details of the electoral process. Historically, the trend has been for "the people" to become more inclusive, most recently with the lowering of the voting age to eighteen prior to the 1974 election. Since 1924 voting has been a legal obligation, and as a result turnout at federal elections is generally in the region of 95 percent.

Australia is an advanced industrial society. This affects both the distribution of political resources in the electorate and the kinds of issues that enter the political debate. In the last decade, education, the social condition of ethnic minorities, the quality of life in the cities, the environment, participation in government and politics, governmental responsiveness, and the extension of social security and health systems have emerged as political issues in Australia, as they have in other advanced industrial nations. At the same time, the voters are still concerned about economic issues, and recent elections have been influenced by the economic uncertainty that accompanies relatively high inflation and unemployment. There is evidence that the electorate has become more dissatisfied with the output of governments and more ready to alter traditional voting habits. There has been a significant shift in the electoral bases of the parties and a consequent change in electoral risks and opportunities for political leaders.

The Distribution of Political Resources

The Vote. In Australian national elections, not all votes are of equal weight. First, the implementation of the federal principle gives greater weight to the votes of electors in the smaller states. The Constitution guarantees to all original states, regardless of population, an equal number of senators (now ten) and at least five members of the House of Representatives even if this exceeds their entitlement on the basis of population. Further, the legislation governing the federal electoral process (the Commonwealth Electoral Act) has included provisions that tend to secure a greater weighting for rural votes in the distribution (apportionment) of electoral boundaries. Again, the system of single-member constituencies in the House of Representatives contributes to the gross underrepresentation of voters who prefer the candidates of a minor party when these voters are widely dispersed. Only when the supporters of a minor party are geographically concentrated are they likely to win representation in the House. With these exceptions, however, the apportionment of seats in Australia for federal House of Representatives elections has been such as to provide relatively fair representation.[1] Insofar as the weighting of votes has been a matter of deliberate policy, it is voters outside the main centers of population who have been advantaged—partly as a price for the political unity of the nation, partly as a function of the influence of the Country party on coalition governments.

Skills, Knowledge, and Money. In dealing with political issues the Australian electorate—like other national electorates—has placed great reliance on small groups of political leaders: particularly the parliamentary leaders of the Liberal, Labor, and Country parties. The principal concerns of Australians are personal and family matters;[2] public life is left largely to those with the motivation, skills, and resources to undertake it. Few members of the electorate belong to political parties (about 4 percent), and fewer still are active in party work.[3] This is not to say that the electorate is uninterested in poli-

---

[1] The constitutional provisions favoring the smaller original states are sections 7 and 24. Joan Rydon, "The Electoral System," in Henry Mayer and Helen Nelson, eds., *Australian Politics: A Fourth Reader* (Melbourne: Cheshire, 1976), pp. 402-414, gives an index of representativeness for Australian federal and state boundaries. For further details on Australian electoral processes, see Ruth Atkins and Adam Graycar, *Governing Australia* (Sydney: John Wiley & Sons, 1972), pp. 41-60.
[2] A recent cross-national comparison of people's main concerns based on survey research was reported in the *Bulletin* (Sydney), April 9, 1977, pp. 14-17. Personal and family concerns predominated in Australia as in other countries.
[3] Don Aitkin, *Stability and Change in Australian Politics* (Canberra: Australian National University Press, 1977), p. 22.

tics. When asked, most voters will express an interest, and a substantial percentage follow politics (especially campaigns) in the media.[4] Following politics through the media (principally television) means following the activities of the political parties and particularly of their leaders. Moreover, whether or not voters are personally active in political work, most associate themselves with one of the major parties. A national survey prior to the 1977 federal election found that about a third of the electorate described themselves "generally" as "very strong" supporters of one of the parties, slightly more than a third as "fairly strongly" attached to one of the parties, and a further one-fifth as attached, but "not very strongly." Overall, some 85–90 percent of the electorate associate themselves with one of the parties.[5]

Political parties therefore have an important place in the functioning of representative government in Australia. A sample survey of Melbourne voters in late 1974 found that, along with organized interest groups, political parties were seen as one of the most effective avenues for influencing government decisions.[6] The same study found a very widespread acceptance of the proposition that, "although they have their faults, political parties are necessary if democracy is to work properly" (82 percent).

How can high levels of partisanship be reconciled with low levels of participation in politics? Relative satisfaction and alienation may

---

[4] Ibid., p. 19ff. A Morgan Gallup survey reported in the *Bulletin*, December 10, 1977, p. 15, found that more and more people were relying on television rather than newspapers for news; 41 percent said they relied most on television for news, 33 percent most on newspapers, 21 percent on radio (N=2,342). I. Saulwick & Associates, National Survey (conducted by Beacon Research, Sydney), November 26-27, 1977, asked: "How much interest have you taken in the election campaign so far? Would you say you have taken a good deal (37 percent), some (34 percent), not much (23 percent), none (6 percent)?" (N=2,112).

[5] Saulwick, National Survey, November 26-27, 1977. This broadly confirmed the finding reported in Aitkin, *Stability and Change*, p. 38.

[6] The 1974 Melbourne sample (N=500) referred to frequently throughout this chapter was a stratified (by sex), clustered probability sample drawn by the Australian Sales Research Bureau. The principal investigators were D. A. Kemp and F. G. Little of the Political Science Department, University of Melbourne. The question was derived from the Almond and Verba, Five Nation (Civic Culture) Study (see Gabriel A. Almond and Sidney Verba, *The Civic Culture: Political Attitudes and Democracy in Five Nations* [Princeton: Princeton University Press, 1963]). The question was: "Suppose several people were trying to influence a government decision. . . . Here is a list of things they might do. The first works through personal and family connections with government officials; the second one writes to government officials explaining his point of view; the third tries to get people interested in the problem and to form a group; the fourth person works through a political party; and the fifth person organizes a protest demonstration. . . . Which one of these methods do you think would be most effective?" Thirty-eight percent of respondents answered groups, 37 percent, parties.

both be relevant. Certainly as dissatisfaction with government output rose in 1974–1975 there was a very large increase in the membership of the coalition parties, particularly the Liberal party. In 1977, dissatisfaction with the performance of the coalition may have been what prompted a section of the electorate to enter active politics for the first time as Australian Democrats. Both these instances show that increasing dissatisfaction with the performance of government will under certain conditions increase levels of participation and, conversely, that lower levels of participation reflect greater relative satisfaction. It is also possible that others are deterred from participation by the centralized character of decision making in the major parties or by a deeper alienation from the social and political system. However, the willingness of most Australians to leave active politics to the parties may well be in part a function of the role the electorate accords to leadership in social life generally and in politics.

The 1974 Melbourne sample responded to a number of items concerning the role of leaders in and outside politics. While simple frequencies in response to such items must be interpreted cautiously, the overall pattern that emerged from the Melbourne interviews seems unmistakable. While "the people" were certainly not to be ignored, an essential role was accorded to leadership. Clear majorities of the Melbourne sample believed that "most of the changes for good in this world depend on the work of a few exceptional men" (69 percent) and that in fact "it will always be necessary to have a few strong able people actually running everything" (81 percent—compare with the 56 percent Herbert McClosky had found some fifteen years before in an American sample).[7] The importance placed on leadership carried over into politics. Some 70 percent agreed that leaders are very important to the success of a political party. (Previous studies have shown that when respondents are asked to name the good and bad features of a party, leadership is a frequent subject for comment.)[8] In the context of attitudes such as these, it is scarcely surprising that the voters overwhelmingly rejected the proposition that "leaders are not really important. People can learn to live together and work together on their own" (88 percent disagreed). The great majority of the electorate believed that "Australians really need a national leader who can give them a sense of direction" (78 percent agreed).

It has generally been to a party's advantage, then, to have a strong national leader to offer the voters. Certainly the Labor party's

---

[7] Herbert McClosky, "Consensus and Ideology in American Politics," *American Political Science Review*, vol. 58 (1964), pp. 361-82.
[8] Aitkin, *Stability and Change*, chap. 15.

rise to power between 1966 and 1972 was associated with the rise—both in the party and in the Parliament—of Gough Whitlam, and the coalition's regaining of power was associated with the election of Malcolm Fraser as Liberal party leader. It is interesting that the Australian Democrats, while they adopted highly participatory procedures for policy making, also had a well-known leader (unlike the much less successful Australia party).

Despite the important role accorded by the electorate to political leadership, there is evidence which suggests that party elites must work in an environment that has strong populistic elements. Few respondents thought that even in theory a benevolent dictator was desirable[9] and a very large majority agreed that "governments should not go ahead with any major policy until there has been thorough public discussion with as many people as possible taking part" (83 percent). When presented with a hypothetical case of conflict between the prime minister and the senior members of Parliament in his own party, 63 percent of the Melbourne sample thought that in the end the prime minister should go along with his senior colleagues rather than force his will on them.[10] In this instance the electorate preferred the organized group to the strong individual. The populism of the electorate may extend also to the social origins of leadership: 71 percent agreed with the statement, "Just because a man is high up socially it doesn't mean he knows any better what is good for the country." Indeed, it has been noted before that the electorate is generally skeptical of politicians, and a substantial proportion believed that "most politicians are looking out for themselves above all else" (51 percent).

If an electorate is going to accord an important role to political elites it may also demand much of them. To the open-ended question, "If a man is to be a good leader of the country, what do you think are the most important qualities he should have?" honesty was the most frequent response; 31 percent volunteered it as their first choice and 44 percent as one of the three most important qualities. Qualities associated with the capacity to reach the political audience and responsiveness to the needs of the electorate were the next most frequently

---

[9] 1974 Melbourne sample. The item was: "In many ways a dictator who has the best interests of his people at heart would be the best form of government." Twenty-four percent agreed, 74 percent disagreed, 3 percent not established.

[10] 1974 Melbourne sample. The question was: "Suppose the Prime Minister disagreed with the senior members of his own party on some issue, do you think in general he should go along with the other people in his own party, or should he have the final say?"

cited first preferences and were among the first three qualities mentioned by 20 percent and 16 percent of the sample respectively.[11] Believability, responsiveness, and capacity to communicate were more frequently cited than education or even experience. These qualities must surely be among the criteria against which leaders are assessed —and the leader whose professional credibility is successfully challenged or whose personal honesty is called into question can expect to suffer electorally.

Linked with the party elites through party funding (especially campaign funding) are the principal elites of the Australian industrial system: the directors of the major corporate enterprises (who have at their disposal company or shareholders' funds) and officials of trade unions (who control the increasingly substantial funds accruing from membership dues). These elites, with the leaders of key primary producers' organizations, have been the sole repositories of the monetary resources needed to support and finance political parties, as well as being the groups that stood to gain the most from direct political action. They are still the principal sources of party funds—trade union officialdom for the Labor party, business corporations for the Liberal party. As such—as well as in their role as powerful and privileged interests—they potentially constitute a challenge to the influence the electors exercise through the vote. Their presence so close to the political parties introduces a tension between electoral and interest politics which continually impinges on the party leaderships in Parliament. It is possible that the electorate recognizes this. Opinion surveys over the years have regularly found a very widespread opinion in the electorate that trade unions and big business have too much power in Australia—generally more respondents seeing trade union power as excessive than big business power.[12] Trade union officials do, of course, have a privileged position in the Labor party structure—a position that is widely disapproved of even by trade union members. There is no comparable affiliation between business interests and the Liberal party, though funding arrange-

---

[11] 1974 Melbourne sample. "Honesty" was coded to include sincerity, integrity, believability, trustworthiness, and straightforwardness. Capacity to reach the audience from the platform refers to performing skills of various kinds, especially being a good speaker, having attractive conduct in public, having charisma. Responsiveness to the needs of the electorate included awareness of needs, approachability, listening to others, willingness to talk with people. Less frequently mentioned qualities included intelligence, education, patriotism, altruism, bargaining and other political skills, strength, dominance.

[12] The 1974 Melbourne sample found 72 percent believing that trade unions had too much power; big business was close behind with 70 percent.

ments and ease of access to political leaders constantly arouse suspicions of excessive influence.[13]

How does the electorate feel about the distribution of power and influence in Australia? A large minority of the Melbourne voters interviewed in late 1974 felt that "the voters" did not have enough power (47 percent), and there was widespread agreement that "people should have more say in government decisions which affect them than they do at present" (76 percent). A 1969 survey of the national electorate had found that only a minority (46 percent) believed that "the people in government" could be "trusted to do the right thing nearly all the time," and a very large proportion (71 percent) were concerned that "some of the people in the government pay more attention to what the big interests want."[14] While only a minority (23 percent) described themselves as "not satisfied" with the state of government and politics in Australia, only 7 percent were "very satisfied." These perceptions were recorded before the unemployment and inflation of the seventies, and before the experience of the Labor government and the constitutional crisis of 1975. By 1977 there was evidence that these events had increased dissatisfaction with the existing political forces. Whether the levels of dissatisfaction recorded in 1969 and 1974 were the norm for Australia or whether they reflected growing concern over the performance of the political system is unclear.

One important change taking place in the distribution of political skills in the electorate can be briefly noted here: the rising level of education, which presumably brings with it a higher ability to absorb and process information, to participate in organized political activity, to mount an argument, to mobilize expertise. Approximately 20 percent of the electorate may now have some "tertiary" education (past the high school level), and this is inversely related to age.[15] The increased proportion with some higher education reflects the great expansion of the university and college system, especially during the

---

[13] An extended discussion of attitudes toward the affiliation of trade unions with the Labor party may be found in Don Rawson, "The Paradox of Partisan Trade Unionism: The Australian Case," *British Journal of Political Science*, vol. 4 (October 1974), pp. 399-418.

[14] Aitkin, *Stability and Change*, p. 293.

[15] The estimate of the educational structure of the electorate at the time of the 1977 election is derived from the November and December national surveys mounted by I. Saulwick & Associates: university degree or some university, 8 percent; other tertiary, 12 percent; trade qualifications, 13 percent; completed secondary, 28 percent; some secondary, 26 percent; primary only, 13 percent; nil, less than 0.5 percent (N=3,998). Only enrolled voters eighteen years of age and over were sampled.

1960s.[16] Those with some higher education have, in turn, played a major role in the development of new organized interests, seeking to realize their objectives through the political system. The rise of these groups has been a prominent feature of the politics of Australia over the last decade.[17] It has also affected the party system and has changed the character of electoral politics in Australia. The Melbourne survey found that almost one voter in five had taken part in a demonstration and that 14 percent had joined a group formed to achieve some political objective.[18]

A National Electorate

Despite the vast geographical spread of the Australian electorate, there has been a clear tendency in recent decades for the electorate to act as one in national elections: changes in support for the parties within states and within individual constituencies have become increasingly similar across the nation. Figure 2–1 charts the relative importance of local, state, and national forces in accounting for movements in party support in the period 1940–1972.[19] The results of the 1977 elections again reveal the presence of a national electorate, with the great preponderance of seats showing swings within several percentage points of the national swing, despite some state and rural/urban differences.[20]

---

[16] The impact of rising educational levels in the electorate is discussed in David A. Kemp, *Society and Electoral Behaviour in Australia* (St. Lucia: Queensland University Press, 1978), chap. 9.

[17] Reference is made to the development and political impact of these groups in Royal Commission on Australian Government Administration, *Report* (Canberra: Australian Government Publishing Service, 1976), chap. 2, esp. section 2.2.

[18] 1974 Melbourne sample. The respondent was asked, "Looking at the list of activities on this card, have you ever . . . handed out leaflets or how-to-vote cards for a political party; joined a group formed to achieve a particular political objective; written to or contacted a member of Parliament; written a letter to a newspaper about some public matter; signed a petition; taken part publicly in a political debate; taken part in a demonstration?"

[19] This figure is derived from an analysis using the "variance components" technique outlined in Donald Stokes, "A Variance Components Model of Political Effects," in John M. Claunch, ed., *Mathematical Applications in Political Science*, vol. 1 (Dallas: Southern Methodist University, 1979), pp. 61-85. Also Donald Stokes, "Parties and the Nationalization of Electoral Forces," in William N. Chambers and Walter D. Burnham, eds., *The American Party Systems: Stages of Political Development* (New York: Oxford University Press, 1967), pp. 182-202. A more extensive analysis of the Australian situation may be found in Kemp, *Society*, chap. 7.

[20] Malcolm Mackerras, *Electoral Monograph no. 5*, Department of Government, Royal Military College, Duntroon, February 1978; Malcolm Mackerras, *The State of Play*, Reference Monograph IX, Australasian Political Studies Association, March 1978. Don Aitkin, *National Times*, February 20-25, 1978, p. 44.

FIGURE 2–1
THE NATIONALIZATION OF THE AUSTRALIAN ELECTORATE, 1940–1972

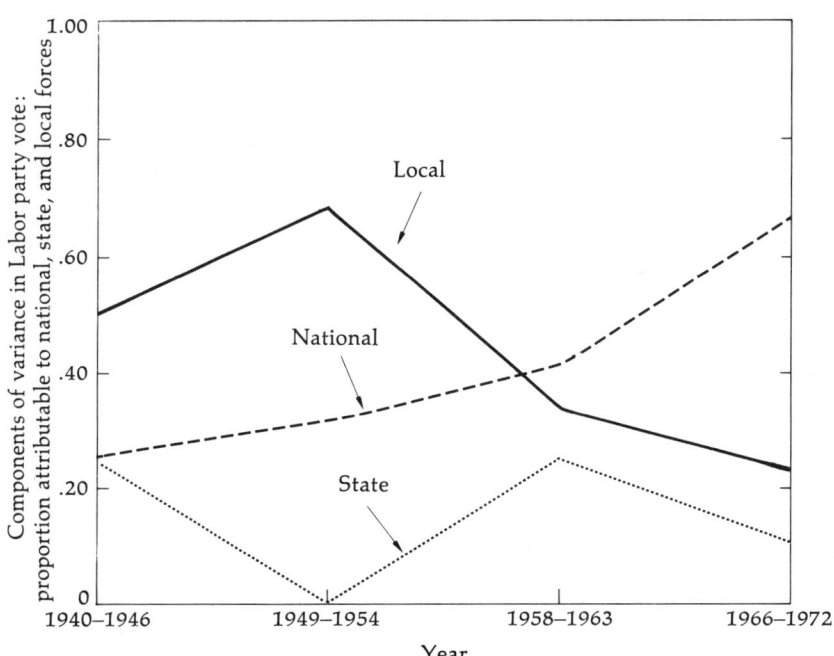

SOURCE: Based on Table 50 in David A. Kemp, *Society and Electoral Behaviour*, (St. Lucia: University of Queensland Press, 1978), p. 227.

It is tempting to see the "nationalization" of the Australian electorate as a consequence of the development of a modern nationwide system of mass communications. Not all advanced nations show this tendency, however. A comparable analysis revealed a growing "provincialization" of electoral responses in Canada.[21] Since Canada is no less advanced than Australia in terms of mass communications technology there must be other relevant factors. It is possible that the significant fact is the existence of nationwide political parties which define national issues and provide a national leadership as a basis for electoral response.

---

[21] Robert Jackman, "Political Parties, Voting and National Integration: The Canadian Case," *Comparative Politics*, July 1972, pp. 511-536.

THE AUSTRALIAN ELECTORATE

Under some circumstances the behavior of the national electorate clearly reflects regional differences—for example when the electorate is called upon to vote in the absence of a nationwide conflict between the major parties. This happens in some constitutional referendums. In the unsuccessful 1967 referendum to amend the constitutional provision that the number of members of the House of Representatives "shall be, as nearly as practicable, twice the number of the senators," the major parties at the national level were agreed, and there were substantial differences between the outcomes in the different states. In referendums where the partisan conflict is as clear as it usually is in a national election, the electorate tends to behave much more uniformly across the states. This supports the view that the political parties have played the key role in the "nationalization" of opinion. By dividing the nation, by focusing its attention on one great partisan contest, the parties also integrate it.[22]

Changing Patterns of Electoral Loyalties

Disciplined political parties have been central features of Australian electoral politics and government for over six decades. During this period the Australian political landscape has remained recognizably the same, with the main lines of contest drawn between the Australian Labor party and the Liberal party (or its predecessors, the United Australia and Nationalist parties) allied with the Country party (since 1974, officially the National Country party). The parties select candidates, promulgate platforms and policy positions, choose the national leaders, and contest the legislative output of the Parliament. They have been the dynamic forces infusing life into the constitutional framework of parliamentary and federal government.

Studies of American and British politics have accorded to the partisan loyalties of the electorate an important, if not central, role in stabilizing the party system and in forming political attitudes. The findings of Australian research, too, show that partisanship is very stable over time and is more stable than voting decisions. The intensity of a voter's attachment to a political party is related to the stability of his past voting behavior (as he recalls it) and inversely related to the likelihood of his voting for another party. American studies have found that party loyalty, or party identification, provides voters with an economical means of orienting themselves to the flow of political events and making decisions at elections. The author of

---

[22] Kemp, *Society*, chap. 7.

the major Australian study concluded that "Australian results bear an astonishing resemblance to similar findings for American and British samples, and the resemblance is powerful evidence to support a thesis that party identification is the corner-stone of the Anglo-American Party systems."[23]

If party loyalties are stable, however, they are not immutable. The study just referred to found that between 1967 and 1969 some 13 percent of voters in a national panel changed their party identification. Clearly, over a decade there is considerable scope for the pattern of party identifications in the electorate to shift. This can occur not only as a result of changes in identification, but also as a result of new identifications (or the absence of identifications) formed by voters entering the electorate or of differential rates of death among existing partisans. If existing parties are unsuccessful in maintaining the level of their core support, so that the proportion of voters without party attachments increases, there would seem to be increasing potential for major changes of support from one election to the next and possibly for the rise of new political parties. It therefore becomes important to know whether the pattern of party loyalties in the electorate has remained stable or has changed under the political, social, and economic pressures of the last decade.

Prior to the 1977 federal election a national survey organization sought to measure the pattern of party loyalties. Respondents were asked: "Generally speaking, in politics, do you think of yourself as Australian Labor Party, Australia Party, Australian Democrats, Democratic Labor Party, Liberal Party or National Country Party?" If any party was named, the respondent was then asked: "How strongly [NAME OF PARTY] do you feel—very strongly, fairly strongly, not very strongly?"[24] Table 2–1 compares the responses to the first question with those obtained in 1967, 1969, and 1978. In the light of the Liberal and National Country party coalition's clear victories in the federal elections of 1975 and 1977, the pattern that emerges is surprising.

Between 1967 and 1977 the percentage of the electorate samples who claimed to be partisans of the coalition parties declined from 47 percent to 37 percent, while the percentage of Labor partisans increased from 37 percent to 39 percent. The 1978 sample (which is smaller and therefore subject to a larger sampling error) shows each of the major political groupings with a larger percentage of partisans

---

[23] Aitkin, *Stability and Change*, pp. 41–42. The following paragraph is also based on this passage of Aitkin.
[24] Saulwick, National Survey, November 26–27, 1977.

TABLE 2-1
Party Identification, Selected Years, 1967-1978
(in percentages)

Party	1967	1969	1977	1978
Liberal	40	40	33	37
National Country	7	6	4	5
Labor	37	39	39	42
Democratic Labor	3	3	1	1
Australian Democrats	—	—	5	4
Other	—	1	1	1
No party	11	10	15	10
Don't know, no answer	2	1	2	—
Total	100	100	100	100
N	(2,054)	(1,870)	(2,112)	(686)

NOTE: The survey questions were as follows: in 1967 and 1969, "Generally speaking, do you usually think of yourself as Liberal, Labor, Country Party or D.L.P.?" In 1977, "Generally speaking, in politics, do you think of yourself as Australian Labor Party, Australia Party, Australian Democrats, Democratic Labor Party, Liberal Party, or National Country Party?" And in 1978, "Generally speaking, do you think of yourself as Liberal Party, National Country Party, Labor (A.L.P.), D.L.P., Australian Democrat or Communist?"

SOURCE: 1967, 1969, Don Aitkin, *Stability and Change in Australian Politics* (Canberra: Australian National University, 1977); 1977, I. Saulwick & Associates, National Survey, November 26-27, 1977; 1978, Dr. B. Headey, National Survey, 1978 (unpublished).

than the 1977 sample but would seem to confirm that Labor had closed the large gap that had separated it from the coalition parties a decade before.[25] Indeed, the 1977 survey showed Labor if anything slightly ahead. The data suggest that despite the Labor party's defeats in the 1975 and 1977 elections it has strengthened its basic support in the electorate. At the same time the coalition parties have lost ground.

Table 2-2 further specifies the nature of the change in the pattern of loyalties that appears to have taken place by showing the percentage of the total electorate who identify very strongly, fairly strongly, and not very strongly with each of the main parties. It suggests an increase in the "solid core" of Labor party support ("very

---

[25] The 1978 survey was mounted by Dr. Bruce Headey, Department of Political Science, University of Melbourne, through the (Morgan) Gallup Organization. The sample (N=686) was a clustered probability sample. It is referred to in this chapter mainly in examinations of relationships between variables rather than in estimates of population distributions.

TABLE 2-2
STRENGTH OF PARTY IDENTIFICATION, 1967 and 1977
(in percentages of total N)

Strength of Party Identification	Liberal		National Country		Labor		Democratic Labor		Australian Democrats		None	
	1967	1977	1967	1977	1967	1977	1967	1977	1967	1977	1967	1977
Very strong	12	11	2	2	15	17	1	a	n.a.	2		
Fairly strong	19	16	4	2	15	17	1	a	n.a.	2		
Not very strong	10	7	1	1	8	7	1	a	n.a.	1		
Total electorate	41	34	7	5	38	41	3	1	n.a.	5	12	15

[a] Less than 1 percent.

SOURCE: Don Aitkin, *Stability and Change in Australian Politics* (Canberra: Australian National University Press, 1977); I. Saulwick & Associates, National Survey, November 26-27, 1977. (Total N, 1967: 1,981; 1977: 1,901.) "Other party" identifiers are omitted from this table.

strong" plus "fairly strong") and a decline in the core support of the coalition.

How certain can we be that these changes have actually occurred and are not just an artifact of the way party identification was measured? Changes in the wording of a question may well alter findings; the party list presented to respondents was longer in the later surveys, when it included the Australian Democrats and, in 1977, the Australia party. In addition, the Democrats were a new party in 1977. How much sense does it make to ask voters whether "generally speaking" they consider themselves Democrats? Party identification is conceptually a persistent element in a voter's orientation to politics. Can this be reconciled with supporting a new party, and if so for how long? In order to test the effect of including the Democrats in the party list in the 1977 sample, a subsample including all the Democrat identifiers in the original Melbourne sample ($N = 193$) was reinterviewed the day after the election. Respondents were asked this time: "Generally speaking, do you usually consider yourself as Liberal, Labor, D.L.P., Country Party, Australia Party or what?" With the Australian Democrats omitted from the list, those who had previously described themselves as Democrats redistributed themselves, principally to the major parties, 41 percent going to the Liberal party and 29 percent to the ALP. None insisted on their Democrat identification. If the Democrat identifiers in the original sample are divided in these proportions between the parties, the major party percentages in Table 2–2 become ALP 42 percent and the coalition 41 percent. While this operation casts some doubt on the stability of the Democrats' support, it does not alter the conclusion that the balance of loyalties between the Labor party and the coalition parties has shifted in Labor's favor. As time goes on, of course, and the longer the Democrats remain a political force, the less justification there will be for removing them from the list. The 1978 sample shows that even in a nonelection year a significant proportion of electors are now willing to describe themselves "generally speaking" as Australian Democrats.

Voters in the 1977 survey showed themselves well able to distinguish between party identification and intended vote or previous vote. While the Labor party scored highest on voter loyalty, the coalition parties were ahead on voting intentions (ALP, 42.9 percent; coalition, 44.4 percent); and when voters were asked to recall their vote in the 1975 election, 52 percent recalled having voted for the coalition, 46 percent for Labor—percentages that are close to the actual totals recorded in that election (coalition, 53 percent; Labor,

TABLE 2–7
Voting Intentions, by Party Identification, November 1977
(in percentages)

	Party Identification					
Voting Intention	Liberal-NCP	Labor	Democratic Labor	Australian Democrats	No party	Total Sample
Liberal-National Country	95	2	19	10	33	43
Labor	—	94	15	7	24	42
Democratic Labor	—	1	62	2	3	2
Australian Democrats	3	3	4	81	19	9
Other	—	—	—	—	5	1
Don't know	1	—	—	—	16	3
Total	99	100	100	100	100	100
Total sample	39	40	1	5	15	100
N	(752)	(774)	(20)	(99)	(292)	(1,937)

NOTE: Columns may not add to 100 because of rounding.
SOURCE: I. Saulwick & Associates, National Survey, November 26–27, 1977.

coalition parties have won the last two elections by comfortable margins? Some clues can be gleaned from Tables 2–7, 2–8, and 2–9. These tables show how party identifiers and nonidentifiers remembered having voted in 1975 and intended to vote in 1977. We cannot hope for an explanation of the election outcomes from these tables, for we still need to know *why* certain exchanges of support occurred, but the movements of support reported by the voters should at least clarify what it is that needs to be explained.

Table 2–7 shows the relationship between party identification and voting intention a fortnight before the election. It must be interpreted cautiously, for there were still substantial improvements in coalition support to come. Nevertheless the swing back to the coalition had begun, and some of the immediate reasons for this may be evident in the table, which shows the coalition in the lead. On the basis of Table 2–7 it would appear that the coalition was more successful than Labor in attracting support from voters who claimed not to identify with any party; it also seems to have been more successful in drawing votes from the supporters of other parties than the other parties were in attracting coalition loyalists. The uncommitted and the weak identifiers were won over by the coalition. The question is, how?

A comparison of the 1975 and 1977 coalition victories shows some important differences. In 1977, despite the coalition's success in holding most of its seats, its share of the first-preference vote was much reduced. In 1975 the coalition parties won 53 percent of the national vote for the House of Representatives in their own right. In 1977, they won 48 percent. Labor, however, also suffered a decline in support. In 1975 Labor won 43 percent of the first-preference vote, in 1977 it dropped to 40 percent. Minor parties and independents in 1975 polled some 4 percent, but in 1977 the minor party and independent vote increased to some 12 percent. Although the final outcome in terms of seats looked like a rerun of 1975, the underlying pattern in 1977 was rather different. Table 2-8 provides some insight into the character of the shifts in support that took place. It does not, of course, show us how the parties were affected by the differential death rates of their supporters, but it does provide some basis for interpreting shifts of support among voters who participated in both elections. Attention should be drawn to the fact that the sample on which Table 2-8 is based was interviewed the week before the 1977 election and that the total distribution of support it shows between the parties, for both 1977 and 1975, is remarkably similar to the actual results in both years. In 1977 this sample was the one that most accurately matched the final national result.

Table 2-8 confirms what the overall outcome suggests—that the fall in first preferences for both the coalition and Labor was the result of a movement of 1975 supporters of each of these parties to the Democrats, with the coalition's losses exceeding Labor's by a ratio of 3 to 2. The only other shift of any size was an exchange between the coalition and Labor, each losing some of its 1975 support to the other. In this exchange the coalition appears narrowly to have come out ahead. Labor made up the difference, however, by its greater success in attracting support from those who had not voted in 1975—almost certainly a function of its greater appeal to the young. It is the emergence of the Democrats that is the chief difference between the two elections. In 1975 Liberal identifiers who defected went to the Labor party; in 1977 they went to the Democrats (see Tables 2-8 and 2-9). Most of those who were later to see themselves as Democrat supporters voted for the coalition in

TABLE 2-8
Vote Switching, 1975–1977
(in percentages of the total sample)

Intended Vote, December 1977	1975 Vote (Recalled)						
	Liberal-NCP	Labor	Democratic Labor	Australia	Other	Did not vote	Total Sample
Liberal-National Country	41.5	3.5	0.1	0.2	0.3	1.7	47
Labor	2.1	34.0	0.1	0.2	0.1	2.7	39
Democratic Labor	0.7	0.6	0.5	0.3	0.1	0.1	2
Australian Democrats	6.1	3.9	0.1	0.1	—	0.6	11
Australia party	0.3	0.2	0.1	0.1	—	—	1
Other	0.2	0.6	—	0.1	0.2	0.1	1
Total sample	54	44	1	1	1		101
N							(1,904)

NOTE: Totals do not add to 100 percent because of rounding.
SOURCE: I. Saulwick & Associates, National Survey, December 3–4, 1977.

1975. In both elections the coalition bettered Labor substantially among nonidentifiers (a fact that demands explanation), but in 1977 the Democrats also won a hefty proportion of the nonidentifiers. Roughly a third of the Democrats' total support was from nonidentifiers.

Table 2–9 suggests that the core of Democrat support comes predominantly from the coalition: 58 percent of Democrat identifiers recalled having voted for the coalition in 1975. But Table 2–7 shows that the non-Democrats who nevertheless intended to vote for the new party in 1977, over and above the core who actually identified with it, were by no means predominantly coalition supporters. They were predominantly nonidentifiers and Labor supporters. To the extent that the Democrats are reduced to their core supporters, therefore, their preferences will probably tend to go more heavily to the coalition.

TABLE 2–9
1975 Recalled Vote, by Party Identification, 1977
(in percentages)

1975 Vote (Recalled)	Party Identification, 1977						
	Liberal-NCP	Labor	Democratic Labor	Australian Democrat	Other	No party	Totals
Liberal-National Country	95	4	35	58	39	53	52
Labor	3	94	25	33	39	33	46
Democratic Labor	—	—	40	3	—	1	1
Australia party	—	—	—	3	9	2	1
Other	—	1	—	—	9	3	1
Not established	1	1	—	3	4	8	a
Total	99	100	100	100	100	100	100
Total sample	39	40	1	5	1	14	100
N	(724)	(736)	(20)	(92)	(23)	(266)	(1,861)

Note: Percentages may not add to 100 because of rounding.
a "Not established" distributed according to percentages of recalled vote.
Source: I. Saulwick & Associates, National Survey, November 26-27, 1977.

Values, Beliefs, and Attitudes of the Australian Electorate

If social structural factors are of relatively limited value in accounting for patterns of partisanship in the electorate, let alone in accounting for voting decisions at elections, where then can we look for explanations? The simplest next step would seem to be to consider how the electorate views the parties: what it thinks it can achieve through politics, what it seeks from leaders and candidates, the criteria it applies in evaluating the parties and issues. This raises the question whether there could be persistent "values" that influence voters' partisanship and political judgment; whether partisanship and voting could be linked to some perceived identity (whether long-standing or temporary) between a voter's main concerns and those of a political party. Even if partisanship (or voting) were based on a connection between the political positions espoused by a party and some generally congruent "outlook" on the part of its supporters, how would one demonstrate this? Is one looking for values or cognitions, beliefs, opinions, or attitudes? Is outlook essentially a matter of voters' priorities, and if it is, priorities among what?

Ideology. Recent Australian research has suggested that "ideology" may have had an important part in the formation of the modern Australian party system[49] and in the stable development of the system over time. There has certainly been remarkable continuity in the terminology of political debate in Australia. For seven decades, the language of free enterprise, competition, individualism, achievement, initiative, incentives, freedom, national development, sound management, responsibility, and loyalty to the Crown has marked the political appeals of the Liberal party (and before it of the United Australia party, the Nationalist party, and the first Liberal party). Equality, cooperation, socialism, solidarity, the working man, nationalism, government action, and anti-imperialism, meanwhile, have been equally characteristic of Labor party appeals. Is it that the parties are stuck in a groove, or do these appeals find real resonance among the voters?

There is considerable evidence that the voters recognize this language of political debate and can identify reasonably accurately the party that is making a given appeal. Different voters seem to respond to different elements within the packages. The parties' "images"—what the voters like and dislike about them—generally reflect the parties' ideologies.[50] As Don Aitkin has written,

> It is ideology, not organisation, which most distinguishes the parties of the twentieth century from their predecessors of the nineteenth century, and it is ideology which encourages the citizen to cleave to his party rather than to chop and change. These ideologies are not fully elaborated: they do not need to be. But they contain an account of the good society and how to arrive at it, an explanation of the present situation of the community and a delineation of its notable champions and villains. Above all, these party ideologies obtain their power because they are related to the social experience of the major groups on which the parties depend for support. For this reason, the ideologies slowly change to accommodate changes in that experience; while the group survives, therefore, the ideology remains relevant.[51]

---

[49] Peter Loveday, Alan W. Martin, Robert S. Parker, *The Emergence of the Australian Party System* (Sydney: Hale & Iremonger, 1977), p. 487.
[50] Aitkin, *Stability and Change*, chap. 15.
[51] Ibid., p. 14.

This account raises several questions. Assuming the parties have loosely structured ideologies, what about the electorate? To what extent can the electorate itself be said to be ideological, and if it is not ideological, how can we best describe what lies behind the appeal of the parties' ideologies for particular voters? Further, in what sense is it true that the appeal of a party's ideological package or of salient parts of that package is related to the social experience of the voter? Is it because the voter has a particular *class* situation that he responds to a particular ideology, or is it some other aspect of social experience that leads him to find certain ideas or verbal symbols attractive? Is ideology best conceived as the *process* by which, say, social class translates itself into partisan preference, or does ideology have an independent force of its own, and if so, which aspect of it is more important in accounting for partisanship? Underlying such questions is the broader conceptual (and empirical) issue: how far is it plausible to give "ideas" independent causal force, and how far are they best conceived as the processes by which social structure translates itself into social (including political) behavior?

There is an ongoing debate over whether mass electorates hold coherent, politically relevant views. The uncertainty is largely a result of the difficulty of measuring coherence with the instruments that are available.[52] Various patterns of coherence are conceivable, with different consequences for partisanship and electoral outcomes. For example, hypothetically all or most voters might fall somewhere on an identifiable ideological continuum (left-right, liberal-socialist, liberal-conservative). Alternatively, there may be a politically relevant ideological continuum that is relevant only for a minority of the total electorate. Or it may be that there are clusterings of coherent viewpoints on issues which nevertheless do not add up to ideologies and which are related to partisanship. The hypothetical possibilities could be multiplied. Moreover, we could distinguish between opinions on issues current in political debate, sets of priority areas for government action, more general orientations to action (as suggested by the sociologist Talcott Parsons and others), between attitudes, beliefs, and values.

Australian research shows that the majority of voters, including most party loyalists, do not recognize the left-right distinction as

---

[52] George F. Bishop, Robert W. Oldenick, Alfred J. Tuchfarber, "Effects of Question Wording and Format on Political Attitude Consistency," *Public Opinion Quarterly*, vol. 42 (1978), pp. 81-92, suggest that some recent conclusions about the increasing consistency of attitudes held by the American electorate are an artifact of changes in question wording and format.

relevant to themselves.[53] Though often used by an elite, this terminology is not part of the currency of the voters at large. The fact that it is recognized more frequently by strong party identifiers than by others, however, supports the case for an ideological element in partisanship.

Several studies of the American electorate have identified an increasing degree of consistency between the opinions voters hold on a number of key issues (such as the size of government, minority welfare, racial integration, crime and urban unrest, the counterculture and drugs, and the cold war). One study found that "the degree of coherence among the political attitudes of citizens has increased substantially since the late 1950s."[54] This greater consistency was not, however, seen to amount to a consistent ideology, "where every specific issue is deducible from a set of general principles."[55] Nevertheless the change was associated with a marked increase in the use of issues to evaluate candidates and predict the vote.[56] A second study identifies a "New Politics" continuum in the American electorate that emerged around the social issues of the late sixties. "The New Politics was the politics of confrontation that divided young and old, hawk and dove, advocates of the counterculture and the dominant culture, disadvantaged groups and middle class America."[57] About a third of the American electorate were found to hold positions at either end of this continuum, so that they could be described as "New Politics ideologues."[58] A voter's position on the continuum affected his assessments of candidates, of policies, and of so-called liberals and conservatives. "The New Politics themes and concerns have added a dimension to political life and have become an important framework within which many people now organize their political beliefs and behaviors," wrote Miller and Levitin.[59]

---

[53] Aitkin, *Stability and Change*, chap. 5. A recent American analysis showing that ideological position defined in a similar way is correlated with vote (but not significantly with party identification) is John D. Holm and John P. Robinson, "Ideological Identification and the American Voter," *Public Opinion Quarterly*, vol. 42 (1978), pp. 235-46. Using a seven-point scale from "extremely liberal" to "extremely conservative," they conclude that "measures of policy orientation derived through voters' stands on closed-ended issue scales or through open-ended references to ideology in evaluating candidates and parties may seriously underestimate the role of ideology in voting behavior" (p. 244).
[54] Nie, Verba, and Petrocik, *Changing American Voter*, p. 130.
[55] Ibid., p. 135.
[56] Ibid., pp. 146-147, chap. 10.
[57] Warren E. Miller and Teresa E. Levitin, *Leadership and Change: The New Politics and The American Electorate* (Cambridge, Mass.: Winthrop, 1976), p. 1.
[58] Ibid., p. 90.
[59] Ibid., p. 242.

While the clusters of issue attitudes and New Politics sentiments were both clearly related to voting, their connection with partisanship was weak. The new attitude clusters in the American electorate did not reinforce, but rather cut across, party identifications formed during the New Deal when economic concerns were dominant. In the American context, in fact, increased attention to issues and to ideology (measured on either a New Politics continuum or a self-assessed liberal-conservative dimension)[60] seemed to be slowly producing a decomposition of traditional party alignments. The American studies underscore the importance of distinguishing between explanations of partisanship and explanations of voting. Issues and ideology were becoming more important for the latter, while cutting across and weakening old partisan attachments.

The Value Cleavage of the Late Sixties. The late sixties and early seventies in Australia, as in the United States, were years when new political issues emerged. Indeed, throughout the Western industrial world during this period similar political issues came onto the agenda: environmentalism, concern for minorities and the position of women, the desire for more participation in government, for less impersonal social relations. These issues ran alongside continuing attention to such matters as inflation, unemployment, economic growth, the treatment of criminal offenders. All of these issues—many of them concerned with the "quality of life"—were actively debated in Australia, particularly under the impetus of the Whitlam-led Labor party. A number of these concerns are closely related to those that define the New Politics in the United States.

A recent cross-national study by Ronald Inglehart has found a striking consistency among Western nations in the patterning of priorities among these issues.[61] Inglehart finds a clear tendency for those who emphasize economic growth, the fight against inflation, and economic stability also to emphasize the importance of maintaining order, fighting crime, and having strong defense forces. He labels this the "materialist" position. At the other end of an underlying dimension (negatively related to the materialist position) he finds those who seek more say on the job, a less impersonal society, more participation in government, and a high priority for freedom of speech. He labels this the "post-materialist" position. Inglehart finds that the

---

[60] Nie, Verba, and Petrocik, *Changing American Voter*, pp. 193, 295; Miller and Levitin, *Leadership and Change*, p. 263.

[61] Ronald Inglehart, *The Silent Revolution: Changing Values and Political Styles Among Western Publics* (Princeton: Princeton University Press, 1977).

relative frequency of these positions varies across nations, as does the extent of generational difference. The proportion of post-materialists he relates to the degree of economic and social advance made by a country, the amount of generational difference to the *rapidity* of change experienced by a country. He also finds a consistent tendency for post-materialists to support the parties of the left and for materialists to support the parties of the right.[62] Inglehart's labeling of the two positions can certainly be questioned. It is used for convenience only in the discussion which follows.

The implications of the materialist/post-materialist dimension for voting and partisanship, Inglehart found, vary from country to country. In Britain, for example, party competition has scarcely focused on this dimension. In France, on the other hand, the "electorate is polarized according to individual value priorities to an exceptional degree."[63] Inglehart confirmed that there is only a weak association between value type (on his scale) and party identification in the United States. He concluded, however, that "on the whole, the relationship between values and voting intention is impressive. We view it as a source of change in the basis of political partisanship."[64]

Australia as an advanced industrial society would be expected to have a significant proportion of post-materialists in its electorate. Moreover, it might be argued that the intensive effort of Gough Whitlam to make Labor the party of concern for the cities and the environment and ethnic minorities, and the continuing interest of state Labor parties in matters of worker participation, might well have succeeded in attracting to Labor support from voters with these concerns. To the extent that young people have been more open to these issues we might begin to find here an explanation for the

---

[62] Ibid., chap. 2, p. 230. Whether Inglehart's labeling of these positions is satisfactory can be questioned. The factor analysis he undertakes on a more extensive set of items (see especially p. 46) supports his use of the shorter scale, but on its face there is an element of acceptance/nonacceptance of authority in the scale he derives from the factor analysis. A correlation analysis of Inglehart's short scale with a scale derived from Robert Bales designed to measure "acceptance of authority" produced a product-moment correlation coefficient of .30. See Robert Bales, *Personality and Interpersonal Behavior* (New York: Holt, Rinehart and Winston, 1970). In this chapter, however, Inglehart's terminology will be adopted. For critical comment see A. Marsh, "The Silent Revolution: Value Priorities and Quality of Life in Britain," *American Political Science Review*, vol. 69 (1975), pp. 21-30; W. M. Lafferty, "Basic Needs and Political Values: Some Perspectives from Norway on Europe's Silent Revolution," *Acta Sociologica*, vol. 19 (1976), pp. 117-136.

[63] Inglehart, *Silent Revolution*, p. 231.

[64] Ibid., pp. 231-232.

observed greater tendency of younger voters to support Labor, even in 1975 and 1977. Inglehart suggests that we may be witnessing

> a change in the social bases of the political parties of the Left, for the Post-Materialists come overwhelmingly from middle class backgrounds, yet they tend to support the policies of the Left. Conversely, the most materialistic individuals tend to be concentrated among low income groups—but support key aspects of the established order.[65]

A recent national survey undertaken by Bruce Headey from Melbourne University allows us to assess the relevance of Inglehart's analysis for Australia. The questionnaire included items used by Inglehart to provide a shorthand measurement of his materialist and post-materialist positions. Voters were asked to give their first and second priorities among the following: fighting rising prices, protecting freedom of speech, maintaining order in the nation, and giving people more say in important government decisions.[66] Those who selected "order" *and* "rising prices" as their first two priorities were labeled materialists; those who selected "freedom of speech" *and* "more say" as their first two priorities were labeled post-materialists. The intergenerational differences in Australia were among the *lowest* in any country. This is consistent with the description of Australia as having many of the characteristics of a "pure" post-industrial society, while having experienced lower rates of economic and social change than most.[67]

How are these positions related to partisanship? Have they actively drawn people to the Labor party in recent years? Table 2–10 shows that there is in fact a clear association between Inglehart's "value-types" and party identification in Australia. Among the quarter of the electorate who could be labeled materialists the coalition parties have a margin of twenty-six percentage points over Labor. Among the 15 percent who are post-materialists Labor has a margin of thirty percentage points over the coalition. The product-moment correlation with major-party identification (measured on a nine-point scale from Very Strong Liberal-National Country to Very Strong Labor) is .21 (accounting for some 4 percent of the variance

---

[65] Ibid., p. 366.

[66] I am very grateful to Dr. Headey for his permission to use an analysis of these items in this chapter.

[67] In *Society*, Kemp employs a characterization of Australia as an unusually "pure" case of an advanced industrial society to interpret data concerning Australian voting patterns over three decades. Australia's relatively low rate of economic growth since World War II has occasioned frequent comment.

TABLE 2–10
"Materialism" and "Post-Materialism" in Australia, by Party Identification, 1978
(in percentages)

Respondent's Party Identification	Respondent's Value Type		
	Materialist	Mixed	Post-materialist
Liberal-National Country	58	40	27
Labor	32	42	57
Australian Democrats	3	4	7
Other	—	3	2
No party	8	11	7
Total	101	100	100
N	(158)	(412)	(98)

Note: "Materialism" and "post-materialism" are here used in the sense defined by Ronald Inglehart: those who emphasize values like economic growth, the fight against inflation, economic stability, law and order, and strong defense forces are materialists; those who emphasize more say on the job, a less impersonal society, greater participation in government, and a high priority for freedom of speech are post-materialists.
Source: Data collected in a national survey (N=686) by Dr. Bruce Headey, Melbourne University. The survey organization was Morgan Gallup.

in major-party identification). As will be seen below, however, this association is independent of occupational class or subjective social class. A voter's position on this materialist/post-materialist dimension has no statistically significant association with either his occupation or his class self-placement. The positions identified by Inglehart (whatever the merit of his labels) do appear to be relevant to an understanding of partisanship in Australia, but can we be sure that this association does not simply reflect the positions taken by the parties on these issues—that people who identify with Labor on other grounds have come to accept their party's position on these values? The simple answer is no, we cannot be sure. On the other hand, the "new" positions have clearly been promoted by many forces in the society. In addition, there is a statistically significant (though not large) positive correlation between education and post-materialism (the product-moment coefficient is 0.17; since $N = 668$, this coefficient is significant at better than the 0.001 level); and one could argue, perhaps persuasively, that these ideas have an origin independent of the parties. But perhaps the educated were simply more alert to the messages of the parties. The logical doubt remains.

To the extent that this difference in values has been a factor behind the voters' choice of party, it is one that may have been operating only in recent years. It may therefore help to account for aspects of Labor's appeal among the young and educated. It is even suggestive for Labor's problems in the two most recent federal elections: the post-materialists are outnumbered two-to-one by materialists among the voters who have no party identification, and these voters have been an important factor in the coalition's victories.

The interest in relating values to partisanship and voting decisions stems in part from the fact that values are conceived of as relatively stable aspects of an individual's orientation to the world, by contrast to mere opinions on current issues.[68] Individualism, for example, is a value that has been seen as a persistent element in Western culture for centuries; or again, certain cultures have been characterized as more achievement-oriented than others. If the dependent variable is known to be relatively stable over time (as party identification is believed to be), then to be useful, the independent variable also must be stable. One of the attractions of social structural explanations of partisanship and political attitudes has been, precisely, that social structure changes slowly and can therefore explain stable phenomena such as persistent loyalties. Inglehart refers to his positions as values, but how certain can we be of their stability over time? Can we be sure they do not reflect mere fashions in ideas? Indeed, their very association with current politics raises questions about attributing to them a causal role in producing and changing patterns of party loyalties and voting behavior.

Application of the Bales Approach to Australia. There are several alternative approaches to the study of values.[69] One of these can be mentioned here, since data are available that will permit us to apply it to partisanship in Australia. This approach was developed by Robert Bales, using items adapted from previous studies and from his own extensive work on individual behavior in small groups. Bales

---

[68] For example, W. J. McGuire, "The Nature of Attitudes and Attitude Change," in Gardner Lindzey and Elliot Aronson, eds., *The Handbook of Social Psychology* (Reading, Mass.: Addison-Wesley, 1969), vol. 3, pp. 187-191; John P. Robinson and Phillip R. Shaver, *Measures of Social Psychological Attitudes* (Ann Arbor, Mich.: Institute for Social Research, 1969), p. 410.

[69] The in-depth interview technique was employed in a Melbourne study that reached conclusions parallel to those flowing from the analysis reported in the text. See Graham Little, *Politics and Personal Style* (Melbourne: Nelson, 1973). Also Graham Little, *Faces on the Campus* (Melbourne: Melbourne University Press, 1975).

developed a number of "value scales" out of a factor analysis of a 144-item "value profile." These scales were designed to measure such values as "acceptance of authority," "equalitarianism," "individualism," and "need-determined expression versus value-determined restraint."[70] Items from these scales were tested on a sample of 193 in Melbourne in December 1977 and administered in revised form as part of the 1978 national survey. Factor analysis confirmed the relevance of the Bales items for the Australian population.[71] One of these scales was interpreted to measure equalitarianism, and it is on this one that attention will be concentrated here. The items used for this scale are set out in Table 2–11.

Most observers would probably agree that equalitarianism is an important political value in Australia, and of course, in some of its aspects it has been seen as a central value in Western societies for centuries. Tocqueville argued that the "passion for equality" was one of the driving forces for change in the United States and that it would eventually transform the American social and political order.[72] It remains a vital subject in current debate on social and political directions.[73] Yet how far and in what respects equality should be pursued has remained controversial. It is possible that voters differ according to whether they believe material equality or social equality to be at issue. Equalitarianism can be expressed in a desire for major social reform or at the level of personal relations. The particular interest here in Bales's scale is that his items are well removed, for the

---

[70] I am grateful to Professor Alan F. Davies (Melbourne University) for drawing my attention to the possible usefulness of Bales's work in this context.

[71] A constrained (four-factor) analysis on a national sample (N=686) produced similar factors to those Bales had found in his American work. The items used for the analysis may be found in Bales, *Personality*, pp. 506-510. Some rewording was effected where the original phrasing was ambiguous in the Australian context or where unduly abstract or artificial language had been employed. Resistance to the wording of some of the items was reported by interviewers in the earlier 193 Melbourne interviews.

[72] Alexis de Tocqueville, *Democracy in America*, translated by G. Lawrence (New York: Doubleday, Anchor, 1969).

[73] John Rawls, *A Theory of Justice* (London: Oxford University Press, 1971); Brian Barry, *A Liberal Theory of Justice* (London: Oxford University Press, 1974); Hugh Stretton, *Capitalism, Socialism and the Environment* (Cambridge: Cambridge University Press, 1976); Christopher Jencks, *Inequality* (New York: Basic Books, 1972); Friedrich von Hayek, *The Constitution of Liberty* (Chicago: University of Chicago Press, 1960). These are a tiny selection from the current vast literature on the subject. For Australia see Theo van Dugteren, ed., *Who Gets What: The Distribution of Wealth and Power in Australia* (Sydney: Hodder and Stoughton, 1976); Sol Encel, *Equality and Authority* (Melbourne: Cheshire, 1970); Michael J. Berry, "Inequality," in Alan F. Davies, Sol Encel and Michael J. Berry, *Australian Society: A Sociological Introduction* (Melbourne: Longman Cheshire, 1977), third edition, pp. 18-54.

TABLE 2–11

Items in Bales's Equalitarianism Scale, Australia, 1978

Item	Rotated Factor Loadings			
	I	II	III	IV
1. There should be equality for everyone because we are all human beings.	0.54	−0.11	−0.00	0.05
2. Everybody should have an equal chance and an equal say.	0.45	0.10	0.05	0.01
3. Poverty could be almost entirely done away with if we made certain basic changes in our social and economic system.	0.43	0.12	0.03	−0.00
4. In a small group there should be no real leaders. Everybody should have an equal say.	0.40	0.08	0.15	0.01
5. A group of equals will work a lot better than a group with a fixed chain of command.	0.38	0.17	0.18	−0.02
6. Everyone should get what he needs. The things we have belong to all of us.	0.36	0.07	0.13	0.10
7. No matter what the circumstances, you should never just tell people what they have to do.	0.27	0.09	0.20	−0.01
8. There has been too much talk, and not enough real action, in doing away with racial discrimination.	0.25	0.02	0.01	0.06

NOTE: The four factors are: I, equalitarianism; II, acceptance of authority; III, need-determined expression versus value-determined restraint; IV, individualism. The order of extraction in the factor analysis was II, III, I, IV. For an explanation of the method see Norman H. Nie, C. Hadlai Hull, Jean A. Jenkins, Karin Steinbrenner, Dale H. Bent, *Statistical Package for the Social Sciences* (New York: McGraw-Hill, 1975), pp. 468–514; Dennis Child, *The Essentials of Factor Analysis* (London: Holt, Rinehart & Winston, 1976).

SOURCE: Headey, National Survey, 1978, using items originated by Robert F. Bales, *Personality and Interpersonal Behavior* (New York: Holt, Rinehart & Winston, 1970). Some items have been reworded.

most part, from the current issue preoccupations of the party leaderships. Thus, they are more likely to capture attitudes formed in the wider cultural environment of Australian society, and if they are found to correlate with partisanship it will perhaps be easier to argue that they are evidence for the relevance of values in explaining the electorate's political judgments.

TABLE 2–12

CORRELATION OF PARTY IDENTIFICATION WITH SOCIAL STRUCTURAL AND VALUE ITEMS, AUSTRALIA, 1978
(in Pearson product-moment correlation coefficients)

	Party Identification[a]	Occupation	Income	Class Self-Placement	Religiosity	Post-Materialism[b]	Equalitarianism
Party identification[a]	1.00	0.25[c]	0.09[c]	0.24[c]	0.16[c]	−0.21[c]	−0.25[c]
Occupation		1.00	0.22[c]	0.40[c]	0.04	0.03	−0.20[c]
Income			1.00	0.05	0.08[c]	0.01	−0.05
Class self-placement				1.00	0.11[c]	−0.01	−0.17[c]
Religiosity					1.00	−0.06	−0.04
Post-materialism[b]						1.00	−0.03
Equalitarianism							1.00

[a] Major party identification is measured on a nine-point scale (1=very strongly Labor, through 5=no ID, to 9=very strongly Liberal).
[b] For the definition of post-materialism see note to Table 2-10.
[c] Statistically significant correlation.
SOURCE: Author's analysis of data from Headey, National Survey, 1978 (N=501).

There is in fact a significant statistical association between a voter's equalitarianism score on Bales's scale and that voter's party: the more equalitarian his values, the more likely he is to identify with the Labor party; the less equalitarian his values, the more likely he is to identify with the coalition. The product-moment correlation between the equalitarianism scale and the major-party identification scale is 0.25 (N=501), indicating that some 6 percent of the variance in major-party identification can be accounted for by a voter's orientation towards equalitarianism as measured by Bales's scale.

Table 2–12, which shows the simple correlations between a number of the major variables discussed, shows further that equalitarian attitudes are associated with both occupation and class self-placement. But although associated with class, equalitarianism is by no means simply the attitudinal process by which class impinges on the party system. Even when we control for equalitarian attitudes, the relationship between occupation and major-party identification is only marginally affected. Class self-placement has much stronger claims to be regarded as a significant part of the process by which occupation is related to party loyalty: when we control for class self-placement, the amount of variance in party identification accounted for by occupation is halved—from six to under three percentage points. Class self-placement still retains some independent explanatory power apart from its link with occupation, but this is much less than is attributable to equalitarianism. Moreover, equalitarianism, as measured by Bales's items, is unrelated to Inglehart's value types statistically, so that both could be used to give independent force to a value-based explanation of partisanship.

Table 2–13 presents the partial correlations supporting these generalizations. Self-perceptions and values are important, and *not simply as processes linking objective situation to vote*. Occupation and income together account for some 6 percent of the variance in party identification; occupation and subjective class together (when their interrelationships are taken into account) account for 9 percent of the variance in major-party identification. When the various value measures are included as well, the total variance accounted for is more than doubled—to 19 percent (the multiple correlation coefficient is 0.433). There is still considerable room for discussion about the most suitable approach to measuring values and the nature of the linkages between values and social experience, but that values in some sense are vital to understanding political partisanship in Australia is scarcely in doubt.

Other techniques are available if one wishes to pursue further the matters raised here. It may prove fruitful to look beyond value concepts such as equalitarianism, on which, theoretically, the whole electorate can be ranked, to specific clusterings of beliefs, norms, and preferences that constitute distinctive outlooks or world views within the electorate. A correlation matrix of responses to a large number of items touching a variety of social beliefs, norms, and attitudes in a Melbourne sample, for instance, found a number of clusterings that were associated with support for one of the major party groupings. A cluster of items related to social conservatism (belief in the importance of the Crown and in the significance of Christianity in the conduct of government) were associated with support for the coalition parties. Another cluster relating to material equality (redistribution of wealth, whether workers got their fair share of what they produced, whether trade unions fought hard enough for workers' rights) were associated with support for the Labor party. When individuals' positions in relation to these and other clusters were known, it was possible to construct a variable that accounted for a high proportion of the variance in major-party voting.[74] This approach

---

[74] For further information see note in Kemp, *Society*, Postscript.

TABLE 2-13
Contribution of Social Structural and Value Items to Party Identification, Australia, 1978
(partial correlation analysis)

	\multicolumn{3}{c}{Association with Party Identification}		
	Simple r	Partial Correlation	Controlling for
Occupation	0.25	0.23	Income
Occupation	0.25	0.22	Equalitarianism
Occupation	0.25	0.16	Income, class self-placement
Occupation	0.25	0.17	Class self-placement
Income	0.09	0.03	Occupation
Class self-placement	0.24	0.16	Occupation
Class self-placement	0.24	0.13	Occupation, income, religiosity, post-materialism, equalitarianism
Religiosity	0.16	0.13	Occupation, income, class self-placement, post-materialism, equalitarianism
Post-materialism	0.21	0.22	Occupation, income, class self-placement, religiosity, equalitarianism
Equalitarianism	0.25	0.21	Occupation, income, religiosity, class self-placement, post-materialism
Multiple R	0.433		
Multiple R^2	0.19		

Source: Author's analysis of data from Headey, National Survey, 1978.

is still being explored, but it has the obvious advantage that it does not assume the society as a whole holds coherent values; instead it makes the more modest assumption that within the society there are reasonably coherent positions and that particular (and different) aspects of the parties' loosely structured ideologies may appeal to discrete but identifiable sections of the electorate grouped according to their world view.

Consensus. So far we have been mainly concerned with discovering what differentiates voters from one another and how they can be grouped to shed light on their political behavior. Equally relevant for political parties seeking to appeal to the electorate, however, is an investigation of those matters on which the electorate is agreed and which influence its political decisions and judgments. Early in this chapter it was suggested that the electorate is largely agreed on the importance of strong leadership that maintains a convincing appearance of being in touch with the people. It was also noted that the electorate seemed to be socially egalitarian in outlook. As one of the most affluent of the world's peoples, Australians have clearly placed a high value on material well-being, and economic issues have consistently been foremost in Australian politics. This is not merely a function of the search for advantage by union and employer elites. It reflects the high priority placed by the voter on material prosperity. Economic issues were once more in the forefront in the 1977 election.

In its search for material well-being the Australian electorate is not notably egalitarian. In late 1974, 87 percent of a Melbourne sample (N=500) agreed with the proposition, "Every person should have the right to become rich if he has the ability," and 85 percent agreed that "the main thing that determines a person's success or failure in life is how hard he works at it." Nevertheless, at a more concrete level significant proportions of the electorate show something less than complete satisfaction with the present distribution of wealth: 47 percent believed that "the working man misses out on his fair share of what he produces," and only 57 percent agreed that "people who make a bit of money have generally earned it." Very few, however, thought that "the only way to get much improvement in conditions in Australia is to tax the rich more heavily" (28 percent). There would seem to be a widespread feeling that the working man could get more, but little desire to see this achieved by attacking the well-to-do. The income tax reductions of the Fraser government during 1977 were criticized by the Labor party for favoring the well-to-do, but there is some indication that they were electorally advantageous to the government in 1977.[75]

For the achievement of a comfortable and happy family life the electorate places a high responsibility on government: 67 percent believed that it is "the government's responsibility to make sure that everyone has a good standard of living." Yet this is not an endorsement of a government-run society: 47 percent felt, for example, that laws nationalizing big business were "wrong in any circumstances," and a further 26 percent felt that such laws might be justified in extreme circumstances, but not now. The view seemed to be rather that government should help the weaker members of society: 66 percent agreed that "the government should give a person work if he

---

[75] The Morgan Gallup Poll reported in the week before the 1977 election that electors preferred personal tax cuts (as legislated by the coalition parties) to payroll tax cuts (as promised by Labor) by 47 percent to 34 percent, with 19 percent classified "can't say, neither, or both." *Bulletin*, December 10, 1977, p. 14.

can't find another job." Past studies have shown the electorate prepared to support improvements in social welfare even though the price was higher taxes.[76]

The electorate has fears concerning the future of the Australian way of life. According to the Melbourne study, a surprisingly high percentage of voters believed that "there are always enemies of our way of life trying to undermine us" (75 percent), while very few were prepared to say that "most of those worries about subversion by communists and others are now things of the past" (29 percent). A national survey in April 1977 asked voters to choose what they thought was the greatest danger to the world from a fixed set of alternatives. There was no consensus, but the most frequently selected answer was "world depression" (18 percent, $N=2,000$), followed by "communism" (17 percent). The Communist question has not been much in evidence in political debate in recent years, but it may well be one of the roots of electoral concern over the power of trade unions since a number of the largest and most militant unions have leaders who are members of Communist parties.

This catalogue sketches possibly important areas of agreement among the electorate. There is a need to examine the extent to which there is a national consensus on important values and beliefs with national samples, and to explore the relationship between values on which there is a consensus and those on which there is not. Consensus may, after all, play an important role in placing boundaries on partisan conflict, since a major party that steps outside a consensus on important matters will probably suffer electorally. To determine which areas of agreement are actually employed as evaluative criteria by the electorate we must await further research.

Conclusion

Here is a plausible perspective concerning the patterns of change observed in the Australian electorate in recent research. A number of changes in Australian society have led to a decline in the significance of social class for political life. These include the differentiation of the occupational structure under advanced industrialism and the growing proportion of the work force engaged in white-collar occupations; the arrival of a society characterized by general affluence, even for blue-collar workers; the absence (at least since the depression of the thirties) of issues with a distinctive class impact; and the emergence of a society in which only a minority see themselves as working

---

[76] Aitkin, *Stability and Change*, p. 277.

class and which has low class consciousness and where a winning electoral strategy cannot be based on class appeals alone. Social change and the lack of distinctive sectarian issues have also led to a decline in the association between denomination and partisanship. On the other hand, different rates of change, contrary trends in occupational status and structure of the work force, and different economic interests in city and country continue to give substance to the urban-rural cleavage.

Post-industrial politics gave rise to a new set of issues, which were skillfully employed by Whitlam, in particular, to attract support to Labor, especially among the young and to some extent among professionals with higher education. The support from this latter category, of course, had the effect of further blurring the connection between class and party. And Whitlam's own personal style weakened the appeal of the Labor party for its traditional blue-collar supporters, who were already becoming less inclined to view their concern with higher real wages and material security as necessarily tied to Labor voting. Value differences in the electorate on post-industrial issues were crystallized and converted by Whitlam Labor into a partisan cleavage at the federal level. In turn, the coalition parties' claim of greater economic competence may have not only attracted the uncommitted who gave priority to this issue but also—and quite incidentally—strengthened the trend toward value-based party identification around post-industrial issues. The way the political issues were formulated in Australia in the early 1970s, then, lined up the parties on a value continuum which, as it happened, exaggerated trends in the bases of partisan support that were already under way. The coalition parties were drawing support more heavily from the older voters, particularly those who stressed security and stability in the social order. Behind these new value differences, however, may lie others of longer standing.

3
The Labor Party and Its 1977 Campaign

Patrick Weller

The shattering electoral defeat of December 13, 1975, left the federal Labor party demoralized. It never really recovered. When the 1977 campaign began, no leading member of the federal parliamentary Labor party (the caucus) seriously believed that Labor could win the election. Apart from a short period of hope when the opinion polls briefly showed the Labor party ahead, the expectation of defeat remained, although no one expected it to be as complete as it was. An understanding of the state of mind that prevailed among members of the Labor party is essential for any review of its progress and problems between 1975 and 1977.

Labor's demoralization took several forms. Immediately after the 1975 election result was known, serious internal squabbling began. Within two days two former ministers launched attacks on the style of Whitlam's leadership. Jim Cairns attacked Whitlam's personality cult; Clyde Cameron, a notorious party in-fighter, claimed that the Liberal campaign was based on mistakes made by Whitlam without consulting the caucus. Whitlam's leadership thus became an issue—indeed the major internal issue—that plagued the party for the next two years.

In part this was because of Whitlam's—and to a lesser extent the whole party's—obsession with the events of November 11, 1975, when the governor general, Sir John Kerr, had sacked the Whitlam government and installed a "caretaker" Fraser government. Whitlam believed that he had been betrayed and deceived, and with considerable justification. It was no surprise that the Labor party was not prepared to forgive Kerr. But the persistent attacks on Kerr's duplicity, the Labor party's decision to boycott any function he attended, and its support, implicit at least, of the rowdy demonstrations against him, were probably electorally counterproductive. On November 11, 1975, Whitlam had told the angry crowds to "maintain their rage." They did. Kerr helped too. His provocative statements, culminating in a speech during his parliamentary farewell in October 1977 that expressed support for the Liberal government's economic policies, continued to politicize the role of the governor general to the extent that it is unlikely to be regarded again as a nonpartisan office. But that was beside the point. In attacking Kerr, Labor too often failed to attack the real architect of the 1975 crisis, Malcolm Fraser. In the first year of his government, while Fraser remained relatively free from criticism, the Labor party became obsessed with the past, not with planning for the future.[1]

The large size of the Liberal majority and Labor's expectation of another lengthy period in the wilderness also had their consequences. Some senior ex-ministers like Frank Crean, Jim Cairns, and Kim Beazley decided to retire at the next election rather than spend a long period in opposition. Perhaps more serious, two younger ministers defeated in 1975 decided not to stand for reelection even though it was expected that both would regain their seats. More generally the 1975 defeat had restored the belief that Labor could only be elected for short periods in times of difficulty, although even the Liberals had not appreciated quite how intractable the economy had become since 1972, in part at least because of international pressures.

During 1976 and 1977 the Liberal government's attempts at economic management often floundered. Inflation was reduced but the costs were high as unemployment continued to rise. According to many precedents the Liberal government should have been under continuous attack, but it was not, primarily because the Labor party remained disunited over the question of leadership.

---

[1] Several books have now been published about the years of the Whitlam government. The best of them are: Clem Lloyd and Gordon Reid, *Out of the Wilderness* (Melbourne: Cassell, 1974); Graham Freudenberg, *A Certain Grandeur: Gough Whitlam in Politics* (Sydney: Macmillan, 1977). For descriptions of recent election campaigns and their concomitant crises, see: Laurie Oakes and David Solomon, *The Making of an Australian Prime Minister* (Melbourne: Cheshire, 1973) and Laurie Oakes and David Solomon, *Grab For Power* (Melbourne: Cheshire, 1974). On the 1975 crisis see Andrew Clark and Clem Lloyd, *Kerr's King Hit* (Sydney: Cassell, 1976); Laurie Oakes, *Crash Through or Crash: The Unmaking of a Prime Minister* (Melbourne: Drummond, 1976); Paul Kelly, *The Unmaking of Gough* (Sydney: Angus & Robertson, 1976); Alan Reid, *The Whitlam Venture* (Melbourne: Hill of Content, 1976); and, of course, Howard R. Penniman, ed., *Australia at the Polls: The National Elections of 1975* (Washington, D.C.: American Enterprise Institute, 1977).

PATRICK WELLER

The Australian Labor Party: Theory and Practice

The Australian Labor party has a long history. It was founded in the various colonies in the 1890s, before Australia became a federation, and the federal party was created when elected representatives from the states met before the first Parliament was opened. It grew rapidly in strength and gained a majority in both houses in 1910. By 1915 it had been in office in all but one of the states and appeared to be becoming the natural governing party. But in 1916 the party split over the issue of support for conscription for overseas military service and lost power. Since then opposition has been, as Rawson puts it, the "normal" state of affairs for the ALP.[2] It has been in office for only thirteen of the sixty-two years since 1916.

But those early years were important because the rules and procedural assumptions on which the party operated were settled then and have scarcely changed.[3] The party drew from its trade union heritage a belief in solidarity and democratic procedures, and the early Labor parties had enshrined these assumptions as norms of political behavior by 1900. In discussions of policy or tactics all members were regarded as having an equal voice, and once debate was finished, all decisions were taken by vote. The decision of the majority was then binding on the party. Further, since in a mass party the participation of every member is clearly unattainable, all officials were elected and were subject to regular reelection. They were regarded as delegates, bound to support and express the views of those who elected them whether or not they personally agreed. This principle was, in theory, as applicable to federal members of Parliament and even prime ministers as it was to branch officials. The system was defended by one of the party's founders in these terms:

> Nothing can more conform to the principles and ideals of Democracy and at the same time more effectively promote the interests and secure the objects for which a party contends than an institution which, enabling all to be heard,

---

[2] D. W. Rawson, "The Labor Campaign" in Penniman, ed., *Australia at the Polls, 1975*, pp. 76-78.

[3] For an analysis of the growth of the machinery of the federal Labor party, see L. F. Crisp, *The Australian Federal Labour Party, 1951-55* (London: Longmans 1955), pp. 1-70, and Patrick Weller, ed., *Caucus Minutes 1901-1949: The Minutes of the Meetings of the Federal Parliamentary Labor Party, Volume I, 1901-15* (Melbourne: Melbourne University Press, 1975), pp. 8-16. For a study of the role of the Labor party, see Don Rawson, *Labor in Vain* (Melbourne: Longmans, 1966).

ensures that after due deliberation the party should speak with one voice.[4]

These assumptions still direct the procedures of the party.

One of the major concerns of the Labor party has been to ensure that its members of Parliament are responsive to the wishes of the rank and file. As early as 1894 in New South Wales the principle was established that the state conference determined policy, which was then binding on M.P.s. At the federal level a similar chain of command was gradually evolved to achieve this purpose, or at least to appear to do so.

The federal conference, now called the national conference, determines party policy. Starting in 1902 it met every third year; it now meets every second year. Up to 1967 the conference consisted of six delegates from each of the six states. In 1967 the four federal parliamentary leaders[5] and the leader in each of the state parliaments were added; and delegates from the Australian Capital Territory, the Northern Territory, and the Young Labor Association have since also been included. The conference meets for five days only. It is an unwieldy body that is not well suited to the intricacies of policy making. It cannot set priorities between the various planks or forecast the political or economic climate in which a putative Labor government must operate. But it is the final court of appeal for disputes within the party, and when it does make a decision, that decision is binding on all members of the party.

The federal (or national) executive was established in 1915 to govern the party's affairs between conferences. Consisting of two delegates from each state branch, it initially was required to meet at least once a year; now it meets at least four times and sometimes far more often. It deals with organizational problems and can "interpret" (but not change) the party platform in cases of dispute. It developed its power only gradually. At one stage, in the mid-1930s, it was almost abolished when a strong state branch, who wanted to be able to direct federal members, sought a reduction of its power.[6] But it survived and even developed the capacity to direct the federal caucus itself. In 1967 the four federal parliamentary leaders were added to the executive, and it has become more wary in its use of its power. Formally it has "plenary power to deal with and decide any matters

---

[4] W. M. Hughes, "The Case for Labor," *Daily Telegraph*, May 30, 1908.

[5] That is, the leader and deputy leader in the House of Representatives and the leader and deputy leader in the Senate.

[6] See the introduction to Patrick Weller and Beverly Lloyd, eds., *Federal Executive Minutes 1915-1945* (Melbourne: Melbourne University Press, 1978).

which, in the opinion of an absolute majority of members of the Executive, affect the general welfare of the Labor Movement."[7] Since it meets more often than the conference, its influence is more far-reaching, and it has become the main extraparliamentary center of power in the federal party machinery.

The Labor caucus (that is, the federal parliamentary party) thus has to act within the procedural constraints created by the party's democratic assumptions and within the policy laid down by the national conference and interpreted by the national executive. In this sense it has less room to maneuver than most other Western parliamentary parties. But those constraints must not be exaggerated. Decisions about parliamentary tactics, about subjects not touched upon by the platform, or about priorities are the responsibility of the caucus. Further it can interpret many of the vaguer or more general platform items and even, occasionally, choose to ignore one. In theory its members are strictly bound, but in practice, because the caucus meets more often and because it must react quickly to government initiatives on a wide range of topics, it is easily the most influential section of the party.

Party rules and procedures are not always followed; there are conventional or pragmatic rules which allow some of them to be partly ignored. But they do provide a general framework within which all party activity is carried on, and, over the long period in which they have been in force, they have acquired a high level of legitimacy. They are now so embedded in the party structure that to try to change them might have far-reaching consequences for the party.

Labor, the Leadership, and Whitlam

Formally at least, the leader of the Labor party is regarded as the first among equals. As a former leader claimed:

> In the caucus of the Labor Party the leader has no more weight by reason of his leadership than the newest member of his party. Every man stands there, as is fitting in a democratic country, upon a level footing. That man's influence is greatest whose arguments are the most cogent. But every man is entitled to be heard, and has an equal opportunity to mould the policy and shape the destiny of the party.[8]

---

[7] The most recent version of the rules of the national executive is published in *The Australian Labor Party: Platform, Constitution and Rules, 1977* (Melbourne: Melbourne Industrial Printing and Publishing Co., 1977).

[8] Hughes, "Case for Labor." Ironically it was Hughes who, as leader, split the party in 1916 because he was not prepared to abide by the principles he laid down here.

The leader is elected by the caucus after each general election. He is bound to accept the decisions adopted by a majority vote of the caucus, the platform endorsed by the national conference, and the edicts of the national executive on organizational matters or on the interpretation of policy between the meetings of the national conference. Any decision he makes may be overruled by the caucus if it was not initially consulted. The democratic forms on which the party is based assume that the leader is a spokesman of the party and restrict his freedom of action.

But those theoretical assumptions, although important, do not, of course, accurately portray the situation. The leader invariably has far more influence than any other member. A wise leader will always keep open his channels of communication with the caucus, to ensure that he understands what the backbenchers feel and that they are kept adequately informed. He can usually rely on a fairly solid group of supporters because at the very least the maintenance of his position represents the status quo. But, more important, if the caucus overrules the leader too often, then his prestige in the community and indeed his electoral credibility can be undermined. His statements and views naturally receive far more weight than those of the average member; he must often react publicly when the caucus cannot meet or be consulted; hence, even if a Labor leader cannot act with as much freedom as his Liberal counterpart, he is not nearly as restricted in his activities as the formal theory of party democracy suggests.

Further, despite the tendency of the Labor party to fight its internal battles with bitterness, intensity, and complete disrespect for any rules that can be manipulated (meanwhile using its kid gloves in its battles with the Liberals), it has often been reluctant to change its leaders. In the federal party's seventy-seven years of existence, no federal leader has been defeated in a ballot. Of the nine leaders that preceded Whitlam, five retired (although not always gracefully), three died, and one walked out and split the party when faced with a vote of confidence. Several challenges to the incumbent have been made, but none has been successful. While the Liberal party, which operates without formal rules or standing orders, is able to move suddenly and decisively against a leader who fails to provide electoral success—or even looks as though he might be unsuccessful—the rules of the Labor party require that proper notice be given and that prescribed procedures be followed. A leader thus always has time to organize his forces. Indeed, in the last twenty years, two leaders at least have long outlasted their period of effectiveness within the Labor party.

H. V. Evatt was leader from 1951 to 1960 even though he could never have won an election after his divisive role in the split of 1955. Arthur Calwell, the party leader from 1961 to 1967, often appeared senile during the 1966 campaign; he had held onto the leadership more because he wanted to stop Whitlam than because he expected to become prime minister.

These precedents help to explain why Whitlam managed to survive to fight the 1977 election. The party's loyalty towards its leaders was important. Then too, Whitlam's ability and faculties had not declined. He may have been tired and his reputation tarnished, but he was still a magnificently entertaining speaker with a commanding presence. He had been one of the most constructive and dynamic political figures in the last thirty years of Australian politics. His personality had dominated the period of the Labor government. Many of the successes—the redirection of foreign policy, the urban and educational initiatives, the equality of pay for women—owed much to Whitlam personally.

But at the same time many of the flaws of his leadership had become more apparent. His philosophy of action—crash through or crash—demanded, rather than nurtured, support. His sharp tongue often unnecessarily offended even his friends. He had failed to unite the cabinet behind a coherent economic strategy until 1975, when it was too late to rehabilitate the Labor party's reputation. Further, many of the more spectacular disasters—such as the bungling of the removal of Vince Gair in 1974 and the long-running loans affair—were also in part Whitlam's own responsibility.[9] In 1975 the opposition used these episodes in the campaign that shattered Whitlam's reputation as an electoral asset, and in the following two years his opponents within the party brought them into the debate over the leadership. In particular they argued (in retrospect justifiably) that Labor could never win another election under Whitlam.

---

[9] See Freudenberg, *A Certain Grandeur*, pp. 288-301 and 317-326 for detailed descriptions of Labor's problems. In 1974 Whitlam had appointed Vince Gair, the leader of the right-wing Democratic Labor party, ambassador to Ireland. He had hoped to improve the Labor party's position in the Senate by having six vacant seats at the forthcoming Senate election. But he failed to secure Gair's resignation, and the premier of Queensland quickly issued the writs for the election. Gair's position thus became a casual vacancy, to be filled by the Country-party-dominated Queensland parliament. For details see Leon Epstein, "The Australian Political System," in Penniman, ed., *Australia at the Polls 1975*, pp. 33-36. The loans affair is the name given to the Labor government's attempt to raise massive overseas loans of Arab money through rather shady businessmen. It failed entirely but it dragged on and discredited the government.

Whitlam survived as leader because no real alternative was prepared to stand. The day after the election Whitlam announced that he would like to be succeeded by Bob Hawke, federal president of the ALP, president of the Australian Council of Trade Unions (ACTU), and, according to the polls, the most popular figure in Australian politics. But Hawke did not have a parliamentary seat and, despite several rumors in the next two years, he never actually put himself forward for party endorsement.[10] There was some doubt whether Hawke himself was prepared to take the risk of entering parliamentary life. In addition Whitlam's arrogance in nominating his own successor aroused such a bitter reaction that Whitlam was forced to announce that he intended to lead the party through the next election himself.[11]

The only plausible alternative to Whitlam was Bill Hayden, who had been treasurer in 1975 and had the reputation of a cautious and capable economic manager. Whitlam publicly stated that he was prepared to stand down in favor of Hayden, but the latter, shattered by the defeat, decided not only to decline the leadership, but even to refuse to stand for the shadow executive. As the only remaining Labor M.P. from Queensland—and even he had survived by the narrowest of margins—Hayden preferred to ensure his own electoral survival and to devote time to private pursuits, including starting a law degree. His refusal meant that by default Whitlam was almost certain to be reelected.

On December 21, 1975, the caucus met and decided to postpone the leadership election until January 21, 1976. Whitlam was then challenged by two men—Frank Crean, recently the party's deputy leader but before that a discredited treasurer, and Lionel Bowen, a right-wing member from New South Wales who had proved a competent and efficient minister, able to keep out of trouble. Whitlam won easily, but the victory was qualified by the caucus's decision to hold new elections for party leader and shadow cabinet in eighteen months, midway through the Parliament's expected life. Whitlam was clearly on probation. The expectation of another ballot in eighteen months had a destabilizing effect on the party. Uncertainty and self-preservation became important, with the party's left wing especially concerned to protect the position of the newly elected deputy leader, Tom Uren.

---

[10] Hawke required endorsement as the Labor party's candidate, preferably for a safe Labor seat. Although two or three sitting members in safe seats did retire in 1977, Hawke was not nominated for any of the resulting vacancies. For comments on candidate selection, see below.

[11] *Age*, December 15, 1975.

During those eighteen months Whitlam's position declined. First, it was revealed that before the 1975 election he had met Iraqi officials through whom he hoped to raise funds for the party. This action alienated both the Jewish lobby in the party and those who firmly believed the Labor party's oft-stated opposition to any overseas funding of Australian parties. Whitlam survived, but only after a bitter debate in the caucus and a censure from the national executive.[12] Later, when he claimed that the caucus contained several "has-beens," a further challenge was considered. Again no alternative leader could be found, but state Labor leaders carefully excluded Whitlam from their local election campaigns and dissociated themselves from the federal party.

In early 1977, towards the end of the eighteen-month period for which Whitlam had been elected, further challenges were discussed. At last, in March, Hayden, who had been elected to the shadow executive after the Iraqi affair, announced he would stand. In many ways Hayden was an enigma; he was immensely hard-working, intelligent, and cautious, although he could be obstinate and rigid once his mind was made up. But he lacked the appearance of overweening self-confidence and arrogance of Fraser and Whitlam. Indeed, he had been genuinely ambivalent about wanting the leader's job.

Hayden's support came partly from the self-styled left wing of the party, partly from those who were totally disillusioned with Whitlam's failure to consult other party leaders, and partly from those who can be loosely termed the economic rationalists. They were on the whole younger, more pragmatic, and more conscious of the need to go slowly in reintroducing reforms. They argued that Hayden's reputation as an economic manager meant simply that he might win an election where Whitlam would not. On Whitlam's side there was considerable residual loyalty and, for many, a desire not to humiliate a once-great leader.

The contest was, unusually for the Labor party, quiet and private. The politicking was intense but not public. The election was held on May 31 and Whitlam just won—thirty-two votes to thirty. The result confirmed Hayden as heir-apparent and was an indication to Whitlam that the party was far from satisfied—an indication he did not heed, for he immediately claimed that those who had voted against him (including nine of the top ten members of the shadow executive) were "out of touch" with the Labor movement.[13]

---

[12] See the description in Kelly, *Unmaking of Gough*, pp. 1-3, 326-345; and Rawson, "The Labor Campaign," pp. 99-102.

[13] *Canberra Times*, June 1, 1977.

Whitlam's isolation grew in the next few months. At the federal conference he was often defeated on issues dear to him—such as proposals to codify the duties of the governor general (which he opposed) and to establish a children's commission (which he supported in preference to a bureau). He was quite alone in defending his government's policy towards Timor.[14] His keynote speech at the conference espousing the need for a sound economic policy was greeted with skepticism. In September, when he publicly disagreed with the party's policy on Timor, the caucus effectively rebuked him again, although further talk of another challenge to his position came to nothing. When the 1977 election campaign began, the Labor party had a leader whose support in the parliamentary party had been reduced even beyond his bare majority of June 1977.

Dissatisfaction with its leadership had been a major reason for the opposition's inability to develop any coherence between 1975 and 1977. Even though the shadow executive included many young and bright members, they seldom gave wholehearted support to Whitlam. Of the four parliamentary leaders of the party, two were not on close terms with him. There was little planning, little united action, few coherent attacks on the government's policy and no serious effort to learn from past mistakes or develop alternative strategies or policy. Whitlam remained the dominant figure—but was no longer constructively so. His personal staff worked more for him than for the party in general. He had few new ideas (although others in the party had even fewer). Whitlam was a wounded and diminished giant. As long as he remained leader the innovations in policy or organization demanded by changed political and economic circumstances were unlikely to occur. He was often isolated at the center of the party, but his position was such that his very presence guaranteed that those around him could neither cooperate with him nor unite effectively without his involvement.

The Perth Conference and the Labor Platform

The Perth conference, held in July 1977, was regarded as an opportunity to rewrite the party platform and to bring into it some of the lessons the party had learned in office. This was a serious under-

---

[14] During the 1975 constitutional crisis the Indonesian army invaded the former Portuguese colony of East Timor. This move appeared to have at least the implicit support of Fraser and Whitlam, even though both publicly condemned it. But during the Perth conference the party moved, despite Whitlam's objections, to condemn the invasion outright, to recognize an independent East Timor, and to suspend military aid to Indonesia.

taking; in the Labor party the platform is considered important. Indeed, under the Labor government a reminder that the platform had endorsed a given measure was often enough to get it through the cabinet. When Whitlam was defending his position from Hayden's challenge in 1977, he contrasted his acceptance of the platform with Hayden's reputed wish to subordinate everything to the demands of economic management. Whitlam declared:

> A lot of people are very cynical and offhand about the platform. They say that I, for instance, have an obsession about the program or the platform. I assure you that if a party has worked as long and as hard as this party has to draw up a platform, then the public should be able to trust the party to carry out that platform.
>
> If it's there, I believe it's the obligation of a Labor Government to bring it into operation. And our Government did—we kept faith. And we're now engaged in a very great revamping of the platform at Perth at the national conference in July.[15]

Even the younger pragmatists in the party, who believed that a future Labor government should act more slowly, agreed that the rewriting of the platform mattered.

Making policy at a national conference is a cumbersome process. Reports are prepared by policy committees that meet infrequently before the conference is convened. They recommend changes to the existing platform or new clauses and proposals where necessary. The process is incremental and the reports are usually the basis for the conference's discussions. In seventy years the party platform has expanded from one page, which included a six-plank "fighting platform" and a ten-plank "general platform," to 113 pages in 1977. The amount of detail varies. In 1977 the new economic policy was couched in generalities that expressed the broad objectives a Labor government would strive to achieve; it did not bind such a government to many specific policies. By contrast, the industrial relations policy attempted to direct the government's every step, even to the extent of requiring it to provide two copies of proceedings before an industrial court to all participants! The excessive detail is ridiculous. Few other democratic parties bind themselves to such a detailed written policy.[16]

The intention was to follow the precedents of the conferences held in 1969 and 1971 where many of the promises that had helped

---

[15] *Age*, March 21, 1977.
[16] See *Platform, Constitution and Rules* for the full details.

Labor win in 1972 were inserted into the platform. The Perth conference was to chart the new directions for the party as it entered the 1980s. But there was a major difference. In the earlier conferences many of the new ideas had sprung from Whitlam himself and had had a rough coherence.[17] In 1977 there was no constructive unity; the committees invariably worked in isolation from one another, and the result was a mosaic of unstructured ideas. Five days of debate could not achieve that unity of outlook.

On the first day, in two resolutions moved by the Labor premiers of South Australia and New South Wales, the conference condemned the Fraser government for its economic mismanagement and for its "new federalism" policy. Discussions then bogged down over the minute details of policy. Only three debates were notable; a fourth, on uranium, was expected to be, but the details of the final resolution were worked out before the issue came before the conference.

In the constitutional debate the conference opted for defining precisely the powers of the governor general, despite Whitlam's wish for a more general statement. It chose to leave the question of removing legal restrictions on abortion up to the conscience of individual Labor M.P.s whenever the matter came before the House. Women delegates argued that the existing law should be changed to allow the decision to be left to the conscience of women, while leading members of the party, including Whitlam, Bill Hayden, Neville Wran, and Don Dunstan, argued for the status quo, fearing that the proposal would offend Catholic members of the party.

During the economic debate the left wing, led by delegates who were also officials of the Australian Metal Workers and Shipwrights Union, Australia's largest and one of its most militant unions, attacked the role of multinationals. It proposed the establishment of a "transnational corporations surveillance authority" and the transfer to public ownership of fringe financial institutions; and it asked support for the proposition that in those underdeveloped countries that were dominated by multinational companies, aid through trade was no longer appropriate. All these proposals were rejected, the last of them with considerable vehemence, as a result of the advocacy of the younger, more pragmatic members of the conference, most of whom were members of Parliament. They were opposed to any doctrinaire paranoia about the activities of multinationals. The final economic platform was general in content.

---

[17] See Freudenberg, *A Certain Grandeur*, pp. 85-179, for the best description of Whitlam's attempt to restructure the party and its policy.

Uranium was the question that dominated the conference. Lobbying was intense all week. Originally the committee report had proposed a moratorium on mining "at least until 1980." The conference rejected a proposal for a total ban on mining and stated that no commitment of Australia's uranium deposits should be made until after a full debate had occurred and the problems of waste disposal had been solved. It endorsed the decision of the royal commission on uranium mining that the government should always allow itself the right to terminate contracts, and declared:

Accordingly an Australian Government will—
(a) declare a moratorium on uranium mining and treatment in Australia;
(b) repudiate any commitment of a non-Labor government to the mining, processing and export of uranium pursuant to agreement entered into contrary to Labor's policy.[18]

It was expected that this policy would be unpopular at first, and of course it could be revised or reversed by the next federal conference in 1979. But because of its specific nature and its likely international consequences, this compromise resolution received more publicity than any other decision taken at Perth.

Yet the whole proceedings of the conference had about them an air of unreality. Whitlam often found himself in a minority and played little part; his intervention was seldom crucial, as it had often been at earlier conferences. It seemed that no one expected the party to have an early opportunity to implement the decisions. Office was a long way off. The final resolutions, especially on economic matters, were usually moderate, but of course few people would read such a detailed policy statement and it did not establish a clear direction for the policy speech. Seldom in the Labor party has the gap between the official processes of decision making, in this case the conference, and the real loci of policy power, the caucus and the shadow ministers, been made more apparent.

The Prelude to the Campaign

When Fraser called an early election in October 1977, the Labor party was not unprepared. In March 1977 the national secretary, David Combe, had forecast that Fraser might hold a poll early because the government realized that unemployment was going to rise early in

---

[18] See *Platform, Constitution and Rules*, p. 26.

1978. Tentative preparations were made. But the uncertainty that prevailed after August 1977 had a paralyzing effect. All activity had to be geared to the possibility of a poll, although Labor clearly did not want one until May the next year.

Some initiatives were taken in expectation of the poll. In August the party released a joint statement from Whitlam and Hayden entitled "A Proposal to Get Australia Working Again."[19] It outlined the policies that Labor would adopt to cope with structural change in the economy. Specific promises were short-term job-creation programs, a regional-employment program, and the implementation of manpower and structural-adjustment-assistance programs to facilitate change in the patterns of industry. It was a modest proposal, but at least it suggested—temporarily—that the Labor party was considering alternative economic policies to put to the electorate.

But unfortunately the illusion of cohesion was destroyed even before Parliament was formally dissolved. After the leadership struggle in May, Whitlam had appointed Hayden joint economic spokesman, with responsibility for the long and medium term. Chris Hurford remained shadow treasurer. This move was sensible. Hayden had a wide reputation as a careful administrator and economic manager. The appointment gave an official imprimatur to his comments. Then, just before the campaign began, Whitlam announced that Hayden would not have an economic portfolio but would be the defense or foreign affairs minister in a Labor government. Considering that much of the proposed advertising had been based on Hayden's economic reputation, it was not surprising that Fraser immediately used the announcement to suggest that Hayden, as a cautious economic manager, was being shifted out of any economic portfolio to allow scope for another spendthrift government. Hayden himself had wanted to broaden his experience, but after two days of pressure Whitlam reversed his statement. Hayden, he now said, would be the minister in charge of the department of economic development that was proposed in the platform and as such the economic head of any Labor government. The incident foreshadowed the series of misunderstandings that would dog the Labor party's economic spokesman throughout the campaign.

Organizing the Campaign

The Labor campaign was organized from a center in Canberra and one in Sydney. In Sydney David Combe was based close to Whitlam's

---

[19] *Canberra Times*, August 12, 1977.

office and to the party's advertising agency, Mullens and Clarke, its pollster, ANOP, and the freelance television producers who provided the material to be used in the party's free television time.

The party did little real research for the election campaign. Although it had commissioned two small polls in September to test the public reaction to the proposed industrial relations bureau and the Lynch budget, it ran no major national poll. To some extent it relied on the results of a poll taken earlier in Queensland and one in Victoria for a by-election, but they had only limited value for a national campaign, and besides, it was dangerous to try to learn federal lessons from state polls. Whereas in 1972 Labor's campaign had been better researched and more scientifically based than the Liberals', by 1977 the position was reversed. Even Labor state campaigns were based on more attitudinal data than was available for the national campaign in 1977. It is ironic that Combe was criticized for paying too much attention to poll results when in fact he was not able to undertake any major research at all.

The advertising planners had the problem of trying to sell a discredited leader. After a week-long campaign in October designed to frighten Fraser off calling the election had failed, the advertisements tried to define the major problem—unemployment—in short shots and then, in longer ones, to explain Labor's solutions. The intention was to take the spotlight away from Whitlam, of whom the electors were inordinately suspicious, and to feature Hayden, Hawke, Dunstan, and Wran. Indeed, only one commercial featured Whitlam alone, and in two others he appeared with other Labor leaders. The Labor party was not taken by surprise by the election; its strategy and campaign slogan had been selected in September. Even so, the campaign was too short to allow them to sell the product or to persuade the electorate to forget its earlier experiences of Labor government.

Both the lack of polling and the limitations of Labor's advertising were partly due to a lack of funds. The Labor campaign was always short of money. In 1975 the emotional reaction to the sacking of the Whitlam government had brought immediate financial support from many individuals in the community and, more important, from the trade unions. In 1977 there was no such mood. Individual contributions amounted to far less. And among some leading Labor supporters there was a fear that the campaign would land the party so deep in debt that it would have financial problems even in the next election, which it could conceivably win. It was the unions' reluctance to provide funds that was most important. According to the federal president of the Storemen and Packers Union, for example, his union, which had contributed $50,000 in 1975, gave only $25,000 in 1977. As he put it, "There was nothing in Labor's campaign to make us want to raise or give more. It was a disaster from start to finish."[20] The six state branches of the ALP, each of which effectively ran an independent campaign in its own bailiwick, have always proved suspicious of the central party bureaucracy and reluctant to fund massive federal campaigns. As a result, state campaigns are usually better researched than federal ones.

There was an attempt to ensure that the communications between various sections of the party campaign were smooth, in the hope of coordinating the statements and itineraries of shadow ministers. A communications center was developed in the national secretariat building in Canberra to do this job. At the same time, information and shadow ministers' statements were fed to the media in a continuous flow.

As in many recent campaigns, the tendency of parties to appeal to the courts or any other relevant tribunal was evident. When the Liberal party gained access to the Labor party's television commercials before their release, Combe accused it of theft and called on the Commonwealth police to investigate. When a Liberal television advertisement featured a segment of the Labor party's policy speech in which Whitlam promised to abolish payroll taxes, Combe complained to the Federation of Australian Commercial Television Stations that the commercial was a breach of copyright. The commercial was remade.

But no campaign organization however sophisticated and well financed (and the Labor campaign was neither) can compensate for a lack of coherence or thought in the party's policy. As the 1977 campaign made clear, organization cannot be a substitute for policy.

The Policy Speech

The Labor party entered the campaign knowing that many voters were suspicious of Whitlam. His popularity, according to the opinion polls, was low (but so was Fraser's). The party could not organize its campaign around Whitlam as it had done in the previous four elections. It could not revive the vibrant memories of the 1972 and 1974 campaign openings in Blacktown Town Hall, with chanting crowds cheering every promise and producing an atmosphere of hope and progress in contrast to what previously had often been a dull affair. Sobriety, caution, and responsibility were to be the basic themes; the

---

[20] *Australian*, December 26, 1977.

concept of a capable team was to replace the image of the dynamic leader.

The new style was noticeable in the delivery of the policy speech that kicked off the campaign. Whitlam's speech was short. Although the event received free television coverage, the Labor strategists chose to fit it into a half-hour program that showed other Labor spokesmen and spokeswomen to advantage. The whole performance was designed to appear moderate. It was held at midday at the majestic Sydney Opera House and scarcely managed to fill all the available seats. The extravagant gestures and theatrical performance of Whitlam, the cheering crowds, and the demonstrations of support and fealty of past years all were missing. So were the zest, the commitment, and the hope.

The contents of the speech were as somber as the atmosphere. Grandiose and expensive promises were no longer seen as useful or productive. Whitlam concentrated on unemployment. He began: "The task before us is to get Australia back to work, to give our young people, our unemployed, our small business people, our migrants a new hope—hope for decent jobs, hope in their future and in the future of their country."[21] Only one specific spending proposal was made: Whitlam followed the suggestions of the August proposals and announced that $500 million net would be spent on job creation schemes by increasing spending on capital works, by expanding apprenticeships and job training, and by offering funds for local employment advancement programs.

The main proposal designed to reduce the level of unemployment was the promise to abolish the payroll tax paid by employers in the hope that this would encourage firms to hire more people.[22] This move had long been advocated by manufacturers' and employers' organizations. In order to finance the promise, Whitlam made an unprecedented appeal to the electorate's altruism. He said:

> We would then, in order to make up the loss of the revenue, ask the Australian taxpayers to trade-off the changes in personal taxation promised in the last Lynch budget in return for this job-creating, inflation-cutting, confidence-restoring tax concession. . . . The Lynch proposals represent the most massive redistribution of wealth, away from lower and middle income earners—the vast majority of Australian taxpayers who earn less than $15,000—in favour of the highest

---

[21] The full text of the policy speech was carried in the *Sydney Morning Herald*, November 18, 1977.

[22] For further discussion of the proposal to abolish the payroll tax see Chapter 8, pp. 235-236, and Chapter 9, fn. 19, in this volume.

income earners, ever attempted in Australia. They were proposals that would give a person on my income $40 a week, but the average Australian wage earner only $3 a week. We ask the overwhelming majority of Australians to forgo nothing.[23]

Few observers believed that the taxpayers would accept this. The remainder of the speech covered the usual range of subjects—immigrants, education, Medibank, social security, the Aborigines, and the environment. But the specific proposals were few; most were commitments to restore Labor reforms that had been dismantled or emasculated by the Fraser government. Little was new or exciting. The presentation and the contents of the policy speech were, perhaps deliberately, flat.

The Campaign

The campaign appeared to begin auspiciously for the Labor party. The resignation of Lynch from his job as treasurer after some questions were raised about his personal finances coincided with one poll that put the Labor party actually ahead. Whitlam regained some of his old zest, ridiculing the Liberal campaign slogan and the private lives and business affairs of the leading ministers. The results of a state by-election in Greensborough, Victoria, and the state election in Queensland suggested that the voters were swinging back to the Labor party. For a brief moment it appeared possible that Labor could actually win. But it was a false dawn. From the beginning of the campaign the party consistently lost ground.

The campaign itself was lackluster and often defensive. Much of it seemed designed to assuage the fears of extremism that the electorate may have held. Bob Hawke was presented as the industrial conciliator, Bill Hayden as the safe and cautious economic manager, Ralph Willis as the man deeply concerned about youth unemployment. Unemployment was the theme that the Labor party harped on at every opportunity.

Fraser accused the ALP of fighting the dirtiest campaign that he could remember, simply because the Labor party refused to allow the resignation of Lynch to die as an issue. That claim itself effectively tarred Labor, at the same time discouraging it from using several possible methods of attack. Meanwhile the Liberals' television commercial entitled "Memories" recalled some of the sensational headlines of Labor's years in government reputedly with devastating effect. Labor

---

[23] *Sydney Morning Herald*, November 18, 1977.

did not retaliate, although it could have. In just two years of Fraser's government, three ministers had resigned—one because of his involvement in a court case, one after accusing the government of interfering in the administration of justice, and then Lynch. In addition, three backbenchers had resigned from the party in protest at the government's economic policies. But little of this was used by the Labor party to any effect. The Labor party's campaign could have been much more aggressive.

Labor's treatment of the uranium issue is illustrative. Party officials feared that the Labor party's new policy would be to its short-term disadvantage, since the polls showed that a majority of people in Australia favored the export of uranium. But during the campaign the question seldom seemed to attract attention. At first the Labor party ran a commercial arguing that the electorate should play it safe. Then in the last week or so of the campaign, when desperate measures were required, the party ran a far more provocative commercial which showed two babies playing with a hand grenade. But by then it was too late to make the export of uranium into the dominant issue it had been expected to be.

The most striking impression that the Labor party's campaign left was one of muddle, particularly on economic matters. The initial policy speech had not made clear where the Labor party stood on wage and tax indexation. The problem with having both Hayden and Hurford as official spokesmen on economic affairs was soon revealed, especially as Whitlam and Hawke also made statements on a future Labor government's economic intentions. These were not always consistent, and the press made the most of the contradictions. On tax indexation, the Labor party kept altering its position. The Lynch budget speech had claimed that, in view of the tax cuts that were to be introduced in February 1978, only half tax indexation (that is, to half of the inflation rate) would be imposed in July 1978. Whitlam declared that the Labor party was in support of full indexation from July 1978; Hayden then argued that full wage indexation would depend on the state of the economy. Later Whitlam accepted that, while Labor would only support full indexation when it was economically responsible to do so, the party would commit itself to immediate, full indexation for people receiving up to average weekly earnings. Hawke declared that the trade unions expected full and immediate wage indexation from a Labor government.[24]

---

[24] See *Australian Financial Review*, November 23, 1977; *Age*, November 24 and 28, 1977; and *Australian*, November 26, 1977, for details of the muddle.

There were other instances of policy making on the run. The Lynch plan would have relieved from any tax obligations 250,000 pensioners and low-income earners. Once the Labor party realized that abandoning the Lynch cuts would require these people to continue to pay taxes, they devised a rebate scheme that would relieve them.[25] Whitlam declared that the rebate scheme had always been part of the policy, but this was clearly not true. Finally, in the last week of the campaign, Whitlam promised that he would reduce inflation by five percentage points (from the OECD figure of 13.1 percent, not Fraser's artificial figure of 9 percent) in a year.

The muddle in which the economic spokesmen found themselves allowed the Liberal government to ridicule the Labor party's proposals. Not only could the Liberals accuse Labor of taking money, in the form of tax cuts, away from the average Australian, they could also—most ironically—claim that the elimination of the payroll tax would give money to major multinationals like Utah, a fully American-owned company that had just announced an annual profit of over $100 million. The prime minister's office could issue without comment four pages of contradictory quotations from Labor party spokesmen on wage and tax indexation.[26] Many of the differences were minor, even semantic, and arose over subjects on which the Liberal government had deliberately confused the population. Nevertheless, the general impression was that the Labor party was full of internal disputes about its policy. Labor spokesmen were only gradually adopting Fraser's own tactic of evading every vital policy issue, especially during elections.

Despite the initial impetus, the incoherence of the party's economic spokesmen was symptomatic of a lack of cohesion in the party as a whole. There were other obvious internal inconsistencies—on the treatment of the Vietnamese refugees who arrived in boatloads during the campaign, for example, and over the effects of and need for various levels of tariff protection. The vaunted communication system did not seem to keep all of the party's spokesmen in contact with one another. The party presented itself to the electorate, as it had for two years, as negative, muddled, and not very different from the party Australia had decisively rejected in 1975.

By the time of the poll on December 10, no one in the Labor party actually expected it to win. On the other hand, everyone expected it to improve its position by fifteen or more seats. But the party in effect won only one new seat—Capricornia, in Queensland.

---

[25] *Australian Financial Review*, November 30, 1977.
[26] *Age*, December 3, 1977.

The other seats that changed hands did so largely as a result of the redistribution. No new seats were won in Victoria or New South Wales, and once again the Labor party won only one seat in Western Australia and none at all in Tasmania. The defeat was as shattering as that of 1975 and the more demoralizing because it was unexpected and had been sustained at a time of consistent unemployment. In many people's view the Labor party needed reconstructing and redirecting if it was ever again to win office.

The New Leadership

Whitlam's leadership was said to be one of the major causes of Labor's defeat. Whatever the truth of that assertion, Whitlam himself speedily and graciously conceded defeat and declared that he would not contest the party leadership. His decision marked the end of an era: Gough Whitlam had dominated Australian politics from his election as leader of the opposition in 1967 to his abrupt dismissal by the governor general in November 1975.

At first it seemed likely that Bill Hayden might be elected leader unopposed, but some opposition began to emerge. One prominent trade unionist attacked Hayden for his support of the tax cut proposals and argued that the only thing that should concern the Labor party was the improvement of the working man's wage. Then Clyde Cameron also began to blame Hayden for Labor's defeat, which, he claimed, was due to the tax cut decision alone. Further, the left wing of the party regarded Hayden's brand of economic conservatism with grave suspicion.

Yet the only other candidate, Lionel Bowen, was a Catholic and a member of the right wing. Whereas Bowen and Hayden probably had similar views on economic management, the free-thinking Hayden was the more radical in his approach to social and moral issues. Bowen's conservative approach had consistently kept him out of trouble and out of the public view. He was far from being a dominant figure, although in the circumstances that was possibly one of his strengths. Several combinations of possible leaders were discussed, and one reason for the growing support for Bowen by the left wing of the party was an attempt to ensure the continued grip of their leading M.P., Tom Uren, on the party's deputy leadership.

In the caucus meeting of December 23, the heir apparent, Bill Hayden, duly defeated Bowen, by thirty-six votes to twenty-eight. Bowen then stood for deputy leader and, after the distribution of preferences, defeated Uren by thirty-three votes to twenty-nine. For the Senate, the party leader, Ken Wriedt, was returned unopposed, while the deputy there was defeated by the talented John Button. The election of the shadow executive saw the choice of several younger people, including for the first time in the party's history one woman, and the defeat of several of the more dogmatic members of the party's left wing.

The new team was described in the press as showing a shift to the right. Like most sweeping claims, this one does not bear careful analysis. The only candidate who was clearly a man of the left was Uren, but the others, and particularly Hayden and Button, were essentially pragmatists, men who were aware of the problems of government, not right-wingers. Whoever won, greater caution was inevitable.

How far Hayden, with his capacity for self-doubt, would manage to survive in the bitter cauldron of the party leadership could not be judged for some time. But what was likely was that the opposition would operate far more readily as a team once most of them were in sympathy with their leader both personally and politically.

The End of Labor?

The immediate reaction to Labor's defeat was that Labor would never again hold power federally because a growing "natural" Liberal majority was suspicious of the Labor party and of its links with the trade unions.

The Labor party's connections with the trade union movement are sometimes considered a disadvantage; they are said to cost the party votes. Even a majority of trade unionists reputedly disagree with the political affiliation of the unions. But to argue that the party should cut its ties with the unions and become an independent social democratic party on the West German model is to misunderstand the nature of the ALP and its historical evolution. Such a split would not only bankrupt a party that depends for much of its financing on union levies, but, given existing expectations, it would be impossible to achieve without major trouble. In two states at least, the Labor machine is virtually synonymous with the local trades hall—that is, the local union headquarters; both are run by the same people. In all states trade unions are heavily represented on state executives and at state conferences of the ALP. Many union officials regard the Labor party as the political wing of the industrial movement and object to the increasing involvement of professionals and academics in the party. Any attempt to disconnect the Labor party from the union movement would, if it were to be amicable, require the agreement of the unions themselves. Since their officials, probably correctly, see that affiliation as useful leverage, their approval would not be forthcoming. Indeed, such a move would probably bring about disintegration of the Labor party as such, and it would not necessarily survive in another form. The shape and operation of pressure groups in Australia naturally bolster and conserve the two-party structure as it developed in the first twenty years of the century. Any major reorientation of the party system is unlikely as long as the two major political groupings do not split—and if the ALP does split (again), early precedents suggest that it is the section that retains its affiliation with the unions that will survive, not the section that tries to become independent from supporting groups. A non-union, independent social democratic party is not at present a possibility in Australian politics.

But it is premature to conclude that the Labor party has no hope of success with the unions still connected to the party. An opinion poll taken immediately after the election suggested that Labor faced especially difficult hurdles in 1977. In particular, it suggested that two factors militated against Labor's winning—Whitlam's leadership and the feeling that Fraser should be given more than two years to solve the nation's problems. (A similar feeling had helped Labor win in May 1974.) By 1980 these circumstances will have changed; Whitlam has stepped down, and Fraser, who will have been in power for five years, will no longer be able to blame high unemployment on the Labor government.

Further, it is a mistake to regard the Labor party as monolithic. Its consistent lack of success at the federal level does not mean that it is a failure as a political party. It has often been successful and effective in the states. Thus the Labor party governed New South Wales from 1941 to 1965, regained power there in 1976 under Neville Wran, and won a further massive victory in 1978; it has ruled Tasmania since 1934 (with a brief gap from 1969 to 1972) and Queensland from 1915 to 1955 (except for the 1929–1932 period); and it has now become the dominant party in South Australia after thirty-five years in opposition.

Nor is success in state elections dependent on federal popularity. Between the two federal Labor disasters in 1975 and 1977, Labor governments were returned to power in South Australia and Tasmania—and in Tasmania the Liberal party won all five federal seats in both elections. In May 1976 the New South Wales Labor party even defeated an incumbent Liberal-Country party state government. Indeed, state Labor parties seem to have more chance of success while there is a Liberal government in Canberra that can be blamed for the problems and financial embarrassments of the states.

The state parties have direct links with the trade unions that are affiliated with them. Delegates elected by trade unions often make up half or more of those who attend state Labor conferences, and in some branches the two organizations have several common officials; thus both the trades hall in Sydney and the New South Wales branch of the Labor party are dominated by John Ducker, while in Queensland two or three unionists control both the unions and the party branch. The unions provide the state branches with most of their funds, which allow them to maintain a considerable organization in the large states. These state branches can survive repeated defeat in federal elections.

By contrast the national organization of the party is thin. Its full-time officials consist of a secretary, an assistant secretary, four media and research officers, and one or two stenographers. The party opened its national headquarters only in 1974. Such power as the national organization has must be exerted through the personal contacts of the secretary, through the federally structured national bodies, and through the federal caucus.

It is easy to equate the party with the federal party, but it is clearly a mistake, even if for journalistic convenience it is understandable. The cohesion and sense of purpose of the state branches do not necessarily depend on the existence or the likelihood of a federal Labor government but can be sustained by success in state politics. To prophesy doom and to forecast the end of the Labor party after the 1977 poll makes for eye-catching headlines, but they are plausible only if Labor's strength in state politics is ignored.

Prospects for the Hayden Labor Party

Between the elections of 1975 and 1977 the federal Labor party did nothing constructive to persuade the swinging voter who had deserted it in 1975 to return. The voters may have had no great incentive to support the government, but there was certainly none to switch back to Labor. For the Labor party, success in the future will depend in part on the performance of the Fraser government, but it will also require a great effort by Hayden and his colleagues to weld the party into a coherent team.

One requirement for the revival of the Labor party is the regeneration of the caucus. Ministers can only be elected from those in the parliamentary party, and those chosen usually have at least a few years of parliamentary experience. As a result ministers are usually people holding safe seats. The present caucus, about sixty-four senators and M.P.s, is thus the core from which future Labor cabinets will be drawn. The choice of people to fill these safe seats is therefore crucial, yet very often they are local party figures who can offer the national party little.

Candidate selection is the responsibility of the state parties, and in each the procedure differs. The influence of the state executives varies; the federal machinery has no involvement at all. In South Australia the state executive carefully controls selection; the colorless occupants of two safe seats were eased out in the last five years and replaced by men of considerable capacity. In Queensland, by contrast, the highly conservative state executive has the power to endorse the choices of local electorate councils and is prepared to use that power to prevent the selection of its opponents; when one electorate council chose an able historian who was a critic of the executive and desired its reform, his nomination was rejected and he was replaced by a more docile supporter.

In Victoria candidates are selected by panels made up of representatives of local branches and the state executive. In 1977 two safe seats were filled by members of the state parliament (one of whom had been a noticeable failure as a state parliamentary leader), while there were attempts to reject two sitting members by transferring endorsement to another party candidate. One succeeded, the other just failed, but the attempts themselves were exceptional; serious challenges to the endorsement of sitting members are too uncommon. In New South Wales, where the choices are usually made by local branches, the executive has less control. The selections for safe seats have often been won by local party members with limited horizons. Local contacts are all important. There are a few noticeable exceptions; when Whitlam retired from Parliament in 1978, for example, the preselection was won by the able John Kerin, a former member for the neighboring federal seat.

State executives have more control over the selection of Senate candidates, who are usually chosen by the state conferences. The first or second candidate on the party's ticket is guaranteed a six-year term, so the choice is vital. Factional alignments are the most important considerations, but people of considerable intellectual and political ability have been chosen in the last four or so years.

Since in most parliamentary democracies parties act as the gatekeepers to office, it is only by running well-qualified candidates in safeseats that a party can guarantee the regeneration of ability in Parliament. Yet the procedures of the Labor party ensure that the internal politics of the state machines will remain the most important determinant of who gains these seats. There is no capacity equivalent to that of the British Labour party to ease able people into Parliament from seats spread over the country. Nevertheless of those who played leading roles in the party in 1978, only three—Hayden, Bowen, and Wriedt—had been ministers for the whole of the 1972-75 Labor government. The change of personnel was swift, but the uneven quality of those selected for safe seats meant that the party still had limited talent from which to rebuild.

After the defeat the national executive convened a committee of party members, academics, and members of Parliament to reexamine the party structure and the directions that it should take. There was also a long debate on whether the party should learn to manage capitalism more effectively or shift radically to the left. Hayden himself argued that Labor lost primarily because it was not seen as an economically responsible party. As economist Peter McCawley commented:

> If Hayden is correct, this may have little to do with the particular economic policies promised by the party several weeks or months before an election campaign, but rather with the general stance of the party on a range of important economic issues over a period. . . . It may be that in a confused, but nevertheless realistic, manner, many Australian electors have come to accept Mr. Fraser's argument that the economic problems of the Australian economy are deep-rooted ones which are somehow or other connected with government spending, the money supply, wage levels, and the structure of Australian industries.[27]

McCawley then argued persuasively that at the very least the Labor party must devise acceptable explanations to justify public spending, must develop a consistent wage policy that was acceptable to the unions, and must create some alternative to the existing protectionist policies in which to develop proposals for structural changes to industry. He neatly summarized the problem:

> Unless Labor spokesmen are prepared to justify higher levels of government spending and taxation, then they had best abandon social welfare goals, because it is clear that the electorate is not prepared to finance government programs through credit creation and inflation. And if these goals are abandoned, why should the electorate vote Labor at all?[28]

---

[27] Peter McCawley, "Where Labor Went Wrong," *National Times*, December 19-24, 1977, pp. 24-25.
[28] Ibid.

Hayden and his colleagues were fully aware of the need to combine an image of economic responsibility with social reformism.

But despite the more fatalistic statements of disillusionment by former supporters and even ministers, the Labor party remained committed to change through evolution and to parliamentary methods. One member suggested that the party had two basic ideals, "a commitment to the constant revision of society, a revision in the direction of more equality; a commitment to democratic means and a pluralist society."[29] The rethinking of the party's policy and approach occurring under Hayden was certain to follow these general lines. At the state level, Labor premiers like Don Dunstan of South Australia and Neville Wran of New South Wales had proved that Labor could win.

The 1977 election showed that the Labor party would not regain its lost seats without effort. Not only must the voters be dissatisfied with Fraser, but, if Labor was to win votes, there must be some positive reasons for change too. The enthusiasm and vision of 1972 were being replaced by caution and pragmatism, albeit connected to a concern for people. Despite the 1977 defeat, the time had not come to write off the Labor party as a force in Australian politics.

---

[29] Bob Carr, *Social Democracy and Australian Labor*, New South Wales Labor Day Committee, Sydney, 1977, p. 6. Carr has been accused by the party's left wing of providing an apologia for the right wing of the party. But factions in the Labor party are often based on personal alignments; often their ideological stands are only symbolic. The left has no coherent ideology, and Carr's pamphlet has been one of the few attempts to draw together the various strands of Labor thinking. Yet it can be regarded as no more than a starting point.

4
The Liberal-National Country Party Coalition

Jean Holmes

Introduction

The Australian Party System. The key to Australian politics still lies with the nation's political parties and party system, as it has since the end of the nineteenth century. Party loyalties define the parameters of voting patterns; the caliber of the party leaders is a central preoccupation of the media; and the party system is the environment that structures the ebb and flow of political interaction in Australian government. Party is the substance of the nation's political life.

Yet many of the generalizations that purport to explain the nature of the Australian party system and its components are singularly uninformative. Frequently described as a two-party system where Labor and non-Labor parties compete for political power, the system also operates as a multiparty system where three major parties and a host of satellite minor parties interact. And it has been described as a two-and-a-half-party system, underlining the importance of the Liberal-NCP coalition, which usually comprises the competitive non-Labor parties, though this fails to convey the nuances of relationships within the coalition.

Furthermore, the federal organizational structure of the Australian political parties imparts its own constraints. The oldest and most developed state, New South Wales, has been a Labor party stronghold for decades, but Victoria, its close rival, is something of a hair shirt to the Labor movement. In the tropical state of Queensland, the National Country party now out-polls the Liberals in the battle for first-preference votes—yet in Tasmania the party had no formal organization at all until the 1960s and its electoral appeal is still minuscule.

Thus the Australian party system is more usefully described as pluralist, where a loose confederation of relatively autonomous state parties provides a base for the nationally organized parties. The latter put forward national policies only after the various political alternatives originating at the state level (which is the forum for the most significant policy initiatives in Australia) have been processed and modified by the parties' federal organizational structures. The state party organizations in turn must process regional demands articulated first at the grass-roots level of the parties before these flow through to the national level. The failure of this intricate network to balance the regional and state interests involved results in the national parties themselves fragmenting along both regional and state lines, effectively preventing the emergence of national policies.[1]

The importance of this process of modifying and generalizing from the regional to the national policy level within the parties is most clearly illustrated today in the state of Queensland. The L-NCP and Labor national parties there are stalemated at the regional level, and the current policy deadlock facing both national party executives stems directly from the failure of the Queensland party machinery to resolve the challenge of its state regionalism.

Despite the essential fluidity of the Australian party system, the history of each of the three major parties spans many decades. The Labor party has had a continuous existence for over eighty years, the Country parties were formed sixty years ago, and the present Liberal party, now thirty-five years old, is a direct descendant of the Nationalist and United Australia parties of the 1920s and 1930s. Their histories have been turbulent, and they have all suffered serious periodic dissension resulting in party splits and new alliances. New minor parties also appear regularly, putting the finishing touch on the pluralist concept of conflict and conciliation among divergent interests.

In the 1970s the downward trend in voter loyalty characteristic of other Western democratic systems has surfaced in Australia. To the extent that stability in the Australian party system has been a function of party loyalties, the appearance of voter volatility could presage a return to the political uncertainties of the last century, when recurring splits and alliances effectively precluded the development of a formal party system. The 1977 federal election campaign initially suggested this possibility. Voter disenchantment with the major parties was highlighted when a new minor party captured 10 percent of the

---

[1] Jean Holmes and Campbell Sharman, *The Australian Federal System* (Sydney: Allen & Unwin, 1977). Chapter 4 contains a full discussion of the federal aspects of Australia's party system.

total vote, and increasing voter volatility caused party support to seesaw throughout the campaign. In Queensland regional differences and a dispute over ministerial portfolios threatened to engulf the established party groupings, and Victoria, the erstwhile "gem in the Liberal party crown,"[2] appeared at last to be considering a massive swing to the Labor party.

Yet despite these ominous signs of emerging political instability, the final voting figures produced an overwhelming Liberal-NCP victory and an apparent return to the status quo. Does this mean that the 1977 election was typical of the ebb and flow of Australian politics, where the party system eventually defines and confines political conflict within traditional norms to produce a customary result? Or did the trends that emerged differ substantially from the patterns which have shaped Australian politics for the past thirty years, presaging a new balance of power for the 1980s? To answer these questions we must turn first to the historical development of the Australian party system and place the 1977 election within its context, before we can assess its overall significance.

The period from 1900 to 1910 is usually seen as an important determinant of the patterns of alignment and consolidation that still characterize Australian political parties.[3] It was in those ten years that the fluid political groupings of the nineteenth century moved towards a dichotomous Labor/non-Labor configuration. Previously Liberal politicians had found alliance with one another both unpalatable and electorally costly, but by the end of the decade they were more than willing to make the compromises necessary to form a parliamentary majority. By contrast, Labor could not bring itself to cooperate with the non-Labor parties as part of the political price for forming a majority. In maintaining its independence as a party in those ten years, it established its contemporary political style, just as the non-Labor parties set up the pattern of alliances they too still practice.

Coalition politics have thus been characteristic of non-Labor since the party system first emerged in Australia. The willingness of non-Labor parties to engage in political alliances has contributed to the description of Australian politics as pragmatic and nonideological, concerned with material gain rather than with political ideals.

---

[2] Sir Henry Bolte, Victoria's redoubtable state premier, described the state this way following the 1969 federal election when it was the only state to stand firm against the swing to Labor. *Age*, October 27, 1969.

[3] Peter Loveday, Allan Martin, and Robert Parker, eds., *The Emergence of the Australian Party System* (Sydney: Hale & Iremonger, 1977).

The parties in turn have been classified as parties of class and interests rather than parties of principles. Labor has been seen to represent working-class interests and to pursue policies of social reform; the non-Labor coalitions have been described as reflecting an amalgam of rural and urban employer interests and a concern to resist any extension of social welfare programs.

It followed that social class was long considered a major determinant in Australian politics, with the corollary that if the solid-seeming interest and class bases of party support were to crumble under the impact of social change, the future of the political parties would be much less secure. It was feared that Australian politics might even revert to the nineteenth-century pattern of unstable alliances and groupings based on personal followings and expediency.[4] Today it is clear that the pervasive tendency to view political conflict in Australia as class conflict has never rested on strong evidence; "class labels are worn lightly by many Australians," as one writer comments,[5] and notions of class consciousness do little to explain the party loyalty of Australian voters.[6]

If social class is not the key, what forces lie behind the fierce voter loyalty still commanded by the major Australian parties? Did the 1977 election pinpoint a change in its quality, an erosion in the bond between party and voter, which does threaten the parties' future, unlike the discovery that the nexus between party and class is weak? Does the slow decline in party loyalty among Australian voters over the past twenty years and the increase in the swinging vote from around 10 percent in 1961 to 20 percent in 1977 constitute a more serious threat to the survival of the present party system?

Firm answers to these questions have yet to be found, but the 1977 election result allows us to infer something about the nature of present-day Australian political parties, despite the lack of content in the old class labels. The voters criticized and even condemned the parties of their first choice, they wavered in their allegiances, some even deserted, but on polling day the old dividing lines held firm. To

---

[4] Peter Loveday and Allan Martin, *Parliament, Factions and Parties* (Melbourne: Melbourne University Press, 1966) describes the faction politics in the early years of responsible government in New South Wales when there were no organized parties.

[5] Don Aitkin, *Stability and Change in Australian Politics* (Canberra: Australian National University Press, 1977) discusses the weak link between class and Australian politics.

[6] David Kemp, *Society and Electoral Behaviour in Australia* (St. Lucia: University of Queensland Press, 1978) examines the declining class basis of politics in Australia, as does his chapter in this book.

Australians their parties are independent political entities, with distinctive and viable, though perhaps poorly articulated, ideologies and organizational structures, surprisingly independent of the social structure. Coalition politics, lacking ideological respectability in other countries, is legitimate and acceptable in Australia, if varied and often turbulent. Our first step towards understanding the relationship between the Liberal party and the National Country party in coalition, therefore, must be to trace each party's identity and ideology. Only then can we assess the strength of party loyalty they can command and give some substance to the stability of that support for the future.

Ideology and the Australian Liberal Party. Systematic analysis of party identification in Australia is still patchy, but existing studies allow us to glimpse the different perceptions that lie behind voters' party choices and the willingness of more than 85 percent of the present electorate to identify themselves with one particular party. For example, the party images teased out by Professor Don Aitkin in a 1967 survey reflect an ideological basis to party loyalty.[7] Liberal partisans stressed the party's free enterprise ideology and its management abilities in government, while Labor partisans saw their party as the protector of the worker and the underdog. Country party supporters saw their party as the farmer's friend, a view shared by non-Country party respondents. Similar social values and style perceptions were relevant to the party differences that emerged in a small postelection survey in 1977.[8] Party preference was more closely correlated with voters' values and beliefs than with their occupation and/or social class, a finding which allowed a value profile to be constructed of each party's supporters. Labor voters identified more strongly than others with egalitarian values, expressing sympathy for the underdog, whereas Liberal supporters emphasized the importance of a stable structure of authority in society and stressed the virtues of individual effort.

Finally a study of federal members of Parliament in 1970 by Hugh Emy found that representatives emphasized the importance of the party's function in reflecting a way of life, in extending the mores and life styles of those who give it their support.[9] For Liberal M.P.s

---

[7] Aitkin, *Stability and Change*, p. 67.

[8] David Kemp, "The Secret Ingredient in Fraser's Success," *Journal of Higher School Certificate Politics* (April 1978), p. 10 ff.

[9] Hugh Emy, *The Politics of Australian Democracy*, 1st ed. (Melbourne: Macmillan, 1974), chap. 16.

the values centered on a doctrine of individualism; they were critical of centralization, socialism, and uniformity and supported individual achievement and responsibility. There was also an authentic strain of conservatism and hostility to change among Liberals, which, when linked with the stress on individual effort, gave substance to their view of Liberalism as a "living tradition of political behavior." Country party M.P.s were even more insistent that their party stood for a way of life, based on customs arising from their rural environment, and Labor M.P.s empathized with the underprivileged in society, stressing the fraternal bond and party solidarity. Party identification learned in childhood, crystallizing in adult perceptions of politics and party style, appears to lie at the heart of Australian party loyalty.[10] It is, as Emy comments, misleading to view Australian political parties in hard material terms as simply the party of X interest,[11] and we must obviously look well beyond social categories to find the contemporary basis for Australian party loyalties. The hypothesis that today's political parties are value-centered and that our politics is the politics of those parties is much more fruitful to an understanding of the forces of present-day Australian politics than a traditional explanation based on the salience of group and class.

L-NCP Platforms and Policies. The party platform is both a major statement of the party's ideology and value orientations (though not necessarily a carefully worked out doctrinal essay) and a justification for its bid for political power. The Liberal party's original federal platform was little more than an abbreviated version of an address given by the party's founder, the Liberal M.P. Robert Menzies (later Sir Robert Menzies), to the inaugural meeting of the various state delegates to its Federal Council on August 31, 1945.[12] These objectives set out in the subsequent official federal platform of the Liberal party remained substantially unaltered for the next thirty years, and it was not until the party was defeated in the 1972 federal election that a serious platform revision was undertaken as part of a full-scale review of the organization and its operations. In 1973 and 1974 the national

---

[10] Robert Connell, *The Child's Construction of Politics* (Melbourne: Melbourne University Press, 1971).

[11] Emy, *Politics*, p. 488.

[12] Graeme Starr and Keith Richmond, *Political Parties in Australia* (Melbourne: Heinemann Educational, 1978). The constitutional arrangements agreed upon by the delegates to the Canberra Conference in October 1944 had included the setting up of a Federal Council comprising seven delegates from each state branch, together with the leader of the federal parliamentary party in the House. It was this body that Menzies addressed in 1945.

party solicited the views of the state branches on general Liberal philosophy and principles and encouraged discussion in settings such as the Women's Group and the Young Liberals, as well as among federal officials. This process culminated in a Draft Federal Platform, which was finally adopted by the Federal Council in October 1974, a few months after the double-dissolution election of May that year.

The new Liberal party platform began with two broad statements of principle, "The Philosophy of Liberalism" and "The Australian Nation," and ended with a summary of objectives. For the first time since the party was formed, it set down in an official document a Liberal party code of beliefs.[13] The stress was on individualism and free enterprise, equality of opportunity, competitiveness and personal incentives, material well-being associated with a stable family life, and the dignity and fulfillment of the individual. It was significant that the new platform (which is still in force) affirmed the value positions Liberal party supporters had always stressed and that distinguished the party from its Australian competitors. It was an antipodean modification of European liberalism, a formulation of liberal doctrines tailored to an Australian political perspective.

One important modification tempers the more conventional liberal view that government intervention in economic life is undesirable. It is true that this has been a persistent strand in Australian non-Labor ideology since the turn of the century, but those supporting this view have not necessarily extended it to the politics of development.[14] Policies favoring development have always had universal appeal in Australia, and non-Labor parties in search of votes have not hesitated to foster schemes for national development, even to the lengths of supporting government enterprises. Primary industry has always been subsidized since responsible government was first granted to the Australian colonies in the 1850s. Secondary industry, including heavy industries such as iron and steel manufacturing and shipbuilding, have been protected by massive tariffs by all governments in the name of national self-sufficiency, and state-run enterprises have always provided transport, communications, and other essential services for the benefit of private enterprise, often at a considerable loss. The ongoing partnership between Australian government and private enterprise has produced a unique liberal ideology in which both laissez faire and state intervention have been stable and permanent elements. Their twin presence in Australian Liberal party ideology has been

---

[13] Starr and Richmond, *Political Parties*, p. 71.
[14] Peter Loveday, "Liberals and the Idea of Development," *Australian Journal of Politics and History*, vol. 23, no. 2 (August 1977), p. 219 ff.

central to the successful coalition policies of the twentieth century, for it has allowed each party to tailor its profile to its supporters' value expectations without the risk of serious ideological conflict.

The Australian Country parties originated during the First World War in the wheat-growing areas. Grain farmers in Australia have always suffered considerably from fluctuations in world markets as well as from the inevitable vicissitudes of weather, and support for state-controlled marketing schemes and wheat pools subsidizing crop prices to growers formed the basis of early Country party policy. Federal and state country parties are the most homogeneous of the Australian political parties, clearly identified with rural interests. Attempts to widen the party's image to counteract its dwindling population base often meet with criticism from party supporters for fear that the change will lead to neglect of the party's traditional base. In 1973, the federal party leader, Doug Anthony, canvassed the possibility of aligning the federal Country party with the ailing Democratic Labor party, a minor anti-Communist party, but the electoral results of the first joint candidates in Western Australia were so disastrous that merger plans lapsed. Little has remained of Anthony's exercise but a name change: the party now calls itself the National Country party of Australia,[15] but in everyday usage its old label, the Country party, is still more common.

In the fashion of the 1970s, the Country party too put together a new platform in an effort to project a new/old image and disassociate itself from some of its outmoded ideological elements. However, it is Australia's only truly regional party, and its voting support is still heavily concentrated in particular country electorates along the Murray River in Victoria, in central New South Wales, and in central and northern Queensland. There is a very real danger that in attempting to "go national" and transcend its rural image the Country party may blur the distinctive features that set it apart from the rural wing of the Liberal party. Organizationally the latter is poised to pick up whatever rural support the Country party loses in the hope of an eventual takeover. Moves by the Country party's leaders to widen its appeal risk undermining its traditional bases of support, for if the party no longer offers to a distinctive segment of the electorate a political party wholly theirs, its future could be threatened.

The dilemma arising from the NCP's desire to retain its independent status yet still command sufficient power to achieve the goals

---

[15] At the state level the party's name varies: in New South Wales, South Australia, and Western Australia it is the National Country party, in Queensland and Victoria the National party, and in the Northern Territory the Country Liberal party.

of those who derive their living from the land is what sharpens its relationship with its big brother in coalition. Conflict over ideology is far less important in the relationship between the partners. Internal conflict arising from the NCP's subordinate role in the coalition has been endemic to the party throughout its sixty years of existence. Some state parties have been willing to enter into coalition cabinets with their urban partners; others, notably the Country party in Victoria, have preferred to extract concessions in return for parliamentary support without joining coalitions. In 1941 a federal Country party leader, Arthur Fadden, even became prime minister of Australia for five weeks, and although the circumstances were partly accidental (in particular, the UAP was in the midst of a leadership crisis), the episode indicates the power that Country party leaders have been only too ready to wield in a coalition situation. It has held major portfolios in non-Labor federal cabinets since the 1920s and has always exercised political clout in excess of its formal parliamentary representation. There is no doubt that its willingness to engage in coalition and concession politics has paid off in policy gains.

However, it should not be assumed that Liberal party supporters have always been content with an arrangement that benefited the Country party more than the Liberals. The Country party's support has been necessary to form a majority in most Parliaments, but there is a significant core of Liberal party opinion today that would like to sever this historical link. In December 1944 when Menzies formed the Liberal party from the remnants of non-Labor he sought to persuade the Country party delegates to join. When they refused, he offered coalition despite opposition from other Liberal delegates. Political leaders are pragmatic in the face of the realities of political power, and the successful Liberal-Country party coalition which began when Labor lost the 1949 federal election owed its formation and survival to Menzies's political skills and perspicacity rather than to his followers' preferences.

The Liberal Party's Structure and Organization. The problem of devising national organizational structures to accommodate the variety of groups and interests that come under the rubric non-Labor in Australia has dogged the "parties of town and country capital" since federation. The National party, launched in 1916 when the conscription crisis split the Australian Labor party, adopted a structure similar to that of the ALP, based on local branches, state councils, interstate conferences, and a national executive, in an attempt to bring the various interests involved into a loose organizational relationship. It did not survive the depression of the 1930s, but in 1931, when it was reorganized under a new name, the United Australia party, and led by a Labor dissident from the right, Joseph Lyons, it retained the familiar ALP structure.

However, power in the new party still lay with the parliamentary representatives and the faction-ridden central executives of the state parties rather than with the UAP electorate organizations. Moreover, the method of financing through independent committees of business and economic interests outside the regular structure of the party also remained—notably committees of the private trading banks, insurance companies, graziers' organizations, land and station firms, and mining and industrial firms. Organizations such as the National Union in Victoria and the Consultative Council in New South Wales, acting as extraconstitutional finance committees, were seen by the electorate to be exerting a highly undesirable influence over the UAP and its policies, so discrediting them by the early 1940s that it became imperative to reconstitute the non-Labor political forces. In September 1944 Robert Menzies, then an M.P., wrote to the various organizations that loosely supported the non-Labor parliamentary opposition, urging unity through the formation of a new national party organization. Few disagreed with the necessity for reorganization, and on October 13-16, 1944, delegates and parliamentary representatives met at Canberra to draw up guidelines.

There was no suggestion that the new party should be other than federally organized, and the seven state divisions still operate independently, each with its own constitution, although the federal organization has strengthened its grip on party affairs since 1974. The present Federal Council consists of:

1. four delegates chosen annually by each state division, the majority of whom shall not be members of Parliament,
2. the president of each state division,
3. the president of each state women's division,
4. a delegate of the Young Liberal movement from each state,
5. each parliamentary leader, and
6. the federal parliamentary leader and deputy leader, and the leader and deputy leader of the Senate parliamentary party.[16]

Since 1973 the proceedings of the Federal Council have been open to the press, and its meetings have become something of a public relations exercise. Policy-making activities have tended to retreat to the less public federal Executive and standing committees, but the real political

---

[16] Starr and Richmond, *Political Parties*, p. 38.

power in the Liberal party rests with the parliamentary leader. He is not bound by organization resolutions, he can appoint and dismiss his ministers at will, and the individual careers of the members of the parliamentary party depend on his electoral appeal and success. It is not a question of the organizational wing of the party being without power (Gorton's poor performance as a Liberal leader in 1971 was partly due to his inability to carry the extraparliamentary organization of the party with him), but rather that the Liberals place a premium on party leadership which ensures the leader's organizational dominance.

In its early years, the party insisted on complete independence in raising and controlling funds. Donations were and still are accepted from individual subscribers only, not from trade groups or associations; branch income through membership subscriptions is based on a bank order system whereby members authorize the party to charge their annual subscriptions to their bank accounts without the need for a renewal authorization each year, and local campaign committees must meet their own administrative costs and election expenses. A central finance committee in each state division oversees its financial affairs, while finance at the federal level is handled by a Federal Finance Committee first set up in 1953. It is composed of the federal treasurer and president, state presidents, and a member of each state finance committee. Since 1973, a National Campaign Committee has coordinated both the state division campaigns and their expenditures in federal elections; secrecy concerning donations is still strictly maintained. Above all, the object is to keep donors and policy makers separate, thus ensuring that the experience of the United Australia party is never repeated.

The second organizational objective distinguishing the Liberal party from the Nationalist party of the 1920s and the UAP of the 1930s was its mass membership structure. Indeed its political significance is derived from its electoral success as a mass party of the right, in the mold of the classic mass parties of the left. Furthermore, its success is linked with the emergence of an articulate middle class in Australia in the 1950s and 1960s, for which it has been the major political channel. Its organization has been built up around the values and beliefs of the Australian middle-class political activist at the local electorate branch level. Membership (which rises somewhat in critical political years) is estimated at around 100,000, but many of these are only nominal members, contributing little beside their annual membership fee of up to $10 through the automatic bank order system.

One other feature that distinguishes the Liberal party's organizational structure from that of other political parties in Australia is the position given to women and the young. The Women's Group and the Young Liberals make important contributions to the party, and both have seen their members elected to Parliament and chosen for ministerial office. Their success is a further indication of the relevance of middle-class values in the organization and of the importance of the Liberal party as a vehicle for keeping those values in the mainstream of Australian politics.

The National Country Party Structure and Organization. The National Country party's structure and organization are similar to those of other Australian political parties. There is a central organization in each state, topped off by a Federal Council and Executive, but the NCP is much weaker at the federal level than its Liberal counterpart. Moreover, an additional tier is added between the local branch and the state branch organization, a district level Electorate Council in each state and federal electorate which brings together individual local branches. These Electorate Councils exercise considerable power, running preselection (candidate selection) contests, coordinating election campaigns, giving a local slant to broad policy objectives, and overseeing local branch activity in their respective federal and state electorates independently of the central federal and state organizations.

Nominal membership figures are high, around 80,000 total. The party's main strength is in Australia's wheat, grazing, and dairying areas, and the majority of its members are small holders and primary producers rather than country town dwellers. Concentrated in certain regions, they give the party a solid core of electoral support and returned nineteen House members and five senators in 1977. Membership fees, paid through a bank order system like the Liberals', have always provided a substantial part of its finances; in addition, it runs a profitable rural insurance scheme. It has never suffered the stigma of being a tool of outside interests as did the Liberal party's forerunners, but the fact that many of its seats are ultra-safe has sometimes made the party organization complacent. The present federal parliamentary leader, Doug Anthony, wants to revitalize the party and strengthen its federal structure as a prerequisite to establishing it on a broader national base because he realizes that the Country party's major problem today is survival. Rural populations are declining (although this trend has shown signs of reversing over the past two years in Australia), and redistribution (redistricting) threatens its parliamentary seats. Its opponents avidly await its disappearance from the Australian political scene.

However, it may be that the Country party reached a plateau of support in the 1977 election; its campaign was well supported by a cross section of the country population, and its basis in Australian economic life is unchallengeable, particularly in the state of Queensland where it has been able to stave off the threat of redistribution without much difficulty. On balance it is probably overly optimistic for the "party of town capital" to assume that its uneasy alliance with the "party of country capital," which has shaped Australian politics over the past sixty years, will be a thing of the past in the 1980s.[17]

The Coalition In Action

The Relationship between the Partners. Not since 1931 has the major non-Labor party attempted to govern outside a parliamentary coalition at the federal level. Even so, a group of vocal Liberals has always been eager to try the experiment again, and the sustained tension between town and country in Australian society is reflected in the political relationships between the coalition parties.

There is no formal machinery for policy coordination between the coalition parties. Instead, the two party leaders have always made ad hoc arrangements, and the Country party leader's relative strength in the coalition has thus been critical in determining the extent to which his party has benefited from the alliance. The NCP's strategy has been to make itself indispensable while maintaining a separate identity, but to some extent it is always the captive of its larger partner. Its price has been significant participation in composite ministries and, more important, the deputy prime ministership for its leader. It has also insisted on holding those portfolios most relevant to its interests.

Moreover, Country party ministers have not hesitated to criticize Liberal party rural policies.[18] Some of the Liberal policies of which the NCP has been critical include price maintenance schemes, subsidies for rural industries, trade and tariff policies seen as inimical to rural interests, and monetary policies that threaten rural incomes and expenses. Redistricting is another source of disputes between the coalition partners. In 1962, when the Liberal party put forward a scheme that would have abolished two Country party seats, its

---

[17] Findlay Crisp, *Australian National Government* (Melbourne: Longmans, 1970).
[18] Ibid., p. 263.

members even threatened to cross the floor of the House and bring down the government.

Country party leaders have also been able to modify and even reverse Liberal policy decisions running counter to NCP interests. In 1962, for example, the party was strongly opposed to Britain's prospective entry into the Common Market, seeing it as a threat to its markets for primary products, and when the Liberal minister Leslie Bury rashly said that in his opinion Country party interests were not seriously threatened, the party sought and attained his resignation from the ministry. Again in 1967, Sir John McEwen, then the Country party leader, forced the deputy leader of the Liberal party, William McMahon, to withdraw from the Liberal party leadership contest following Harold Holt's death by drowning in December that year. McEwen simply announced that he would not serve in a McMahon government—a use of political muscle almost unparalleled in Liberal-Country party relations. The Country party also won a significant victory in 1971 when it forced the Liberal party to reduce its devaluation of the Australian dollar from 8.5 percent to 6.3 percent, thus protecting rural export incomes.

A somewhat farcical illustration of the Country party's willingness to engage in independent action within the coalition occurred when the parties took their place in opposition in the federal Parliament for the first time in 1972. The leader of the Country party moved swiftly to ensconce himself and his staff in the more spacious deputy opposition leader's office suite one jump ahead of the Liberal deputy leader, Phillip Lynch. In the ensuing squabble, the squatters prevailed, demonstrating that the Country party's power in the coalition, even in opposition, was still significant.

At the state level, the coalitions are more fragile. Prior to the 1974 federal election, Liberal party leader Billy Snedden was forced to intervene when the Liberals in Victoria threatened to field candidates against sitting Country party members. In 1976 the Queensland Liberal party decided that in the future it would contest selected Country party federal seats. For the past decade Liberal and Country party candidates have run against one another in several districts in Queensland state elections, and in Victoria and Western Australia there have been occasions when Country party candidates have exchanged ballot paper preferences with Labor party candidates. Three-cornered electoral contests have always been the practice in Western Australian state elections, and in 1972 the Country party in that state voted to become an independent center party.

In summing up the relationship between the coalition partners, it can be said that over the years Liberal-Country alliances have been enduring but uneasy at the federal level and customary but uncertain in the states. Generally they have been quite peaceful in New South Wales, but in Queensland and Western Australia they have been marked by deep resentments on occasion flaring into open hostilities. In Victoria, the Country party has been an ineffective rural opposition ever since the Labor party split in 1955 which allowed the Liberals to form state governments in their own right with the help of the minority Democratic Labor party's second-preference votes. In South Australia and Tasmania the Country party appears not to be a viable electoral force. Thus Australia's federally organized party system makes maintaining the coalition a difficult balancing act for the country's two chief non-Labor parties. The ability of NCP federal party leaders to handle coalition strategies successfully is undoubtedly the key to continuing Country party success in the federal sphere into the 1980s.

The Return to Power, 1975. The Liberals' defeat in 1972, after twenty-three continuous years in office, first sent the party into shock, then galvanized it into rebuilding a party machine grown tired and unresponsive during its long years in power. Members began by reexamining the party's federal constitution and platform, a task that involved activists from all levels of the party. It took two years to complete. A "new federalism" policy was hammered out in a policy document issued late in 1975 acknowledging the relevance of federalism in Australian government for the first time in the party's history. The principle of federalism with its emphasis on preventing a concentration of political power and guaranteeing political freedom is now an integral part of Liberal party doctrine.

The 1972–1974 revision also upgraded the function of the outside organization in policy formulation, previously dominated by the parliamentary wing. For the first time since 1949 the Liberals, now in opposition, were forced to rely on the party's own resources for policy advice. Cut off from the expert public service advisers on whom party leaders had depended all their long years in office, they revitalized their own policy advisory committees between 1972 and 1974, giving them the task of bringing forward new policy alternatives and consulting with outside groups as well as with the state branches.

The 1972 setback was also responsible for the innovatory decision to appoint a National Campaign Committee to mastermind all future election campaigns. The lack of coordination between the states so apparent during the 1972 federal election campaign had highlighted for the Liberal party the problems of running a national campaign in a federal system. Chaired by the parliamentary leader, the new National Campaign Committee includes the deputy leader, the federal party president, the senior secretariat officers, and the state general secretaries. Its task is to lay down a campaign budget and strategy based on research, to authorize a national advertising agency, and to coordinate itineraries and publicity. Each state division has agreed to delegate some of its authority in federal campaigns to the committee, to provide financing for the committee's media campaign, and to cooperate in the implementation of the committee's decisions. Tony Eggleton, former Prime Minister Harold Holt's successful press secretary, was appointed director of communications for the committee.

However, there was still one serious obstacle to the party's return to power, namely the leadership issue. With Sir Robert Menzies's retirement in 1965, his protégé Harold Holt had become party leader, leading the party to a sweeping election victory the year after. Holt's accidental death in December 1967 had opened the way for a bitter struggle between three aspiring successors that was not to be resolved until after the 1974 double-dissolution election. Senator John Gorton, who succeeded Holt, proved a maverick party leader, unconcerned with the task of tending the party machine and buttressing party loyalties; eventually, after being deposed as leader and dismissed from the cabinet, he even resigned from the party. He was followed as leader by William McMahon, a long-time treasurer in the Menzies governments and deputy leader under Holt. McMahon's original bid for leadership in 1968 had been thwarted when the leader of the Country party, Sir John McEwen, had announced that the Country party would not serve in a McMahon government, and in the interests of maintaining the coalition McMahon had withdrawn from the leadership contest. By 1971 McEwen was in retirement and the new Country party leader, Doug Anthony, was willing to support McMahon, enabling his second leadership bid to succeed. He stood down a year later when the coalition lost the 1972 federal election, and the West Australian Billy Snedden was elected in his stead.

It has been argued that Snedden was to be no more than a caretaker leader, fit only for leading the party in opposition. This view underrates the organizational reforms put in train by Snedden during his stint as leader which were to prove so important to the party's return to power in 1975. It was on his initiative that a parliamentary executive was set up, with spokesmen in various policy areas, each supported by a committee, to work on much-needed new policy proposals. The Liberals were able to go into the 1974 federal election campaign reasonably well prepared as a result of Snedden's efforts; senior ministers, bereft of the back-up of their personal staffs and public service advisers, had proved woefully inadequate for the task of reshaping the party in opposition, and his initiative had ensured that the framework of a new party platform, supported by broad policy outlines, could be put forward for testing in the 1974 election campaign. The Liberals were almost returned to office at that election when the Whitlam Labor government was reelected by a scant handful of votes in marginal seats and its parliamentary majority reduced to 5 seats in a House of 127.

However close, the outcome was still a Liberal defeat; as party leader, Snedden was held accountable, in his turn to be deposed by Malcolm Fraser, whose rise to the party leadership parallels that of Menzies. Sir Robert had been isolated in the party in 1939, just as Fraser had been in the Gorton period in the 1960s. Menzies had come back as party leader in 1944 to weld the fragmented and split anti-Labor forces into political unity, and Fraser too was elected leader by the demoralized Liberal party in the aftermath of the 1972 and 1974 defeats. Menzies went on to lead his regrouped forces to electoral victory in 1949, just as Malcolm Fraser led a revitalized Liberal party to a similar victory late in 1975. Although more aloof and reserved in manner than Sir Robert Menzies, Fraser is a strong party leader in the Menzies tradition and has now held that office longer than any Liberal leader since Sir Robert.

The 1975 election was held amidst the bitterness of a constitutional crisis, arising from the governor general's dismissal of the Whitlam Labor government when it could not pass its supply bills in the Senate. The campaign was particularly acrimonious, and its echoes have not yet completely subsided in Australia. Labor campaigned exclusively on the constitutionality of an election forced on them by the Liberals' improper use of their Senate majority to deny supply to a properly elected Labor government, refusing throughout the campaign to modify their strategy of single-minded insistence on this constitutional outrage. The coalition parties ran a more traditional campaign emphasizing the failure of the Whitlam government to provide effective federal leadership and economic management, and on election night Malcolm Fraser proved to have gauged the mood of the electorate more accurately than Gough Whitlam. The L-NCP opposition parties were returned to power just three years after their first postwar federal electoral defeat. It was a landslide victory, with the coalition parties winning an unprecedented lower house majority of fifty-five seats—an even more decisive vote of electoral confidence than the 1966 Liberal victory. It was Fraser's night of triumph.

The Coalition Government, 1975–1977. The Fraser government began its first term in office by announcing cuts in government spending and in the size of ministerial staffs and a rise in interest rates in a mini-budget aimed at reducing the national deficit. They also introduced a 40 percent investment allowance to stimulate capital investment, provided for emergency loans to ailing secondary industries, and restored subsidies like the superphosphate bounty to rural industries. Finally, in a goodwill gesture towards organized labor, they retained the Prices Justification Tribunal, set up by Whitlam in 1973 to monitor price rises, despite a Liberal campaign promise to abolish it. Fraser's cabinet maintained his party's opposition to wage indexation, however, and when the trade union case for full wage indexation came before the Conciliation and Arbitration Commission for decision, the government put its case before the court as part of its anti-inflationary policy.[19]

The new cabinet also decided to reverse the previous Labor government's decision to recognize the incorporation of the Baltic states into the Soviet Union. Fraser's foreign policies have continued to stress the Soviet threat to world peace, along with the importance of European markets for Australian primary products. But despite such policy concessions to the National Country party's interests, the 1975 coalition government has been Fraser-style government with parallels in the early Menzies period. The prime minister excluded from his first ministry rebel party figures such as Don Chipp (who resigned from the party in 1976 to found the Australian Democrats). He set up six standing committees of cabinet with full executive powers in an apparent attempt to spread the cabinet's work load, but chaired four of them himself and decided on the agenda for all six. Even minor decisions such as the appointment of a chairman of the Australian Broadcasting Commission were often made by Fraser himself in his first term.

---

[19] In Australia, award wage rates (those set by arbitration, which is compulsory) are determined by an intricate and widespread network of wage boards, tribunals, and the federal Conciliation and Arbitration Commission. The judgments handed down by these bodies are binding on both employers and unions. The government has no special power to determine awards and wage levels, but must present its case against union applications for wage increases in accordance with the proper procedures. The independence of Australian arbitration authorities is a recognized feature of the Australian economy.

LIBERAL-NATIONAL COUNTRY PARTY COALITION

As a prime minister, Fraser also pursued an individual line in representing Australia overseas. He acted as a spokesman for Third World nations in the Pacific and Indian Ocean area at the Commonwealth Heads of Government meeting in London in 1977, opposing apartheid policies; he accepted the dissolution of the Southeast Asia Treaty Organization and supported in its place the proposed Australian and Southeast Asian regional alliance; he did not support President Carter's proposal to demilitarize the Indian Ocean. Overall, despite Australia's growing unemployment problem (around 7 percent of the work force) Fraser's position as party leader and coalition prime minister appeared securely established by mid-1977, and he decided to consolidate it by calling an election for December 1977, after only two years in office.

The 1977 Election

The Pre-campaign Period, 1977. Malcolm Fraser has become a master at exploiting the media in a rather special way.[20] Although his personal image does not project particularly well, he is most skillful at using the media's resources to promote his political decisions and to win a measure of public support for them before they become open political issues. When as defense minister, Fraser clashed with Prime Minister Gorton over the latter's decision to involve the Australian army in a potentially threatening engagement in 1971, his press briefings were central to the conflict, leading initially to Fraser's resignation from the Gorton ministry and his apparent defeat, but ultimately to the prime minister's downfall. In 1975 when the media were giving wide coverage to Billy Snedden's disastrous performance as Liberal party leader, Fraser publicly reiterated his loyalty, thus avoiding any ill will for broaching party solidarity while his own candidacy was pushed in private by his followers. The media also played a key part in the Liberal prelude to the 1975 double-dissolution campaign. Reporters inquiring about the possibility of a dissolution of Parliament in 1975 were told by Fraser that unless "extraordinary and reprehensible" circumstances existed, a government with a majority in the House should complete its term of office. When asked what would constitute such circumstances, he was reported to have told members of newspaper editorial boards in an informal meeting that all major Australian newspapers would need to call for such an election before it could be considered justifiable. This was a clear instance of Fraser's use of the media link as a political resource. It

---

[20] *Age*, October 24, 1977, p. 8.

meant that when the Liberals forced the 1975 double-dissolution election, the party received full media attention. With such a long lead up to the actual event, the party was able to conduct a reasonably normal election campaign, while Labor was forced to emphasize the crisis quality of the election. Labor's bitter accusation that constitutional convention had been breached enabled the Fraser campaign to stay on course, pointing to the scandals and poor management of the economy that had characterized Labor in government, and finally coast to victory.

In calling for an early election in 1977, the prime minister used a similar media strategy. For some months beforehand, speculation about the possibility of an early poll went unchecked (despite the complete absence of any conventional parliamentary reason for one) until eventually an early election seemed inevitable, if not positively necessary to clear the air. In the end, the Liberals risked little by forcing the Australian people to the polls a year ahead of time for no very good reason. "The Media Danced as the Prime Minister Called the Poll Tune," read the headlines. Few political leaders have remained as aloof from day-to-day contact with the media, particularly from the press, as Malcolm Fraser, and none has benefited more from his unseen and careful handling of its powers and resources.

The Structure of the Campaign. With the timing of the election carefully orchestrated to avoid a poll in 1978, when the economic situation might be worse, the Liberal party assembled its campaign structure. A redistribution due to population shifts since 1968, already under way, was hurriedly completed and the electoral rolls finalized, an undertaking which abolished three Country party seats and marginally improved Labor's position. Opinion polls showed Labor to be slightly ahead—44 percent compared with 43 percent for the coalition—and needing a swing of 6.4 percentage points away from the government to win the election. A close contest seemed inevitable.

Labor's precampaign hopes were never realized. Some four weeks later, after the votes were counted, it emerged that all the government's sitting members had been returned and the coalition had lost only one seat in the House. Every Liberal senator was also reelected. Backbenchers in marginal seats who had expressed severe misgivings about the prime minister's election timing were jubilant, and Fraser's judgment was completely vindicated by the outcome.

On the surface it had been a dull election, free of divisive issues. It is only on closer examination that the importance of the campaign's contribution to the Liberal victory becomes apparent. Critical to the success of that campaign were the organization and planning for which the National Campaign Committee of the Liberal party is now responsible, both before and during an election campaign. It decided on the main themes for the 1977 campaign as a result of in-depth surveys, and by and large the Liberals fought around these issues as originally planned. They were:

- the success of the government's economic policies,
- the groundwork laid for economic recovery,
- responsible and stable government,
- new policies consistent with the Liberals' economic objectives ("doing the job," reducing inflation, and creating a favorable climate for employment opportunities),
- a fair but firm approach to industrial relations,
- the link between the ALP and extremist union leaders,
- the alternative—ALP divisiveness, confusion, and extravagance, Whitlam's disastrous track record—and
- the threat posed by Labor to the economic recovery achieved over the last two years.

Once the campaign proper began, the federal director of the Liberal party, acting as secretary to the Campaign Committee, was formally vested with the committee's authority and became responsible for the coordination and implementation of the campaign. For the 1977 election, a campaign headquarters was established in Melbourne, close to the party's advertising agency. It operated twenty-four hours a day for the duration of the campaign so that there was always someone available to handle problems as they arose. The party director traveled with the prime minister throughout the campaign, coordinating his front-line strategy with the party's overall plan. In 1977, for the first time, the top Liberal speakers' schedules (including the prime minister's) were also coordinated and supervised from campaign headquarters. Daily contact with campaign headquarters was maintained by party staff traveling with the prime minister and by other ministers. Two strategy meetings were held at headquarters each day, and the advertising agency and the committee kept in constant touch with state division officers.[21] Nothing was left to chance.

Although the coalition parties lost ground in the opinion polls when Labor opened its campaign some ten days before them, in the

---

[21] I am indebted to the Federal Secretariat of the Liberal party for these details.

end they gained a considerable advantage from having early warning of the opposition's economic policies and election promises on unemployment. They were able to counter the Labor proposals and still have sufficient time to make their own impact, while Labor's early start appeared only to give it more time to display its inconsistencies and economic ad hockery.

An effective part of the Liberals' campaign "fine-tuning" was their decision to play up the three issues that countered the ALP's emphasis on unemployment, namely, tax reform, the dangers of Whitlam-type government, and the fragmented and confused Labor leadership. Contrary to the general assumption, the Liberal party's preliminary research had shown that unemployment was not a major electoral liability for them; it was a major *election* issue, but the voters blamed Whitlam rather than the Liberal party, and the government had much less to fear from it than Labor realized.

Another vote-winner for the Liberals was their imaginative advertising program. One particularly successful gimmick, known as dial-a-tax-cut, consisted of a recorded telephone message spelling out the actual increases in take-home pay that voters would receive under a Liberal government. More than a quarter of a million voters used it. Equally effective were the campaign television and radio advertisements quoting headlines from Labor's tumultuous term in office while a tune called "Memories" played in the background. Voters could recall those events too readily for Labor's comfort.

For all its careful, detailed planning, the Liberal campaign managed to retain enough flexibility to meet the challenge of what came to be known as the Lynch affair. The Liberal treasurer, Phillip Lynch, made headlines when it was revealed by the opposition that he had profited, through a family trust, from property deals capitalizing on the inflationary price spiral that the Liberal government had undertaken to contain over the past two years. This disclosure threatened the Fraser government's economic credibility as a responsible and stable government laying the groundwork for economic recovery, and at the prime minister's bidding Lynch resigned from the ministry. His obvious reluctance to do so added to the drama, as did the subsequent pictures of him undergoing surgery for a kidney ailment. However, his illness was undoubtedly a bonus for the Liberals, for it effectively removed Lynch from the campaign and prevented the opposition from exploiting the issue to the full. The prime minister procured the treasurer's resignation on the grounds that his personal affairs ought not to become an election issue, then silenced further controversy with Lynch's illness. "Out of sheer plain decency," Fraser said, "Mr. Lynch's personal affairs should not be dragged into the campaign." Further ALP attempts to make electoral capital out of the issue of ministerial pecuniary interests allowed the prime minister to accuse them of deliberately running a dirty campaign because their policies were so inadequate. Fraser's decisiveness and fighting strength held party support together for the week or so that Lynch's business affairs dominated the media, and the credit for turning what could have been an explosive issue into a fizzle went to him. Although the disclosure that the treasurer's personal business activities had run counter to the government's declared policies of economic restraint was potentially damaging for the Liberal party, the Lynch affair appeared to have little effect on the poll outcome. What it did was to consolidate Fraser's grip on the Liberal party leadership.

Thereafter the Liberal campaign ran according to plan. Fraser campaigned in all of the states, addressing around forty meetings during the nineteen-day campaign. He took part in innumerable radio and television programs and news conferences and participated in the party's advertising campaign, stressing the theme that the Liberal government had laid the foundations for economic recovery over the past two years and now offered a stable and responsible future: "Doing the Job" was the Liberals' campaign slogan, and the prime minister embodied its message.

The Liberal party promised a continued fall in inflation, tax cuts that would put money in the voters' pockets, new investment to promote growth and development, and more jobs. They hammered away at Labor's failure to think through its tax and wage indexation policies and stressed the ALP's economic ineptitude on every count. Moreover, their advertising campaign was flexible enough to capitalize on whatever issues the party-sponsored private twice-weekly polls revealed as likely scoring points. Once the tide of opinion turned in their favor midway through the campaign, the Liberal machine never faltered.

A somewhat bizarre footnote to the formal party campaign was the parallel campaign run by the former Liberal premier of the state of Victoria, Sir Henry Bolte. He sponsored his own press, radio, and television messages, capitalizing on the earthy style that had stood him in good stead in his seventeen record-breaking years as Victoria's premier. "In under Three Years Labor Tore the Guts Right out of Australia," proclaimed his headlines. Although Liberal party officials displayed some embarrassment at this outburst of the old-fashioned Bolte style, his theme was in line with the "Memories" advertisements and on balance probably aided the Liberal cause. It also had the merit of enlivening a campaign focused mainly on the bread-and-butter issues of tax reform, inflation, and unemployment. By the end of November, the L-NCP vote was running at 44.3 percent in the polls, compared with Labor's 42.9 percent,[22] and it went on gathering momentum over the final two weeks of the campaign, to culminate in an overwhelming victory for the coalition.

The National Country Party Campaign. As always, the NCP ran its own separate campaign, stressing its raison d'être as a party, the importance of attending to the needs of the rural electorate. The leader's policy speech promised funds for a new national water resources program, a reduction in the fuel tax, the abolition of probate duties on estates passing between husband and wife and parent and child, provision for carry-on loans to tide farmers over market delays in the beef industry, and so on, through a wide range of rural concerns.

The NCP leader, Deputy Prime Minister Anthony, had lost ground during the first Fraser ministry, partly through illness and partly as a consequence of his support for the abortive merger with the Democratic Labor party in Western Australia and Queensland. His 1977 campaign performance, though not sparkling, was important for him because it restored some of his lost support and headed off moves to replace him as party leader. His choice of Queensland to open the National Country party campaign was symbolic: its premier, Johanes Bjelke-Petersen, is perhaps the best known, if the most eccentric, of the Country party leaders in Australia, and Anthony was guaranteed a welcome in the state with the highest Country party vote.

Some observers find that the NCP's rural image sits oddly with its razz-ma-tazz campaign style. Jazz bands play "Tiger Rag," marching girls parade, supporters fly streamers over party cavalcades, and platform proceedings are often in the hands of former beauty queens and celebrities. The country fair atmosphere of the NCP's campaigns successfully translates its understanding of the rural values that underlie its supporters' loyalty. So long as the party differentiates itself from the rural wings of the Liberal and Labor parties and reinforces its voters' conviction that their party is the farmers' friend, it is likely to survive in Australia.

Doug Anthony also added an NCP twist to "Memories," saying, "Mr. Whitlam just does not like country people. He wrote them off

---

[22] *Age-Poll*, November 26, 1977, conducted by Irving Saulwick & Associates, Melbourne.

once with his record inflation, high interest rates and antagonistic attitudes, and he will do it again. Don't put the big spenders back in office." It was a simple but effective message in rural areas threatened by rising costs, falling incomes, and a disastrous drought.

In keeping with his stress on the party's independent status, the NCP leader advocated a policy of even greater tax relief than the Liberal party promised. He admitted that these proposed wider rebates were not yet an accepted coalition policy, but added "I have no doubt that Mr. Fraser will be sympathetic." It was an accurate description of the coalition partners' campaign relationship. Though the NCP asked for rural concessions on behalf of its supporters, it recognized its subordinate role in the government and the need ultimately to wait upon Liberal party decisions. Only once did signs of dissension between the two leaders surface during the campaign, in the midst of the Lynch affair. Anthony showed little support for Fraser's strategy of labeling the criticism of Lynch a "campaign of smear and innuendo," commenting that it depends on how close you are standing to flying mud whether you see a campaign as dirty!

The NCP campaign was generally more successful than many had expected in the light of the party's declining electoral base. It had lost three seats as a result of the redistribution carried out prior to the election, and it lost one more on December 10 in Victoria where its organization was weak. But nationwide it held its voting percentage to 10 percent, and in Queensland it polled a heartening 26 percent.[23] It may well have reached a plateau, for the 1977 election demonstrated that the NCP has a solid core of support concentrated in certain rural electorates where it is seen as having the interests of the country at heart. Its future clearly depends on its ability to retain an electoral ratio favorable to country districts and a policy that runs counter to the one-man one-vote sentiment strongly held by city voters, particularly ALP supporters, who are sharply critical of country electorates with up to a quarter fewer electors on their rolls. The NCP's value to the Liberal party as a coalition partner is also crucial, particularly since the record Liberal majorities in 1975 and 1977, making Country party support technically unnecessary, have called its role in the coalition into question. Finally, its success in wielding power within the coalition in the past has also been a function of the effectiveness of its own party leaders: the contribution to the party's position made by strong leaders like Arthur Fadden and

---

[23] Malcolm Mackerras, "No Change: Analysis of the 1977 Election," *Politics*, vol. 13, no. 1 (May 1978), p. 131 ff.

Sir John McEwen should not be underestimated. For the NCP the 1977 election campaign promised survival into the 1980s.

The Lessons of the Campaign. The coalition parties' separate campaigns reflected their careful planning and effective deployment of resources. Campaign readiness is one of the major tasks undertaken by the Liberal Federal Secretariat, which is now more or less continuously involved in preparation for election campaigns. Planning for the next election is always as far advanced as is practical. Research projects designed to identify election issues and attitudes and help develop the advertising agency's media campaign continue to be carried out between elections, although at a slower pace, and as the campaign proper develops, further survey monitoring ensures that the overall strategy remains consistent with the flow of events. The emphasis is on both quantitative and qualitative in-depth polling. In 1977, this combination of research techniques alerted the Liberals to the fact that the unemployment issue was a paper tiger: the quantitative surveys showed it to be salient, but the in-depth research revealed that the majority of swinging voters blamed Whitlam rather than Fraser. The view that "one man's wage rise is another man's job" was widely held in the Australian electorate. Labor assumed that the voters would blame the Liberals for unemployment and planned its campaign accordingly. It centered its policy proposals on abolishing payroll taxes and tackling unemployment indirectly through savings to employers that would enable them to increase their labor force. However, the electorate preferred the more direct Liberal offer of personal income tax cuts translated through rising consumer demand into job creation.

Another instance of the coalition's careful deployment of their resources was their use of the leaders' time. The Liberal party decided against wasting the prime minister at meetings where no more than about fifty people would see him, instead planning extensive use of radio and television to reach tens of thousands of listeners and viewers. Today the committee cuts back on public meetings, leaving more time for media work. The party's free time on radio and television is also carefully allocated, and its paid advertisements are spread thinly in newspapers since it has found that saturation advertising gives less value for campaign dollars.[24] In 1977 the Liberal party claimed to have spent much the same as the ALP on its campaign, around $2 million. The Liberals used skilled consultants as

[24] Tony Eggleton, "The 1977 Campaign: a Liberal Viewpoint," *Journal of Higher School Certificate Politics* (April 1978), p. 20 ff.

well as the secretariat personnel for the daily briefings at campaign headquarters and made extensive use of a media monitoring technique developed by a former member of Snedden's staff.

To some extent the ALP activists' belief that they were the "victims of media imbalance in 1977,"[25] along with their conviction that the Liberals had an unfair advantage in media advertising, greatly outspending Labor, reflects the ALP's failure to understand the sheer professionalism of the Liberal party's campaigns since the 1972–1974 reorganization. It is uncertain whether this same efficiency could elect a prime minister if his party lacked electoral credibility.

On the other hand, the Liberals' planning strategies are primarily aimed at uncovering the electorate's political beliefs, attitudes, policy priorities, and reactions to the government's record. Not until these have been charted does Liberal campaign planning get under way. Since the National Campaign Committee was first set up, hit-or-miss campaigns have become a thing of the past in the Liberal party. Perhaps it is now up to the Australian voters to extend their political education and increase their knowledge and awareness so that they can hold their own against the sophisticated and persuasive strategies that political parties now have at their command.

Australian Democracy and the 1977 Election Outcome

The election results on December 10 gave the Liberal party sixty-seven seats, compared with its previous sixty-eight, and the NCP nineteen compared with its previous twenty-three (although three Country party losses were due to redistribution; the party's seat total was twenty in 1969 and 1972). The ALP won thirty-eight out of a total of 124 House seats compared with thirty-six in 1975 out of a total of 127. Thus the 1977 federal election was a no-change election, leaving the relative power of the major political parties untouched. The state variations, which were considerable, are set forth in Table 4–1.

The superficially dull election campaign centering on bread-and-butter issues had returned a Parliament almost identical to the outgoing one, restoring the reigning L-NCP Fraser government.

Yet it is too simple a view to see the 1977 election as a non-event in Australian electoral history. About 20 percent of the voters changed their party preferences during the campaign, and the numbers acknowledging no party loyalty increased from 9 percent in 1972 to

---

[25] David Combe, "Labor: Election '77 and Prospects for 1978" *Journal of Higher School Certificate Politics* (April 1978), p. 29 ff.

TABLE 4–1
PARTY DISTRIBUTION OF HOUSE OF REPRESENTATIVES SEATS,
BY STATE, 1977

State	Liberal	NCP	ALP	Total Seats
New South Wales	18	8	17	43
Victoria	20	3	10	33
Queensland	9	7	3	19
South Australia	5	—	6	11
Western Australia	9	—	1	10
Tasmania	5	—	—	5
Australian Capital Territory	1	—	1	2
Northern Territory	—	1	—	1
Australia	67	19	38	124

SOURCE: Commonwealth Electoral Office.

approximately 15 percent. Over 70 percent of these swinging voters made up their minds on how they would vote during the campaign, taking right up to polling day to decide in many cases. For them the campaign images presented by the political parties and their leaders were important, and the changing party fortunes charted by successive opinion polls reflected their reaction to the unfolding campaign.[26]

The campaign ran officially from November 17 to December 10, and as Table 4–2 shows, it was decisive to the Liberals' victory. With increasing voter volatility likely to affect Australian politics in the 1980s, the importance of campaigns—and the problem of finding the financial resources necessary to fight them—can only increase. The Liberal party, while determined never to incur the kind of financial links with outside organizations that brought the United Australia party to disaster in the 1930s, may find financing one of its most intractable problems in the next decade.

The 1977 campaign also saw the major parties campaign on clearly different ideological solutions to the problems of inflation and economic recession. Conventional wisdom has long held that Australians take an instrumental view of government; William K. Hancock's conclusion in 1930 that "Australian democracy has come to look upon

---

[26] The data on swinging voters quoted here are taken from a postelection survey conducted by the department of political science at the University of Melbourne. The results are reported in Jean Holmes, "The Swinging Voter in Australia—1977 and After," *Journal of Higher School Certificate Politics* (April 1978), p. 3 ff., and the data are held in the department.

TABLE 4–2
Voting Intentions Before and During the 1977 Federal Election Campaign
(in percentages)

	Voting Intention		
Party	September 24–25	November 26–27	December 3–4
ALP	43.7	42.9	39.3
Liberal	36.5	38.9	41.1
NCP	4.2	5.4	5.1
DLP	3.1	1.6	2.1
Australian Democrats	8.8	9.7	10.8
Other	3.5	1.5	1.7
Total	99.8	100.0	100.1
N	(1,908)	(1,927)	(1,921)

NOTE: The survey question was: "If a Federal Election for the House of Representatives were held tomorrow, for which political party would you probably vote?" The fixed-choice card handed to the respondent listed the parties shown in the table.

SOURCE: *Age-Poll*, September, November, December, 1977. Conducted by Irving Saulwick & Associates, Melbourne.

the state as one vast utility whose duty is to provide the greatest happiness for the greatest number" still seems to hold.[27] A 1978 survey, the results of which are set out in Table 4–3, found that economic growth and a stable economy were still Australians' most important public policy priorities.

Almost half the respondents chose pragmatic economic policy goals as their top priority, including not only 50.5 percent of Liberal respondents but also 40.8 percent of Labor supporters. It is in the respondents' second choices that ideological differences between the parties appear. Liberals ranked stability and maintenance of law and order second in importance, whereas Labor supporters were more oriented towards egalitarian values and their implementation by government. The means by which economic objectives are to be achieved in Australia have a party slant, further evidence of the relevance of the value dichotomy in Australian politics described earlier.

Labor's 1977 election policies for economic recovery stressed programs for the underprivileged unemployed, and when the Lynch

---

[27] William Hancock, *Australia* (London: 1930), pp. 61, 65.

TABLE 4-3
POLICY PRIORITIES AND VOTING INTENTIONS, MARCH 1978
(in percentages)

Policy Priority	Party				Total
	ALP	Liberal	NCP	Australian Democrats	
Economic growth, stable economy, fight against rising prices	40.8	50.5	42.4	40.4	44.8
Strong defense forces, maintaining law and order, fight against crime	20.8	34.7	43.1	20.7	27.5
Greater participation at work, more say in government decisions, protecting freedom of speech	28.0	8.2	8.6	21.9	18.4
More humane society, more beautiful environment, ideas more important than money	10.5	6.6	5.9	17.0	9.3
Total	100.1	100.0	100.0	100.0	100.0
N	(795)	(178)	(740)	(85)	(1,798)

NOTE: $x^2 = 40.79$ df $= 9$ $p<.001$. The survey question was, "Now would you look again at all of the goals listed on the three cards and tell me which one you consider most important, and which one you consider next most important, and which is the least important from your point of view?
- achieving a high rate of economic growth
- making sure that this country has strong defense forces
- seeing that the people have more say in how things get decided at work and in their communities
- trying to make our cities and countryside more beautiful
- maintaining order in the nation
- giving the people more say in important government decisions
- fighting rising prices
- protecting freedom of speech
- having a stable economy
- progress towards a less impersonal more humane society
- the fight against crime
- progress towards a society where ideas are more important than money."

SOURCE: *Age-Poll*, March 1978, conducted by Irving Saulwick & Associates, Melbourne.

affair blew up, they tried to support their theme by stressing the abuse of ministerial privileges by the Liberals. The latter centered their campaign on tax cuts and individual incentives and rewards within an orderly framework of government as the solution to the country's economic problems. The National Country party in turn emphasized the threat to the rural way of life posed by current economic trends and pushed for subsidies and development schemes to help country people defend themselves in a hostile physical and economic world. The new minor party, the Australian Democrats, turned away from instrumentalism, exhorting the voters to return to the basic principles of Australian democracy, and while they too supported economic objectives as their first policy choice, thereafter they divided almost equally between the remaining three priorities. The postelection survey also indicated that Australian Democrats had a different perspective on politics. More than 70 percent of the voters who switched to the Democrats expressed dissatisfaction with both the major parties and their policies and gave this as their main reason for supporting the new minor party. It polled over 9 percent nationally and almost 12 percent in some states. Australian Democrats distributed their second preferences more or less equally between Labor and non-Labor; they appeared to defect equally from both and were equally dissatisfied with their ideological alternatives. Other voters stayed with the major parties in the House vote but used their Senate votes to express increasing dissatisfaction with the major parties; nearly 9 percent of the postelection survey said that they voted for different parties in the House of Representatives and the Senate, and two Australian Democrat senators were elected as a consequence.

The new minor party's success in the 1977 election was a reflection of the groundswell of dissatisfaction with both Labor and non-Labor that has developed in Australian politics in the 1970s. Linked with increasing voter volatility, it presages a change in the balance of forces in the Australian party system for the 1980s. The pluralist and federalist structure of the system may well be adequate to accommodate the new voting interests that are emerging, but it is important that the major parties retain their role as the spokesmen for the consensus value positions in Australian society. Otherwise the instability inherent in the structure of the party system may well overwhelm the balancing mechanisms described earlier and the pattern of Australian party politics change irrevocably.

Finally, the 1977 election campaign saw something of a generation gap emerge in Australian politics. Figure 4–1 reflects this, breaking down voting intentions by the voter's age. Those over

FIGURE 4–1
Voting Intentions, By Age, 1977

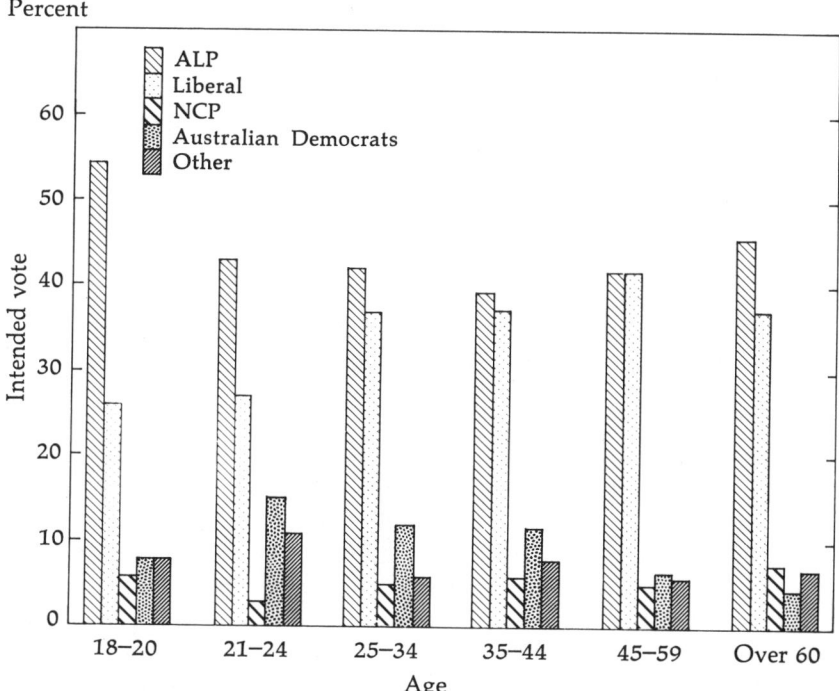

Source: Age Poll, September 1977.

twenty-five divided more or less evenly between the Liberal and Labor parties, while the Democrats' main support came from the middle group, the twenty-one to forty-four year olds. Voters under twenty-five were twice as likely to support Labor as the Liberals, and NCP support was evenly distributed throughout the age cohorts, dropping off only among the twenty-one to twenty-four year olds.

A cleavage between those voters who had grown up in the prosperous Australia of the mid-1950s and 1960s and those whose less optimistic world view had been shaped by the uncertain 1970s appeared to surface in the 1977 election. The Liberal party, with its ideological roots in the Protestant work ethic, will be less in tune with a generation for whom unemployment, through no obvious fault of their own, has been a significant social experience. Liberal leaders with their emphasis on individual incentive and reward will be less likely to see any necessity for government policies to offset the problems of the young. By contrast, Labor with an ideology attuned to the less fortunate in Australian society, and with its emphasis on social egalitarianism, can much more readily put forward proposals for reform. If the electorate does blame the Fraser government for youthful unemployment in the 1980s, the Liberals could once again face serious internal conflict and, fragmented and split by dissension, lose power as they did in 1972 to an opponent pledged to right social injustice.

Figure 4–1 contains more comfort for the NCP. Its support appears to have leveled out across the age cohorts, and this, together with the present population shift away from the cities into rural areas, suggests that a separate rural political party is still viable in Australia. NCP numbers may once more be crucial in maintaining the coalition's strength in the 1980s, a situation the Country party is well equipped to exploit to its continued benefit.

Conclusion. There seems little doubt that the 1977 federal election in Australia, for all its apparent tranquility, was something of a watershed for the coalition parties. A significant and growing minority of voters appeared to be turning away from the two-party pattern that has dominated Australian federal politics for the past three decades. They expressed their dissatisfaction with the simple ideological approach to economic problems that has characterized election alternatives over this period. As major party identification declines among Australian voters, and voter volatility increases with higher education, the pluralist party system will need to tackle again the task of shaping electoral alternatives at the margins where so many Australian elections are decided, just as it has done in the past. Party stances that have characterized Australian politics since the Liberal party first emerged as a political force in the 1950s are now breaking down and fragmenting under the stress of social change. New political movements are once more appearing in response to that change, just as they did in the 1940s out of postwar change. In retrospect, the 1977 federal election may mark the first intriguing glimpse of political Australia in the 1980s, a prospect that holds both promise and threat for the thirty-year L-NCP coalition.

5
The Australian Democrats

Paul Reynolds

Political scientists have often debated whether Australia has a two-party or a three-party system[1]—in particular, whether the National Country party should be included with the Liberal party as forming a single non-Labor entity in a bipartite system, or whether it can be seen as essentially independent of its major coalition partner and thus the smallest component of a tripartite system. Either way, the minor or third parties are excluded, perhaps on the assumption that, because of their size, such groups will always be bit players in a scene dominated by two or three main actors. At the same time, the minor parties, which have constituted a durable feature of the party system since the early 1950s, clearly deserve some consideration.

Minor parties (excluding the NCP from this category) were virtually unknown in Australia prior to 1954, with the exception of the Communist party of Australia and the short-lived Lang Labor party in New South Wales. Since then, however, a succession of third parties have competed, with mixed success, in Australian politics. The most memorable, at state and federal levels, have been the Democratic Labor party (DLP), the Queensland Labor party, the National Alliance, the Liberal Reform Group, the Australia party (AP), the Liberal Movement, the New Liberal Movement, the Workers' party, the Progress party, and the Australian Democrats. This list, however, is deceptive in that many of these parties were closely related to each other or to major parties. The Queensland and Democratic Labor parties, for example, eventually merged; the DLP amalgamated with the Country party in Western Australia to form the National Alliance; the Liberal

---

[1] See for example, Jack M. Barbalet, "Tri-partism in Australia: the Country Party," *Politics*, vol. 10, no. 1 (May 1975), for a useful discussion and analysis. Barbalet argues the case for a three-party system.

Reform Group became the Australia party; the New Liberal Movement was that portion of the Liberal Movement that did not rejoin the South Australian branch of the Liberal party; the Workers' party of 1975 gave way to the Progress party of 1977, while the Australian Democrats, with varying success in each state, incorporated the remnants of the Australia party.

The DLP, which began in 1955 as Australia's first, and to date most successful minor party, had combined hard-line right-wing policies on defense and foreign affairs with moderately left-wing policies on social welfare and immigration. However, owing to the priority it gave to anticommunism over its other policies, it was usually regarded as a minor party of the right. It was the Australia party and its Liberal Reform Group predecessor that first gave organizational expression to the idea of a minority party of the center. Forged initially out of middle-class hostility to the Vietnam War and to the conscription policies of Liberal-Country party governments in the 1960s, it gave an option to those who were dissatisfied with the old polarization of politics: on one side, an apparently trade-union dominated ALP led by Arthur A. Calwell mouthing the socialist rhetoric of the 1930s, and opposite it the post-Menzian coalition government, which had grown complacent, lazy, and insensitive to criticism in its long years in power.

AP support declined as the ALP, led by E. G. Whitlam, was revitalized. In the late 1960s and early 1970s Labor addressed itself to the problems of contemporary Australia, especially the inadequacy of public facilities (in education, health, welfare, housing, transport, environmental protection, and the like), and sought a new role for Australia in world affairs, unencumbered by slavish adherence to the military aspects of the Australian-American alliance. The AP succumbed, then, to the threat that is ever present for small center parties, namely seeing their base eroded by whichever major party most closely approximates their own aims and aspirations.

In some ways the political situation after the 1975 election resembled the situation following the 1966 election. In both cases the conservative coalition parties had won landslide victories, with the ALP left weak and demoralized. A lopsided parliamentary majority resulted in the government's having more to fear from discontent within its own swollen ranks than from the impotent parliamentary opposition. In 1967 Prime Minister Harold Holt became the target of criticism from within the government as the coalition faltered at the Senate elections of that year. His death in December 1967 was an occasion for bloodletting within the Liberal party over the question of its leadership, culminating in the government's near defeat in 1969 and its loss of office in 1972.

After the 1975 election the government's conservative policies on industrial matters, social welfare, and foreign policy disturbed some, while its autocratic style under Fraser's leadership caused disquiet among those who saw themselves as small "l" liberals. In any event, however, it was neither the politics nor the style of the first Fraser government that proved to be the catalyst for the rejuvenation of the center party idea in Australian politics, but the exclusion of Don Chipp from the cabinet and ministry Fraser formed on December 18, 1977.

The Emergence of the Australian Democrats

Chipp, the son of working-class parents, had held the middle and lower-middle-class seats of Higginbotham and Hotham for the Liberals since 1960. He had been a junior minister under Gorton and had distinguished himself as the minister for customs and excise in the ill-fated McMahon government. As that government appeared to be sliding inexorably towards electoral defeat in 1972, Chipp made his reputation as a sensitive minister who warned of the dangers of drug abuse and also liberalized the repressive censorship laws, thereby earning the wrath of conservatives in his own party and the hatred of the DLP.[2]

With Labor in power after December 1972, Chipp became opposition spokesman for international trade, then for health and welfare. When Billy Snedden was challenged by Fraser for the position of leader of the opposition, Chipp was one of his leader's most ardent and articulate defenders. He and Andrew Peacock worked unceasingly in the week that preceded the party ballot of March 21, 1975, to save Snedden's position, but to no avail. Fraser and Chipp were as far apart as it was possible to be while remaining within one party; Chipp retained his shadow portfolio, but because of his championing of Snedden, he was unlikely to advance in a government led by Fraser. This presumption was reinforced by Chipp's denunciation of Medibank, the Labor government's popular public health scheme, at the end of August 1975. His stand on this question was repudiated by Fraser, who, after the 1975 election victory, left him on the backbench. As Chipp's biographers remarked, "The conservative wing of the coalition, with the exception of Peacock, held the positions of power, and liberals such as Snedden (who became Mr. Speaker) were left on

---

[2] Paul L. Reynolds, *The Democratic Labor Party* (Brisbane: Jacaranda Press, 1974), pp. 84-89.

the outer. It looked as though Chipp's final break with the party was inevitable."³

It took Chipp another fifteen months to break with the Liberal party. He resigned in a speech to the House of Representatives on March 24, 1977, in which *inter alia* he criticized the government's economic policies, its attitude to the trade union movement, its stand on uranium mining, its failure to implement election promises in the field of social welfare, and various of its foreign policy positions. He continued by attacking the established parties as being beholden to pressure groups and vested interests—Labor to the trade unions, the National Country party to the rural sector, and the Liberals to big business. He concluded by stating: "I wonder if the ordinary voter is not becoming sick and tired of the vested interests which unduly influence the present political parties and yearn for the emergence of a third political force, representing middle-of-the-road policies which would owe allegiance to no outside pressure group. Perhaps it may be the right time to test that proposition."⁴

It is possible to analyze Chipp's actions at two levels. He has been accused of political ambition, of deserting his party to seek political advancement elsewhere when he failed to gain the spoils of office. In this he is reminiscent of some of the DLP leaders who, failing to attain ascendance within the ALP, went outside it to form their own party as an alternative vehicle for gaining their political goals. Undoubtedly there is an element of this, too, in the aspirations of some Australian Democrats who had been prominent in the old AP.

On the other hand, Chipp's move gave a focus to those who were increasingly dissatisfied with the course Australian politics had taken over the past five years. The Labor government of 1972–1975 had shifted the consensus in national politics from the concerns of the 1950s and 1960s to questions of social reform, independence in foreign affairs, a "moral" stance on minority rights, constitutional reform, and concern over the "new" issues—environment, women's rights, government involvement in the quality of life, artistic and cultural expression, and an assertive national indentity. Such matters had been widely discussed among the opinion leaders and attentive public, with one of Labor's major achievements being to bring them within the scope of legislative and bureaucratic decision making. The economic

---

³ Tim Hewatt and David Wilson, *Don Chipp* (Camberwell: Widescope International Publishers, 1978), p. 71. "Left on the outer" means excluded from the inner circle.

⁴ *Commonwealth of Australia Parliamentary Debates, Hansard* (House of Representatives), no. 5 (March 22-24, 1977), pp. 555-558.

recession, however, had driven the mass electorate's concerns back to the basic questions of economic politics. The coalition parties were perceived as being the more competent economic managers and the guarantors of national living standards during a period of profound economic uncertainty, characterized by escalating unemployment and high inflation. Certain sections of the middle-class electorate, however, were not prepared to see the priorities Labor had emphasized totally swamped by a return to conservative economic management. For the most part they were younger, white-collar, and better educated voters who were in comparatively secure economic positions and for whom party loyalties were neither fixed nor immutable.

At the end of the 1960s and in the early 1970s this group had emerged as a significant segment of the swinging vote; in 1972 they largely gravitated to the ALP.[5] It is probably fair to assume that, politically, they became more heterogeneous as Labor's term progressed, some remaining with the government, others gravitating to the Liberals. And they were undoubtedly subjected to strong cross-pressures by the constitutional crisis of November 1975. At all events, this is the kind of constituency most likely to be receptive to the claims of a third center party that would emphasize the value issues they wished to see remain on the national agenda. The subordination of all areas of public policy to economic considerations by the Fraser government, plus its tough-minded and at times arrogant style, were increasingly unlikely to retain the loyalties of those of this group who had supported the Liberals in 1975. Similarly a demoralized ALP, preoccupied with formulating its own economic solutions, was not an automatic alternative. Although Chipp's resignation speech talked of "the ordinary voter," those who would be attracted to the type of party he seemed to have in mind were hardly likely to be average.

The Democrats in the State Elections

When Chipp resigned in March, an early federal election was not expected. As it turned out, he and his followers would have about eight months to organize and to contest one national and two state elections.

In response to his resignation speech various people contacted Chipp, and a groundswell of sorts seemed to be developing. For the next four or five months supporters set about organizing the party in all of the states, establishing a National Steering Committee, and

---

[5] David Kemp, "Swingers and Stayers: The Australian Swinging Voter, 1961-72," in Henry Mayer, ed., *Labor to Power* (Sydney: Angus and Robertson, 1973).

generally gathering personnel, ideas, and policy. When the election was announced for December 10, there were several thousand members, including a number of ex-Australia party and New Liberal Movement followers in South Australia, but most recruits had never belonged to any political party.

Even in their early days the Australian Democrats saw their task as encompassing a number of concerns. Their overriding motivation was alienation from "traditional" politics. This was not merely a matter of feeling equally repelled by both major parties, but rather an aversion to all machine politics of the type the established political forces were seen to practice. Although the Australian Democrats lacked a comprehensive ideology, they were attracted to the notions of participatory democracy and individual responsibility. Decision making within the party was to be devolved as far and as often as possible to rank-and-file members. The organization was to be as open as practicable and to have a minimum of formal structure. "Small is beautiful" was an appealing notion to the Democrats, who generally distrusted big business, big unionism, growth for its own sake, and unbridled consumption patterns based on consumer-oriented economic expansion. There was a Poujadist flavor to some of their ideas, along with perhaps more marked echoes of the New Left's emphasis on the bureaucratization of society and the consequent alienation of man from his world. Their radicalism lay in their commitment to attacking prevailing concepts of social organization, elitist decision-making processes, and the overwhelming power of the major public and private bureaucracies.

In response to these general concerns, the party instituted a system of internal decision making which was reminiscent of that employed by the Australia party. Policy options were set out in the party's journal, which was mailed to all members. The rank and file then voted on these options, returning their choices to the member of the National Executive responsible for collating the results. The option receiving the greatest support then became the party's policy on that issue. In this way the Democrats hoped to involve all members in decision making on policy matters, to foster a sense of involvement within the party by devolving decision making, and to point to, and embody, a model for decision making in the wider society.

In conformity with this general approach, the party convened meetings with interested people to discuss its policy ideas and to gain additional information in the areas of policy it was exploring. It was both reaching within itself for opinions that would reflect the consensus of its membership and simultaneously going beyond itself to seek expertise in order to remain in touch with informed opinion in the wider society. This combination of approaches indicated a degree of originality and flexibility. That the proportion of members voting on policy ballots varied between 12 and 25 percent, and that these policy discussion sessions, though open to the public, were generally not well attended did not dampen the enthusiasm of the Australian Democrats for this novel approach to politics and issues. Inevitably the process had scarcely begun in earnest before these and all other considerations were subordinated to the business of waging electoral campaigns. The calling of a snap election in South Australia in September, where the Democrats had the best "old" base from which to work (the New Liberal Movement having integrated with the Australian Democrats), provided an opportunity even the half-formed party could not afford to miss. This election was followed by a state by-election in the outer Melbourne seat of Greensborough, another state election in Queensland, and the federal election in December.

The South Australian results were moderately encouraging. The election night returns were: Labor, 52 percent; Liberals, 40.8 percent; NCP, 1.6 percent; Australian Democrats, 3.5 percent; others, 2.1 percent.[6] This statewide result obscured the fact that the Australian Democrats had contested only twelve of the forty-seven seats, and in these they polled an average of 13.2 percent. Mitcham was won with a 32.4 percent AD vote plus ALP second preferences. Their candidate for this seat was Robin Millhouse, who had been deputy leader of the Liberal Movement and leader of the New Liberal Movement before leading his organization into the ranks of the Australian Democrats. The AD showing suggested that the new party had achieved a fairly broad base of support. Of the remaining eleven seats it contested, eight were held by Labor and three by the Liberals, with the AD gaining an average of 11.7 percent of the vote in the former and 11.2 percent in the latter. Its second best result was 13.8 percent in Playford (Labor), where the AD had the advantage of the donkey vote,[7] and its worst was 7.6 percent in Kavel (Liberal).

The next electoral test was significant in that it occurred in the state seat of Greensborough, Victoria, which encompassed half the federal division of Diamond Valley, one of the ring of marginal seats on Melbourne's outskirts. Greensborough had been won by the

---

[6] *Sydney Morning Herald*, September 19, 1977.

[7] The candidate who heads the alphabetical list on the ballot is reckoned to have an advantage of about 2 percent over his opponents, as this proportion of the electorate votes straight down the ballot, irrespective of party. Party labels are not placed on the ballot in Australia.

Liberals in 1969, by Labor in 1972 and 1974, and retaken by the Liberals in 1975. It was populated by younger, mainly middle-class voters whose attitude would be crucial in determining whether the Australian Democrats could find a receptive following in the large cities. The party was well led, with an attractive candidate and an effective organization. The state Liberal government was handicapped during the by-election by a Royal Commission inquiry into the land transactions of the Housing Commission and by media reports of hearing evidence that appeared to implicate two senior ministers. In addition, Victoria was gripped by a prolonged power strike which had disrupted industry and caused personal hardship. The strike was instigated and led by militant unionists, and it was thought that this would harm the ALP's chances of taking the seat from the government. In the end the Australian Democrats polled strongly, winning 17.5 percent; the DLP took 5.9 percent, the Liberals 34 percent (a swing against them of 18.8 percentage points), and Labor 42.6 percent (a decline of 4.6 percentage points). In the urban voting booths the Democrats won between 20 and 24 percent, but in the rural ones only 13 to 14 percent. The ALP won the seat with 57.8 percent of AD second preferences, thereby boosting the third party's hopes of influencing, through its preferences, the federal election a month later and of having a significant impact on the Queensland poll, to be held the following week.

The Queensland branch of the Australian Democrats, founded on July 1, 1977, had gained 800 members in its first six months of activity. Owing to the pattern of settlement in that state, the Democrats' impact was greatest in Brisbane and the southeast (the populous areas), while the provincial towns and rural areas proved harder to penetrate. They contested twelve of the eighty-two seats, taking 1.6 percent of the state vote. In the seats they contested they gained 10.4 percent, but again they did best in urban areas, collecting an average of 13.2 percent in the five Brisbane and South East Zone electorates contested.[8] Their best results were in the blue ribbon Liberal strongholds of Toowong (19.2 percent), Kurilpa (14.1 percent),

---

[8] For the purposes of state politics, Queensland is divided into four electoral zones: South Eastern, Provincial Cities, Country, and Western and Far Northern. In each a different quota is struck to ascertain the number of seats for the zone. The quota for the South Eastern zone is currently 16,368 electors, which entitles the zone to forty-seven seats. In the Provincial Cities zone a separate quota is struck for each seat in each city. As with the quotas in the three other zones, a 20 percent variance is permitted above and below the quota. In 1977 the Provincial City electorates varied in size from 13,166 (Port Curtis) to 18,213 (Mackay). The Country zone has a quota of 11,151 voters and fifteen seats. The Western and Far Northern zone has a quota of 8,586 and seven seats.

and Greenslopes (12.7 percent)—this last seat being the scene of a bitter intracoalition contest between rival Liberal and National candidates. In their three rural electorates the Democrats averaged 9.5 percent; in Cunningham there were even signs that they were poised to displace Labor as the second party, winning 10.8 percent to the ALP's 13.6 percent.[9] In their provincial city contests they gained 7.7 percent, a disappointing result but testimony to the difficulties any new party faces in constructing an organization in a state as far flung as Queensland and presided over by a highly conservative state government entrenched in power by an electoral system based on vote weighting.

In this prelude to the 1977 federal election, certain features of the Australian Democrats' support had become apparent. The electorate seemed to be generally receptive to the idea of a third political alternative. The continuation of economic recession in the two years following the Liberal victory of 1975 was highlighted by the stubborn persistence of high unemployment, especially among the young. Many who had seen the Liberals as the economic saviors in 1975 when Labor presided over the economic slump, had become disillusioned. For the Labor deserters in 1975, Whitlam's continuing in the position of ALP leader probably epitomized the inadequacy of the Labor alternative. That potentially volatile section of the electorate therefore had not been finally claimed by either major party in 1977.

In the preceding state elections the Australian Democrats had shown the strength and nature of their appeal to those prepared to abandon the major parties. The Australian Democrats' appeal, however, was neither inevitable nor universal, and certain factors appeared to be crucial in mobilizing their potential support. The party had to be organized in such a way as to capitalize on any dissatisfaction felt with the major parties. In Greensborough the local organization was efficiently led, generated enthusiasm at the grass-roots level, and campaigned with all the trappings of a major party.[10] In South Australia, there was a residue of the Liberal Movement-New Liberal Movement organization to assist the new party, as well as a Democrat already in Parliament, Robin Millhouse.[11] In Queensland the organization was

---

[9] The National party (as the NCP is known in Queensland) polled 75.6 percent.
[10] See Hewatt and Wilson, *Don Chipp*, pp. 87-90, for a description of the Democrats' campaign.
[11] The South Australian branch seems to have given most attention to the problems of organization and its contribution to electoral success. See Australian Democrats South Australian Division, *Report and Recommendations of the Committee appointed to review the Organisation and Boundaries of Branches in South Australia*, February 1978.

not sophisticated enough to mount a systematic assault on major party seats in areas likely to be receptive to the Australian Democrat alternative. Only one of the South Coast electorates was contested, and only two outer Brisbane ones, which were analogous to Greensborough. The organization selected nonmetropolitan seats in a haphazard way, concentrating its provincial efforts in only two towns (Toowoomba and Cairns), with little discernible strategy for the rural areas. Hence, after the Queensland results the Australian Democrats did look like a third force of sorts, but one whose appeal was highest in those middle-class urban seats where there was a concentration of younger voters. It had made little impact in rural areas, despite a brief flirtation with the increasingly militant Cattlemen's Union, while its record in working-class Labor areas was patchy.

The National Elections

There can be little doubt that the intervention of the Australian Democrats in the 1977 federal election profoundly influenced the result. It was the first House of Representatives election since 1958 where there was a swing against both major parties. The ALP gained 39.8 percent, a drop of 3.0 percentage points over 1975 and the party's worst result since 1931. The Liberal vote fell by 3.6 percentage points, to 38.1 percent, while the NCP dropped 1.3 percentage points, to 10 percent. The Australian Democrats' 9.4 percent of the vote in the House election was equal to the DLP's best result (1958), while their 11.1 percent in the Senate was equal to the DLP's best Senate figure (1970). Two AD senators were elected, Chipp in Victoria with virtually a full quota in his own right (16.2 percent) and Colin Mason in New South Wales (8.3 percent), who was returned on ALP second preferences. The party was narrowly beaten for the fifth Senate seat in South Australia (11.2 percent) and in Western Australia (12.5 percent).

The election result did not show a swing to all minor parties; the Progress party, for example, took a poor 0.7 percent. Rather, it was a triumph specifically for the Australian Democrats. The Senate result did not give them the balance of power in that chamber (the hope of all minor parties), but it ensured them a national platform from which to expound their views for six years.[12]

---

[12] The Australian Democrats acquired their first senator, in South Australia, when Janine Haines was appointed to fill the seat vacated by Steele Hall, who had retired to contest a House seat. Hall had been elected as a member of the Liberal Movement, to which Haines had also belonged; by the end of 1977, however, the Liberal Movement had ceased to exist. This posed a problem since state governments are required by law to replace a deceased or retiring senator with an

The pattern of AD support that had been revealed in the previous state and by-elections was confirmed in the national result (see Table 5–1).

The ADs polled above their national average in Victoria, South Australia, and Western Australia, but within those states their performance was not uniform. A number of factors seem to have influenced their showing. In South Australia, the Democrats had established themselves as heirs to Liberal Movement support; in 1975 the LM had won 6.2 percent of the South Australian vote, which the Democrats came close to doubling two years later. The history of Liberal-New Liberal Movement activity had given them a base from which to work. Victoria, where the ADs seemed to be stronger organizationally than elsewhere, was Chipp's power base. His office and staff were located in Melbourne, and his media exposure was greatest there. Moreover, the ADs apparently had a strong appeal to potentially volatile sections of the metropolitan vote. In all six of the Liberal seats in Melbourne that had been won by the ALP in 1972 and 1974 the Australian Democrats did better than their national average for the House, as the following figures show:

Seat	Australian Democrat vote (in percentages)
Issacs	17.1
Casey	16.8
Diamond Valley	16.3
La Trobe	14.2
Holt	12.8
Henty	10.0

In addition, the ADs gained their best result, 18.4 percent, in Chipp's old seat of Hotham.

It also appeared that the Australian Democrats won votes where one of the major parties suffered losses disproportionate to those of the other major party. In the nation as a whole, the ALP and the

---

appointee of the same party. On the grounds that many former members of the Liberal Movement had joined the Australian Democrats, the state government recommended that the balance of Hall's term be filled by an Australian Democrat, and the party chose Haines.

The requirement that casual Senate vacancies be filled by members of the same party as the retiring or deceased senator had been the subject of a national referendum passed just a few months before Haines's appointment, on May 21, 1977. The issue had become lively during the constitutional crisis of 1975, when a crucial Senate vote went against the Labor government only because a state government had refused to replace a deceased ALP senator with a member of the ALP. See Leon D. Epstein, "The Australian Political System," in Howard R. Penniman, ed., *Australia at the Polls* (Washington, D.C.: American Enterprise Institute, 1977), p. 40.

TABLE 5-1
Results in House Seats Where the ADs Polled Above Their National Average, 1977
(vote in percentages, swing in percentage points)

Seat Type	AD Vote	Swing from Other Parties, 1975–1977			
		Liberal	ALP	NCP	LM
South Australia, Liberal, metropolitan	14.4	−2.0	−2.6	—	−8.2
Victoria, Liberal, metropolitan	14.2	−6.9	−5.5	—	—
South Australia, metropolitan	12.6	−3.6	−1.2	—	−6.9
Western Australia, metropolitan	12.6	−5.4	−8.4	—	—
Victoria, metropolitan	12.5	−6.6	−4.7	—	—
South Australia, ALP, metropolitan	11.6	−4.3	−0.2	—	−6.0
Victoria, all seats	11.4	−2.5	−4.5	−3.3	—
Western Australia, all seats	11.3	−5.0	−7.2	−1.0	—
South Australia, all seats	11.2	−4.0	−0.0	—	−6.2
Ten safest Liberal seats	10.9	−2.6	−4.5	—	—
Victoria, Liberal, nonmetropolitan	10.3	−0.6	−3.5	−5.4	—
Victoria, ALP, metropolitan	9.8	−4.3	−3.6	—	—

NOTE: Dashes indicate that the party concerned did not contest these seats in either 1975 or 1977.
SOURCE: Author's calculations from official election returns.

Liberals lost support at similar rates, but in Western Australia Labor's vote fell 7.5 percentage points, to 32.6 percent, its worst state result. Table 5–1 suggests that the erosion of Labor support was greatest in Perth (the only large metropolitan area in Western Australia), with the Australian Democrats being the main beneficiary.

Finally, the Australian Democrats made a strong impact in safe Liberal seats, where they established themselves as a viable non-Labor alternative for middle-class voters disenchanted with the Liberal government. In South Australian Liberal metropolitan seats, non-metropolitan Liberal seats in Victoria, and the country's ten safest Liberal seats, ALP support fell at a faster rate than support for the Liberals, with the Australian Democrats again benefiting. In this type of seat the Australian Democrats' voting strength resembled that of the Liberals in Britain: the Liberals perform strongly in safe Conservative constituencies, particularly in southern England, and even replaced Labour as the second party in many of these in the election of February 1974. The Australian Democrats, then, appear to be on their way to becoming an alternative middle-class party in Victoria and South Australia.

TABLE 5–2

Results in House Seats Where the ADs Polled Below Their National Average, 1977

(vote in percentages, swing in percentage points)

Seat Type	AD Vote	Swing from Other Parties, 1975–1977		
		Liberal	ALP	NCP
Tasmania, all seats	3.2	+0.3	−1.1	−1.3
New South Wales, NCP seats	5.0	−0.4	+5.9	−3.8
Victoria, NCP seats	5.2	+16.2	−6.2	−16.2
New South Wales, ALP, nonmetropolitan	5.4	−0.2	−5.1	+2.3
Queensland, nonmetropolitan	5.5	−6.5	−4.0	+2.7
Queensland, all seats	6.5	−2.9	−1.0	+3.0
New South Wales, nonmetropolitan	6.6	−3.2	−2.2	+2.6
New South Wales, Liberal, nonmetropolitan	8.0	+2.1	−3.8	—
New South Wales, all seats	8.0	−3.7	−2.8	−0.7
Ten safest ALP seats	8.2	−5.7	−2.5	—
Victoria, nonmetropolitan	8.6	+7.4	−3.9	−11.3
New South Wales, Liberal, metropolitan	8.7	−8.1	−6.6	—
Western Australia, nonmetropolitan	9.0	−4.5	−5.3	−1.2
New South Wales, metropolitan	9.0	−4.9	−3.3	—

Source: Author's calculations from official election returns.

Table 5–2, which groups in various categories the seats where the Australian Democrats polled below their national average, shows up their areas of weakness. The party clearly holds limited attraction for country voters, making little impression in seats where the NCP vote held (New South Wales and Queensland) or where the Liberals gained at the NCP's expense (Victoria) or where NCP losses were only marginal (Western Australia). Again like the British Liberals, the Australian Democrats are not particularly attractive to working-class voters, especially in New South Wales. In those working-class seats where the ALP is dominant, the party did not capitalize on the decline in Labor's vote. Similarly in the ten safest ALP electorates (six of which are in New South Wales), the Australian Democrats did worse than in similar Liberal bailiwicks. New South Wales as a whole proved to be infertile ground for the Australian Democrats, despite having been the best state for the Australia party in the 1960s. Even where the Liberals were dominant in that state, the Australian Democrats failed to win as much support as they did in similar areas in Victoria, South Australia, and Western Australia.

Tasmania recorded the lowest swing of any state, the ALP vote falling by 1.4 percentage points, the Liberal vote rising by 0.5 percentage points. This lack of movement in voting patterns froze out any hope the Australian Democrats had of making an impact. In addition, prior to the election the party had virtually no organization in Tasmania, the last state where it had established a branch, and three months afterwards the National Executive was still attempting to build a viable organization.

Unlike previous minority parties the Australian Democrats did not direct their second preferences towards, or away from, any major party. This policy was in accord with their general philosophy of offering as much freedom of choice in politics as possible, but it may also have been based on the calculation that by not directing preferences they would maximize their attraction for dissatisfied supporters of all parties. As it transpired, the distribution of AD preferences, shown in Table 5–3, reflected the party's success in drawing support equally from the coalition parties and the ALP. Malcolm Mackerras suggests that the aggregate figures probably slightly understate the extent to which AD voters preferred Labor over the government parties and that, taking into account ballot position and the variance it produces, the ratio should be 52:48 in Labor's favor.[13]

In many ways the timing of the 1977 election was inopportune for the Australian Democrats. The party had to face a major electoral test less than a year after its foundation and with its organization only a skeleton in most of the states. It was handicapped by a lack of money; its total income from July 1977 to February 1978 was only $40,215, while its campaign expenses alone came to about $44,000.[14] It had only one national figure in Don Chipp who, though the media attention he received was generally favorable, was placed under great strain having to carry the burden of the national campaign almost single-handed. The jibe that the party was a "one-man band" was, if disputable, virtually inevitable. Despite these handicaps, the party's first venture into national politics was impressive. The most tantalizing question one was left with was whether the Australian Democrats would survive at the level of support they achieved in 1977, whether

---

[13] Malcolm Mackerras, *Australian General Election and Senate Election*. Statistical Analysis, Electoral Monograph no. 5, Department of Government, Faculty of Military Studies, University of New South Wales at Duntroon, 1978.

[14] *Statement of Income/Application of Funds, 25.7.77 to 8.2.78 (Not Audited)*, presented to February 1978 meeting of National Executive, Australian Democrats.

TABLE 5-3
DISTRIBUTION OF AD PREFERENCES, BY STATE, 1977

State	Number of Seats Contested by the AD	Percentage of AD Preferences Given to:	
		L-NCP	ALP
New South Wales	8	51.7	48.3
Victoria	11	47.0	53.0
Queensland	6	52.4	47.6
South Australia	3	50.8	49.2
Western Australia	5	53.1	46.9
Australian Capital Territory	1	48.2	51.8
Northern Territory	—	49.5	50.5
Australia	34	49.9	50.1

SOURCE: Official election returns.

they would improve on this figure to become a serious and continuing threat to major-party hegemony, or whether they would decline.

Judgments as to the survival chances of any minor party are necessarily risky. To survive at all, a party needs a cohesive electoral base. The ALP and the Liberals achieve this in terms of social class, the NCP through its regional and rural identity, while the DLP held together a constituency based on social class and religious factors for over twenty years.[15] The Australian Democrats cannot claim to have attracted any more than a narrow and unstable following. According to a postelection survey in Melbourne, the Democrats' support "came significantly from those voters who had weak loyalties to the major parties. Some 30 percent of the Democrats' votes appear to have been drawn from those who acknowledged no party loyalty at all. This helps to account for the fact that the Democrats' voters tended to be better educated than voters for the major parties."[16] An important corollary is that these voters are among the most volatile in the electorate, and thus no party can claim their habitual loyalty. Any party that becomes overdependent upon such voters risks finding its electoral base swiftly eroded in response to changing circumstances and expectations in the wider electorate.

---

[15] See Paul Reynolds, "The Role of the Minor Parties," in Howard R. Penniman, ed., *Australia at the Polls* (Washington, D.C.: American Enterprise Institute, 1977), pp. 162-163.

[16] David Kemp, "Values and the Australian Electorate," *National Times*, January 16-21, 1978, p. 20.

The history of minor parties in Australia does not offer encouraging precedents. The DLP lasted for twenty-three years, the Australia party for less than ten. The Australian Democrats claim that they are an entirely different party from the DLP and therefore can avoid the mistake of becoming irrelevant to the fundamental needs of the society. If that is so, then it is imperative for their survival, let alone their growth, that they widen their electoral appeal from the group already identified as their constituency. This will involve clarifying policies and presenting an image rather broader than that projected in 1977.

The paradox for this new party is that its ultimate destiny is inextricably interwoven with those of the two main parties. The Australian Democrats made a strong showing in 1977 because sections of the electorate were disenchanted with the government but were not prepared to support Labor. If the ALP is able to reshape its policy making, to present a more appealing image under its new leadership, and to rejuvenate its organization (as it did in 1966 after a similarly bad defeat), then the Australian Democrats of 1977 could well be Labor supporters by 1980.

The best medium-term hope for the Australian Democrats is the increasingly high level of public dissatisfaction with the Fraser government's performance and continued skepticism about Labor's ability to offer a credible alternative. In other countries, center parties have performed best when there is disenchantment with a conservative government and sections of the middle class are unwilling to gravitate to the working-class-based alternative party. The Australian Democrats reaped this type of support in 1977 and added to it a segment of Labor support. However, one significant finding of Kemp's survey in Melbourne was that Labor won a plurality among the youngest electors (those under twenty-five): about 45 percent claimed loyalty to the ALP and 30 percent to the Liberals.[17] If this result is applicable to the nation as a whole, Labor's chances for recovery look good, while the Australian Democrats' hopes for continuing support at the same or a higher level seem more remote.

---

[17] Ibid.

6
The Polls, the Public, and the Reelection of the Fraser Government

Murray Goot and Terence W. Beed

During an election, to talk about politics is to talk about the polls. The polls are prominently reported, widely respected, and closely watched. The front pages now carry the same sort of information on parties and their leaders as the sports pages carry on horses and their riders. To a nation of gamblers, the polls have been the basis of some very good bets.

For the 1977 race the need for an up-to-the-minute racing form was as great as ever. As in the past, the two major parties were the focus of attention, but the relatively late entry of the Australian Democrats raised new questions about the election outcome: the rapid growth in their support revealed a higher level of electoral volatility than had been the case for some years. The polls seemed fairly well agreed about major national issues such as unemployment and inflation, but less so on uranium and taxation. And they were less forthcoming on the question of which party any of the issues would favor. Leaders were shown to be held in fairly low regard. There was a fair measure of agreement over how the race developed: an even start, Labor setting the pace over the first couple of weeks; then the government, with the Lynch resignation and the Fraser policy speech, throwing out its challenge. Halfway through the campaign the government moved to the front, opening an ever increasing lead and going on to win.

During the long months of preparation the different pollsters registered different levels of party support. All four—the Australian

---

We wish to thank Peggy Ridley for research assistance, Karl Gunasinghe for clerical assistance, and Pat Keane for typing and layout. The Australian Research Grants Committee provided financial support through the project "Opinion Polls in Political Decision Making."

Nationwide Opinion Poll (ANOP); the *Age* poll/*Herald* survey run by Irving Saulwick and Associates with interviews conducted by Beacon Research Co. Pty Ltd.; the Australian Public Opinion Poll (APOP) conducted as the Gallup poll for the Herald and Weekly Times newspaper publishing group by the McNair Anderson market research organization; and the Morgan Gallup poll—picked the winner, though they offered different forecasts of the winning margin. One of them, in retrospect, argued that early support for Labor had been engineered by Liberals wanting the race to appear closer than it really was. The winning margin surprised almost everyone. Not for the first time, punters consulted the racing form but overlooked the weights.

The Pre-Campaign Period, 1976–1977

Polling Patterns. The frequency with which the polls monitor party preference is largely determined by the pollsters themselves and the media that carry their results, but it is partly a matter of the political climate as well. In the eighteen months between the reelection of the Whitlam Labor government in May 1974 and its final defeat in December 1975 Morgan took thirty-two readings, APOP twenty, ANOP and the *Age* poll at least a dozen between them.[1] In the two years between the election of the Fraser government in December 1975 and its reelection in 1977, Morgan and APOP between them took only forty-three readings; ANOP and the *Age* poll sixteen. Whitlam's 1974 victory had been narrow, and a hostile Senate threatened to throw the government out at any time. Fraser's winning margin had been wide and the next election would be held at a date of his own choosing.

Morgan's first survey of voting intentions after the election of December 1975 was conducted in mid January 1976, APOP's in mid March, and the *Age* and ANOP's not until April. During the first half of 1976 the Morgan Gallup poll's interest was spasmodic; publishing results fortnightly, it next asked about intended vote in March and again on four subsequent occasions in the first nine months of 1976. The other pollsters did so even less frequently. APOP, polling monthly, asked about voting intentions six times during 1976; the *Age* did so each time it was in the field, which meant quarterly; and ANOP, for publication at least, only twice.

From October on, the interest of Morgan Gallup quickened; it asked about voting intentions five times in less than two months. From

---

[1] Terence W. Beed, "Opinion Polling and the Elections," in Howard R. Penniman, ed., *Australia at the Polls* (Washington, D.C.: American Enterprise Institute, 1977), pp. 229-231.

January 1977 a party preference question was included each month, with three in August (when Parliament was debating the budget) and two in October (the eve of the expected election announcement). APOP ran a voting intention question in February, then monthly except in March and July. The *Age* poll stuck by its quarterly schedule; and ANOP, after February, published no further figures until the *National Times* and the television program "Four Corners" commissioned a survey for the first half of October.

The Trend in Party Support. With a new prime minister in office and a Labor party greatly damaged by its political opponents and the media, the coalition's honeymoon lasted well into 1976.[2] After Whitlam's reelection in January as leader of the parliamentary Labor party, the government's stocks may even have risen. In March the National Executive of the ALP censured Whitlam, David Combe (the federal secretary), and Bill Hartley (a member of the ALP executive in Victoria sympathetic to the Palestine Liberation Organization) for their part in the proposed donation of Iraqi money to the 1975 campaign fund. In April the government's lead over the opposition in public opinion polls was still within two or three points of the ten-point lead opened up by the 1975 election.

In June, notwithstanding his stump oratory about Australia's having "a tourist [Whitlam] for a Prime Minister," Fraser made the first of several overseas trips, visiting Japan, China, Canada, and the United States. Both APOP and the *Age* poll showed the gap between government and opposition to be narrowing, but slowly. The first half of 1976 saw cuts in federal expenditures highlighted by plans to downgrade the national health and medical insurance plan, Medibank. In July the issue came to a head with a one-day national strike, the first since federation, "to defend and extend" Medibank.[3] The first of the Ranger reports giving a cautious "yes" on the question of uranium mining was published in September; Medibank, in its downgraded form came into operation on October 1; and on December 17, Sir

---

[2] Roger Douglas's analysis of coalition support between 1956 and 1972 showed that in the first six months the honeymoon effect for a new prime minister explained 11 percent of variance in support for the government, after controlling for unemployment, inflation, and industrial unrest. In 1974 Labor's second honeymoon lasted no more than a month or two. Roger Douglas, "Economy and Polity in Australia: A Quantification of Commonsense," *British Journal of Political Science*, vol. 5 (July 1975), pp. 346-347, 354; Beed, "Opinion Polling," p. 235.

[3] A short time later, Morgan asked whether voters approved or disapproved of the Australian Council of Trade Unions strike. Seventy percent, including 50 percent of intending Labor voters disapproved; 22 percent approved. Morgan Gallup poll No. 128, July 17-24, 1976.

REELECTION OF THE FRASER GOVERNMENT

FIGURE 6–1
VOTING INTENTIONS: SUPPORT FOR L-NCP, JANUARY 1976–OCTOBER 1977

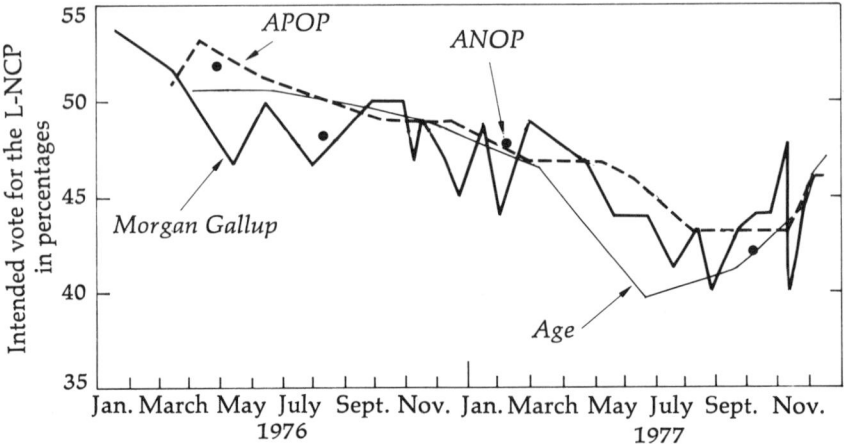

SOURCE: ANOP, Morgan Gallup, APOP, and Age poll press releases, 1976–1977.

Henry Bland resigned as chairman of the Australian Broadcasting Commission (ABC) after a stormy five months. By the end of the year APOP and the *Age* poll still had the government four to five points ahead of Labor.

The Morgan Gallup poll in 1976 told a different story (see Figures 6–1 and 6–2). For Morgan the honeymoon ended more abruptly (a view shared by ANOP), with May–August 1976 a period in which the government's ascendancy was only marginal. In September the government's fortunes revived, in November they slumped, and by the end of December the opposition was actually ahead. Morgan's findings were erratic: between March and May 1976 the gap between government and opposition closed by eleven points; from May to June it grew by five points; by August it was down again by four points, inflating by five or six points in October, declining, rising, and declining again by the end of December.

In 1977 there was greater agreement among the polls. Until May, the four national referenda and the unsuccessful challenge to Whitlam's leadership by Bill Hayden argued for a clear if narrow government lead. From June to August, however, Morgan and APOP put the opposition ahead. During this period Fraser went overseas again; the governor general, Sir John Kerr, announced his resignation, effective from December; Lynch presented to Parliament a budget that promised

FIGURE 6–2
Voting Intentions: Support for the ALP, January 1976–October 1977

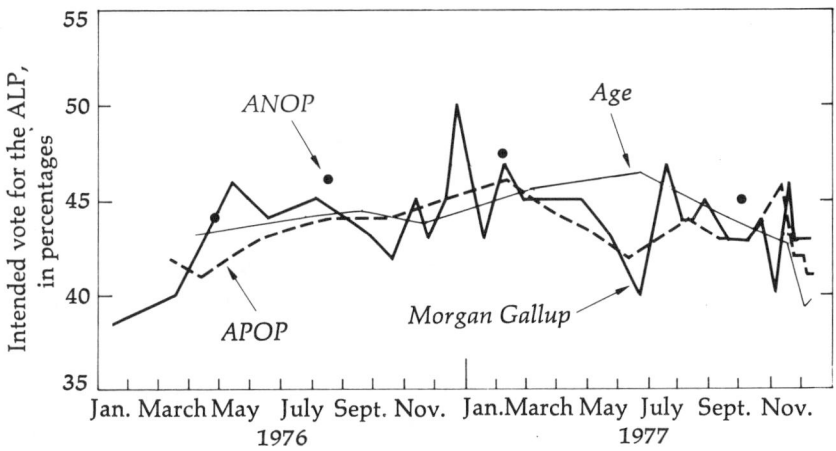

Source: ANOP, Morgan Gallup, APOP, and Age poll press releases, 1976–1977.

personal tax cuts starting in February 1978; and the government formally announced its decision to go ahead with uranium mining. In September the *Age* poll put the opposition ahead. In October, so did ANOP, but the same month Morgan and APOP found the parties neck and neck.

In general, the gap between the two sides changed when support for both the ALP and the coalition changed. The coalition's losses, as one would expect, were the opposition's gains, and vice versa. But more striking were the exceptions—the extent to which the loss of support on one side was not matched by a gain on the other.[4] If the voters were generally unenthusiastic about the main parties, as many believed they were, this is exactly what one would expect. An unusually large number of voters crossed not from Labor to the coalition (or vice versa) but from a major party to a minor party. The minor party, of course, was the Australian Democrats (AD). Asked in

---

[4] The rank-order correlation coefficients for the two major parties' support as identified by three of the pollsters in 1976-1977 are fairly low:

	Correlation ALP × L-NCP	Number of Surveys
Morgan Gallup	−.46	(23)
APOP	−.22	(9)
Age	−.39	(7)

December by ANOP whether it mattered which side won, over 80 percent of L-NCP and ALP voters said that it did; 40 percent of the Australian Democrats said it did not.[5]

Formed early in May 1977, the Australian Democrats showed up immediately in the polls. From 4 percent in May/June, support for the Democrats jumped to 6 or 7 percent in June/July. In October, Morgan Gallup put it back at 6 percent but ANOP boosted it to 7 or 8 percent, APOP and the *Age* poll to 9 percent (see Figure 6–3).

Where were the Democrats coming from? Since Don Chipp himself was an ex-Liberal most of his followers might also have been former Liberals. On the other hand, the Liberals were to go on and win the election by almost the same margin as in 1975, while the Australian Democrats too would poll strongly. This suggests that AD voters may have been former Labor voters. The truth lay somewhere in between.

Since none of the polls matched intended vote with past vote we are forced to rely on other less direct evidence. According to APOP and the *Age* poll a change in support for the Democrats was generally accompanied by a change in the same direction for the coalition and in the opposite direction for the ALP. This suggests that AD voters may have been disillusioned Labor voters rather than erstwhile Liberals. On the other hand, evidence from the largest number of surveys, those conducted by Morgan Gallup, shows almost no relation between fluctuation in support for the Australian Democrats and support for either the ALP or the coalition. This favors the proposition that support for the AD came from both sides.[6]

Other evidence confirms this. In September and again in October APOP asked voters whether they might consider voting for the Australian Democrats. On each occasion those who said they would included equal numbers of Labor and non-Labor voters. All the polls asked intending Democrats which party would receive their second preferences. Early figures favored the coalition but later ones showed the two major parties to be almost equally favored.[7] Finally, there is evidence from a McNair survey of 360 Sydney voters in six "swinging"

---

[5] ANOP, "ANOP-National Times/Four Corners Campaign Study," press release [December 2, 1977].

[6] The rank-order correlation coefficient for the Democrats' and the major parties' support from May to December 1977 are as follows:

	Correlation, AD × ALP	Correlation, AD × L-NCP	Number of Surveys
Morgan Gallup	.12	−.05	(16)
APOP	−.45	.27	(8)
Age	−.93	.97	(5)

[7] See Table 6-4.

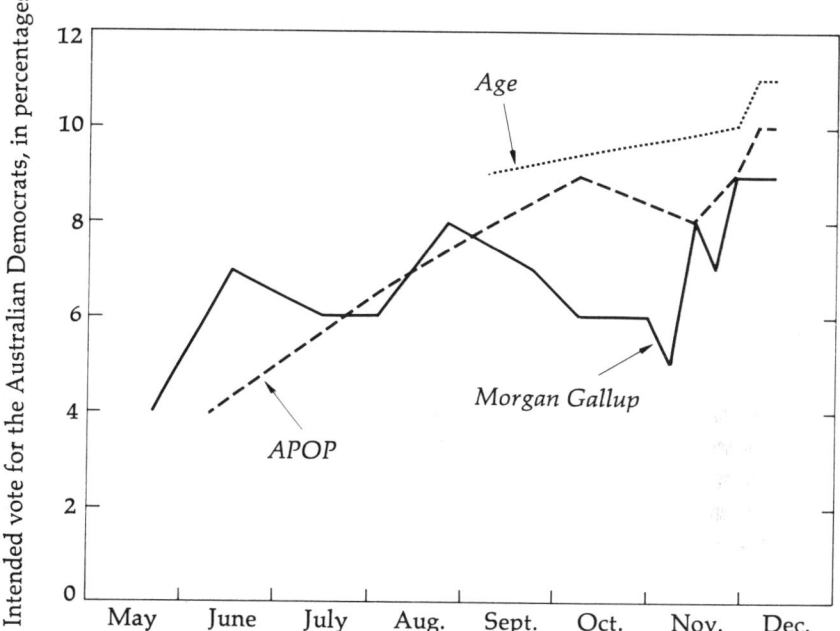

FIGURE 6–3
VOTING INTENTIONS: SUPPORT FOR THE AUSTRALIAN DEMOCRATS, MAY–DECEMBER 1977

SOURCE: *Newsletter of the University of Sydney Sample Survey Centre*, vol. 1, no. 4 (December 1977), p. 2; Age Poll Reprint Series, June 1977.

seats on election day itself: of those who had voted AD, 73 percent gave dissatisfaction with the major parties as their main reason.[8]

An Early Election. The rise of the AD made it increasingly likely that the government would go to the polls early, calling elections for both the House of Representatives and the Senate. The electorate itself was divided over the merits of an early election (see Table 6–1).[9] Liberal and Country party voters, who had nothing to gain and everything to lose, were less well disposed to the idea than Labor's sup-

---

[8] McNair Anderson Associates, *Reason for the Return of the Fraser Government: The Federal Election December 10, 1977*, Report prepared for Australian Broadcasting Commission, December 1977, p. 5.

[9] At one point, election analyst Malcolm Mackerras accused the *Age/Herald* of asking a question that made voters appear to be opposed to an early election when they really were not. The papers themselves were opposed to an early poll. Mackerras's charge was subsequently withdrawn. *Age*, October 13, 1977, p. 5; *Sydney Morning Herald*, October 13, 1977, p. 3.

TABLE 6–1

Attitudes to an Early Election, by Intended Vote, July–October 1977
(in percentages)

Pollster, Date of Survey, and Intended Vote	For	Against	Undecided
Morgan Gallup (July 23–30)			
ALP	36	56	8
L–NCP	25	64	11
AD	49	43	8
Total	40	50	11
Age (September 18–25)			
ALP	47	52	1
L–NCP	37	62	1
AD	41	59	—
Total	41	57	2
ANOP (October 1–8)			
ALP	54	35	11
L–NCP	37	50	13
AD	40	49	11
Total	45	43	12

Note: The survey questions were as follows:

• *Morgan:* "As you may know there has to be a half-Senate election before June next year. Do you think there should be an election for the House of Representatives at the same time or should the House of Representatives see out its full term until December next year?"

• *Age:* "The Australian Government does not need to call an election for the House of Representatives until the end of 1978. Nevertheless, there has been some talk recently about the possibility of an early Federal election. Which of the following statements comes closest to your view? (1) Any Government would be sensible to call an early election if it thought that it would be to its political advantage to do so; (2) The Federal Government should bring Senate and House of Representatives elections back in line by holding an election for both around next May; (3) Electors are entitled to expect a Government to govern for three years before they are asked to vote again."

• *ANOP:* "Do you think that the Prime Minister would be justified or not justified in calling an early Federal election for the House of Representatives this year?"

Source: Morgan Gallup Poll No. 175 computer report; *Age*, October 10, 1977; ANOP, "ANOP-National Times/Four Corners Attitude Survey," press release [c. October 13, 1977].

porters. The government could bank on its own supporters' forgetting the question of the merits of an early election once an election was called. But there was always the chance that a preemptive assault against the Democrats would backfire. Polls in September and October suggested that Don Chipp and his followers were almost as strongly opposed to an early election as L-NCP voters.

Unemployment and Inflation. The fate of the government was widely agreed to depend on the levels of unemployment and inflation. This was hardly new. In the postwar years it had become an article of faith that governments could not afford to have high inflation, much less high unemployment.

It was an assumption that had stood the test of time. Unemployment, in particular, had been associated with the near defeat of the Menzies government in 1961 and the defeat of the McMahon government in 1972. Unemployment and inflation had dogged Labor in 1975. An econometric analysis of fluctuations in the level of support for the federal government over the years 1956–1972 showed that while unemployment was a better predictor of government support than inflation, nearly half the variance in government support could be explained in terms of their joint effect. "Two percent unemployment [100,000 people] still seems to be regarded as excessive," wrote Roger Douglas in 1975, "and the data suggest that even in 1972 6 percent inflation was regarded as too high."[10] Douglas, sensibly warned against extrapolation: "What is currently unacceptable may over time come to be regarded as tolerable." But he retained the established model: it was the performance of the government that was generally seen to matter, rather than the performance of the opposition. The government would be rewarded (or at least would not suffer) if inflation were reduced, and it would be punished if unemployment increased.

The quarterly figures on unemployment and the rate of change in the consumer price index were eagerly anticipated and closely analyzed. A good deal was made of where one started in identifying trends, what one excluded as a freak occurrence, and, in the case of unemployment, which set of figures one used—the Commonwealth Employment Service's figures on the registered unemployed (CES), the Australian Bureau of Statistics's sample-based estimates of those looking for full-time work (ABS), or a new sample survey series established by the Morgan Research Centre.[11]

---

[10] Douglas, "Economy and Polity," pp. 353, 357. For more recent argument over the specification and validation of this form of econometric model see the *American Political Science Review*, vol. 69 (December 1975), pp. 1232-1269.

[11] For a discussion of ABS and CES figures, see John Steinke, "Measurement of Unemployment in Australia," *Journal of Industrial Relations*, vol. 20 (June 1978), pp. 146-162.

REELECTION OF THE FRASER GOVERNMENT

While the government boasted its success in reducing the "underlying rate" of inflation, the opposition attacked it for promoting policies that "deliberately created" unemployment. With inflation coming down and unemployment going up the political consequences were difficult to disentangle. But the evidence, at least for the period prior to the campaign, suggests that the government was being punished for higher unemployment rather than rewarded for lower inflation (see Figures 6–4 and 6–5).

The unemployment pattern was marked by seasonal factors but the change was clearly upwards. In the summer months (November 1975–February 1976) unemployment increased sharply as school leavers entered the labor market. After February there was a drop and only a slight rise by November, but between November 1976 and February 1977 unemployment soared. After February it fell away only slightly. The new plateau was 40,000 (ABS) to 60,000 (CES) higher than in 1976. In December, as the voters went to the polls, unemployment was again rising (see Figure 6–4).

FIGURE 6–4
UNEMPLOYMENT IN AUSTRALIA, 1976–1978

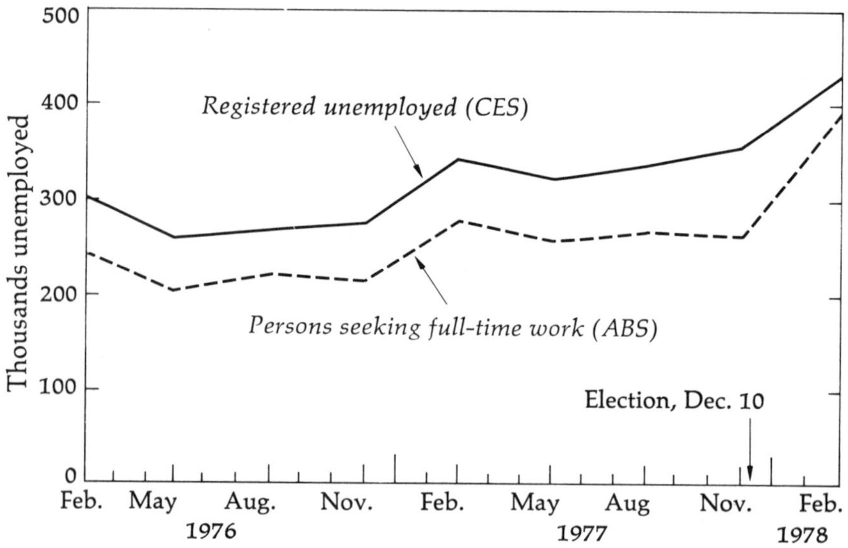

SOURCE: Australian Bureau of Statistics, *Labour Force*, 1976, 1977; Reserve Bank of Australia, *Statistical Bulletin*, May 1978.

FIGURE 6-5
Relative Increase in Consumer Price Index 1975–1978
(base 1966/67 = 100)

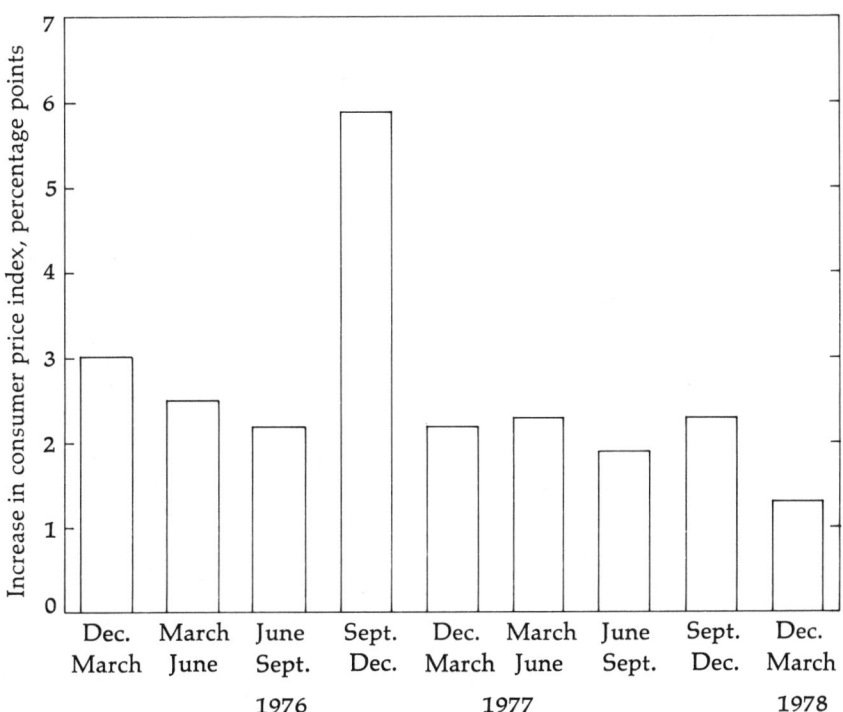

Source: Reserve Bank of Australia, *Statistical Bulletin*, April 1978, p. 295.

In the pre-campaign period the rise in the number of unemployed coincided with a decline in the coalition's support. The consumer price index, meanwhile, seems to have been a less reliable guide to the government's fortunes (see Figure 6–5). In its worst quarter, ending in December 1976, the government's future looked reasonably bright. Three polls—the *Age*, APOP, and Morgan—put the government an average of three to five points ahead of the opposition. During and after the period of the lowest increase, the September 1977 quarter, the polls had the government behind Labor or at best level-pegging. With a rise in unemployment, support for the government seems to have fallen; even by October a fall in inflation had brought the government no joy. Yet six weeks later, with unemployment still up, the government was returned to office having hardly lost a seat.

An explanation is not far to seek. Politics cannot be reduced to economics, nor do voters judge the government alone. Instead—and especially during a campaign like that of 1977, with an opposition not long out of office and a government determined to make its predecessor's poor performance on the economy the centerpiece of its own campaign—they judge the relative merits of government and opposition.

The Campaign Period

The Polling Pattern. Beginning with the announcement of the election, on October 27, the Morgan Gallup poll released its party support figures on a weekly basis. Between October 29–30 and December 3–4 there were six releases. Except for the last weekend, the samples ranged in size from 1,035 to 1,245.[12] The gain in immediacy meant an increase in sampling variance and therefore of possible error, though the poll did not draw attention to this. On the last weekend, December 3–4, the sample size was increased to 2,475. During the last week of the campaign a number of these people were reinterviewed.

Prior to December 3–4 the results of the Morgan Gallup poll were carried by the *Bulletin*, a national weekly published each Wednesday by Consolidated Press. This made the interval between field work and publication about ten days. The results of the December 3–4 survey were not processed in time for the last *Bulletin* of the campaign. These results and the results of the reinterviews were carried by the *Australian* on December 9 and the *Weekend Australian*, published by News Ltd., on December 10–11.

The Morgan Research Centre was the only organization to conduct a survey each weekend. McNair, for the Australian Public Opinion Poll, started on the second weekend and polled on four weekends out of a possible six. In each of the last two weekends of the campaign interviews were conducted with about 2,000 people; that is, about as many as were usually interviewed over two weeks. Like Morgan, the APOP asked voters to mark their party choice on a piece of paper and to place it in a cardboard "ballot box."[13] A small number of voters were reinterviewed during the last days of the campaign. All surveys were done under contract to the Herald and Weekly Times and published in the Melbourne *Herald* and *Sun-News Pictorial* as well as in the interstate papers published by this group.

---

[12] Though sample size for November 5-6 and November 19-20 was not published at the time.

[13] Until 1973 the APOP contract was held by the Morgan Research Centre, which explains why Morgan and APOP polls have a certain amount in common.

Irving Saulwick & Associates conducted two surveys for the *Age* and *Sydney Morning Herald*, papers owned by John Fairfax & Sons. The *Age* and *Herald* polls were conducted at the end of the fourth and fifth weeks of the campaign, on the first and second weekends after the prime minister's policy speech. Their findings on party support in the House of Representatives were announced on Wednesdays within three days of the surveys; results for the Senate followed on Thursdays. There were reinterviews on the last Wednesday of the campaign. ANOP was the only organization not to conduct surveys during weekends. They argued that since the campaign had "shown signs of producing a degree of volatility in the electorate," the gap between interviewing and publication should be as short as possible.[14] ANOP's joint clients were the *National Times*, a weekly owned by John Fairfax & Sons and published on Saturday evenings, and the ABC television program "Four Corners," which also appeared on Saturday night.

ANOP conducted its first survey, known as Campaign Monitor One, on Wednesday, November 16, the day after Whitlam's policy speech; its second (not for ABC or the *National Times*) on November 23, the day after Fraser's policy speech; and the third on Thursday and Friday, December 1–2. Monitors One and Two were "strictly controlled" telephone surveys of 1,000 and 500 voters, respectively, while Monitor Three consisted of 1,410 reinterviews (1,050 on Wednesday and 360 on Thursday) from a sample of 3,000 voters interviewed in October. Two out of three respondents were interviewed by phone; the rest were visited at home. ANOP claimed that it "knew the full demographic and political characteristics of telephone and non-telephone owners" and "could make accurate adjustments" in terms of a representative national sample.[15]

The first survey was little more than a dry run, promoted by ANOP as "the first attempt in this country to devise questions, conduct interviews, analyse and publish results from a major national political survey, all within a three day total period."[16] Interviewing was completed within twelve hours of the *National Times* deadline and eighteen hours before the final deadline for "Four Corners." Even so, by election day ANOP's final poll was the least recent of them all—

[14] ANOP "ANOP-National Times/Four Corners Campaign Study," p. 1.

[15] Rod Cameron, "The 1977 Federal Election: ANOP Analysis of the Campaign Trends and Results of a Special Study on the Day after the Election," press release, pp. 1–2.

[16] ANOP "ANOP-National Times/Four Corners Campaign Study," p. 1. Results for party preference from the second monitor were not officially released until after the election.

and it knew that, rightly or wrongly, it would be judged by the results of its final poll. Clearly, to take account of last-minute changes in a volatile electorate ANOP needed to hitch its star to a different wagon. Ideally, it needed a daily vehicle (publication late Saturday was not practicable when the election itself was on a Saturday), and because of the Broadcasting and Television Act, that meant a daily newspaper.[17] Whether such an outlet would have been available in the last week of the campaign is another matter. All the metropolitan dailies were owned by three companies, each of which, as it turned out, had its dailies tied up with one or another of ANOP's rivals.

The Questions. The voters were asked, by each of the polls, how they would vote at a federal House of Representatives election. The *Age* poll asked, "If a Federal election for the House of Representatives were held tomorrow, for which political party would you probably vote?" APOP and Morgan asked voters to indicate their first preference if an election were "held today." ANOP asked a similar question. APOP added a regular question about whether voters might change their minds before December 10; Morgan asked this only once, on the last weekend of the campaign. In the last two weekends APOP also asked respondents whether or not they intended to vote the same way as in 1975.

Considerable interest was taken in the Australian Democrats. APOP, over the first two weekends in November, asked its respondents whether they would consider giving "Mr. Don Chipp's Australian Democrats" their first preference, and if so, to whom they would give their second preference. The *Age* poll, ANOP, and APOP also recorded the second preferences of voters who intended to vote AD. Morgan Gallup did not do so until the last few days of the campaign.

The question of party support in the Senate was somewhat neglected. Given that support for the Australian Democrats was likely to be important, especially in the Senate, this neglect is curious. In part, no doubt, it reflects the fact that once samples are broken down by state they are extremely small and therefore unreliable. Only the *Age* poll placed as much emphasis on the Senate as on the House. In both of its surveys it asked voters how they would vote in the Senate. Morgan asked this question on four weekends but none of the results were released until the last week of the campaign. APOP asked about the Senate in its last two surveys but would only indicate

---

[17] Under the Broadcasting and Television Act, the broadcasting of material bearing on the election on radio and television has to stop at midnight on the Wednesday prior to an election, all Australian elections being held on Saturdays.

FIGURE 6–6
Voting Intentions for the House: Gap between the Coalition and Labor, October–December 1977

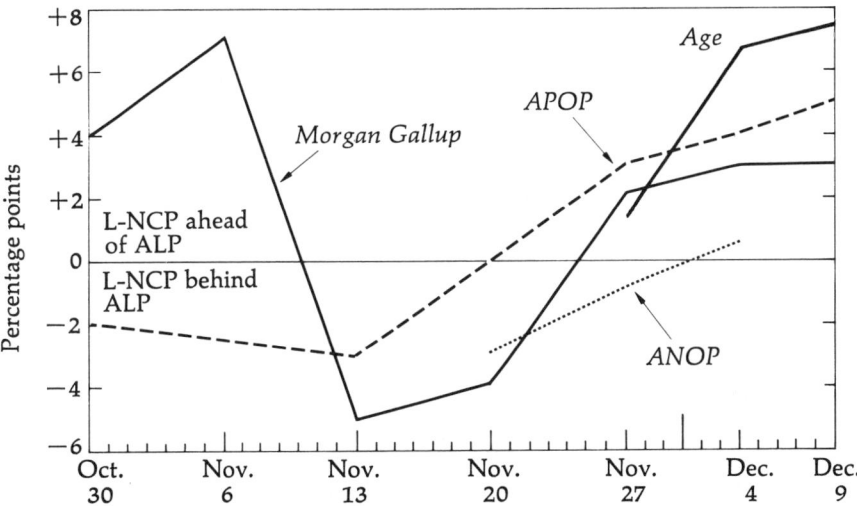

SOURCE: *Newsletter of the University of Sydney Sample Survey Centre*, vol. 1, no. 4 (December 1977), p. 2.

the proportion likely to vote the same or differently for the two chambers. As with referenda, ANOP steered clear.[18]

Trends in Party Support. Throughout the campaign the polls showed considerable shifts in party support (see Figure 6–6). Government and opposition started off fairly even, but in the first two to three weeks of the campaign the government appeared to fall behind. Only in the last two weeks did all the polls put the government ahead, with its lead, if anything, increasing (see Table 6–2).

As of October 27, the day on which the election was announced, none of the polls showed the government ahead. The most recent survey, carried out by the Morgan Gallup poll on October 15–22, showed the government and opposition tied; so did the APOP survey

---

[18] Murray Goot and Terence W. Beed, "The Referenda: Pollsters and Predictions" in Dean Jaensch, ed., *Politics of the "New Federalism"* (Adelaide: Political Studies Association, 1977), pp. 86-95.

TABLE 6–2
Voting Intentions for House and Senate: The Coalition's Lead Over Labor, October–December 1977
(in percentage points)

Date of Survey	House of Representatives				Senate	
	Age	ANOP	APOP	Morgan	Age	Morgan
October 29–30				4		
November 5–6			} −3	7		
November 12–13				−5		} −6
November 16		−3				
November 19–20				−4		
November 26–27	1.4		3	2	0.8	3
December 1–2		0.5				
December 3–4	6.9		4	3	9.5	3
December 6–8	7.3		5	3		

NOTE: ANOP conducted no surveys on voting intentions for the Senate; APOP included a Senate question in its last two surveys but did not publish its findings on party preference. See APOP Special Poll No. 1, press release, December 7, 1977.

SOURCE: *Newsletter of the University of Sydney Sample Survey Centre*, vol. 1, no. 4 (December 1977), p. 2.

taken October 1–8. An ANOP survey of October 1–8 put Labor three percentage points ahead.[19]

Once the question of whether or not there should be an early election had been settled and a date fixed, the polls moved in the government's favor. Over the first and second weekends of the campaign the Morgan Gallup poll put the government four percentage points ahead (October 29–30), then seven (November 5–6). By the end of the third week, however, both Morgan and APOP put the government behind: APOP, with its sample spread across the second and third weekends, had the government three points behind; Morgan having had the government seven points ahead, now had them five points behind. According to Morgan the government had slipped seven points (from 47 to 40 percent) while the opposition had picked up five (40 to 45 percent). A shift of at least 500,000 voters from one camp to another in the space of a week was difficult to credit.

---

[19] ANOP, "ANOP-National Times/Four Corners Attitude Survey," press release [c. October 13, 1977].

This apparent reversal in party support occasioned considerable public comment. Asked about it on the ABC television program "Monday Conference," Gary Morgan, managing director of the Morgan Research Centre, argued that the figures were correct. They could be explained by a number of factors: favorable publicity for the ALP and Don Chipp following the by-election for the state seat of Greensborough in Victoria; bad publicity during the following week for the Liberal government in Victoria over the alleged rake-off in the purchase of land by the State Housing Commission involving land developers, Liberal politicians, and public servants; bad publicity for the federal government over "record unemployment"; an anti-Liberal swing in the Queensland state election on the second weekend; and the arrest in Brisbane of 172 demonstrators marching for the right to demonstrate in the streets.[20]

Any effect from the Queensland election could not have been felt before the last Sunday. State politics in Queensland or Victoria might wash over into federal politics, but did the Morgan Gallup poll show this? APOP produced evidence for the impact of the "lands affair" in Victoria, but not Morgan. Between the first two weeks of October and the first two weeks of November—a period of four weeks, not one—APOP reported that the government's nine-percentage-point lead in Victoria had been converted to a deficit of one point. In New South Wales it moved from four points behind to two behind (see Figures 6-7 and 6-8). The corresponding Morgan figures are erratic. But for the week in question, with more on the lands affair and comment on the result of the by-election, the figures show the swing against the government to have been less in Victoria than in New South Wales. The press release,[21] which only cited the figures from Victoria and implied that the government's low standing there may have been due to the lands affair, failed to mention the shift in New South Wales and to that extent was misleading.

The only general cause cited by Morgan for the massive swing was unemployment; more precisely, the publicity given to the unemployment figures. But, as we have already seen, while announcements of "record unemployment" earlier in the year may have eroded government support, they hardly caused an instant landslide. In fact, the most likely cause is simply sampling variance. Had the results for the two weekends (November 5-6 and November 12-13) been released as one—the practice adopted in the precampaign period—they would have placed the government one point ahead, not five behind.

[20] "Monday Conference," ABC Television, November 28, 1977.
[21] Morgan Research Centre, November 18, 1977.

FIGURE 6-7
VOTING INTENTIONS FOR THE HOUSE IN NEW SOUTH WALES:
GAP BETWEEN THE COALITION AND LABOR, OCTOBER–DECEMBER 1977

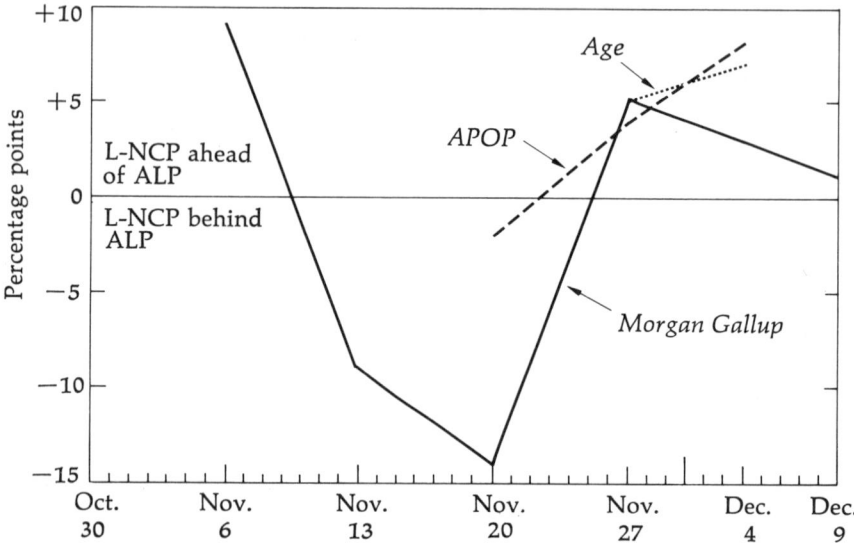

SOURCE: Computer Tabulations Morgan Gallup Poll and APOP, October–December 1977.

Where the Morgan Gallup poll was almost certainly right, however, was in suggesting that support for the government was slipping. Surveys conducted between the end of the second week and the end of the third week all put the opposition three to five points ahead. For government and opposition the midpoint of the campaign—the resignation of Lynch (November 18) and Fraser's policy speech (November 21)—was a turning point. From the fourth week until the election itself all the polls put the government ahead. All of them showed the government's lead increasing, but the *Age* poll showed the biggest swing. According to its figures the government increased its lead by a healthy five points in the House of Representatives and a massive eight points in the Senate, all in the space of a week. Again, it is unlikely that such a shift actually took place. In all probability the first of these two surveys underestimated the margin of support for the government while the second overestimated it (at least in the Senate).

This periodization of the campaign—a fairly even start, a swing to Labor, then a swing to the government—is borne out by the

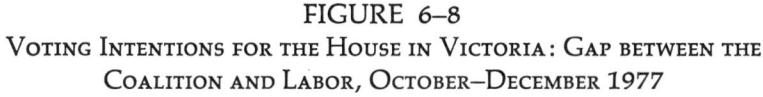

FIGURE 6–8
VOTING INTENTIONS FOR THE HOUSE IN VICTORIA: GAP BETWEEN THE
COALITION AND LABOR, OCTOBER–DECEMBER 1977

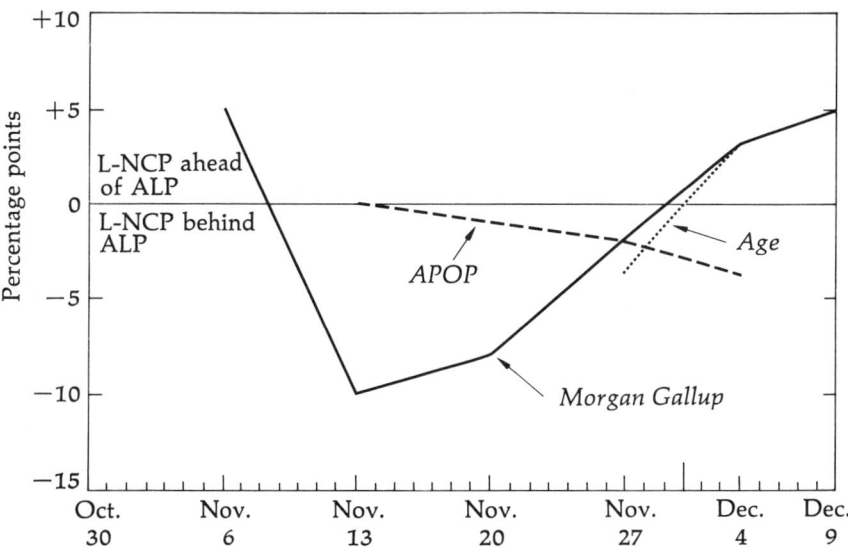

SOURCE: Computer Tabulations Morgan Gallup Poll and APOP, October–December 1977.

national figures. It does not apply to the figures for the separate states. The state figures, at every point, defy reconciliation. To illustrate, we need only consider the two most populous states, New South Wales and Victoria (Figures 6–7 and 6–8). APOP showed the government to be ahead of the opposition and gaining in New South Wales, behind and slipping in Victoria. In the last weeks of the campaign, Morgan Gallup put the government ahead but slipping in New South Wales, coming up from behind in Victoria. The *Age* and *Herald* polls had the government gaining in New South Wales in the House of Representatives, slipping in the Senate; and in Victoria coming from behind in the House yet surrendering its lead in the Senate.

As election day drew near the proportion of those interviewed who were undecided as to the party they would support (or who refused to say) remained fairly stable: about 4 percent in the *Age* poll,

TABLE 6–3

Voting Intentions for the House: Possible Party Switchers, 1977 Campaign

(in percentages)

Pollster and Date of Survey	Yes	No	Undecided
APOP, November 5–12	16	77	7
APOP, November 26–27	15	80	5
APOP, December 3–4	10	87	3
Morgan, December 3–4	8	90	2

NOTE: The APOP survey question was not stated; Morgan asked respondents which party would "probably receive your first preference," whether they might change their mind, and if so in what direction.

SOURCE: APOP Poll No. 01/11/77; Poll No. 01/12/77; Special Poll No. 1, Press release December 7, 1977; Morgan Gallup Poll No. 191.

5 percent for Morgan, and 6 percent for APOP.[22] The number who declared a preference but said they might still change their minds did, however, diminish from one-in-six in November to about half that number in early December (see Table 6–3). APOP surveys revealed that as many as one-quarter of those who reported how they had voted in 1975 were going to vote differently in 1977.[23] In the 1960s a similar question put by Morgan Gallup had generally produced a figure around one-in-eight.[24] The analysts' references to a volatile electorate were clearly not without foundation.

What of the Australian Democrats? According to an APOP survey in November, 33 percent of voters (including 28 percent of ALP and 28 percent of L-NCP voters) "would consider" giving the Democrats their first preference; in September APOP's figure had been 31 percent (26 percent of ALP voters and 25 percent of L-NCP voters).[25] The number who would actually vote for the Democrats was, of course, much smaller. But according to three of the polls this number grew during the campaign. The *Age* poll, APOP, and Morgan put support for the Australian Democrats at 6 to 9 percent in October,

---

[22] ANOP did not publish a figure.

[23] In the November 26-27 survey the figure was 25 percent; on December 3-4, 27 percent. APOP Poll No. 01/12/77; Special Poll No. 1, December 7, 1977.

[24] Murray Goot, "Growth and Decay: Party Support between Elections," in Henry Mayer, ed., *Labor to Power* (Sydney: Angus and Robertson, 1973), pp. 265-271.

[25] APOP Poll No. 06/9/77; 04/11/77.

TABLE 6–4

Voting Intentions: Share of Australian Democrats'
Second Preferences Going to the Coalition
(in percentages)

Date of Poll	Age	ANOP	APOP	Morgan
October 1–8		65		
November 16		55		
November 19,20				
November 23		52		
November 26,27	56		56	
December 1,2		48		
December 3,4	51		57	
December 6–8			54	45

Source: *Age*, November 30, December 7, 1977; ANOP, "ANOP-National Times/Four Corners Campaign Study"; APOP Poll No. 01/12/77, Special Poll No. 1, Special Poll No. 3; *Australian*, December 9, 1977, for Morgan.

rising to between 9 and 11 percent in December. ANOP put support for the Democrats at 8 percent in October and 11 percent in December with a peak of 13 percent in mid-November.[26]

A high proportion of Democrats, however, indicated that they might vote for another party. According to APOP about one-in-three indicated this throughout November, dropping to one-in-five on the first weekend in December. The Morgan poll taken on December 3–4 confirmed the last figure for House and Senate. According to all four polls, AD preferences would divide fairly evenly between government and opposition (Table 6–4). The figures suggest a movement towards the opposition during the campaign, but both the movement itself and the numbers on which it is based are small.

The Forecasts. Inevitably the polls were treated as racing forms, their last surveys as final selections. Three (all but ANOP) attempted to predict the support the parties would get. On the last Tuesday and Wednesday before the election the Morgan Research Centre reinterviewed 347 of the 2,475 voters who had participated in Morgan's last full survey. The result "showed a slight swing to the ALP and Australian Democrats" but not enough to change the figures from the full survey. On a two-party-preferred basis, the government was expected to "win narrowly"—51 percent to 49, or a margin of sixteen

---

[26] Cameron, "The 1977 Federal Election," p. 2.

seats. In the Senate, however, the government was expected to lose two percentage points. "The L-NCP is likely to obtain 3 out of 5 Senate [seats] only in Queensland," reported the *Weekend Australian*. "This means they will lose Senate control."[27]

The APOP conducted follow-up telephone interviews on the last Wednesday of the campaign with 110 "swinging voters" in Sydney and Melbourne first interviewed the previous weekend. "There was a degree of movement among about half of the swinging voters with Labor losing ground while the Liberals and Australian Democrats improved marginally." On the basis of these reinterviews and "some NSW and Queensland country interviews which arrived too late to be included" in the results from the full survey, APOP adjusted the figure for the ALP downwards and that for the L-NCP upwards by one percentage point.[28]

On October 7, Saulwick reinterviewed 228 voters for the *Age*. Eight percent said they did not know how they would vote, though three-quarters of these had expressed a definite voting intention the previous weekend. The newly undecided came in roughly equal numbers from the Liberals, Labor, and the Australian Democrats. Both the government and the opposition did slightly better than the previous weekend, but the two-party-preferred vote remained the same, 54 to 46 percent. The figures, as usual, were given to the first decimal point and readers were warned, as usual, that the estimate should be treated cautiously.[29]

All the polls "picked the winner" in the House, while the *Age* (but not Morgan Gallup) did so in the Senate. All underestimated support for the government. Apart from the *Age* poll (which overestimated support for the minor parties), all of them overestimated support for Labor. In the Senate the *Age* poll was almost exactly right, but the Morgan Gallup poll was nearly six percentage points out in its estimate of the gap between the government and the opposition. Indeed Morgan had predicted that the government would lose control of the Senate. In the House, the *Age* finished first, APOP and Morgan last.

---

[27] *Weekend Australian*, December 10-11, 1977, p. 1. Whether reinterviewing was done by telephone or otherwise is not clear; sample size is incorrectly given as 2,735 and Thursday as the third day of reinterviewing. The survey is accurately reported in "L-NCP to Win Narrowly," Roy Morgan Research Centre, press release, December 8, 1977.

[28] APOP Special Poll No. 3, press release, December 9, 1977. Swingers were those who had indicated in the full survey that they might change their minds or were undecided or intended to vote one way in the House and another in the Senate.

[29] *Age*, December 9, 1977.

TABLE 6–5
Results of House Election and National Voting Intention Polls, October–December 1977
(in percentages)

	ALP	L–NCP	AD	Other	Sample Size
Election Results	39.6	48.1	9.4	2.9	
Opinion Poll Forecasts					
ANOP					
November 16	43	40	13	4	(1,000)
November 23	43	42	12	3	(500)
December 1–2	42.5	43	11	3.5	(1,410)
Age					
November 26–27	42.9	44.3	9.7	3.1	(2,000)
December 3–4	39.3	46.2	10.8	3.7	(2,000)
December 7	39.7	47.0	10.8	2.5	(228)[a]
APOP					
November 5–13	46	43	8	3	(1,953)
November 26–27	42	45	9	4	(1,960)
December 3–4	42	46	10	2	(2,048)
December 8	41	46	10	3	(110)[b]
Morgan Gallup					
October 29–30	42	46	6	6	(1,055)
November 5–6	40	47	5	8	(1,003)
November 12–13	45	40	8	7	(1,035)
November 19–20	46	42	7	5	(1,083)
November 26–27	43	45	9	3	(1,245)
December 3–4	43	46	9	2	(2,475)[c]
December 7–8	43	46	9	2	(347)[a]

[a] Reinterviews from December 3-4.
[b] Telephone interviews with "swinging voters" in Sydney and Melbourne.
[c] Reported as 2,735 in the press release and *Weekend Australian,* December 10-11, 1977.

SOURCE: Press releases and computer reports by Morgan Gallup Poll and APOP, October-December 1977; *Weekend Australian,* December 10-11, 1977; Rod Cameron, "The 1977 Federal Election," for ANOP; and *Age,* November 30, December 7 and 9, 1977.

Did Voters Really Change Their Preferences? ANOP's final survey was more a guide to the trend than a firm prediction of the actual result. In a statement issued after the election, ANOP argued that in the nine days between their last survey and the election itself they would have expected the swing to the government to continue and to

TABLE 6-6
Results of Senate Election and National Voting Intention Polls, October–December 1977
(in percentages)

	ALP	L–NCP	AD	Other	Sample Size
Election Results	36.8	45.6	11.1	6.6	
Opinion Polls					
Age					
November 26–27	42.2	43.0	11.5	3.3	(2,000)
December 3–4	37.1	46.6	11.7	4.7	(2,000)
Morgan Gallup					
November 12–20	44	38	8	12	(2,118)
November 26–27	41	44	11	4	(1,245)
December 3–4	41	44	11	4	(2,475)

Source: Press releases and computer reports by Morgan Gallup Poll, November–December 1977; *Age*, December 1 and 8, 1977.

cost the ALP a further 1 point in support.[30] On this basis ANOP would have expected the government to lead by 2.5 percentage points, compared with the 8.5 points it actually achieved. This would have put ANOP slightly closer to the final result. More important, while its forecast of ALP support remained within the range of sampling variance, the forecast of support for the L-NCP did not.

Why, ANOP now asked, had it not done better? Its answer: the voters, intending all along to return the government, had not answered survey questions about their voting intentions sincerely. The "rises in Labor support in early November," when all the polls put Labor ahead and showed an increased level of support for the Australian Democrats were "purely illusory."[31] The "measured voting intentions were more expressions of discontent with the government (and to a lesser extent both parties) than a commitment to vote against the coalition."

---

[30] This and subsequent references are to Cameron, "The 1977 Federal Election."
[31] Professor Solomon Encel argued that the *Age* and ANOP surveys were the most accurate because they showed "several months before the elections, that the ALP would not win." On this basis, of course, all the polls were accurate—with ANOP, arguably, the least accurate. Encel merely appeals to authority: the Chifley dictum that elections are usually won six months before polling day. The point, however, is to establish this. *National Times*, January 9-14, 1978, p. 16. Encel was subsequently appointed to an ALP committee inquiring into the reasons for Labor's defeat.

The idea that voters will show their displeasure with the government's performance by expressing support for the opposition, only to recoil when faced with an election, is not new. As Roger Douglas points out, it underlies the conventional wisdom that support for the government increases as an election approaches. But there is another possibility not considered by ANOP. Where voters are dissatisfied with the opposition, for instance its leadership, they might express support for the government, returning to the opposition only when the crunch comes. For the period 1956–1972 Douglas found no evidence of any prodigal voters.[32]

For ANOP, 1977 threw up a "unique political situation—two largely discredited parties, a new third force, two unpopular major leaders, and a confused electorate." The "implications" of the situation were not lost on the firm. Pollsters ask questions on the assumption that the answers given are sincere—hence the publication of results free of commentary, the reader's attempt to correlate results with events, and so on. To assume anything different alters the situation radically. Those who do make other assumptions include both the most sophisticated interpreters of polling material and those most suspicious of survey research.

Evidence gathered by ANOP "throughout the year and particularly in the December 1–2 monitor" revealed two factors of major significance operating against Labor:

> a strong anti-Whitlam feeling in the community and particularly amongst swinging voters—such feeling manifesting itself in a tendency not to believe what the Labor leader said; a resolution not to vote a government out of office after two years, notwithstanding the fact that it was not a popular decision of the prime minister's to call an election. . . . The key reason, our research showed, for Labor's winning in 1974 concerned this same factor.[33]

Earlier research had not shown that these factors would mean that Labor could only improve its position by 1–1.5 percentage points over 1975, so ANOP undertook a "day-after-the-election" study to "discover the relative importance of these and other factors in the vote decision." On Sunday, December 11, ANOP approached 530 New South Wales voters who in one or more of ANOP's campaign monitors had expressed the intention to vote ALP or AD and who had not changed their minds by the time of the last monitor on December 1–2. Interviews were obtained with 505 voters, 443 of whom had

---

[32] Douglas, "Economy and Polity," pp. 348-349, 354.
[33] Cameron, "The 1977 Federal Election," p. 5.

intended voting Labor, 62 Democrat. Of these, 5 percent had actually voted against their stated intention; 22 percent more had at least "considered" doing so; and a further 1 percent had not voted. Of the 5 percent of intended Labor voters who changed their vote, three-fifths switched to the government, the other two to the Democrats. The 3 percent of the intended Democrat voters who changed their vote all went to the L-NCP. Thus the coalition gained six percentage points (three from Labor and three from the Australian Democrats). Why this apparent shift? About one-third of all switchers or near-switchers mentioned dislike of Whitlam as the reason for their weak loyalty to Labor. Another third were confused, especially by the claims and counterclaims over taxation, or felt the government deserved more time in which to prove itself, or both. No other factor was mentioned by more than a fraction of the respondents.

What is unconvincing in all this is not the late swing (picked up as well by the *Age*) or the reasons offered for it but ANOP's attempt to isolate both from the campaign itself—despite its own final campaign monitor in which 21 percent of all voters, including one-third of the Australian Democrats, had agreed that the campaign had had some influence on the way they would vote.[34]

ANOP attributed the mid-November rise in support for Labor to the Lynch affair. In its last campaign monitor 11 percent of Labor voters admitted that the affair had had "some influence" on their vote; so did 28 percent of AD voters. Four in every five Labor voters who claimed to have been influenced had merely been confirmed in their preference for Labor, but one-in-five was actually converted. This represents no less than 2 percent of Labor's entire support. Among the Democrats, three were converted as a result of the Lynch affair, for every one reinforced. A plurality of voters thought Labor was running the "dirtiest" campaign, but this 28 percent of the electorate may have been Liberal voters anyway. Data gathered the day after the election showing that Lynch had not been a key consideration in the voters' choice have little bearing on whether he would have been crucial had the election been held three weeks earlier. The fall in Labor support, as ANOP notes, coincided with the resignation of Lynch, a move the Liberal party hoped would kill the issue. There is nothing in ANOP's evidence to show why they could not have been right.

The reasons most often advanced for the defeat of Labor—opposition to Whitlam, confusion, and (usually related to this) the need to give the government another chance—argue precisely for the

---

[34] ANOP, "ANOP-National Times/Four Corners Campaign Study."

importance of the campaign. The very fact that anti-Whitlam memories existed before the campaign started ensured that the anti-Labor parties would work to keep them alive. Outside the context of the campaign, Labor's confusion over economic policy and its argument with the Liberals over taxation would be incomprehensible.

ANOP research had shown that voters could be opposed to Whitlam and in favor of the government's lasting beyond two years, yet prepared to vote Labor. The margin by which the government was returned surprised ANOP. The campaign against Labor gave precisely those sentiments identified by ANOP a life and force they might otherwise have lacked. On ANOP's own evidence it does not follow—as ANOP has claimed—that "Labor was never in the race in an election in 1977" or that the "results would not have been a great deal different no matter what sort of campaign Labor waged."[35]

The Issues and the Outcome

One way of explaining movements in party support is by correlating them with movements in economic or other factors. The campaign was most widely analyzed in terms of unemployment and inflation. As we have seen, analyses of short-term fluctuations in party support can be attempted without direct reference to what voters see the issues to be or to any assumption about the position of the opposition, real or perceived.

A more common strategy, however, has been to view campaigns through the issues as perceived by the voters. What issues concerned the voters and how were the parties seen in relation to them? When voters were asked to explain their party choice, what accounts did they give? This last allows us to see the campaign in terms of factors like leadership as well.

The Issues. Ideally one needs to look at the issues through the eyes of the swinging voter, but since none of the polls made a serious attempt to isolate the swingers we must deal instead with the electorate as a whole. What issues made an impact?

Butler and Stokes argue that an issue can have substantial impact only where it satisfies three conditions.[36] First, salience. Voters need

---

[35] Cameron, "The 1977 Federal Election," p. 3.
[36] David Butler and Donald Stokes, *Political Change in Britain* (London: Macmillan, 1969), chap. 15. For Australia, see Don Aitkin, *Stability and Change in Australian Politics* (Canberra: Australian National University Press, 1977), chap. 14.

to know about the issue and acknowledge its importance to them. Second, there should be a consensus on the issue. If public opinion is split, it is unlikely to affect the net balance between the parties. Third, the parties themselves need to be differentiated on the issue. If the parties are equally likely or unlikely to meet the agreed view, neither side can gain, no matter how important the issue or how united the public.[37] Which issues met these criteria?

Salience. In the course of the campaign each of the four polls asked voters to identify the most important issues or the most important problem facing the government. ANOP asked a question about issues and another about problems in October; and it repeated the "problem" question in December, along with a question on the major issue. The *Age* poll included questions on the issues in surveys conducted a week apart in November. APOP asked about the issues once, halfway through the campaign, and again on election day for the ABC. Morgan included a long list of issues twice early in the campaign but not thereafter. The results of these surveys, though not exactly comparable, are summarized in Table 6–7.

Unemployment, almost invariably, was mentioned ahead of any other issue. Most of the polls put inflation and/or economic management second. Most people believed that unemployment and inflation would get worse (see Table 6–8). Responding to an *Age* poll in October,[38] 51 percent of a sample agreed that inflation should be fought, "but only if unemployment is not increased as a result"— another way of stating the priority of unemployment over inflation. A further 24 percent said "fight inflation even if it means an increase in unemployment." Industrial issues (strikes, union power), uranium, honest government (including, presumably, Lynch), social welfare (including Medibank and pensions), and education finished well back in the field, with less than 10 percent seeing any of them as the most important issue. Taxation (cuts in personal taxes versus cuts in payroll taxes) and the party leaders, foreign policy and defense, counted, on this reckoning, for nought.

Consensus. The issues the voters cared most about were indeed consensus issues. That unemployment meant less unemployment; inflation, less inflation; industrial unrest, fewer strikes, is something we can safely assume. No doubt "sound economic management"

---

[37] Conditions two and three tacitly assume an electoral situation of the British or Australian kind with the electorate fairly evenly divided between government and opposition.
[38] *Age*, October 29, 1977.

TABLE 6-7
PUBLIC RATINGS OF THE MOST IMPORTANT ELECTION ISSUES AND OF PROBLEMS FACING THE GOVERNMENT, 1977 CAMPAIGN
(in percentages)

Issue	ANOP October 1-9 (I)	ANOP October 1-9 (II)	Morgan November 12-13	Morgan November 19-20	Age November 26-27	APOP November 26	ANOP December 1-2 (III)	ANOP December 1-2 (IV)	Age December 3-4	APOP December 10
Unemployment	44	28	51	53	27	39	52	74	29	41
Inflation	25	15	36	33	16	33	29		16	34
Economic management			7	6	16	7			15	
Industrial unrest	6	7	25	26	11		3		10	4
Social welfare/Medibank/health	1	1	28	29	9	4	5		9	5
Uranium	12	35	23	26	5	5	4		5	6
Taxation	1	1				2		16		3
Education	1	1	17	18		7	1			6
Honesty					13				13	
Disclosure of MPs' private financial affairs	1									
Early election			7	7	1				<1	
Leadership	1	1								
Overseas ownership			8	8	<1				<1	

(Table continues on next page.)

TABLE 6-7 (continued)

	ANOP October 1-9		Morgan			Age November 26-27	APOP November 26	ANOP December 1-2		Age December 3-4	APOP December 10
Issue	(I)	(II)	November 12-13	November 19-20				(III)	(IV)		
Foreign policy/defense						<1				<1	
Other	6	7	9	7			} 3	3	2		10
Undecided	4	4	72	73		<1		3	8		1
Total	100	100	1	3		100	100	100	100	100	100
			100	100							

NOTE: The survey questions and techniques were as follows:

• ANOP used three different questions: "If there was an early Federal election for the House of Representatives this year, what do you think the most important issue would be in the campaign?" (column I); "What is the most important problem facing the Federal government?" (columns II and III); and "The Labor Party has said that the major issue of the election is unemployment. The Liberal Party has said that the major issue is taxation. Who do you think is closer to the mark, the Labor Party or the Liberal Party?" (column IV).

• Morgan Gallup handed respondents a card listing the twenty-one main election issues and asked them to say which three would be most important to them at the federal election on December 10. The entries are percentages of respondents who named the issue as one of the three most important; thus, the Morgan columns do not add to 100 percent.

• Age poll respondents were given a list of ten issues and asked to rank them in importance; the figures given here are for the issues ranked number one.

• APOP asked on its November survey, "Here are a number of important issues in this election. Which one do you think is the most important issue?" The respondent was then handed a list of seven issues. On December 10 the APOP asked essentially the same question of 360 Sydney voters, this time using a list of eight election issues.

SOURCE: Age, December 1, 1977, and December 9, 1977; ANOP "ANOP-National Times/Four Corners Campaign Study"; APOP Poll No. 03/12/77; Morgan Research Centre press release November 25, 1977; ANOP-National Times/Four Corners Attitude Survey"; ANOP "ANOP-National Times/Four Corners Campaign Study"; APOP Poll No. 03/12/77; Morgan Research Centre press release November 25, 1977; McNair Anderson, Reasons for the Return of the Fraser Government, report for the Australian Broadcasting Commission.

TABLE 6-8
EXPECTATIONS ABOUT INFLATION/PRICES AND UNEMPLOYMENT, 1976–1977
(in percentages)

	APOP		Morgan November 1976	APOP			Morgan November 1977
Issue and Response	March 1976	August 1976		March 1977	September 1977		
Inflation/Prices							
Rising	66	61	78	75	66		72
Stable	3	4	10	3	4		13
Falling	25	31	9	18	25		10
Don't know	6	4	3	4	5		5
Unemployment							
Rising	56	72		71	75		
Stable	3	2		3	2		
Falling	36	23		22	19		
Don't know	5	3		4	4		

NOTE: APOP asked: "Over the next few months do you expect that Australia will have a declining or increasing rate of [inflation, unemployment]?" Morgan did not publish the text of the question asked.
SOURCE: APOP Poll No. 05/9/77; Morgan Gallup Poll, Nos. 505, 520A, November-December 1977 and press release, November 4, 1977.

TABLE 6–9

VOTERS' VIEWS ON TAX CUTS, BY INTENDED VOTE,
NOVEMBER–DECEMBER 1977
(in percentages)

Intended Vote	Cut Payroll Tax	Cut Personal Tax	Undecided
L–NCP			
Morgan	18	66	16
ANOP	15	71	14
ALP			
Morgan	54	27	19
ANOP	68	22	10
Australian Democrats			
Morgan	35	51	14
ANOP	38	42	20
All Respondents			
Morgan	34	47	19
ANOP	41	44	15

NOTE: The Morgan Gallup survey was conducted November 25-26; ANOP's December 1-2.
SOURCE: Morgan Gallup Poll, November 25-26; ANOP "ANOP-National Times/Four Corners Campaign Study," December 1-2.

included "competence" and the absence of "scandal." A consensus on these issues and on these terms was simply taken for granted by the pollsters. Where there was no consensus, on the other hand, the polls were busy. They showed that on taxation the electorate divided between those who favored cuts in direct taxes and those who favored cuts in the payroll tax. This issue, created by the parties, saw the voters in turn divide along party lines (see Table 6–9).

Similarly with uranium. Of those who considered uranium an important issue (see Table 6–7), some opposed mining and some favored it. In the electorate as a whole opinion favored mining but fell well short of a consensus (see Table 6–10).

Distinctiveness. Where were the parties seen to stand in relation to the issues? Only one of the polls, APOP, tackled the question in anything like a comprehensive manner. The evidence from its survey, combined with what little there is from ANOP, Morgan, and telephone surveys conducted in Melbourne and Sydney for the Liberal party,[39]

---

[39] Discussed in detail in Murray Goot's chapter, "Monitoring the Public, Marketing the Parties."

TABLE 6–10

Voters' Views on Uranium, by Intended Vote,
September–October 1977
(in percentages)

Intended Vote	Favor Mining and Export of Uranium	Oppose Mining and Export of Uranium	Undecided
L–NCP			
Age	77	17	6
APOP	72	19	9
ALP			
Age	32	63	5
APOP	34	56	10
Australian Democrats			
Age	46	47	7
APOP	50	42	9
All Respondents			
Age	53	42	5
APOP	52	38	10

NOTE: The Age Poll's survey was conducted September 24-25, APOP's October 1-8.
SOURCE: *Age*, October 17, 1977; APOP Poll No. 02/10/77.

is presented in Table 6–11. On this evidence the government enjoyed a substantial advantage over the ALP on three issues, inflation, economic management, and taxation. Only the first two were rated important by the voters and only the first two can possibly be seen as consensus issues. That its image on the issues of inflation and the economy more generally was an important factor in the government's win is underlined by the Liberal party surveys, which showed that on the economy the margin in favor of the government "increased dramatically" following the prime minister's policy speech and that on inflation it increased as the campaign progressed—that is, as the polls showed an upturn in support for the government itself. At the same time, according to the Morgan poll, most voters thought 1978 would be a better year for them than 1977. In 1975 and 1976 they had been less optimistic (see Table 6–12).

Between September and November the number prepared to describe economic conditions as "very good" or "good" rose, the expectation that the next six months would bring "poor" or "very poor" conditions fell, and the expectation that the government would

TABLE 6-11
VOTERS' RATINGS OF MAJOR PARTIES, BY POLICY AREA, 1977 CAMPAIGN
(entries are percentages of N who prefer the stated party's policy)

Policy Area	APOP		Morgan		ANOP		Liberal Party Surveys[a]		McNair[b]	
	L-NCP	ALP	L-NCP	ALP	L-NCP	ALP	L-NCP	ALP	L-NCP	ALP
Unemployment	31	34						+	40	46
Inflation	43	22					++		48	36
Economic management			46	22			++			
Industrial unrest	29	23					+	+	42	35
Social services, pensions, Medibank	24	29								
Income tax/payroll tax	30	21	47	34	44	41	++		41	37

Uranium	26	28			38	45
Education	20	26			31	41
Best policies for Australia, overall			49	37		
Team of ministers			41	35		
Prime minister			41	35		
Disclosure of MPs' private financial affairs			40	32	29	40
N	(2,028)	(1,074)	(1,410)	(350)	(360)	

[a] Based on telephone surveys conducted in Sydney and Melbourne in November 1977. Plus signs indicate the party favored by the voters: two pluses indicate a substantial advantage; one each, a balance.

[b] Based on interviews with 360 Sydney voters after they left selected polling booths in six "swinging" seats—Barton, Lowe, Macquarie, Phillip, Robertson, St. George—on December 10.

SOURCE: APOP November 26-27 to December 3, 1977, Poll No. 03/12/77; McNair Anderson, *Reasons for the Return of the Fraser Government*; Morgan Gallup October 15-22 (prime minister), November 25-26 (taxes), November (the economy, ministers); ANOP, "ANOP-National Times/Four Corners Campaign Study," December 1-2, 1977; Liberal party, unpublished data.

TABLE 6-12
Voters' Assessment of the Outlook for the Coming Year, November 1975, 1976, and 1977
(in percentages)

Next Year Will be:	November 1975	November 1976	November 1977
Better	37	48	57
Same	19	16	15
Worse	37	28	21
Undecided	7	8	7

NOTE: The survey question was: "As far as you are concerned, do you think 1978 [1977, 1976] will be better or worse, than 1977 [1976, 1975]?"
SOURCE: Morgan Gallup Poll Nos. 505, 520A, November-December 1977.

TABLE 6-13
Voters' Assessment of Economic Conditions, Selected Months, 1977
(in percentages)

Economic Conditions are:	March	June	September	November
Very good/good	11	11	12	16
Fair	45	42	46	47
Poor/very poor	43	47	41	36
Undecided	1	—	1	1

NOTE: The survey question was: "Would you say that economic conditions today are very good, good, fair, poor, or very poor?"
SOURCE: *Age* Poll, December 3, 1977.

be returned increased (see Tables 6-13, 6-14, and 6-15).[40] As expected, unemployment did not work in the government's favor; but it did very little for the opposition either (see Table 6-11). It was this, more than anything else, that took observers by surprise. While the voters believed that the government should have been doing more to create jobs, they did not hold it responsible for unemployment (see Tables 6-16 and 6-17). As with inflation, four out of five of the causes named were factors other than the government, and the unions and the unemployed themselves accounted for at least half.[41] The number of

---
[40] One can speculate that this may have been based on the polls themselves.
[41] On inflation, see the Morgan Gallup poll conducted at the end of May and early June: "Unions blamed for strikes, inflation," Morgan Research Centre, press release, n.d.

TABLE 6–14

Voters' Assessment of the Economic Outlook,
Selected Months, 1977
(in percentages)

Economic Outlook is:	IAESR August 1977	Age September 1977	IAESR October 1977	Age November 1977	IAESR November 1977	ANOP December 1977
Very good/ good	19	20	18	26	25	33
Fair/average	33	33	30	33	29	32
Poor/very poor/bad	39	44	39	30	27	25
Undicided	9	4	13	12	18	10

NOTE: IAESR (the Institute of Applied Economic and Social Research, in Melbourne) asked: "Now turning to economic conditions in Australia as a whole—do you think that during the next twelve months we will have good times financially, or bad times, or what?" The *Age* poll asked: "In six months' time, do you feel economic conditions will be very good, good, fair, poor, or very poor?" ANOP asked: "Thinking about the economy next year, Do you believe it will get better, get worse or will it stay the same as it has been this year?"
SOURCE: University of Melbourne Institute of Applied Economic and Social Research; *Age* Poll, December 3, 1977; ANOP, "ANOP-National Times/Four Corners Campaign Study," December 1-2, 1977.

respondents who feared for their jobs may have been down compared with the figures for 1975 and 1976; it was certainly not up (see Table 6–18). In short, where Labor held an advantage over the government, either the margin was small, as with unemployment, or the issue was of low priority, as with education, or it was one, like uranium, that divided the electorate fairly evenly.

TABLE 6–15

Party Expected to Win 1977 Election, September–November 1977
(in percentages)

Party Expected to Win	Age September 24–25	Morgan Gallup October 15–22	APOP November 5–12
L–NCP	50	50	59
ALP	44	32	28
Undecided	6	18	13

SOURCE: *Age*, October 10, 1977; Morgan Gallup Poll, press release (undated); APOP Poll No. 01/11/77.

TABLE 6–16
VOTERS' ASSESSMENT OF THE GOVERNMENT'S EFFORT TO CREATE JOBS, OCTOBER 1975, 1976, AND 1977
(in percentages)

The Government is:	October 1975	October 1976	October 1977
Doing enough	35	35	27
Not doing enough	58	55	64
Undecided	7	10	9

SOURCE: Morgan Gallup Poll, press release, November 4, 1977.

TABLE 6–17
VOTERS' ASSESSMENT OF THE CAUSES OF UNEMPLOYMENT, OCTOBER 1975, 1976, AND 1977
(in percentages)

Cause of Unemployment	October 1975	October 1976	October 1977
Government	33	27	32
Employers	8	10	12
Trade unions	36	42	43
People not wanting to work	48	30	36
World economic pressures, foreign countries	32	25	30
Others/no answer	3	6	6

NOTE: The respondent was handed a card listing five "causes of unemployment" and asked which, if any, were the main causes of present unemployment. The columns add to more than 100 percent because some cited more than one cause.
SOURCE: Morgan Gallup Poll, press release, November 4, 1977.

TABLE 6–18
VOTERS' ASSESSMENT OF THEIR JOB SECURITY, OCTOBER 1975, 1976, AND 1977
(in percentages)

Response	October 1975	October 1976	October 1977
Present job safe	76	78	82
Chance of unemployment	21	17	15
No answer	3	5	3

SOURCE: Morgan Gallup Poll, press release, November 4, 1977.

What of the Tax Cuts? For many it was taxation that brought the election to life; some even saw this issue as decisive. Curiously, the *Age* poll did not include taxation in its selection of "important issues"; nor, perhaps for reasons of time, did Morgan Gallup. While the Liberals had the edge on taxation (see Tables 6–9 and 6–11), surveys by ANOP and APOP ten days to a fortnight before the election found few voters prepared to say that taxation was the main issue.

Perhaps it was simply slow to surface. Certainly the Liberal party's research suggests this. By the end of the campaign over 10 percent of its telephone sample were naming taxation as the major issue. This put it into the middle range of issues rather than at the top. A small Morgan poll conducted three days before the election went further. It purported to show that taxation was not just an important issue but the "decisive" one. This conclusion it reached on the basis of interviews with 180 "swinging" voters (voters who felt they might not vote according to their current preference) and voters intending to support the Australian Democrats. Those interviewed were asked what "personal benefits" they could expect in the event of a Liberal (or Labor) victory (see Table 6–19). Not surprisingly, more people mentioned having to pay less tax than mentioned any other personal benefit.

Gary Morgan, managing director of Roy Morgan Research Centre Pty Ltd., was not alone in predicting that Whitlam's payroll tax proposal had given the Liberals a winning issue.[42] But whether people would be motivated by personal rather than impersonal considerations, instrumental rather than affective values, was something that needed to be established, not simply assumed. Len Reason, in charge of the Liberal party's account for the advertising firm of Masius, was also convinced of the selling power of taxation. When it was unemployment rather than taxation that showed up most strongly in the party's research he simply dismissed the research: "If someone with a clipboard and horn-rimmed glasses knocks at your front door and asks you your favorite pastime, you are more likely to say reading historical novels than having sex."[43] Unemployment, Reason argued, connoted altruism; tax cuts avarice. Voters were answering not sincerely but strategically.[44]

---

[42] Personal communication, November 18, 1977.

[43] [Len Reason] *The Anatomy of a Political Merchandising Idea* (Melbourne: Masius, Wynne-Williams & D'Arcy-MacManus, December 10, 1977).

[44] For the distinction between sincere and strategic or sophisticated voting, see Robin Farquharson, *A Theory of Voting* (Oxford: Basil Blackwell, 1969). Butler and Stokes implicitly assume that voters are sincere.

TABLE 6–19
Personal Benefits Expected by Swinging Voters from Liberal or Labor Victory, Election Eve, 1977
(in percentages)

Personal Benefits Expected	If Liberals Win	If Labor Wins
Lower taxes	28	7
Lower inflation/better economy	13	3
Continuity of government	4	—
Lower unemployment	—	9
Aid to the underprivileged	—	8
Medibank, education	—	4
Other	3	4
None	52	65

NOTE: These figures are derived from a Morgan survey of swinging voters in Melbourne and Sydney (swinging voters being defined here as those who feel they might not vote according to their current preference). N= 180 (minus an unspecified number of Australian Democrats).
SOURCE: Morgan Research Centre, press release, December 9, 1977.

The argument is less than convincing. The assertion that only altruistic motives have public acceptance is curious—not least when it comes from within the advertising industry. It is surely closer to the mark to argue that the demand in Australia for more goods and services, more money to spend on them (lower taxation), and lower prices is widespread, openly self-serving, and unabashed.

The argument for taxation as the overriding consideration assumed that the voters were self-regarding rather than other-regarding; that (according to Reason) it is necessary to clothe self-regarding acts in other-regarding rhetoric; and, initially at least, that taxation and unemployment fitted in at opposite ends of this spectrum of motives. When Liberal party research, towards the end of the campaign, showed more people openly supporting tax cuts, Reason did not take this as a contradiction of his view but, on the contrary, as a confirmation of it: ". . . people became franker as they grasped the very acceptable proposition that they could help the unemployed by taking money, an unusual (perhaps unique?) opportunity to be selfish and altruistic simultaneously." [45] This twist in the argument ran counter to the Liberal party's own evidence. Labor was more closely identified than the Liberals with cutting unemployment; as taxation

---
[45] Reason, *Anatomy*.

became more salient, unemployment became less salient, and only in the fine print did Liberal party advertisements connect tax cuts with the creation of jobs.

David Kemp, meanwhile, presenting the results of a day-after-the-election survey conducted through the Department of Political Science at Melbourne University, confirmed that the election was not a vote for lower direct taxes or lower payroll taxes. He argued instead that it was a vote "against turbulence and change, for stability and order."[46]

Beyond Issues. In the last analysis the concern to track down "the issues" of the election assumed that the outcome hinged on them. This, implicitly, was the position of the polls themselves. In asking voters to identify the important aspects of the election the polls actually confined themselves to "the issues" and in so doing assumed the rationality of electoral choice. But the connection between issues and electoral outcomes is not necessary, it is contingent. When asked to nominate the important issues in an election voters may react strategically, treating the question as a test of their general knowledge and political awareness rather than a simple request for information about the things that motivate them. Or their answers may merely reflect the major issues pushed by the parties and mentioned in the media. In 1977, unemployment may have been just such an issue.

Where voters are asked not for "the issues" but for their party preference and the reasons for it, the situation, in principle, has changed. Voters may still mention issues but they are no longer confined to them. Answers to questions of this kind typically include habit or tradition (in which case the important issues are irrelevant); party image, economic interests, and ideology (all much more general than discrete issues); and, of course, the party leaders themselves.[47]

---

[46] David Kemp, "The Secret Ingredient in Fraser's Success," *National Times*, January 16-21, 1978, p. 21. Kemp's conclusion is based on correlations between a series of opinion items and the two-party vote. The items that correlated most strongly were those related to acceptance of authority (Liberal) and to sympathy with the underdog (Labor). These items included "the importance of young people putting their youthful rebellion behind them; the importance of children learning obedience and respect for authority; the need for discipline, determination and the will to work among youth." It could be argued, however, that any conclusions about the significance of this polarization for the outcome of the election would have to be based on evidence about the absolute levels of authoritarianism in the electorate. See R. W. Connell and Murray Goot, "The End of Class, Re-Run," *Meanjin*, vol. 38, no. 1 (1979).

[47] For Australia, see D.W. Rawson and Susan M. Holtzinger, *Politics in Eden-Monaro* (London: Heinemann, 1958), pp. 134-135; Creighton Burns, *Parties and People: A Survey Based on the La Trobe Electorate* (Melbourne: Melbourne Uni-

Only McNair approached the voters in this way. In its election-day study McNair asked 360 Sydney voters how they had voted and why (see Table 6-20). Specific issues were mentioned by only one voter in six. Liberal voters mentioned the economy, especially inflation; none mentioned taxation. Most voters talked in much more general terms. As Liberals saw it, the government had "better policies" than the opposition and was doing a "good job"; Labor was not to be "trusted." These results confirm our earlier analysis while placing it in a wider context. Almost as many voters mentioned the leaders as mentioned specific issues.

Leaders. As much as any issue it was the performance and credibility of Fraser and Whitlam that excited comment, not only during the campaign but before it. Much of the speculation centered on Whitlam: could the party win again with Whitlam as leader? The polls themselves were almost as much concerned with the standing of the leaders as they were with the standing of the parties. In the media the ratings of the two men were compared directly, as if to suggest that the contest was as much between them as between the parties.

What relation was there between changes in support for the leaders and changes in support for the parties? In 1976 and throughout 1977 the Morgan Gallup poll took regular soundings of party and leader support. On twenty-three occasions—nine in 1976, fourteen in 1977—questions about the leaders and a question on voting intentions were asked in the same survey. This allows us to construct a time series for each of the leaders and for the Labor and Liberal-National Country parties and to compare movements in one series with movements in any other. Similar readings were taken by APOP (three in 1976, six in 1977) and by the *Age* poll (three and four respectively). Morgan and McNair asked "Do you approve or disapprove the way Mr. [Fraser, Whitlam] is handling his job as [Prime Minister, Leader of the Opposition]?" The *Age* poll asked, "If you personally had to give [Fraser, Whitlam] a mark out of ten for his popularity with you,

---

versity Press, 1961), chap. 12; J. Goodhew, John Power, and T. Valentine, "The Survey," in John Power, ed., *Politics in a Suburban Community* (Sydney: Sydney University Press, 1968), p. 153; Terence W. Beed, Murray Goot, Stephen Hodgson, and Peggy Ridley, *Australian Opinion Polls 1941-1977* (Sydney: Hale & Iremonger and the University of Sydney Sample Survey Centre, 1978), pp. 341-342; McNair Anderson Associates, *Reasons for the Swing to Labor: The Federal Election December 2, 1972*, report prepared for the Australian Broadcasting Commission, December 1972; *Reasons for the Return of the Whitlam Labor Government: The Federal Election May 18, 1974*, report prepared for the Australian Broadcasting Commission, May 1974; *Reasons for the Swing Back to the Liberals: The Federal Election December 13, 1975*, report prepared for the Australian Broadcasting Commission, December 1975.

TABLE 6-20

Voters' Explanations for their Vote Choice, 1977 Election
(in percentages)

	Vote		
Reasons Offered for Vote Choice	L–NCP	ALP	AD
Tradition: always vote this way	10	15	
Performance			
Trust Liberals, distrust Labor	15		
Did a good job	14		
Made a mess	7	11	73
Deserve a(nother) chance	6	9	30
Leaders			
Anti-Fraser		12	
Anti-Whitlam	14		
Pro-Chipp			19
Policies			
Pro-worker/standard of living		22	
Policies better for Australia	29	18	
Anti-socialism/welfare state	9		
Pro-private enterprise/small business	6		
Issues			
Economic management	11		
Inflation, wages/prices	6		
Unemployment		10	
Uranium		5	
Local member doing a good job		5	

Note: The survey question was "Why did you vote this way?" Since some respondents mentioned more than one reason, the columns add to more than 100 percent.
Source: McNair Anderson, *Reasons for the Return of the Fraser Government.*

what mark would you give?" A score between seven and ten meant the leader was popular. For each of these series the Spearman rank-order correlation coefficient was calculated (see Table 6–21).

The evidence suggests that support for Fraser did not entail opposition to Whitlam or support for Whitlam opposition to Fraser. On the evidence of the Morgan poll, support for the one varied quite independently of support for the other. The surveys by APOP and the *Age* poll indicate a positive-sum, not a zero-sum, relationship, with support for the two leaders rising and falling together. As one would expect, support for Fraser went hand-in-hand with support for the government. And, in general, when support for Fraser went one way

TABLE 6-21
CORRELATION BETWEEN SUPPORT FOR THE MAJOR PARTIES AND
SUPPORT FOR THEIR LEADERS, 1976–1977

	Rank-order Correlation Coefficients		
	Morgan Gallup	APOP	Age Poll
Fraser × Whitlam	−.01	.53	.56
Fraser × L–NCP	.79	.75	.92
Whitlam × L–NCP	−.21	.16	.36
Fraser × ALP	−.27	−.60	−.57
Whitlam × ALP	.54	−.02	−.46
Number of surveys	(23)	(9)	(7)

SOURCE: Authors' computations, based on the results of questions about support for the two major parties and for their leaders included in thirty-nine surveys conducted between January 1976 and December 1977.

support for the opposition went the other. Whitlam, during these two years, seems to have played the lesser role. None of the polls show his impact on the ALP to have been as strong as Fraser's on the Liberal-National Country party coalition; indeed, on the evidence of the *Age* poll, support for the Labor party and for its leader varied inversely. None of the polls show Whitlam's impact on the government to have been as strong as Fraser's on the opposition—which supports the finding, valid since the late 1960s, that the performance of leaders of the opposition has mattered less than the performance of prime ministers.[48]

This, in turn, suggests that the election was not lost by Whitlam so much as won by Fraser. At least, not lost by Whitlam on account of anything he might have said or done as leader of the opposition. For who can doubt that the Liberal party's advantage over Labor as an economic manager rested largely on the voters' memories of Whitlam in government. Whitlam was the first former prime minister in a generation to contest an election as leader of the opposition. It was Whitlam's performance in government that the Liberals attacked during the campaign, not his performance in opposition.

---

[48] Murray Goot and R.W. Connell, *Social Patterns in Public Opinion* (forthcoming).

7
Monitoring the Public, Marketing the Parties

Murray Goot

The dependence of parties on public opinion research, though not new, is growing. Parties monitor opinion through polls published in the press and they commission polls of their own. In the sixties such activity was irregular and unsystematic. Now, market research has a bearing on almost every aspect of an election: its timing, the issues, the presentation of the leaders, the segment of the electorate to which the parties address their appeals, the slogans, and the advertising.

Research practices are not politically neutral, and market research is no exception. The right to participate in deciding what to ask, when, how, and of whom is invariably restricted to a few; so, usually, are the results. Research of this kind favors big parties over small, parliamentary leaders over the rest of the parliamentary party, party officials and pollsters over the party rank and file.

Though poll findings are highly abstract and in that sense remote from actual social situations, political developments, and, often, the thought patterns of the voters, they have nonetheless come to be seen as providing a "scientific" or "professional," hence authoritative, account of "what the voters want." Polling has increased the pressure on politicians to follow "public opinion" rather than to lead it: to follow, either by adjusting policies or by adjusting the image of the

---

This chapter could not have been written without the help of each of the parties. The ALP, the Australian Democrats, and the Progress party allowed me access to their polls and their pollsters. The Liberal party provided limited access to its results, while the NCP allowed me to look at its survey on condition that the findings were not disclosed.

Thanks are due to a number of people in politics, market research, advertising, and the media. Thanks are also due to Peggy Ridley for research assistance, Pat Keane for typing, and Terence W. Beed for comments on two earlier drafts. The Australian Research Grants Committee provided financial support through the project "Opinion Polls in Political Decision Making."

policies. Polls have been used much more by those who believe in adjusting party policies or images to the shape of the market—or to that segment of the market known as the swinging vote—than by those who want to shape the market to the thinking of the party. Polls appeal to pragmatists and opportunists both.

The public and private polls overlap. Both measure support for the parties, the standing of party leaders, and reactions to issues. Three of the commercial pollsters publish their findings on a regular basis and offer subscriptions to detailed computer reports.[1] Privately commissioned polls are tailored to a party's needs, asking questions on voting intentions and whether these might change, questions not only on the overall standing of leaders but on their particular qualities. They can ask open-ended, not just precoded, questions, can be analyzed by nonstandard as well as standard variables, and can be timed according to the party's requirements. When speed is an important consideration, they can make use of telephone interviews. Finally, their confidential results can be selectively leaked to browbeat opponents, boost party morale, or generate a bandwagon effect.

People who participate in private polls are told neither the sponsor nor the purpose of the research. Parties generally do not want it known that they have commissioned research and they do not want the interviewees, in particular, to know lest the knowledge skew their responses. Indeed, where parties choose well-known public opinion firms to do their research they have an added advantage in that the interviewees are likely to be under the impression that they are participating in a survey intended for publication and may therefore be more eager to participate.

In 1977 the Liberal party and its leader used surveys more extensively than any of the other parties. Survey information came from work conducted outside the party but most was commercial research commissioned directly by the party. Surveys were undertaken, advertising ideas tested, well in advance of any election. During the campaign the party continued to monitor public opinion and the impact of its own advertising as well as Labor's.

Labor commissioned considerably less research than the Liberals, but, if anything, it squeezed what it had even harder. Only one preelection survey was conducted. It was supplemented by surveys carried out for the state branches of the party and by the public polls,

---

[1] However, except for the Liberal party, which subscribed to the Morgan reports, none of the federal parties appears to have subscribed to any of these reports. For the minor parties, because they are small and geographically clustered (notably in the country), public polls are less useful than they might otherwise be.

especially those published in the *National Times*. Little was done to test ALP advertising.

The National Country party and the Progress party also commissioned research, but less of it than the major parties, and it was less useful. The Australian Democrats did a survey themselves, rather than hiring a professional pollster, but they basically depended on the public polls and leaked private polls. No party talked more of principle than the Democrats, but no party's use of the polls was more opportunistic.

The Liberal Party

Ongoing Research. The Federal Secretariat was responsible, under the federal (campaign) director, to the Federal Campaign Committee for the coordination and implementation of any campaign. It divided the interelection period into three stages: ongoing, pre-campaign, and campaign. From 1976 to May 1977 the Morgan Research Centre conducted private research for the Liberals on an ongoing basis. In March 1977 the Secretariat was strengthened by the appointment of Martin Rawlinson, formerly a lecturer in political science at the Mitchell College of Advanced Education, to the new position of manager, policy research and development division. Rawlinson, acquainted with the academic literature on political behavior and with theories of voting, had the kind of background the Secretariat wanted.

Under his supervision the Secretariat clipped the public opinion polls from the Sydney, Melbourne, and national press. It also subscribed to the computer sheets of the Morgan Gallup poll, which broke down all findings by voting intention, sex, age, occupation, state, metropolitan/nonmetropolitan residence, education, and occasionally nationality and "life cycle."[2] The Secretariat paid special attention to the young, who were thought to be less strongly committed to particular parties and more susceptible to the prevailing political mood than older voters; to blue-collar workers, more of whom had crossed over to vote Liberal in recent years; and to white-collar workers, more of whom had voted Labor in the early 1970s than ever before.

During 1976, the Liberals commissioned at least one survey. On the basis of this and the public polls, the party's director, Tony Eggle-

---

[2] "Life cycle" meant whether voters were under thirty-five and single; under thirty-five and married; thirty-five and over, married with child; thirty-five and over, married without child; or over thirty-five and unmarried.

ton, was able to assure the prime minister that the governor general, Sir John Kerr, was no longer an electoral liability.[3]

Then in March 1977, just before Rawlinson's arrival, there was another private survey "to test the water." According to this survey, most voters felt the government had not done enough about unemployment or inflation; most favored tax reductions but did not support further cuts in government spending; most thought Fraser was trying to do what was right, but only two-in-five thought him a strong man with the right ideas. Fraser was seen as honest and respected, but also a person who changed his stand too often. He had fallen short in explaining his policies, but most voters felt the government had not yet had enough time to do its job.

The Morgan Research Centre provided an interpretation of its results, either at meetings or over the phone, and an analysis was also made within the Secretariat, principally by Rawlinson. His reports on both private and public polls were forwarded to members of the Federal Executive, state directors, and the federal parliamentary leaders. The prime minister would have heard of these from Eggleton, with whom he was in daily contact. Every six weeks or so until the campaign proper, a one-day conference was held in Melbourne with the party's advertising agents Masius, Wynne-Williams. The Secretariat set the agenda, chaired the meetings, and provided the political intelligence, including information gleaned from the polls.

The Pre-Campaign Period. Following the referendum in May and on the assumption that a half-Senate election, with or without a simultaneous House election, would take place later in the year, the Secretariat moved from an "ongoing" to a "pre-campaign" state of preparedness. Two national surveys were commissioned: one in July, the other after the announcement of the budget in August. In addition to its concerns of March, the party was now interested in Don Chipp's followers and in the states, particularly Victoria.

Contact between the Secretariat and Masius became more frequent as the agency devised and tested campaign slogans and advertising approaches under the ultimate direction of Len Reason. Eggleton, Baudino, and the agency had worked together for the first time in 1975. Out of that success had developed a close relationship based on what they called "professionalism" and political like-mindedness.

---

[3] *National Times*, December 12-14, 1977, p. 5. Between August and December 1976, the public polls showed 47-57 percent in favor of Sir John Kerr's continuing in office, 34-39 percent against. As to whether Kerr had acted properly in dismissing Whitlam, voters divided sharply along party lines. Morgan Gallup Poll No. 133, August 1976; No. 144, November 1976; *Age*, December 10, 1976.

The Morgan team had rather less regard for Masius. They felt that the agency's staff spent too much time throwing ideas around the office and too little time looking at the results of research, or at least the results of Morgan's research. Morgan regarded its meetings with Eggleton, Rawlinson, and Reason as productive, those attended by the agency's lesser lights as unproductive. But Morgan's attempts to deal with Eggleton and Fraser directly met with only limited success.

While Morgan did the large-scale research, Masius—or people hired by them—conducted small-scale surveys on specific questions that concerned the Secretariat (the government's performance, for example, or attitudes toward unemployment). The reactions and remedies that emerged from this work with small groups in turn would inform the party's slogans and advertisements, as well as the questions to be asked by Morgan nationwide.

On the last Friday in August members of the Secretariat, with Gary Morgan, gathered in the offices of Masius to review the findings of both kinds of research. As a subsequent Morgan poll would confirm, the voters were naming unemployment as the main election issue. In 1975 under Whitlam and in 1976 under Fraser, the poll had shown trade unions and "people not wanting to work" to be the most frequently mentioned causes of unemployment. In 1977 the situation had changed only marginally. Like the parties and the press, the voters were still complaining about people not wanting to work[4] (this point was later made in a campaign ad), but even more were blaming the unions. Only 20 percent of the responses laid the blame at the door of the government. At the same time the voters thought the government was not doing enough to create jobs. Within weeks the cabinet had allocated $1 million to publicize its employment and job-training schemes: NEAT (National Employment and Training Scheme), the Special Youth Employment Training Programme, and CRAFT (Commonwealth Rebate for Apprentice Full-Time Training). From mid-October until mid-November, halfway into the campaign period, the minister for employment and industrial relations, Tony Street, appeared in a series of television, radio, and full-page press advertisements promoting the Commonwealth Employment Service with the slogan, "We Help Australia Work."

The Melbourne meeting recommended that the party adopt the slogan "Right to Work" as its campaign theme. This acknowledged unemployment to be the electorate's most widely felt concern and the

---

[4] In one poll, 52 percent agreed that young people often were not looking for jobs. APOP, September 1977.

unions to be the culprits. But the party also came up with other slogans—"Australia on the Move" and "Get Australia Moving." "Our nation is on the move" were the opening words of the prime minister's policy speech. Like the slogan on which the party finally and rather belatedly settled, "Doing the Job," these latter slogans were to take the spotlight off unemployment and the heat off the unions.

Meanwhile, the last weekend in August, the party's Platform and Policy Review Subcommittee of the Joint Standing Committee on Federal Policy met in Melbourne at the Southern Cross Hotel. Set up originally to revise the 1974 platform, the subcommittee had been diverted into preparing policy recommendations for a policy speech in the event of an election.

At the August meeting, David Kemp, a political scientist at Melbourne University and former senior adviser to the prime minister, described in detail the results of a Melbourne survey he had conducted in 1975 along with a colleague, Graham Little.[5] This research, he argued, revealed a consensus of electoral opinion "on a number of matters relating to social relations, the nature of the individual, the role of government and the role of political leadership." Particularly pertinent, in view of the party's own research showing unemployment to be the single most important issue, were the items on work. "The main thing that determines a person's success or failure in life is how hard he works at it" was a proposition with which 85 percent of the sample agreed; only 24 percent were prepared to say that "by and large it is good fortune rather than anything to do with the individual [that determines] how well he does in life." But the sentiments that emerged were less those of free enterprise capitalism than of welfare state liberalism. Two out of three respondents agreed that "the government should give a person work if he can't find another job"; only one out of three thought it "not really the government's responsibility to make sure that everyone has a good standard of living." Kemp's influence on the committee, as Fraser's policy speech would show, was substantial. He was uncommon in having a well thought out philosophy of liberalism, and he was highly regarded as a student of electoral behavior. In addition, having worked with the prime minister, he could be looked to as the man to gauge what could be sold to Fraser and what could not. His results not only correlated with those from the party's commissioned research (that the voters saw unemployment as being caused by people's not wanting

---

[5] David Kemp, "Political Parties and Australian Culture," *Quadrant*, December 1977, pp. 3-13. During the election Kemp was retained by the party as a consultant.

to work and the government's not doing enough to create jobs), they seemed to explain them.

Early in September a meeting of the Federal Campaign Committee was convened. With the prime minister in the chair, the committee approved the campaign strategy devised by the Secretariat and presented by Len Reason. The Campaign Committee was aware that support for the government in the opinion polls was no greater than support for the ALP, that support for Fraser was no greater than support for Whitlam (see Table 7–1), and that under these circumstances their market researchers could not predict a government victory. They were also aware that the Australian Democrats might hold the balance and that voters and editorialists, state branches of the party, and Liberals in the Parliament[6] all were opposed to an early election.

For Fraser none of these objections was convincing. On the basis of the party's 1975 experience, Eggleton argued publicly that once an election were called the whole question of whether or not it should have been called would be rapidly overtaken by the need to choose between Liberal and Labor. That, in the last analysis, would be settled by people's memories of the Whitlam years. Whatever campaign strategy were adopted, the government would pull ahead of the opposition. As the electorate became polarized, support for the Democrats would fall. In Liberal surveys 60 percent of intending Democrats had said they might change their minds, and if they did, Eggleton predicted, "a great majority . . . [would] come back where they belong." Outside Victoria, he argued, the Democrats could not hope for more than 6 or 7 percent of the vote.[7]

The Campaign Period. A month later, with the *Age* poll suggesting that Labor voters were more confident of a Labor win in 1978 than in 1977 and the electorate overall predicting a coalition victory in a 1977 election, the Secretariat entered what it already called the "campaign period." An election had yet to be called, but as the *Sydney Morning Herald* observed, the prime minister was performing "the remarkable feat of deploring speculation while at the same time

---

[6] On state branches, see *Sunday Times*, October 16, 1977, p. 1; October 17, 1977, p. 6. The clearest exception was Western Australia. There were divided opinions in New South Wales where Sir Kenneth Anderson (president) and Sir Eric Willis (opposition leader) opposed Fraser's move. On the Liberals in Parliament see *Sydney Morning Herald*, October 10, 1977, p. 1; October 11, 1977, p. 1. Reasons for opposition included "the Government's falling popularity at the polls" and the possibility that Australian Democrat preferences might prove decisive.

[7] *National Times*, October 24–29, 1977, p. 14.

TABLE 7-1

Support for Government and Opposition, Parties and Leaders,
August–September 1977
(in percentages)

		Party		Leader	
Pollster	Date[a]	L–NCP	ALP	Fraser	Whitlam
Morgan	August 6	43	44		
Morgan	August 13	43	44	36	39
APOP	August 14	43	44	43	44
Morgan	August 27	40	45	42	42
Morgan	September 10			37	38
APOP	September 11	43	43		
Morgan	September 25	43	43		
Age	September 25	41	44	26	26

[a] Where surveys were conducted over two weekends the date listed is that of the second weekend.

SOURCE: Morgan Gallup Poll Nos. 177, 179, 181; APOP computer sheets, August–September 1977; *Age*, October 15, 1977.

stimulating it."[8] If he opted for December, an announcement would have to be made by the end of October. Telephone surveys were now commissioned. These would confirm the prime minister's final decision. They would also provide a bench mark against which to assess shifts in public opinion once the campaign got under way.

The first of these surveys was carried out in the middle of October, the weekend of the Cunningham by-election held to fill the vacancy caused by the death of the former Labor minister for minerals and energy, R. F. X. Connor. With none of the swing against the government that might be expected in a by-election, the result gave the prime minister considerable cheer. On October 22 there was another survey and on Thursday, October 27, the election was announced. Telephone polls were now conducted each weekend and occasionally during the week. These involved 300 to 400 interviews, each lasting about twenty minutes. Interviewing was confined to Sydney and Melbourne with about one-half of the sample in each city.

[8] Editorial, *Sydney Morning Herald*, October 11, 1977, p. 6. In the Secretariat, where the Federal Council of the Liberal party was meeting, the walls were plastered with slogans like "Australia on the move"; "15.4% inflation under Labor"; "Unemployment under Labor up 172.6%." *Mercury*, October 17, 1977, p. 1. At the time the election was announced Reason was still saying that the main campaign slogan would be "Get Australia Moving." *Australian Financial Review*, October 28, 1977.

The earlier, larger Liberal surveys had been part of the Morgan consumer omnibus.[9] This enabled the party to get its questions into the field on almost any weekend. But Morgan's telephone polls offered the party a number of advantages over the omnibus: they could be conducted at any time, not just at weekends; since only 300 to 400 interviews were conducted, compared with about 1,000, they were cheaper; they were quickly executed ("let your fingers do the walking"), which meant feedback within hours at a lower unit cost; they had a lower nonresponse rate since people are less likely to hang up on an interviewer, Morgan claimed, than to turn him or her away in person; and better interviewers could be obtained since fewer were required. Typically, Eggleton and Rawlinson, in Canberra, would draft a questionnaire on Wednesday or Thursday and discuss it on the phone with Gary Morgan in Melbourne. Morgan would then print the questionnaires. Those to be used in Sydney would leave Melbourne on the 11 a.m. flight on Friday. Most of the interviewing was done in both cities from the company's offices, which saved time and cost and made control and checking easier. Any questionnaires sent to interviewers outside were delivered and picked up by courier. From Sydney the questionnaires were flown back to Melbourne to be coded (in the case of the open-ended questions) and fed to the computer. Since the Liberal party was able to pay for long periods of overtime, the computer reports could be on the plane and in the Secretariat's hands the following day, even a Sunday.

But the telephone surveys had disadvantages too. Though too little is known about their biases, it is clear that not every dwelling has a phone (Morgan says 75 percent of Australian homes have phones, 80 percent in Melbourne) and that telephone samples must pick up a disproportionately large number of the better-off. To compensate for this bias, which was interpreted as a class bias in favor of the Liberals, all the undecideds were allocated to the ALP. Again, telephone books (like electoral rolls) include numbers that are no longer connected and exclude new subscribers. Any number that did not answer was simply dropped and another number substituted. Finally, to make up for the difficulty of catching young voters at home, interviewers began by asking to speak to the youngest male/female voter in the house; even so there was some bias depending on when the call was made.

Telephone surveys are much more difficult to complete quickly in country areas than in urban ones, and the cost rises outside the cities

---

[9] The most regular omnibus surveys in Australia are those run by Morgan and McNair.

where the poll is based. This the party had to live with. It was some consolation that since the questions on voting intention and support for the leaders were identical to those used on the Morgan Gallup omnibus the results of the telephone surveys could later be read against a wider backdrop. More important, Sydney and Melbourne were located in the states where most of the voters lived. By assuming uniformity of electoral swing, Morgan was able to generalize from its results. And Melbourne was a window onto the state that was occasioning the Liberals the greatest anxiety.

Thus, as well as being asked whether they approved or disapproved of the way Fraser was handling his job as prime minister or Whitlam his as leader of the opposition, Melbournians were asked whether they approved or disapproved of the way Dick Hamer was handling his job as premier of Victoria. Again, voters were asked their party preferences in the House of Representatives and, on two occasions, in the Senate. If the Australian Democrats were to win any seats in the Senate, the first would be in Victoria. And the Liberals were equally concerned with the distribution of AD second preferences.

The purpose of the surveys was as much to pick up the themes that should be highlighted by the party as to discover those that might best be hidden. Respondents were asked to point out, in their own words, where "Mr. Fraser's Liberal Party" had let them down; likewise, "Mr. Whitlam's Labor Party." They were also asked to name the one "best thing done by the government in the last two years."

Before being asked how they would vote, respondents were asked, "What one thing, more than anything else, would cause you to vote for a particular party or candidate?" The party thus avoided the assumption that elections must be about the issues or even the leaders. Certainly the party's advertising agency needed information that was not restricted by such assumptions. On the telephone it was impossible to present the respondent with a list of possible issues and ask him or her to select the most important, as was done in the omnibus surveys. Instead, voters were asked which of the two parties,[10] Labor or Liberal, would "be best" for controlling inflation, reducing unemployment, controlling unions and industrial troubles, improving the economy, reducing taxes, and providing honest government.

The idea, throughout the campaign, was to keep as much continuity in the surveys as possible, but inevitably some questions were dropped and others added. A question on which party would be

---

[10] The questions usually did not refer to the National Country party or to the coalition. The Liberals sought to keep the questions brief and in any event doubted that the respondents would understand the term *coalition*.

better for lowering interest rates, for example, was omitted because a large number of "don't know" and "indifferent" responses were being recorded. After Whitlam's policy speech on November 15 a new question was added: "In February, the Liberal Government's personal tax cuts apply. Mr. Whitlam said if Labor is elected these tax cuts wouldn't apply, but payroll tax would be abolished. Next February, would you prefer personal tax cuts or payroll tax to be abolished?"

These surveys also asked which leader, Fraser or Whitlam, was campaigning better and which party, Labor or Liberal, would govern best; they also asked about the parties' advertising. Of the several ways of measuring advertising effectiveness, the party accepted the method of unaided recall developed by George Gallup and the late Claude Robinson. Voters were asked whether they recalled "seeing or hearing any advertisements for the (Labor/Liberal) party within recent times." Those who did were asked to name or describe the ad and to say whether it had made them more or less favorable to that particular party. The responses, however, were not cross-classified with the data on swinging voters.

None of the precoded or closed questions elicited views on policies other than taxation. Instead, they sought the voters' views on the relative merits of the parties in different areas. The questions were couched in terms that assumed an electorate of undifferentiated interests ("the electors"), a consensus on economic and political ends (reducing unemployment, improving the economy, reducing taxation), and the dominance of the values of liberal capitalism (honest government, controlling unions and industrial troubles). The class framework within which these questions were asked may be glimpsed in responses to the *Age*'s surveys on the election issues.[11] Voters who described themselves as middle class or upper-middle class were more likely to mention trade unions, economic management, and inflation as election issues than were those who described themselves as working class or even lower-middle-class voters. The reverse was true of social services (which were not covered by the Liberal surveys) and of course unemployment. On honesty in government there was no differentiation.

What of the other issues, including the Lynch affair, the land scandals in Victoria, and uranium? Within days of Lynch's resignation, snap polls in Sydney and Melbourne had established that the voters did not think the allegations against Lynch should be an elec-

---

[11] *Age*, October 27, 1977.

tion issue.¹² In Sydney, a survey of 532 people commissioned by the Australian Broadcasting Commission (ABC) and conducted by Nanette Dykes Market Research indicated that over 70 percent held this view. This was the poll that made the greatest impression on the Liberals, coming as it did soon after the televised confrontation between the prime minister and George Negus, Canberra correspondent for "This Day Tonight," on the Lynch affair. On the other hand, the Sydney radio station 2GB received as many calls saying that Lynch should be an issue (260) as that he should not (259), while a Melbourne survey of 290 voters conducted by the Computer Telephone Service put the figure opposed to making Lynch an issue at just over 60 percent. Backed by his market researchers, Fraser had decided that if the media would not kill the story Lynch would have to go. A survey of fifty "leading businessmen" showed the majority opposed to Lynch's being reinstated as treasurer after the election.[13]

Support for the coalition reached its lowest point just prior to Lynch's resignation; his departure coincided with an upturn in the party's fortunes. According to the News Ltd. press, Liberal surveys "found a strong sympathy element emerging, with many of those polled now see[ing] Mr. Lynch as the underdog, ill in hospital, in pain and unable to defend himself."[14]

Fraser had much less control over allegations in connection with the land deals in Victoria, and this worried him. Before calling the election he was reported to have asked the party to commission a survey "urgently" to find out whether the allegations would rebound against the federal government.[15] A week after the election was announced Eggleton was reported to have informed him that voter reaction to "the aura of scandal surrounding the land deals" was showing up "strongly in party surveys," a trend that had "emerged only in recent weeks."[16] When interviewed ten days later on ATV-0, Eggleton conceded that the land deals had emerged as a strong issue at the November 5 Greensborough by-election at which the Liberal government of Victoria had suffered a setback. But, he noted, the same polls that had predicted that the Liberals would not do well there had also suggested that the lands scandal was strictly a state issue: it would not be reflected in a federal poll.[17]

---

[12] *Australian*, November 24, 1977, p. 1; *Daily Telegraph*, November 24, 1977, p. 2; *Advertiser*, November 24, 1977, p. 20.
[13] *Sydney Morning Herald*, November 23, 1977, p. 3.
[14] *News*, November 23, 1977; *Australian*, November 30, 1977.
[15] *Sun-Herald*, October 9, 1977, p. 15.
[16] *Inside Canberra*, November 4, 1977, p. 1.
[17] *Age*, November 14, 1977, pp. 4-5.

The party had conducted some research on uranium as an issue though not as much as it might have had the issue not been taken up so intensively by the public polls. Even as the government formally announced its decision to mine and export uranium, it was noted that support for uranium was gradually losing ground, not gaining. Fraser, in an interview with Laurie Oakes, argued that "you get a noticeably different answer depending on how you frame your question. One sort of question is 'Are you in favor of exporting uranium?' Another is 'Are you in favor of the continued mining and export of uranium as Australia has for the last 20 years, for the production of energy for peaceful purposes?'"[18] The Morgan Gallup poll had already tried a question similar to the latter, with results not very different from those of questions less obviously designed to elicit a favorable response.[19] More important, party strategists were convinced that uranium was a low priority issue in the electorate. They refused to take at face value an early ANOP finding that uranium was the number one issue. People mentioned uranium merely because it was in the news, the Secretariat reasoned, but to imagine that they would vote on this basis was naive.

A post-budget Morgan Gallup poll indicated that 42 percent thought the budget would worsen unemployment; only 10 percent thought it would help reduce it.[20] In response to the series of questions "Which party do you think would be best for . . ." asked before and during the campaign, the only issue on which Labor consistently came out ahead of the Liberals was unemployment. This was largely because of the solidarity of those Labor voters who said there was no chance at all that they would change their vote. On the eve of the prime minister's policy speech Morgan Gallup indicated that about 60 percent of Labor voters and 40 percent of L-NCP voters placed unemployment among the top three issues of the election.[21] According to the party's private surveys, unemployment became a less salient issue as the campaign progressed.

Since, in the public mind, the unions and the unemployed themselves were responsible for unemployment, the party's first inclination had been to turn its defense of the unemployment figures into an attack on the unions. August had seen the start of an eleven-week

---

[18] *Age*, November 15, 1977, p. 5.
[19] *Newsletter of the University of Sydney Sample Survey Centre*, vol. 2 (June 1978), pp. 2-3.
[20] Morgan Gallup Poll No. 179, August 20-27, 1977.
[21] Morgan Gallup Poll No. 186, November 11-12, 1977; No. 188, November 19-20, 1977.

strike by maintenance workers employed in Victoria by the State Electricity Commission. There had also been strikes by air-traffic controllers and postal workers; and the government had rushed the Commonwealth Employees (Employment Provisions) Act through Parliament under which it would have power to sack or suspend Commonwealth government employees who went on strike.

The strikes had occasioned a good deal of speculation about a "law and order" election. Not only Fraser but many Labor members of Parliament considered the strikes to be playing straight into the hands of the government. In response to the party's polls, voters spontaneously mentioned strikes and unions as election issues. It was in this context that the Liberal party produced its "Right to Work" slogan—an attempt to turn a traditional union demand against the unions and cut the labor movement off from its own history.

But the day before the election was announced the strike in Victoria ended. Liberal strategists knew that in the absence of a current and well-publicized dispute industrial relations issues would be difficult to push. And in fact, after the strikes, unions only showed up as a salient issue in polls when respondents were presented with lists of possible issues, never in response to open-ended questions. Moreover, party research prior to the election (and through the campaign) showed the electorate to be evenly divided over which of the parties would be better at "controlling unions and industrial troubles."

Widely publicized Labor research indicated that the prime minister had emerged from the confrontation in Victoria with his credibility damaged.[22] The party's own research, contrary to Labor's, argued that the public wanted the unions "brought into line"; and many, including Kemp, thought Labor's connection with the unions made the party electorally vulnerable, widening the gap between a militant leadership and a moderate membership. A third of the way through his policy speech Fraser attacked Labor's leaders as "partners in obstruction with extremist union leaders. The extremist unions are all affiliated with the Labor Party," Fraser said. "That's why it is Labor's official policy to put unions above the law." The government's approach had been to pass laws "protecting individual unionists" and giving "responsible rank and file unionists the chance to make their voices heard."

But the Campaign Committee took the view that the prime minister was not to be too openly associated with this debate. Union-

---

[22] *Sun News-Pictorial,* November 7, 1977, p. 8.

bashing was fine in local campaigns and in the local media but divisive in national politics and unbecoming to a national leader. In the party's national advertising the subject of the unions was avoided.

In "Doing the Job" the party came up with a slogan that captured the sentiments most frequently expressed by those voters who approved of the job Fraser was doing. It worked in the contrast with Labor that was to become the motif of the government's campaign: "When you consider the future don't forget the past. Liberals are doing the Job." In the concept of "the job" it appealed to the politics of consensus: lower unemployment, lower inflation, proper economic management, lower interest rates, and the like. In Kemp's survey, 78 percent had agreed that "what we need now is a common cause that all Australians can get behind and work for together."[23]

The government was ahead of Labor on inflation and the economy generally. As early as January the party had been told, on the basis of research in the states by Quantum Market Research, that though people said unemployment was the number one issue, inflation was what they really cared about. Notwithstanding an August poll in which 32 percent had said the budget would increase inflation, against 10 percent who thought it would reduce it,[24] the government's lead over the opposition on inflation was substantial and grew as the campaign progressed. Inflation and unemployment, the prime minister and treasurer insisted, were inseparable. Unemployment would only come down as inflation came down. "LABOR'S INFLATION 19%" said the large balloon on one page: "LIBERAL HALVES IT: 9%" was the modest message on the balloon opposite. These double-page spreads appeared in newspapers across Australia in the first week of the Liberals' campaign. In the same week the government's margin as the party most likely to improve the economy increased dramatically. Though these advertisements were only run in the first week, almost 40 percent of the Melbourne-Sydney sample recalled them unaided in the final week.

According to the Liberal party's own research the Liberals started behind Labor as the party of lower taxation. The tax cuts promised in the Lynch budget for February had proved a public relations flop. In the week after Fraser's election announcement more voters expected taxes to rise in 1978 than expected them to fall (41 percent to 25 percent).[25] It was only when Whitlam pledged that a Labor gov-

---

[23] Kemp, "Political Parties," p. 8.
[24] Morgan Gallup Poll No. 179, August 20-27, 1977.
[25] Morgan Gallup Poll No. 187, October 29-November 6, 1977.

ernment would eliminate the payroll tax instead of cutting personal taxes that the whole campaign came to life. According to a Liberal senior strategist, "Until Labor put that up, we didn't have an issue to really fight on.... The economy was a difficult thing to make into a decisive issue because of its complexity.... Labor's tax plan has given us something to focus on. I said the day of their policy speech that it would cost them the election."[26] Almost all the preplanned marketing strategy was thrown away as the party "danced to the polls."[27]

The week the prime minister opened the government's campaign the Liberal party placed full-page ads in papers across the country proclaiming, "LABOR GIVES NOTHING. LIBERAL GIVES TAX CUTS." In the second and third weeks of the three-week campaign the party's tax ads played down any reference to Labor's proposals, concentrating instead on the details of the Liberal tax cuts and advising people of the number they should dial if they wanted to know whether they were among the 225,000 who pay tax now but "will pay none after February 1." In the first six days, according to agency estimates, 250,000 "dialled a tax cut."[28] A television commercial in which the new treasurer, John Howard, explained the tax cuts and gave people the number to phone was recalled by more than 40 percent of the voters interviewed in the telephone polls. No Labor commercial was recalled by more than 10 percent.

The Morgan Gallup poll taken the weekend after the Liberal policy speech showed 47 percent favoring the government's tax cuts to 34 percent favoring the opposition's.[29] The party was in no doubt that its tax message was getting through. In both aided and unaided recall the tax cuts rose quickly into the middle rank of the important reasons for voting Liberal.

By the end of the campaign Fraser's personal rating in all the polls—private and public—had improved, while Whitlam's had not (see Table 7–2). The prime minister played a larger part in Liberal advertising than did the leader of the opposition in Labor advertising, and Liberal ads were aimed more at undermining Whitlam than Labor ads were aimed at exposing Fraser. "A REPEAT OF PAST HISTORY?" asked the full-page ads in the last week of the campaign, above the picture of a sleazy-looking Whitlam. On television, the Liberals jolted the viewers' memories of the Whitlam years: the sacking of a succession

---

[26] *Sydney Morning Herald*, November 28, 1977, p. 1.

[27] *Australian Financial Review*, December 14, 1977, p. 1.

[28] [L. Reason], *The Anatomy of a Political Merchandising Idea* (Masius, Wynne-Williams & D'Arcy-MacManus [Aust.] Pty. Ltd., December 10, 1977).

[29] *Bulletin*, December 10, 1977.

TABLE 7-2

POPULARITY OF FRASER AND WHITLAM, OCTOBER–DECEMBER 1977
(in percentages; differences in percentage points)

Poll	Date[a]	Fraser	Whitlam	Difference
Morgan	October 29	41	36	5
Morgan	November 5	38	30	8
Morgan	November 12	37	33	4
APOP	November 13	41	30	11
Morgan	November 19	38	39	−1
Morgan	November 26	40	35	5
APOP	November 27	46	42	4
Age	November 27	31	30	1
ANOP	December 1	39	40	−1
Morgan	December 3	44	36	8
APOP	December 4	46	40	6
Age	December 4	34	29	5

NOTE: APOP and Morgan asked whether voters approved or disapproved of the way each leader was handling his job. The *Age* asked, "If you had to give each leader a mark out of 10 for his popularity with you, which mark would you give him?"; marks between 7 and 10 were classified as "popular." ANOP asked whether voters were satisfied or dissatisfied with Fraser as prime minister and Whitlam as opposition leader.

[a] Where surveys were conducted over two weekends the date listed is that of the second weekend.

SOURCE: Computer sheets, Morgan Gallup and APOP, October–December 1977; ANOP, "ANOP-National Times/Four Corners Campaign Study"; *Age*, December 2, 1977, December 8, 1977.

of ministers, high inflation, high prices, high unemployment ("Memories" one), all this and a "tax rip-off" too ("Memories" two). The telephone polls assured them that the prime minister was campaigning more effectively than his rival.

Party research, it was reported, revealed Fraser's "toughness" to be one of his strengths; his "upper crust" demeanor and apparent ruthlessness among his weaknesses.[30] The importance of these qualities was confirmed by Kemp, who argued, with evidence from his Melbourne survey, that the electorate demanded strong leadership, policy making based on wide discussion, and egalitarian attitudes in social relations. Fraser responded by giving the electorate all of these things—or rather the appearance of them. Strength of leadership was encapsulated in the party's slogan "Liberal—Doing the Job"; wide discussion was symbolized by the uranium debate; and Fraser was

[30] *Mirror*, November 23, 1977, p. 2; *News*, November 23, 1977, p. 7.

portrayed, with the help of the media, as the easy-going, gregarious leader his intimates knew him to be. He was pictured wearing an Eastern Suburbs football jersey, pulling beers in Easts' club, driving racing cars, acting the clown at a carnival to launch Victoria's fitness campaign, and so on.

Whitlam, according to Kemp, "missed badly" on egalitarianism. Certainly the Liberals' private research suggested that voters saw Whitlam as arrogant and, in the aftermath of Kerr and Lynch, as a mud-slinger. Even the majority of the Labor voters identified in these surveys disapproved. His support was confined to the hard-core Labor vote, those who said there was "no chance at all" that they might vote for another party. Though the number who felt "Mr. Fraser's Liberal Party" had "let the electorate down" was no smaller than the number who felt "Mr. Whitlam's Labor Party" had "let the electorate down," the attack on the opposition was more widely based and more sharply focused. The government's critics were drawn mostly from Labor's ranks. Except on the issue of employment their barbs were too widely scattered to cause the government much discomfort. Labor's critics, on the other hand, were drawn not just from the ranks of L-NCP voters but from Labor ranks as well.

On the specifics of where "Mr. Whitlam's Labor Party had let the electorate down," the proportion referring to Labor's "economic mismanagement" or "profligate spending"—memories of its days in office—rose in the course of the campaign from one-in-five to two-in-five. About 5 percent mentioned the loans affair. On open-ended questions the Liberal party's "Memories" ads were mentioned by over 60 percent of respondents. "Memories," as Eggleton later wrote, "may go down as one of the best-remembered advertisements ever produced in an Australian election campaign."[31]

The Labor Party

The Labor Secretariat was as quick as the Liberal Secretariat to assess the chances for an early election. In March 1977 the national secretary, David Combe, warned the party that there would be an election later in the year. The organizational wing of the party, including a majority of the members of the Executive, believed an election in 1977 to be no more than a possibility. In May, the state secretaries and the Campaign Committee, led by Combe, started discussing the mechanics of organizing a campaign.

---

[31] Tony Eggleton, "The 1977 Campaign: A Liberal Secretariat Viewpoint," March 1978, p. 9. (A mimeographed document prepared for publication in a student newspaper.)

In March, Combe had argued that unemployment was likely to be so bad by 1978 that the government would surely be tempted to go to the people early. That an early election was on the cards had been confirmed by a number of events in Canberra. Following the reelection in mid-February of the coalition in Western Australia, Vic Garland, an M.P. from Perth, had been overheard in Kings Hall (the parliamentary vestibule) telling a colleague that an early election was being considered. Garland had contacted Fraser suggesting that the result in Western Australia was a guide to a federal poll, and Fraser had assured him that an early election had been "under active consideration for some time." A few miles away in Fishwyck, the Liberal party's printer, it was understood, had already been alerted.

Combe refused to accept that the government's referendum in May was intended to avoid an early election or to delay it as long as possible—the official line given to journalists. Fraser, of course, had not committed the government to an early poll; but neither had he forsworn it. Labor had sought legal advice on whether an election could be held on the existing boundaries. In March the government introduced legislation for a redistribution; in October it was passed. Senator Doug McClelland's argument that the Liberals would not have time to carry out the redistribution was treated with skepticism within the Secretariat.

There were many in the parliamentary party who refused to take Combe's warning at face value. Convinced that Labor could not win with Whitlam, they read Combe's statement as an attempt to secure Whitlam's hold on the leadership. If the party agreed that an early election was likely, a challenge to the leadership would be unlikely.

Combe's critics conflated effect and intention. In doing so they not only misread his statement in the immediate sense but misjudged his general position as well. Since the days of Mick Young, the secretary had owed his position not to the support of a particular faction that would stick by him through thick and thin but to his ability to boost Labor's parliamentary representation. It would therefore have been more rational, though not necessarily more accurate, for the caucus to have read Combe's statement as a plea to have Whitlam dumped, and dumped quickly. For like his critics within the party, and Labor's critics without, Combe privately agreed that Whitlam's continuing leadership made it less likely that Labor would regain office.

While in public Combe argued that an election late in 1977 would be "unnecessary and improper," his private concern was that "two years would be too short a period of time for the Party to achieve forgiveness within the electorate and too short a period of time for patience with the Government to be exhausted"; in short, "that Fraser could not lose it and Labor could not regain sufficient credibility to win it."[32]

A Research Hiatus. It was not only Whitlam's leadership that provided problems for Labor strategists during the first half of 1977. There was, above all, the uncertainty about whether he would still be the leader at the next election. The choice lay between Whitlam, the darling of the party's rank and file, and Hayden, a possible election winner (see Table 7-3) whose defeat of Whitlam might cause massive disaffection within the party. The choice was not settled until the end of May, when Whitlam survived Hayden's challenge by the narrowest of margins.

The uncertainty cost time. The party conducted no surveys of public opinion before June on the grounds that Whitlam might be replaced as leader; even the planning for any research in June or July was curtailed on the grounds that a new leader would be too recently installed for any reading of the electorate's reactions to have meaning.

Again, no research was likely to be undertaken without the approval of the Federal Executive, a body that met only once every three months and was usually preoccupied with some special issue (such as the situation within a particular state branch). In the wake of the 1975 campaign, which was believed to have left the party up to $500,000 in debt, the Executive was more concerned to raise funds than to spend them. For the federal party the principal source of funds was the states. But contributions from the states failed to raise the required sums.

After 1975, and with the enthusiastic support of the National Secretariat, the states spent money on their own research. In at least one state this included money donated during the 1975 campaign but not forwarded to Canberra for what was judged to be a hopeless cause. In 1976, elections were held in Victoria, New South Wales, and Tasmania; in 1977, in Western Australia, Queensland, Victoria (the Greensborough by-election), and the Northern Territory. For each of these elections survey research was commissioned by the state branch.

Labor's surveys were done by ANOP, and both the party and journalists sometimes treated the firm's public polls as if they had been commissioned by the ALP. Party strategists took note of the

---

[32] "Report of the ALP National Secretary, David Combe, on the 1977 Federal Election Campaign," p. 3.

TABLE 7-3
Support for Whitlam and Hayden as Labor Leader, April and June 1977
(in percentages)

	April 1977	June 1977
Whitlam	37	40
Hayden	50	43
Neither	2	2
Undecided	11	14

NOTE: The survey questions were, in April, "Who has a better chance of leading the Labor party back into power in the Federal Parliament—Mr. Whitlam or Mr. Hayden?"; and in June, whether Mr. Whitlam or Mr. Hayden would attract more support as leader of the opposition (the exact wording was not released). Figures may not add to 100 percent because of rounding.
SOURCE: APOP Poll Nos. 01/4/77, 03/6/77.

results published by the other polls as well. They had high regard for both APOP and Saulwick's *Age* poll but less for Morgan Gallup. Indeed, following the publication during the campaign of a Morgan poll purporting to show that the coalition's support had jumped from 40 to 47 percent while the ALP's had slumped from 45 to 40 in the course of a week, the party circulated to Labor candidates a four-page critique of Morgan's methods and history.[33] The circular concluded by recommending two pollsters (neither of which had ever been retained by the party) and by warning for the sake of morale that even these were likely to underestimate Labor's final vote:

> If opinion polls are to be taken seriously between now and December 10, the McNair Anderson poll [APOP] and those published in the *Age* and the *Sydney Morning Herald* are generally conceded to be far more reliable, but there will be a number of "sleepers" in this election which will not be recorded in any public opinion poll.
> They certainly will not be running against Labor.

Unlike the Liberal party, Labor's National Secretariat did not subscribe to Morgan's computer sheets.

---

[33] "Secrets of Morgan Gallup Poll Revealed," Australian Labor Party 1977 National Campaign Bulletin [c. November 18, 1977]. Whitlam had openly attacked the Morgan poll during the 1975 election. Terence W. Beed, "Opinion Polling and the Elections," in Howard R. Penniman, ed., *Australia at the Polls* (Washington, D.C.: American Enterprise Institute, 1977), p. 234.

The party's pollster provided the states with tabulated data, written reports, oral interpretation, and advice on strategy. Survey results were passed to the state branches through the state secretaries group (which included the national secretary) and through the National Campaign Committee, whose meetings were attended by both the market research and the advertising men.[34] State surveys, meanwhile, were of limited use to the National Campaign Committee. The only questions on federal politics regularly included in these surveys were items on voting intentions and satisfaction with the leaders, which added little to the information available from the major national polls. In 1977 only the surveys conducted for the ALP in Victoria in August contained material of much federal relevance. State research was certainly no substitute for research funded by the federal party.

The Budget and Industrial Conflict. The research plans sketched by the National Secretariat in February bore no fruit until September, despite the market researchers' warning that a research-based campaign needed a lead-time of six months. No fruit, that is, until after the party's federal conference in July and the presentation of the budget in August.

During August the National Campaign Committee agreed that an early election was imminent. It approved an advertising campaign proposal prepared by Mullins, Clarke, and Ralph from data gathered by the state branches, which "defined the issues as unemployment, broken promises, economic competence, the unions, and uranium."[35] In the second week of August the party's first advertisement appeared—a full page in the national press, signposting a press conference at which Whitlam and Hayden would launch a plan "To Get Australia Working Again."

The Campaign Committee, worried that the government was going to either run on the budget or provoke a violent industrial confrontation as the excuse for an election, decided to commission national research. This research concentrated on the impact of the August budget, specifically the tax cuts heralded for February 1978 and the government's tougher industrial line highlighted in August by the Commonwealth (Employment Provisions) Act. This act gave the Commonwealth government power to sack or suspend any of its

---

[34] The committee comprised the party's officers and its four parliamentary leaders.

[35] "Report on Controlled Paid Media," Appendix (ii) to the "Report on the 1977 Election Campaign to the Federal Executive," p. 2.

employees who went on strike and to lay off employees whose jobs had been affected by other workers' strikes. The details of the survey, including the wording of the questions, were left to Combe and the party's pollster. A sample of 1,200 living in capital cities was chosen to allow speedy interviewing and rapid processing of results. The fieldwork was completed in the last two weeks of September.

The results, reported orally to the Campaign Committee, were mixed but they did bring the party some aid and comfort. The public's reaction to the budget was not as bad as earlier APOP or Morgan polls had suggested (see Table 7–4), but awareness of the tax concessions was still low. About one-third of those who approved of the budget thought it the "best that could be managed under difficult circumstances" or "not as severe as expected," and this was double the number mentioning tax concessions. Asked how the tax cuts would affect them personally, six out of ten respondents claimed they would make no difference. Those who said they would be better off were no more numerous than those who said they would be worse off; and those who said they would be better off were concentrated among the higher income groups.

Industrial relations were covered by three questions. Forty-two percent judged strikes to have gotten worse over the past year or so. The number who thought things had improved was the same as the

TABLE 7–4

REACTIONS TO THE PRE-ELECTION BUDGET, AUGUST–SEPTEMBER 1977
(in percentages)

Reaction to the Budget	ANOP	APOP	Morgan
Good/very satisfied/somewhat satisfied	47	32	12
Bad/somewhat dissatisfied/very dissatisfied	31	39	24
No opinion/neither satisfied nor dissatisfied/average budget	22	29	52

NOTE: ANOP asked: "Thinking about the budget that the federal government brought down a few weeks ago. Overall, was it a good budget or a bad budget?" N=1,200, capital cities only, September 17–24, 1977. APOP showed voters a card listing five possible degrees of satisfaction or dissatisfaction and asked them to state how satisfied they were overall with the recent budget in terms of its effect on Australia (the exact wording was not released). N=1,995, September 3–10, 1977. Morgan asked: "Altogether, would you say the Federal budget was a good budget, an average budget, or a bad budget?" N=2,075, August 20–27, 1977.
SOURCE: ANOP; APOP Poll No. 02/9/77; Morgan Gallup Poll, No. 179.

TABLE 7-5
Voters' Perceptions of the Outlook for Labor Relations, September–November 1977
(in percentages)

Outlook	APOP September 1977	Morgan November 1977
Strikes and disputes will increase	74	57
No change	3	17
Strikes and disputes will decrease	17	15
Undecided	6	11

NOTE:
- APOP asked, "Over the next few months, do you expect that Australia will have a declining or increasing number of strikes or industrial disputes?" N=1,995.
- Morgan asked, "Will 1978 be a year of strikes and industrial disputes, or a year of industrial peace?" N=2,352.

SOURCE: APOP Poll No. 05/9/77; Morgan Gallup Poll, Poll Nos. 505, 520A, November-December 1977.

number who thought things had not changed. An APOP survey conducted at the same time indicated that three voters out of four expected strikes and industrial disputes to increase "in the next few months." In November, according to a Morgan poll, 1978 was expected to be a bad year for industrial disputes (see Table 7–5).

On the question of what the government should do in the face of strikes by its own employees, opinion divided evenly between those who thought the government should have the power to suspend or dismiss its employees and those who thought it should not. The *Age* poll and APOP both reported a split more favorable to the government but a split nonetheless (see Table 7–6). The 44 percent who backed the government in Labor's poll expressed themselves not in antiunion or antistrike terms but in terms of being anti-public servant. The 47 percent who opposed the government did not defend public servants as such but, in response to an open-ended follow-up question, appealed instead to the more general principles of the "right to strike" (40 percent), "freedom of speech" (20 percent), and "human rights" (15 percent).

The vulnerability of public servants was already known to the government through a Morgan Gallup poll taken in July.[36] Over half the Morgan sample agreed that too many people were employed by

---

[36] Morgan Gallup Poll No. 172, July 9-16, 1977.

TABLE 7–6

ATTITUDES TO COMMONWEALTH EMPLOYEES ACT, SEPTEMBER 1977

(in percentages)

	ANOP	Age	APOP (a)	APOP (b)
For	44	54	55	42
Against	47	43	40	53
Undecided	9	4	5	5

NOTE:
- The ANOP question was: "The Federal government has recently passed a Bill in Parliament which enables the government to suspend or dismiss Commonwealth Public Servants who take industrial action. Do you agree or disagree with this Bill?" N=1,200, capital cities only, September 17-24, 1977.
- The *Age* question was: "The Government has recently passed legislation which will allow it to suspend or dismiss Government employees who are striking and to stand-down [lay off] Government employees who cannot work as a result of the strike. Do you yourself approve of this legislation? disapprove of this legislation?" N=2,000, September 24-25, 1977.
- APOP asked: "Do you agree or disagree that the Federal Government should have power (a) to suspend or dismiss Government employees who take industrial action? (b) to stand-down Government employees whose work is affected by a dispute?"

SOURCE: ANOP; *Age*, October 22, 1977; APOP Poll No. 07/9/77.

the federal government (as against too few or about enough). Some 63 percent felt that federal employees did not "work as hard" as workers in nongovernment jobs; 52 percent thought they were paid more than nongovernment employees, and 68 percent said they had more "fringe benefits," such as time off, holidays, sick leave, pensions, and the like.

What could be done to lessen the number of strikes? Labor's poll showed 40 percent to be pro-conciliation (secret ballots, arbitration, collective bargaining conferences between labor and capital) or anti-big stick. A further 20 percent were pro-big stick or anti-conciliation, calling for penalties and fines, the abolition of unions, and the jailing —even the shooting—of strikers.

On this evidence, the government had no more hope of winning votes through industrial confrontation than it had of winning votes through tax cuts. In the event of an industrial conflict and the emergence of strikes as an issue[37] there might even be votes to be won by

---

[37] Neither Labor nor Liberal strategists expected strikes to be an issue in the absence of a major strike. *National Times*, October 24-29, 1977, p. 16.

Labor, provided it did not take a divisive stand. People believed the strike situation to have deteriorated (notwithstanding statistics which showed the actual situation to have improved) and wanted governments to be firmer. But this did not mean (contrary to Morgan's research) a bout of "union bashing." If the government's legislation were to be an issue, Labor should come forward and criticize some unions—to show that it too disapproved of "bad unions"[38]—at the same time denouncing heavy-handed solutions of the kind that could be associated with the government.

In November, fearing that Fraser was about to fight the election on an anti-union "law and order" platform, the party publicized its research. Both Whitlam and Hawke, in their comments on the outcome of the by-election for the state seat of Greensborough in Victoria, argued that the swing against the Liberals confirmed research which showed that the antiunion moves during the power strike in Victoria would rebound against the government.[39] Research in Victoria, as in Greensborough specifically, was reported to have shown 54 percent dissatisfied with the government's industrial relations record and 60 percent believing the power strike to have been wholly or partly justified.[40] An earlier *Age* poll reported that 52 percent of the people interviewed thought Hawke's involvement in settling strikes constructive as against 19 percent for Fraser.[41]

As a result of Hawke's standing in the polls[42] the Campaign Committee used him in a "have bag, will travel" commercial. This featured Hawke, the industrial trouble-shooter, living out of a suitcase in motel rooms, prepared to travel anywhere in the cause of industrial peace. The government would have had difficulty matching this had the unions ever become an issue; the publicity Labor gave its own research helped ensure that they did not.

---

[38] As in New South Wales, the idea was to give advance warning to the unions in question so they could discount the attacks.

[39] E. G. Whitlam, "Greensborough By-Election," press release, Sydney, November 6, 1977, No. 152; *Australian Financial Review*, November 7, 1977, p. 4; *Australian*, November 7, 1977, p. 1.

[40] *Age*, November 9, 1977, p. 5; *Inside Canberra*, November 11, 1977, p. 1. Two surveys were sponsored by the Victoria branch of the ALP: an urban-provincial study of Melbourne, Bendigo, Geelong; and a small survey in Greensborough itself, principally to see how much money was worth sinking into the campaign.

[41] *Age*, July 25, 1977; *Sydney Morning Herald*, July 25, 1977.

[42] According to the Morgan Gallup poll, for instance, in June and again in August, 57 percent approved of the way Hawke was handling his job as ACTU president. Morgan Gallup Poll No. 168, June 11-18, 1977, and No. 179, August 20-27, 1977.

Uranium. The industrial issue most feared by Labor was a dispute over the export of uranium. The party was divided over uranium. Some branches, notably those in Victoria, were opposed to the mining or export of uranium; others, like the Queensland branch, were not. The party's Federal Conference in Perth had adopted a "wait and see" policy and decided to launch a program of public education on the difficulties and dangers associated with uranium. Following the conference the party had made uranium one of its two campaign themes, adopting the slogan "Uranium—Play it Safe" and commissioning four television commercials at a cost of $8,000-$9,000 each.

While the issue of uranium itself was not covered in the party's national research it was touched on in other surveys including surveys for the Victoria and Northern Territory branches. It also received considerable coverage in the public polls. As the election drew near, all the polls on uranium showed a slide away from the government's position. The government was still ahead but the margin had been cut. ANOP described the shift as "an unusually rapid one." On issues of "social importance, like abortion, prison reform, and homosexuality, the drift in public opinion was usually only 0.5 percent to 1 percent annually, but the antiuranium movement had public opinion changing at a rate of 3 percent or 4 percent a month."[43] The shift was confirmed by the ALP's surveys in Victoria. An August survey put support for uranium at 55 percent; in Greensborough, in late October, the figure was 46 percent.[44]

How important an issue was uranium likely to be? ANOP was the first of the public opinion polls to pose the question. In the first two weeks of October ANOP asked, "What is the most important problem facing the Federal Government?" and "If there was an early Federal election for the House of Representatives this year, what do you think the most important issue would be in the campaign?"[45] These questions are clearly distinct: they are not alternative measures of the same thing. The first invites voters to indicate what they, personally, think the government should be concerned about; the second invites voters to more or less guess the issues the parties or the media might, at some later date, be pushing. The answers to the "problems" question put uranium into third place, with 12 percent of the responses; on the "issues" question it came in first, with 35

---

[43] Alice Bates [pseud.], "The Election Issue That Never Was," *New Journalist*, no. 30 (April 1978), p. 5.

[44] *Sydney Morning Herald*, November 8, 1977, p. 8; November 9, 1977, p. 14.

[45] ANOP, "ANOP-National Times/Four Corners Attitude Study," press release [c. October 13, 1977].

TABLE 7-7
Attitudes toward the Mining and Export of Uranium, by Sex, September–October 1977
(in percentages; differences in percentage points)

Sex	Favor Mining and Export of Uranium	Oppose Mining and Export of Uranium	Undecided
Men			
Age	57	39	5
APOP	57	35	8
Women			
Age	49	44	7
APOP	46	40	14
Difference			
Age	8	5	2
APOP	11	5	6

NOTE: The *Age* poll was conducted September 24-25, APOP's October 1-8.
SOURCE: *Age*, October 17, 1977; APOP Poll No. 02/10/77.

percent. The sponsors of this survey, the *National Times* and "Four Corners," published the results of the "issues" question but ignored the results of the "problems" question. "A new poll shows uranium replacing unemployment as the dominant issue in an early campaign," was how the *National Times* introduced ANOP's study.[46]

Apprised of the situation, Combe still thought the issue should be pushed. Not only was the tide running against the government but the biggest shift in opinion "had been among women, the middle class and the middle aged, those sections of the community from which Labor usually has most difficulty in attracting votes."[47] On industrial issues the party's research had shown women to be less tough-minded than men; on uranium the differences were even more marked. As both the *Age* poll and APOP showed, men were significantly more in favor of the mining and export of uranium than were women; women were more opposed and more uncertain (see Table 7–7). Among the under twenty-fives the difference between men and women was reported to be sixteen percentage points.[48] Sex differences

---
[46] *National Times*, October 17-23, 1977, pp. 8-9.
[47] Bates, "The Election Issue That Never Was," p. 5.
[48] *National Times*, November 14-19, 1977, p. 4; *Sun*, December 6, 1977, p. 5. For Greensborough see *Mirror*, November 8, 1977, p. 11.

TABLE 7-8

RESULTS OF ANOP SURVEY ON URANIUM, BY PARTY PREFERENCE

(in percentages)

Time Allowed for Debate on Uranium Has Been:	Total	Party Preference		
		L-NCP	ALP	AD
Too short	46	29	54	59
About right	32	45	27	22
Too long	14	19	12	14
Unsure	8	7	7	5

NOTE: The survey question was "Thinking about the amount of time that has been allowed for public debate on the uranium question—has it been too long a time, too short a time or about right?"

SOURCE: "ANOP-National Times/Four Corners Attitude Study," October 1/2-8/9, 1977.

of this magnitude are rare indeed. At the same time women under twenty-five were, in the words of the party secretary, "underproducing" for Labor. If the party were to make women its target, uranium was the issue to play up. Labor research had discovered that those opposed to the mining and export of uranium were more likely to give reasons for their position than those in favor, who generally fell back on the government's right to decide. This was interpreted to mean that voters opposed to uranium felt more strongly about the issue than those in favor.

There were also the Australian Democrats to consider. On uranium, the distribution of opinion among AD voters was closer to that of Labor voters than to that of L-NCP voters (see Tables 7-8 and 7-9). The number of AD voters was increasing and they were certainly regarded as strong on the issue. Trends in the distribution of AD second preferences suggested a movement towards Labor.[49] As this became clear, Whitlam's speeches came to emphasize the similarities between Labor and the Democrats.

But the party was so divided on uranium and Combe's authority as campaign director was so circumscribed that Labor's fourth uranium commercial, arguably the best, was held back. This was a thirty-second television spot showing two babies playing with a hand grenade while a voice warned that the mining and export of uranium played "with the future of generations to come." In Sydney it had

---

[49] See Goot and Beed, Chapter 6 in this volume, Table 6-4 and Figure 6-3.

TABLE 7-9

RESULTS OF MORGAN GALLUP SURVEY ON URANIUM, BY PARTY PREFERENCE
(in percentages)

Mining and Export of Uranium Worries Respondent	Total	Party Preference		
		L–NCP	ALP	AD
Yes	62	54	70	71
No	31	40	23	23
Can't say	7	6	7	6

NOTE: The survey question was, "Is there anything about the mining and export of uranium that worries you?"
SOURCE: Morgan Gallup Poll Nos. 492 and 493, October 1977.

been screened by the party's market research consultant before about five groups of ten women. Half had been "favorably disposed," 30 percent said "it makes you think," and 20 percent were reported as feeling "brutally sick" or "horrified."[50] It was the only Labor advertisement to be tested. Yet despite "proof that the advertisement was a winner" the campaign committee held off until the last desperate week. A party official was reported to have commented that those who voted not to screen it were by and large the people who took a pro-mining stand.[51]

Uranium, of course, was not a consensus issue. But the party attempted to wrap it in consensus rhetoric. In the television overture to the policy speech Don Dunstan, the South Australian premier, told voters that uranium "should be above politics." In another commercial he praised South Australian M.P.s for voting on the issue "independent of party affiliation and according to their conscience." The voters should "vote as the Liberals did in South Australia," to "play it safe."[52] Tom Uren, the party's deputy leader, a man of the left at the forefront of the antiuranium movement, accepted the fact that he rated poorly in the polls. He embraced the idea of the Dunstan commercial, but he knew that if he did not the chance of uranium's being an issue would diminish.

Dunstan himself had changed his mind on uranium; and in September at the South Australian election he had seen the issue

---

[50] *Mirror*, December 6, 1977, p. 11.

[51] Bates, "The Election Issue That Never Was."

[52] For example, *National Times*, November 21-26, 1977, p. 23. The two minute commercial was described as "the longest yet seen in political advertising in Australia." *B & T Weekly*, vol. 28 (November 17, 1977), p. 1.

come "upon us slowly, from nowhere, in about three weeks," creating a "vague and unarticulated disquiet."[53] Dunstan's public standing was very high. During the year he was variously rated as the "most effective State Premier" and, with Sir Robert Menzies, the man the public most admired.[54]

In its final address of the campaign the party referred to uranium as the number three issue in the polls. But Labor's soft-pedalling may, in the end, have cost it votes. Those who felt strongly about uranium, more strongly than Dunstan, may have found the Australian Democrats more attractive. Chipp made his position clear: "The Australian Democrats are the only party with a policy of unequivocal opposition to uranium mining. The Fraser Government supports uranium mining. Mr. Whitlam and Mr. Keating are now equivocating on the issue."[55]

Unemployment. It was to be unemployment, not uranium, that consumed most of Labor's energy.[56] From the campaign's earliest days until the National Press Club luncheon at the end, unemployment was Whitlam's major theme. The number of unemployed was higher than at any time since the thirties; no government since the war had survived with unemployment at even half this level. Not to run on unemployment would have been to ignore the media, to betray the party's working-class base, and, so it seemed, to defy the polls.

Unemployment became everyone's issue, but for differing reasons. There were those, traditionalists included, for whom unemployment had to be the first priority of any campaign. At a time when so many were out of work a Labor party worthy of the name had no choice. The question was not what would win votes but what was right.

Others, including a younger, university-educated coterie, close to the National Secretariat and to the journalists in the press gallery,[57]

---

[53] *Weekend Australian*, November 19-20, 1977, Mag. p. 4; November 26-27, 1977, Mag. p. 4. Dunstan's change of mind was also mentioned in his commercials.

[54] *Advertiser*, March 30, 1977; *Sun-News Pictorial*, September 17, 1977; *National Times*, October 24-29, p. 15.

[55] Policy speech, reprinted in Tim Hewat and David Wilson, *Don Chipp* (Camberwell: Widescope, 1978). For uranium, see p. 121.

[56] "Our brief to Mullins, Clarke and Ralph, our advertising agency was to concentrate on unemployment and the government's failure in this regard—this was done and done well." *Radical*, April/May 1978, p. 2.

[57] The gallery "became pro-Labor (or at least pro-Whitlam) in the late 1960s and early 1970s ... then anti-Fraser after 11 November 1975." David Solomon, *Inside the Australian Parliament* (Sydney: George Allen & Unwin, 1978), p. 156. The press gallery is made up of political journalists who cover Parliament and Commonwealth elections.

embraced unemployment as the major issue only by default. These were the men (and occasionally women) for whom the Whitlam years had been a turning point. Politically hard-headed, they had been attracted by Whitlam's choice of issues, his style, his physical presence. These were the things they wanted to recapture: a leader who could be marketed and with whom Labor could emerge as a party of government rather than a party of opposition. Campaigning on unemployment conjured up nothing so much as the cold drabness of Arthur Calwell's rhetoric. Unemployment was an unpleasantness; to campaign on it was to risk being labelled a whinger. But apart from unemployment what was there? After all, 1977 was not 1972: the party had to avoid programs that made it look like a free-spender. To campaign on government scandals would only work if the government were manifestly failing in other and more important areas and if the Labor party could not be tarred with the same brush. The accusations against Lynch were welcome, but Labor would benefit most by leaving them to the media.

Finally, there were those for whom almost any issue would do if it offered the chance of winning. By no means new to the party, they were interested in riding public opinion, not in challenging it. In recent years they had come to regard opinion polls and market research as the surest means to this end. Success in state elections had strengthened their hand and their assurance.

The polls allowed these three lines of thought to coalesce. With all the polls showing unemployment to be the main issue and the state of the economy second, the traditionalists felt vindicated and the Whitlamites were able to rationalize their failure to come up with any alternative. Those who would have been guided by the polls anyway now knew which way to go.

Labor strategists realized that many voters attributed the high level of unemployment to the unwillingness of the young to work, so any suggestion that the party was soft on shirkers had to be avoided. Instead the ALP advertising campaign set out to show that Labor wanted "Australia and Australians to get back to work." One commercial featured a businessman having to lay off workers, another showed a man qualified as an architectural draftsman reduced to driving taxis, another a young woman formerly with a "good job" in an advertising agency, now a cleaning woman, and another a struggling farmer; the message apparently was that Labor was sympathetic to the problems of businessmen, professionals, young women, and farmers—people not always known as Labor's supporters.

That Labor fought on unemployment did not mean, as Liberal officials believed, that the party was unaware of the attitudes underlying public concern. Party strategists realized that only a minority of voters believed the government had caused the unemployment. But they also knew that voters looked to the government to reduce unemployment and that on this score the government must be vulnerable. In Labor's Victorian survey, 71 percent of voters thought the government's handling of unemployment "bad" or "very bad"; apart from Medibank no other issue was as frequently named as a government failing. Voters thought the government had not done as well as Labor might do.

Whitlam's remedy for unemployment was the abolition of the payroll tax, which presupposed that labor costs in large firms were one of its principal causes. While Whitlam's understanding of the causes of unemployment may well have been informed by public opinion polls, the solution he offered was certainly not derived from public opinion research. For the first time since 1972 the ALP leader kept the policy speech to himself until it was delivered. As Combe, a strong believer in market research, was bitterly to observe: "Despite the several meetings of the National Executive which were held pre-election, at none of these were we able to have any meaningful discussion about what Labor would be proposing. That must never happen again."[58]

What Labor would have offered instead of Whitlam's pledge, of course, is another matter. In the televised prelude to the policy speech, prepared in ignorance of Whitlam's move on the payroll tax, there was hardly any explanation of the causes of unemployment (even in terms of the consequences of the government's anti-inflationary strategy). By way of solution, the party offered little more than vague pledges from Ralph Willis, shadow minister for industrial relations, to "create job opportunities" and to boost "the confidence" of the young so that they would not drop out of the labor market (and into the unemployment statistics). While Whitlam's view of the causes of unemployment hardly challenged widespread anti-Labor and antiunion assumptions, his remedy certainly called for a period of public education longer than four weeks. In his rise to power, Whitlam himself had been the first to insist on that.

Leadership. In the advertising footage that preceded the policy speech, viewers were told that in public "acceptance and approval" Whitlam had the better of Fraser. This was a reference to the party's Septem-

---

[58] "Report of the ALP National Secretary," p. 4.

TABLE 7–10
POPULARITY OF WHITLAM AND FRASER, SEPTEMBER–DECEMBER 1977
(in percentages)

Response	Fraser			Whitlam		
	Sept.	Oct.	Dec.	Sept.	Oct.	Dec.
Satisfied	36	34	39	41	38	40
Dissatisfied	57	58	54	48	53	52
Unsure	7	8	7	11	9	8

NOTE: The survey question was, "Are you satisfied or dissatisfied with the job [Mr. Fraser, Mr. Whitlam] is doing as [Prime Minister, Leader of the Opposition]?"
SOURCE: ANOP: N=1,200, capital cities only, September 17-24, 1977; ANOP, "ANOP-National Times/Four Corners Campaign Study"; ANOP, "ANOP-National Times/Four Corners Attitude Study."

ber survey, which was confirmed by an ANOP survey in October (see Table 7–10). Research commissioned by the party's state branches covered the strengths and weaknesses of the state leaders. The national survey, less comprehensive, had only asked voters whether they were satisfied or dissatisfied with the job Whitlam or Fraser was doing.

In October, ANOP showed Labor to be ahead of the government on first preferences, and its campaign monitor of mid-November showed Labor to be ahead in two-party preferred terms as well.[59] But ANOP was not the only poll to raise Labor's hopes. In his reflections on Labor's defeat, Mick Young, an M.P. from South Australia and a member of the Federal Executive, admitted ruefully that throughout 1976 and 1977 "our moods ran hot and cold reading what the latest pollster said."[60] Of the campaign period in particular, David Combe wrote: "Regrettably many of us who had retained a realistic appraisal of our prospects did yield, however briefly, to the luxury of optimism in early November when the McNair and Morgan polls showed us winning and ANOP showed a close result."[61]

In its day-after-the-election study ANOP argued that Labor could never have won with Whitlam.[62] As early as 1976, the party

[59] ANOP, "ANOP-National Times/Four Corners Campaign Study," press release [December 2, 1977].
[60] *Australian*, December 24, 1977.
[61] "Report of the ALP National Secretary," p. 3.
[62] Rod Cameron, "The 1977 Federal Election," press release [c. December 11, 1977], discussed in Goot and Beed, "The Polls."

had been advised that it was most unlikely that Whitlam could ever recover enough credibility to win. This was confirmed, in September 1977, by a report so sensitive apparently that not even all the members of the executive knew of it. But Whitlam would have known he was always keen to know, and the worse the news the more it would have mattered. The news also reached other members of the caucus, some of whom tried to have the New South Wales Labor government offer Whitlam a position, possibly on the judiciary—a move that would have left the leadership open for Hayden.[63]

After the election some party officers were to complain that they had not been informed of the liability Whitlam's continuing leadership constituted. But they could hardly deny that the party's advertising had gone out of its way to play down the leader and play up the team. Indeed nothing like this had been done since 1966, when the party had been led by Arthur Calwell. The team Labor advertisements promoted was not the team the voters were being asked to vote into office. Dunstan and Hawke, together with Hayden (treasurer in the last Whitlam government) and Wran (premier of New South Wales), had two things in common: prominent positions in the Labor movement and high ratings in the polls. In March 1977 and again on the eve of the challenge to Whitlam in May, Dunstan, Hawke, and Hayden had emerged as equally popular alternatives to Whitlam as leader of the opposition (see Table 7–11). In Labor's final telecast Hawke and Hayden were referred to as "arguably the most respected political figures in Australia." Dunstan and now Wran were the most popular of the premiers.[64]

Of the four—Hayden, Hawke, Dunstan, and Wran—only Hayden would have held office in any Labor government that might have been elected. In the public's estimate of who would make the best treasurer he easily outshone Lynch and almost all the other candidates combined. Indeed, in his home state of Queensland, Hayden's popularity outran Whitlam's.[65]

---

[63] *National Times*, October 21, 1978, p. 12.

[64] In March, in response to an APOP question "Who is the most effective State Premier in Australia?" 39 percent said Dunstan, 18 percent Bjelke Petersen, 14 percent Wran, 9 percent Hamer, 5 percent Court, 1 percent Neilson. At midyear Dunstan was approved by 75-80 percent of South Australians, Wran by 73 percent in New South Wales, and Court by 59 percent in Western Australia, according to the Morgan Gallup poll. APOP March 1977; Morgan Gallup Poll No. 485, July 1977.

[65] *Sun-News Pictorial*, October 14, 1977, p. 5; *Sydney Morning Herald*, October 31, 1977, p. 1; ANOP, "ANOP-National Times/Four Corners Campaign Study"; *Age*, December 3, 1977, p. 10.

TABLE 7-11

POPULARITY OF LABOR LEADERS, MARCH–MAY 1977

Leader	March 26–April 2	May 14–May 21
Whitlam	19	18
Hayden	26	19
Dunstan	21	20
Hawke	14	20
Wran	6	7
Uren	<1	1
Other	6	5
Don't know	10	10

NOTE: The survey question was "If you were a Labor voter and helping to choose the Leader of the Opposition who would you prefer?" Figures may not add to 100 percent because of rounding.
SOURCE: Morgan Gallup Poll Nos. 156 and 164.

That the media would spotlight Whitlam was something party strategists could hardly hope to avoid. Whitlam's announcement that the party would abolish the payroll tax put paid to any chance that he might be simply one of a number of Labor leaders or frontbenchers featured in the campaign. In trying to explain and clarify Labor's taxation policies, the team of Whitlam, Hayden, and Hurford (shadow treasurer), far from neutralizing Whitlam, merely added to the liability. As ANOP's day-after-the-election study was to reveal, one-third of those who had considered switching from Labor had not done so because claims and counter-claims had left them confused.[66]

The National Country Party

The Liberal and National Country parties form a coalition to govern, and they present a joint government program, but they remain electoral rivals. While the main threat to the Liberal party comes from Labor, the NCP is threatened from both sides, Labor and Liberal. Moreover, the loss of a seat to the Liberals is twice as damaging to the NCP as the loss of a seat to Labor since it not only reduces the party's absolute strength but also more sharply diminishes its relative strength within the coalition. At election time the Liberals and

---

[66] Cameron, "The 1977 Federal Election."

the NCP commission their own advertising. Their research is separately commissioned and the findings are closely guarded.[67]

In 1977 surveys were conducted for the federal branch of the party in two electorates, Calare in New South Wales and Indi in Victoria. The research was commissioned, at the behest of the party leader, in October shortly before the election was announced. The decision to conduct research in only two electorates reflected the pressures of time. The party's former marketing director, Barry Cassell, had failed to persuade Doug Anthony that a continuing research program was something the party could not afford to be without. Anthony, however, was warming to such research, partly because he saw it as a way of checking the performance of individual M.P.s. He shared the belief that in the country the caliber of individual candidates is a significant factor in electoral swings. The party was particularly concerned with those seats—ten in all—in which there were to be "three-cornered" contests; that is, seats in which both coalition partners, as well as Labor, would be running candidates. In 1977, Indi, Calare, and Capricornia (in Queensland) were the seats in which sitting NCP members were opposed by the Liberal party as well as Labor.

Calare had been won by the (then) Country party in a 1960 by-election. Previously held by the Liberal party, it was not contested by the Liberals again until 1975. On that occasion, the Country party held off the challenge fairly comfortably, even though it had to rely on Liberal preferences to do so. In 1977 there were changes in the electoral boundary. Calare, once a safe seat, was now marginal, not only for the NCP but for the government. Indi had traditionally been a much safer seat for the NCP than Calare and its boundaries had not been altered. But the Liberal party, which had not contested the seat since 1969, decided to try again, and Anthony was concerned about the image of the local member, R. M. (Mac) Holten.

The survey was placed with the Melbourne firm, Spectrum Research, by the party's advertising agent, Compton Advertising. The party had wanted surveys in seven seats—including Capricornia, where the sitting member, Colin Carige, was conducting a survey of his own—but in the time available Spectrum could only manage two. Spectrum did the quantitative work first, the qualitative second.

In the first phase 130 telephone interviews were conducted with voters in each of the two electorates. Though interviewees were told

---

[67] At an earlier election a copy of a survey conducted for the Liberal party by Morgan had been mailed to the NCP. On being informed of this Anthony issued instructions that Morgan never again be employed by the NCP.

that the questions would only take eight or ten minutes, the interview schedules were much longer than those used by other parties. The respondents were asked how they had voted in 1975 and in 1972 and how they would vote if there were an election in December (a hypothetical question in the absence of information about which parties would be running candidates); what they thought of the local member and local problems; what they thought of the federal party and national problems; which of a series of favorable and unfavorable descriptions they would apply to the party leaders; and their age and marital and work status, as well as the occupation of the head of the household. Much of the interviewing focused on the qualities and performance of the local member and the three party leaders. There were twenty-one questions on each. The patchy reporting of the results, however, made comparisons difficult: only positive ratings appear to have been leaked for Anthony and only negative ones for Whitlam.[68]

Phase two consisted of three group discussions in each electorate. The first two groups comprised "working" men and women aged eighteen to twenty-eight and thirty-five to sixty respectively. The third group was made up of "nonworking" women eighteen to twenty-eight and thirty-five to sixty years of age. The areas covered were much the same as in the first phase. The sample, drawn from phase one, was deliberately biased towards swinging voters—those who had changed parties since 1972 or felt they might change, those who had voted for minor parties, and those who had not voted before.

A report of the research, dated November 9, was handed to Anthony, not to the party organization. Copies were not forwarded to either of the local members, nor were they apprised of the results. In the past, the results of such surveys had been disseminated, but this time the leader was determined to ensure restricted access to the report, thereby avoiding damage within the party as well as difficulties with its coalition partner. Anthony and the party's advertising agents ignored the figures on voting intentions and looked instead at the recommendations. On a number of matters, however, the party was hemmed in by coalition policy—a point the electorate had perceived. Anthony, having taken policy initiatives during the 1972 campaign (notably on oil pricing), had subsequently carried the blame in some quarters for the coalition's defeat. Once bitten, twice shy.

The policy speech started with the economic issues: unemployment, inflation, interest rates, wages, and government spending.

---

[68] *Age*, November 21, 1977, p. 9.

Whitlam had caused the rot; only the government could protect "your future," "freedom," and the "Australian way of life." The coalition was described as the "Fraser/Anthony government" (in contrast to the Whitlam government), emphasizing the importance of the leaders and the idea of Anthony as an equal partner.[69] Throughout the speech, the National Country party (the National party in Queensland) was referred to by its former name, the Country party. This emphasized its loyalty to the country against the ambitions of some of its branches, notably Queensland, to take the party into the cities.

At the 1975 election, the Queensland branch had commissioned some research of its own and had gone very much its own way.[70] In 1977, even though federal research did not touch on either of the vulnerable Queensland seats (Leichhardt and Capricornia), the Queensland branch commissioned no research and was content with the national effort, though it did place advertisements (other than how-to-vote instructions) in the Brisbane *Courier Mail*. These were devoted exclusively to attacking Whitlam: "He took away Australia's pride, now he wants to take away your money." In the end, the party lost Indi but held Calare. Riverina and Capricornia, seats that had looked more vulnerable than Calare, were lost as well.

The Minor Parties

The Australian Democrats. The Democrats carried out a very large survey in 1977, weeks before any election was announced, and they carried it out themselves. While the survey might have given the leadership a broad indication of public attitudes to particular issues, including some not covered by the commercial opinion polls, this was not—in Chipp's view—its principal purpose. The party wanted to give its members something to do. It had been established along participatory lines and its members were already determining policies, even the party name, by a plebiscitary process. A survey of voters extended this sense of participation.

---

[69] Doug Anthony, *Policy Speech*, n. d., John McEwen House, Canberra. For evidence that the appearance of a subservient relationship between the NCP and the Liberal party was damaging the NCP in Farrer and in Anthony's own seat of Richmond, see Elaine Thompson and Tom Wheelwright, "An Analysis of the 1977 Federal Election in NSW," *Politics*, vol. 13 (May 1978), pp. 143, 145.

[70] Margaret Bridson Cribb, "The Country Party," in Howard R. Penniman, ed., *Australia at the Polls* (Washington, D.C.: American Enterprise Institute, 1977), p. 154.

The survey was also designed to enable the party to publicize itself and to exemplify its principles in action. The ballot to decide the party's name closed on August 22; the result was announced on September 1—just as the survey began. The interviewers introduced themselves as members of "Don Chipp's (Australian) Democrats," then explained that Chipp wanted to know people's views on a number of issues, that the party was committed to the view that political decisions should reflect the wishes of the electorate. The party stood for a "nonconfrontationist" political style: the questionnaire avoided any reference to parties or leaders; it concentrated on issues.

The survey was a test of the membership's commitment to party work and a test of the party's "ability to organize a very simple exercise at Member, Branch and Divisional level, with a reasonable timetable." Party funds were limited—not least by the leadership's own belief that parties should declare the source of their funds. A survey drawing on the voluntary efforts of the members could be carried out for less than $600—a sum that would not have bought the party answers to more than two of its questions in a commercial omnibus survey.

The idea for the survey originated with Bill Dart, a Melbourne charter flight operator and one of the party's two national vice-presidents. In July he mentioned the idea to Chipp and drafted twelve statements covering a wide range of issues. On each issue voters were to be asked whether they agreed strongly, agreed, disagreed, disagreed strongly, or were neutral/undecided. Chipp and the national executive approved of the format and of three of the questions—uranium, party funding, and child endowment (the family allowance paid regularly to mothers). For the other nine Chipp substituted nine of his own (see Table 7–12). By the beginning of September, Dart had the survey under way.

Questionnaires for 23,000 interviews and instruction sheets for 2,300 interviewers were mailed to the party's 120 branches spread across each of the states and the territories. Interviewers were asked to conduct ten interviews wherever they could—at work places, clubs, and so on. The niceties of systematic sampling were ignored. Each branch was to tabulate its own results and to return these and the questionnaires by the end of the third week in September.

About 700 members took part and 7,168 interviews were completed. A number of members disapproved of the questions and declined to participate; some participated but refused to ask all the questions. Some of the branches were very slow to submit returns; others failed altogether. The best response, predictably, came from

TABLE 7–12

The Australian Democrats' Nationwide Survey, September 1977
(in percentages)

Item	Agree	Disagree	No Opinion
1. Young parents in Australia should be able to transfer child endowment entitlement in a lump sum against the cost of a first home.	64	27	9
2. If a 35-hour week drastically reduced unemployment but greatly increased costs, would you accept a pro rata reduction in wages on a shorter working week?	42	47	11
3. Employers and trade unions should be sued in civil courts for breaches of agreement.	79	12	9
4. The threat of unemployment is deterring you from immediately purchasing consumer goods.	30	58	12
5. Direct taxes should be reduced before indirect taxes such as sales tax.	64	26	10
6. Money should be diverted from tertiary education to pre-natal care and pre-school facilities.	35	53	12
7. City people should pay more (up to 3 cents per call) so that country people can have the same telephone costs as city people.	38	52	10
8. All political parties should disclose all sources of funding.	89	7	4
9. Declared homosexuals of either sex should not be allowed to teach in schools.	31	58	11
10. Australia would be better served by the abolition of state governments and the creation of autonomous regional bodies responsible for such matters as health, welfare, and education.	40	46	14
11. The government's Welfare, Education, and Health departments provide service to the public which satisfies the applicants' needs.	41	47	12
12. Australia should not mine uranium until we find a totally safe way to handle the wastes.	65	27	8

SOURCE: "Report of the Australian Democrats on the AD Nationwide Survey No. 1-1977."

Chipp's home state, Victoria, where 1,774 interviews were completed. Western Australia (the state where the party was first founded) was next with 1,486; then Queensland 1,174; New South Wales 975; South Australia 967; the Australian Capital Territory 361; the Northern Territory 249; and Tasmania 193. The cost, including return postage but excluding services rendered without charge, was half the $600 budgeted. Dart judged the number of interviews insufficient "to achieve wide public recognition of the Democrats' public intentions to 'ask the people,'" but large enough to be representative of electoral opinion.

The results, weighted by state, were released on October 15 (see Table 7–12). Agreement was greatest on the disclosing of party funds, suing employers and trade unions for breaches of the law, a moratorium on uranium mining, a reduction in personal taxes before cuts in indirect taxes, and permitting child endowment to be paid in lump sums to finance first homes. The survey results gave Chipp some idea of the issues he could play up and alerted him to areas where he should be cautious.

In addition to the survey, votes of the membership were taken to determine party policy. For these, the arrangement of the ballots remained in the hands of the party's leaders. On the ballot for the party name, no fewer than fifty-six possibilities were listed; the provisional name, Australian Democrats, the choice of the Steering Committee, was placed at the top of the list and subsequently topped the poll.[71] On uranium, members were given four options—one unconditionally pro-uranium, three opposed:

(a) That uranium be exported without hindrance
(b) That uranium not be exported at all
(c) That there be a five-year stay of uranium export to allow public debate
(d) That there be an indeterminate stay of uranium export and that it be accompanied not only by public debate but also by constructive action by Australia to stimulate, and itself initiate, a massive international programme of research and development of safe and inexhaustible supplies of energy, whatever their nature.

Not surprisingly, perhaps, this last option received 795 votes, the others about 100 votes each.[72]

---

[71] *National Journal of the Australian Democrats*, no. 3/77 (July 25, 1977), p. 24; 5/77 (September 5, 1977), p. 3. "Australian Democrats" beat all the others combined, 949 votes to 123.

[72] *National Journal of the Australian Democrats*, no. 4/77 (August 15, 1977),

In the policy speech delivered on November 23, Chipp tackled the issues in the order in which they had been ranked in ANOP's poll on the most important problem facing the federal government conducted early in October for the *National Times* and the ABC: unemployment, inflation, uranium, and industrial relations.[73] In general terms, Chipp explained, the party stood for honesty, tolerance, and compassion; he returned to this theme over and over again. According to the polls, these were the positive qualities the general public associated with Chipp's name.[74]

Had the party been able to afford it, Chipp would almost certainly have commissioned private research of his own. As it was, he learned from Labor that those who opposed the mining and export of uranium felt more strongly on the issue than those who favored it. Uranium, Chipp was advised, was a "sleeper." From then on he pushed the party's uranium policy into every speech.

The Democrats' uranium policy was clearly closer to Labor's than to the government's. Similarly with industrial relations.[75] The party's slogan "Get Australia Together" had been devised months earlier by Nichols-Cuming, a Melbourne advertising agency with an interest in third-party politics. At the time, industrial relations had been a prominent issue. The Democrats were entering a plea for "conciliation, not confrontation," and like the Labor party, Chipp half expected the government to engineer a confrontation over the export of uranium yellow cake. The Democrats were certainly useful to Labor: attacks on the government launched by Chipp were more likely to get media coverage than those launched by Whitlam.

But the Democrats were equally capable of opposing Labor. Chipp knew that research showed Labor to be doing badly among rural voters, who had not forgiven Whitlam for cutting the super-

---

p. 20; no. 6/77 (September 26, 1977), p. 2; no. 7/77 (October 17, 1977), p. 2. The result was option (d) 795, (b) 102, (c) 99, (a) 82.

[73] Goot and Beed, "The Polls," Table 7-7; Hewat and Wilson, *Don Chipp*, pp. 114-124.

[74] Hewat and Wilson, *Don Chipp*, pp. 93-94. Hewat and Wilson's claim that these were associated in the voters' minds with Whitlam (rather than Chipp) is mistaken.

[75] A survey of 148 major-party candidates conducted by the National Campaign for a Democratic Constitution found the Democrats' views closer to those of the ALP candidates on a number of issues (holding federal elections at fixed intervals, further limiting the powers of the governor general, amending the Constitution by simple majority, and curbing the powers of the Senate). Not surprisingly, however, the Democrats' views were closer to the Liberals' on the question of abolition of the Senate; and only a minority of Democrats thought Australia should become a republic, a change supported by almost all the Labor candidates. *Australian*, December 8, 1977, p. 6.

phosphate bounty or for telling them that they had "never had it so good." Chipp's campaign in the countryside spared Labor nothing. Since the same research showed NCP support to be holding firm, he confined his attacks on the NCP to denouncing their "broken promises."

The polls on party support affected morale and heightened Chipp's expectations. He used them for propaganda—to show that the party was a "real alternative" and that a vote for the Australian Democrats would not be wasted. As early as July, after Chipp's resignation from the Liberal party but before the new party had been established, one poll reported that 60 percent of voters thought a center party would be a good thing, 20 percent said they would vote for a center party candidate if one were to stand in their electorate, and 29 percent said they would consider doing so.[76] In the course of the campaign all the polls showed a swing to the Democrats. According to APOP about a third of the electorate "would consider" voting AD. On the night of the election Chipp was hoping for a senator in each state or 18 percent of the national vote.[77]

Progress Party. Two years after its birth early in 1975, the Workers party split, retaining its name in South Australia but elsewhere becoming the Progress party. According to Barry Brachen, the Progress party's chairman in New South Wales and number one Senate candidate in 1977, two forces precipitated the split: an inflexible constitution guarded by an authoritarian organization; and the results of a survey, conducted by party members, indicating that the voters were disconcerted by a party of unfettered free enterprise that also claimed to represent the interests of workers and the organized labor movement. Those who could not abide the party's rigid procedures or who felt it had taken the wrong name formed the Progress party.[78] By September there was little to cheer about when the Morgan organization informed the party, through John Singleton, that the number intending to vote PP in the Senate was negligible.

One difficulty the party faced was that of adapting its philosophy, derived from Americans like Ayn Rand and from the Austrians von Hayek and von Mises, to Australian ways of thinking. One solution

---

[76] *Age*, July 22, 1977; *Sydney Morning Herald*, July 22, 1977. The poll, conducted by Irving Saulwick & Associates, is incorrectly attributed to ANOP in Chipp and Larkin, *Don Chipp*, p. 193.

[77] Chipp and Larkin, *Don Chipp*, pp. 200, 207; for AD support see Goot and Beed, "The Polls," Figure 3.

[78] Corrobrated by Peter Sawyer, *Bulletin*, June 11, 1977.

was to pinpoint particular policies and to show that the party's outlook, far from being a fringe view, actually echoed ordinary common sense.

The party was fortunate in having a sympathizer in Sydney who worked in market research. With the campaign under way he wanted to do something for the party, so he offered to tag a couple of questions onto a survey that was being run. The survey was conducted in the capital cities over two weekends, November 19-20 and 26-27. There were 1,000 interviews and two questions:

> Thinking about tertiary education, things like Universities and Colleges of Advanced Education, which of these statements do you most agree with:
> (a) tertiary education should be free
> (b) students should pay fees each year for tertiary education while they are studying
> (c) students should pay for tertiary education, but not have to pay until after they finish studying, by way of low interest loans?

> When a government wishes to resume land for any reason, do you think that it should pay for the land at market value, at less than market value, or at more than market value?

The results were gratifying. While 45 percent thought higher education should be free, 51 percent thought it should not: 16 percent favored fees paid while studying, 35 percent favored low interest loans. Predictably, only 1 percent thought the government should pay less than market value for any land it resumed; 62 percent favored market value; and 35 percent favored something in excess of this. The results, released to the press, were almost completely ignored.[79] The party itself, through its advertising, did little to publicize either cause.

Final Observations

For the campaign, the Liberal party spent the best part of $150,000 on survey research; the federal ALP, something under $10,000; the NCP about $14,000; and the other parties, virtually nothing. The difference between spending and not spending was, in part, the

---

[79] The education question was carried by the *Courier-Mail*, December 2, 1977, p. 14.

difference between having a media tycoon to foot the bill and not having one.[80] It was certainly not a matter of not wanting to spend.

Surveys played an important part in the campaign but they did not totally dominate it. At vital points the leaders made their judgments on independent grounds: Fraser's decision to call the election; Whitlam's decision to fight on taxation. There were also institutional constraints. There were, for example, limits to what the marketers could do with the Labor party, given that Whitlam was the party's leader; and there were limits on how far the NCP could promote a separate sense of identity, given that it was a partner in a coalition.

The introduction and extension of surveys into political campaigning has not been achieved in the absence of opposition. If victory stifles criticism, nothing is better calculated to raise doubts than defeat. After the election, a left-wing union official from Victoria wrote of the "alarming degree" to which "the ALP does not manage its own affairs at all," with some of the most critical decisions being "taken in the offices of opinion surveyors, public relations firms and advertising agents."[81] Even Mick Young, an active and early proselytizer of the technique, had to confess, "we are fast becoming a generation of political activists without the courage or conviction to make a decision lest we unleash the wrath of the pollsters."[82]

---

[80] After the campaign Labor's national secretary, David Combe, renewed his call for public funding of campaigns. *Age*, February 24, 1978, p. 8.
[81] *Nation Review*, January 19-25, 1978, p. 9.
[82] *Australian*, December 24, 1977, p. 2.

8
A Lean Campaign for the Media

C. J. Lloyd

After a decade unsurpassed for political incident, which included three memorable elections, the 1977 campaign was a distinct letdown for the media. The last federal election campaign of the 1970s was difficult and often frustrating to report and interpret. As a consequence, much of the media coverage was unoriginal and lacking in insight although the major political parties were resourceful in their media strategies. It was an election campaign where what the media did to the parties was less important than what the parties did to the media.[1]

The Electoral Context

The media were instrumental in building up an atmosphere conducive to an election at the end of 1977. Throughout the year, there were important questions of electoral strategy that pointed to an early election. The government would face an election for half of the Senate before the end of June 1978. An attempt to amend the Australian Constitution so as to bring elections for the Senate and the House of Representatives into line had been defeated in May at a national referendum. With a House of Representatives election due at the end of 1978 the prime minister, Malcolm Fraser, could either hold a Senate election before June 1978 and a House of Representa-

---

[1] The chronicling of the first Fraser government and the elections of December 1977 has been extremely meager. The only work of substance on Fraser's political career and his policies is John Edwards, *Life Wasn't Meant to be Easy* (Sydney: Hale and Iremonger, 1977). There have been no general accounts of the 1977 elections. Two books on the Australian Democrats contain material on Australian politics between 1975 and 1977 and on the 1977 election campaign: Tim Hewat and David Wilson, *Don Chipp* (Melbourne: Visa, 1978) and Don Chipp and John Larkin, *Don Chipp: The Third Man* (Adelaide: Rigby, 1978).

tives election six months later or he could hold both elections at the same time. There were obvious disadvantages to holding separate federal elections so close together, and it was clear once the constitutional amendment was defeated that Fraser would move to hold joint elections for both houses.[2]

These joint elections could be held at the end of 1977 or the middle of 1978. There were advantages either way. At the end of 1977, the government would avoid the problems of rapidly rising unemployment which always reached a seasonal peak in January–February as "school leavers" entered the labor market. (The Australian university and school year runs from February–March to November–December.) In May–June 1978 Fraser would have the political advantage of substantial tax cuts due to be implemented from February 1, 1978. Another important factor was the formation of a new political party, the Australian Democrats, in May 1977. The founder of the Democrats, Don Chipp, was a former minister in the Liberal–National Country party governments of the late 1960s and early 1970s. He had not been reappointed to the ministry when Fraser became prime minister in December 1975. Chipp was one of the best known and most widely admired political figures in Australia, and his defection created political problems for Fraser, particularly after the Democrats performed creditably in a sequence of state elections. It raised the threat that if a half-Senate election were held separately from a House of Representatives election, the Democrats and the Labor party might poll well enough to challenge government control of the Senate.

These issues were canvassed extensively in the media in the months immediately following the presentation of the 1977–1978 budget in August 1977. This budget included tax cuts and other concessions that were compatible with an early election. Both party machines had been alerted for an end-of-year election. The Labor party had begun planning early in the year, although most of its

[2] Elections for the Australian Senate and the House of Representatives have been out of step since the end of 1963. The House of Representatives has a maximum term of three years but may be dissolved earlier with the agreement of the governor general. Half of the Senate is elected every three years, and senators are elected for a six-year term. The Australian Constitution provides that proposals for constitutional amendment must be submitted to a national referendum and must be approved by both a national majority and a majority in at least four of the states. Fraser stated his justification for the election on the Australian Broadcasting Commission (ABC) current affairs television program "This Day Tonight" on November 29, 1977: "We believe that since there had to be an election in either December or April or May, it is better to get it out of the way so that Australians can know the course they are on and know it for a good firm period ahead" (transcript p. 5).

senior members and officials felt that an election was unlikely. After the budget debate, the party's leader, Gough Whitlam, and its principal economic spokesman, Bill Hayden, announced a modest program of public works and other stimulatory measures to reduce unemployment which Labor would implement if elected. This Whitlam-Hayden plan was the central element of the Labor party's contingency plan. By October, there were unequivocal signs that Fraser was maneuvering for an early election, and the Labor party embarked on an advertising campaign in the press at the substantial cost of $110,000. This campaign was designed partly to influence the Liberal party's Federal Council meeting in mid-October against an election and partly to give the Labor party a week of uncontested campaigning just in case an election at the end of the year could not be avoided. It pointed up the extravagances of the coalition government and drew attention to weak points in its performance.

The media, meanwhile, were drawn into intensive speculation about the likelihood of an election. Though they recognized that this only served Fraser's tactical purposes, they were unable to avoid it. Once the rumors began, Fraser did not have to fan the flames. The media resented being used by Fraser in this way, but they were trapped by their own demands. The prime minister could deplore the speculation and state firmly that it did not emanate from him or his government, but he did not make the only move that would have quelled it: a firm declaration that there would be no election. All of the talk served Fraser's purposes by discomposing his opponents and making an election seem inevitable. One of the subsequent justifications for the election was the need to end the uncertainty that was damaging the economy.

One problem facing the government was the lack of major issues that could justify the decision to go to the country. Industrial disputes seemed likely to give the government an issue in September, when a wave of national strikes culminated in the disruption of power supplies to Melbourne, Australia's second largest city. Another possible issue was uranium. Anti-uranium feeling had built up significantly during the second half of 1977, and there were some clashes between police and protesters as shipments of uranium yellow cake departed from Sydney and Melbourne.

But neither industrial disputes nor uranium materialized as a big enough issue to serve as the basis for an election. When Fraser eventually made his announcement late in October, his main justification was the need to synchronize elections for the two houses of Parliament—a valid but unexciting concern. Sustaining media interest and public attention for the three weeks of the campaign would be a challenge.

The Labor party had signalled that it would concentrate its campaign on unemployment. The government, meanwhile, faced the risk that hastily improvised issues might fail to make an impact, while unexpected and unwelcome ones might catch on in the overheated atmosphere of a campaign. As it turned out, just such a brushfire dominated the media during the weeks between Fraser's announcement on October 27 and the opening of his campaign on November 22.

The Media and the Issues

The Lynch Affair. Allegations about the financial affairs of the federal treasurer, Phillip R. Lynch, broke at an unfortunate moment for the government. The Lynch affair escalated quickly and reached its raucous crescendo in the media on the eve of the government's campaign launching, when Lynch's resignation effectively stifled its potential to damage the government.

Lynch's predicament arose when a Royal Commission was appointed by the state government of Victoria to investigate charges of malpractice by the State Housing Commission in some of its land dealings.[3] The unfavorable publicity generated by the inquiry damaged the state's Liberal government and created apprehension in the Victoria division of the Liberal party that its federal electoral prospects might be jeopardized. Lynch became involved in a peripheral way when allegations were made to the Royal Commission that a trust company associated with the Lynch family had financed a land purchase which was the subject of evidence put before the inquiry. The suggestion that Lynch was involved in the purchase of land at a place called Stumpy Gully had been put to the inquiry by Peter Leake, who some years earlier had been chairman of Lynch's campaign committee in his electorate.

The reference to Lynch at the inquiry was taken up vigorously by the Labor party in the federal Parliament. Lynch at first responded cautiously to questions from the opposition leader, Gough Whitlam. In carefully considered written replies, he denied that a private company owned by a trust, whose beneficiaries were his wife and three children, had invested in residential land while he was treasurer.

---

[3] In Australia, the state governments are responsible for providing low-income and welfare housing through state housing authorities, with funds provided by the federal government.

He admitted that a land investment had been undertaken by the trustee company while he was deputy leader of the opposition, between 1973 and 1975, but he denied that this purchase was in any way connected with land purchases that the Royal Commission was investigating.

These admissions provoked a wide-ranging investigation by the media of Lynch's financial circumstances, involving his accountants, lawyers, and mortgagors. It disclosed that the transactions at Stumpy Gully had made a respectable profit. Lynch had also purchased two luxury apartments at Surfers Paradise, a resort area on the Queensland Gold Coast, and these received wide publicity.

The media investigations uncovered an extraordinary range of material in the early weeks of November. Much of it was irrelevant but some was embarrassing to Lynch. It was revealed that Lynch's purchase of an apartment in the Golden Gate building at Surfers Paradise had been assisted by an extremely generous mortgage. The family trust was found to reduce Lynch's income tax payments, though the treasurer had often expounded the need to crack down hard on tax avoidance schemes.

The Labor party was unable to exploit Lynch's embarrassment fully in the federal Parliament, which had completed its session. The state Parliament of Victoria was still in session, however, and in its Legislative Council, Labor party member Bill Landeryou accused Lynch of profiting by nearly $110,000 from land dealings. The allegations were exaggerated and the attack, under parliamentary privilege, was unfair, but as a principal instigator of the media onslaught on the Labor government's attempts to raise loans overseas in 1975, Lynch could expect no quarter from the ALP.[4]

Landeryou's accusations were made on November 15 and were accompanied by extensive media coverage. Whitlam followed with restrained but pointed criticism in the policy speech on November 17 that launched the ALP campaign. Interest in Lynch's personal finances was heightened by the vulnerability of the treasurer, who was recovering from treatment for kidney stones. His problems were described in a media statement by his principal private secretary, Andrew Hay:

---

[4] For accounts of the "Loans affair" and Australian politics up until the end of 1975, see Laurie Oakes, *Crash Through or Crash* (Melbourne: Drummond, 1976); Paul Kelly, *The Unmaking of Gough* (Sydney: Angus and Robertson, 1976); Clem Lloyd and Andrew Clark, *Kerr's King Hit!* (Sydney: Cassell, 1976); Alan Reid, *The Whitlam Venture* (Melbourne: Hill of Content, 1976).

> Over recent days there has been a series of extremely inaccurate and false reports in the media, and comments of a scurrilous and unfounded nature made yesterday [November 15] in the Victorian Parliament concerning the pecuniary interests of the Treasurer and his family. These reports have caused great distress to Mrs. Lynch and to her three children. The Treasurer has been, during this time, confined to hospital following an operation and under medical advice has been unable to deal with the allegations that have been made.[5]

Strenuous efforts in defense of Lynch were made by his wife, his lawyers, his accountants, and his personal staff. The investigations had, after all, revealed no evidence of impropriety. This was explicitly conceded on one radio current affairs program that had been a principal investigator:

> HUW EVANS: We've inquired into the story at some length over the past ten days, I expect, or so. We've been scrupulous in the facts that we have presented and at no stage have we indicated involvement in anything illegal and that I think is the general consensus of the media presentation of the facts so far.[6]

But despite the consensus that Lynch had done nothing illegal, the government—for the first time—faced unfavorable media coverage that threatened to be as damaging as the coverage of the Labor government in the climactic months of 1975.

The dangers of the Lynch affair were brought home to Fraser when he held a press conference late on the afternoon of November 18 to comment on the Whitlam policy speech. The prime minister spoke for a quarter of an hour about the high cost of Labor's policies and outlined a strategy for exploiting it during the election campaign. Then (after days of silence on the Lynch affair) he told the reporters that he had not received details from Lynch's accountants about the treasurer's pecuniary interests and therefore would make no comment. But Fraser, who had wanted the conference to be an attack on the Labor party, was inundated with questions about Lynch:

---

[5] Treasurer, press release no. 144, November 16, 1977, statement by Mr. Andrew Hay, principal private secretary to the treasurer.

[6] "PM" Broadcast, November 17, 1977, transcript p. 2. "AM" and "PM" are ABC radio current affairs programs. The transcripts were obtained from the Commonwealth Parliamentary Library and the Australian National Library, Canberra.

REPORTER: With respect, Mr. Fraser, three weeks before an election when serious questions are raised about the propriety of the Treasurer, is it fair to the electorate for you not to comment?

MR. FRASER: Yes, certainly it is very fair to the electorate not to comment when I am waiting for a report from the Treasurer which he has instructed should be given to me. When the Treasurer is ill in hospital. . . .

REPORTER: Is your Government now on the defensive as the Labor Government was in 1975, answering allegations?

MR. FRASER: Oh good heavens no, good heavens no.[7]

Fraser abruptly broke off the conference and strode from the room, after three times refusing to state that he retained faith in his treasurer or that Lynch would still be treasurer if the coalition were returned to government. To television viewers across the country, the episode evoked a strong impression of a government in crisis.

The media's concentration on the Lynch affair was paramount in Fraser's decision to force the treasurer's resignation, announced late on the afternoon of November 19. In his letter of resignation to the prime minister Lynch wrote:

> I now wish to inform you that, in the interests of my party and the colleagues with whom I have served over many years, I am prepared to stand aside as Treasurer in the present Government. . . . I am confident that my action in standing aside as Treasurer will prevent the Australian people going to the poll on quite the wrong issue and in a poisonous atmosphere.[8]

This assessment proved correct. After one final barrage of bad publicity, the issue quickly subsided. Fraser was able to point to Lynch's compliance with the strict Westminster tradition in his policy speech and campaign interviews:

> What Phillip Lynch has done is to stand our government in stark contrast with that of the previous administration because he has acted from the highest principles of the Westminster system. Charges—things were said and he knew that there was no chance of a fair judgment of these

---

[7] "PM" Broadcast, November 17, 1977, "P.M. Holds Press Conference," transcript pp. 3-4.

[8] P. R. Lynch to J. M. Fraser, November 18, 1977, correspondence released to the media by the Prime Minister's Office, Canberra, *Sydney Morning Herald*, November 19, 1977.

particular matters during the heat of an election campaign, you know, acting out of the highest principles he made the decision to stand aside.⁹

Whitlam, meanwhile, applied his caustic wit to Lynch's abrupt departure from the campaign, referring to the "sanitized" version of the Fraser policy speech—"deleted, deloused and de-Lynched."¹⁰ He ridiculed the family trusts, tax evasion schemes, and perks of the "rich squatters" who, he claimed, ran the Liberal and National Country parties.¹¹ Whitlam had particular fun with the Liberal campaign slogan "Doing the Job":

> And then of course on the platform and behind it, there was that beaut sign—Liberal, Doing the Job. Now I must confess I thought—that's a bit vulgar . . . (laughter), that's not the sort of thing that gentlemen say in front of blue-rinsed ladies! So I thought I had better go to the dictionary and see if I'm wrong . . . and this is how it's defined: Job in the Oxford English Dictionary: "a transaction in which duty or public interest is sacrificed for the sake of private or party advantage." Now I thought, this is too good to be true. They couldn't have come clean with the public so entirely.¹²

The Lynch affair petered out into a desultory exchange over the pecuniary interests of politicians. This produced some interesting material for the media. Fraser defended the use of family trusts by farmers and small businessmen who wanted to keep their assets together. When asked if he had a family trust, the prime minister responded: "Oh yes, I do. They're designed to benefit the family and keep the farm together."¹³ Other senior politicians divulged the details of their pecuniary interests, including Whitlam who revealed that he and his wife had bought an apartment through a trust account controlled by their lawyers. "My other assets," Whitlam said, "are a house, barrister's chambers, and a Ford Cortina in Sydney and

---

⁹ "AM" Broadcast, November 21, 1977, transcript p. 1.

¹⁰ "PM" Broadcast, November 21, 1977, "Mr. Whitlam Campaigning in Queensland," transcript p. 2.

¹¹ Squatter is Australian idiom for a large rural landholder. It derives from the settlement of Australia during the nineteenth century when land was appropriated by squatting on it.

¹² "AM" Broadcast, November 24, 1977, transcript p. 1. This was a tape of Whitlam addressing a public meeting in Adelaide. "Blue-rinsed ladies" is a common epithet for the more genteel female supporters of the Liberal party.

¹³ "PM" Broadcast, November 3, 1977, "Mr. Fraser Interviewed on Family Trusts," transcript p. 1.

$3000 debentures in Prospect County Council."[14] Labor's principal economic spokesman, Bill Hayden, disclosed a list of personal assets so meager that government spokesmen derided his ability to manage the national economy.

Whitlam tried to keep the issue alive throughout the campaign, stressing the need for politicians to account strictly for their pecuniary interests and striving to arouse moral outrage in an indifferent electorate:

> "Trust": one of the noblest words, one of the noblest ideas in the English language! And another noble word, "family": the basis of our society, the basis of our community. Only a Fraser Government, the Government of family trusts; only a Fraser, a Lynch, an Anthony, a Sinclair could join these words together and debase them into a tax dodge. Put these rascals out![15]

But the legitimacy of tax loopholes and land speculation is deeply ingrained in Australia, and Whitlam's moral strictures fell on deaf ears.

Lynch spent much of the election campaign secluded in the hospital, inaccessible to the media. Only once did television audiences see film footage of him, standing on a hospital balcony in robe and pajamas. His wife, Leah Lynch, made a strong attack on the media for their investigative reporting:

> Various aspects of the media have really pursued my husband's business affairs through legal documents, company documents and so forth for months now. It has been a highly orchestrated performance. A lot of the taxpayer's money has been used in fact to pursue his downfall. . . . I feel, the media has a lot to answer for.[16]

Taxation. With the Lynch affair effectively removed from the campaign, tax policy became the dominant issue. In the months preceding the election, Labor's main policy and propaganda efforts had

---

[14] Leader of the Opposition, November 24, 1977, Media Statement: "E. G. Whitlam—Pecuniary Interests." In the state of New South Wales, Australian lawyers who work as advocates in the courts are called barristers. Each barrister buys or leases chambers where he conducts his practice. A Ford Cortina is a relatively modest car manufactured in Australia. Australian semi-government authorities raise funds in the capital market by debenture issues.
[15] E. G. Whitlam, Address, Brisbane City Hall, text p. 7. Doug Anthony and Ian Sinclair were the leaders of the National Country party.
[16] "Willesee at Seven" (Channel 9 Network current affairs program), December 5, 1977, transcript pp. 2-3.

been directed to unemployment. When Whitlam's policy speech was in preparation, there was a feeling among his advisers that the Whitlam-Hayden plan was not substantial enough to carry a major election campaign and that it would not adequately dramatize unemployment. Accordingly, a late decision was made to include an innovatory proposal to abolish payroll taxes as an incentive to the private sector to create more jobs. This central commitment was reinforced by subsidiary proposals designed to stimulate employment. The relevant section of Whitlam's policy speech read:

> We therefore propose to ask the Premiers [of the states] to agree to forgo the collection of payroll tax. In return we would give the States an indexed general purpose grant equal to the revenue they forgo. We would then ask the taxpayers to trade-off this job-creating, inflation-cutting, confidence-restoring tax concession for the changes in personal taxation proposed in the last Lynch Budget.[17]

Whitlam proposed an extremely daring political trade-off. In the federal budget for 1977–1978, Lynch had announced personal tax cuts that would apply from February 1, 1978. The government had expected to win considerable political advantage from these concessions, but their presentation to the electorate was handled badly. Government spokesmen and public officials made conflicting statements about how the tax cuts would be applied. The media had been extremely critical, and opinion polls had shown a low level of awareness among voters about the impending tax reductions. Whitlam argued that the government's proposals were weighted in favor of higher-income earners and away from the great majority of Australians, who would get very little. The polls had shown clearly that unemployment was by far the most important electoral issue, while taxation had not been particularly prominent. Accordingly, Whitlam's campaign was framed around an idealistic appeal to the Australian electorate to forgo their tax cuts so that the burden of the payroll tax might be removed from the private sector, which would then be free to spend on job-creating investment.

---

[17] E. G. Whitlam Policy Speech, Sydney Opera House, November 17, 1977, text p. 8. In five of the six Australian states every employer of more than six workers, and in Queensland every employer of more than ten workers, has to pay payroll tax. The average annual payment is around $500 per worker. Since the tax is collected by the states, it could only be abolished if they were willing to cooperate and if the Commonwealth paid them compensatory grants. The Labor strategy was to reduce the cost of labor for private firms without reducing the spending power of the workers.

The Labor party's campaign organizers were caught off balance by this unexpected policy innovation. They knew that advertisements relating directly to the policy speech would have to be prepared at the last minute, but they had not foreseen anything like the challenge of putting together media material to convince the electorate that it should reject a tax cut.

Labor's tax proposal presented the government, which had been shaken by the Lynch affair, with an unexpected opportunity. It had bungled its first attempt to sell its tax cuts when the budget was presented in August and the new tax rates were announced. Now it had been given a second chance—in the favorable context of an election. Fraser knew how great his luck had been. A few hours after Whitlam announced his party's policy, Fraser interrupted a prepared speech to comment: "I was delighted when I heard that he had made that particular promise because $3.25 billion worth of tax cuts is worth having and to have it rubbed out at one stroke is not something that I think most people would want."[18]

This set the course the Liberal party would pursue throughout the campaign. Fraser argued that substantial tax cuts put money directly into the hands of consumers, and more consumption created more jobs. As demand rose, employers were encouraged to hire more workers, and lower marginal tax rates increased incentive and production. By implication, consumers who accepted tax cuts and spent the extra money were helping to overcome unemployment by creating more jobs. This altruistic theme was taken up enthusiastically by the Liberal party's advertising agents and media strategists.

The party quickly prepared advertisements condemning Labor's payroll tax proposal and exploiting the impending February tax cuts. When the party's National Campaign Committee met on November 22, it decided to concentrate its media material on the taxation issue. The subsequent campaign on taxation had many ironies. Fraser was able to depict Labor as a high-tax party which was diverting resources from workers and small-income earners to the big corporations, many of them foreign-owned. The abolition of payroll taxes, Fraser said, would give the industrial giants huge windfall profits: General Motors $10 million, Dunlop $11–13 million, Ford $7 million, Utah $2 million, and the Bank of New South Wales $11 million. A government whose creed was private enterprise was fighting to protect small-income earners from socialists scheming to give more resources to big business!

---

[18] "AM" Broadcast, November 18, 1977, "Mr. Fraser Addresses a Dinner for the Morgan Trust Company of New York," transcript p. 1.

LEAN CAMPAIGN FOR THE MEDIA

The media were divided on the merits of Whitlam's payroll tax trade-off. Initially the scheme had support from important elements of the press, including Rupert Murdoch's *Australian*, which had been a persistent advocate of the abolition of payroll taxes throughout the year. But there was also criticism, on economic grounds; in particular, the accuracy of the costing estimates provided by Whitlam was questioned. During the campaign, the skepticism expressed in the print media hardened into a pervasive feeling that the trade-off would not work.

The electronic media's treatment of the issue was dominated by a vigorous advertising campaign. A late survey taken by the Morgan Gallup poll showed that among marginal voters, the tax cuts were perceived as the main benefit of a government victory. This was a marked turnaround from the preelection polls, in which tax cuts had ranked low among important campaign issues.

Whitlam was left in the invidious position of pushing an unpopular cause. This he did with characteristic force:

> The central issues in this election are unemployment and economic management. Labor has already advanced proposals, practical proposals for a direct attack on the problems of jobs and prices. Labor has made proposals; Labor has announced a strategy. The coalition parties have not. Their concern seems to have been restricted to death duties. How splendidly appropriate is that concern when one considers that uranium is also an issue in this election.[19]

But Whitlam was unable to kindle any compassion for the jobless in the peculiar circumstances of the 1977 election.

In addition, the ALP was bedevilled by a series of contradictions between statements made by its various spokesmen. As early as November, Whitlam's announcement that the party's principal economic spokesman, Bill Hayden, would be foreign affairs and defense minister, not treasurer, if Labor won the election created problems for the party's campaign strategists. They had shaped the campaign around the Whitlam-Hayden plan to conquer unemployment and were anxious to use Hayden as a foil for Whitlam's lack of credibility in the electorate. The change aroused so much criticism that Whitlam backed down and announced that Hayden would be given a new portfolio, economic development, in a Labor government. Labor entered the campaign period with its economic responsibilities split among four

---

[19] E. G. Whitlam, Press Club Luncheon, Adelaide, November 24, 1977, text p. 3. Fraser's policy speech had included a promise to abolish federal estate and gift duties over the life of the next Parliament.

senior spokesmen apart from Whitlam. This made coordination extremely difficult and increased the chances of damaging conflicts between spokesmen.

The government had partly financed its February tax cuts by retreating from a policy of full tax indexation to partial indexation for the remainder of the 1977–1978 fiscal year.[20] Lack of clarity about this indexation policy had been one of the factors dampening the impact of the tax cuts when they were announced in August. Now confusion over indexation caused problems for Labor, which had to frame an approach consistent with its proposal to abolish the tax cuts to finance the abolition of payroll taxes. The party's national policy was support for full wage and tax indexation, but in fact there were pronounced differences of approach within the party.

Inevitably these strains were exposed in the media during the campaign. When questioned by the media about tax indexation early in the campaign, Whitlam was ambivalent, at one point indicating that the February tax cuts might only be postponed and not abolished by a Labor government, then having to correct himself. Whitlam's comprehension of indexation often seemed defective, and he was uneasy when questioned about it.

To make matters worse, the Labor party's treasury spokesman, Chris Hurford, committed an unfortunate gaffe. Hurrying to catch an early morning plane at a provincial airport, he was phoned by a radio interviewer who asked him to explain Labor's policy on tax indexation. Hurford replied that he couldn't answer because he had read only the local newspaper, the *Cairns Post*, that morning.[21] Fraser seized on this unfortunate answer and ridiculed Hurford mercilessly throughout the campaign: "In the background of all this confusion and disarray is poor Mr. Hurford, who said he couldn't say what Labor's policy on tax indexation was because he had only read the *Cairns Post*, a shocking slur on a fine newspaper."[22]

---

[20] Wage indexation was introduced by the Labor government in 1974. Percentage adjustments to wages for cost-of-living increases were set by the Commonwealth Industrial Court. The Fraser government continued the indexation in a modified form, which resulted effectively in partial indexation, that is, only part of the increase in living costs was compensated for by wage increases. It also introduced a proposal for full tax indexation, which it later modified to partial indexation, to help finance the major tax cuts announced in the 1977-1978 budget. Whether by accident or by design, Australia has been in the forefront of the worldwide move for lower income taxes.

[21] "AM" Broadcast, November 23, 1978, transcript pp. 1-3. This episode illustrates the communications problems of coordinating a campaign over Australia's vast distances.

[22] J. M. Fraser, Hobart Evening Rally, November 28, 1977, text p. 4.

It was late in the campaign before Hayden was able to present a coherent and authoritative statement of policy on wage and tax indexation. By then, the damage had been done, as was acknowledged in a postelection report by the ALP federal secretary, David Combe:

> Perhaps the varying statements early in the campaign from the Leader and our economic spokesmen on tax indexation and wage indexation gave more of an appearance of conflict than reality justified. Perhaps, also, the seeming confusion on tax indexation was more a by-product of the payroll tax proposal than anything else. Nevertheless, the appearance of confusion and conflict gave to the journalists covering the campaign (and thereafter, the Government) the opportunity they had been seeking to attack our economic competence and credibility.[23]

Tariff Policy. In the last half of the campaign, tariffs emerged as another policy issue to confound the Labor party. It was raised by an industry group, the Australian Confederation of Apparel Manufacturers (ACAM). Clothing, textiles, and footwear industries had been damaged by a 25 percent tariff cut and the relaxation of other protectionist policies by the Labor government. During the campaign, the confederation approached Labor party spokesmen seeking assurances that the Labor party would continue policies designed to maintain employment and productivity in these vulnerable industries. The discussions exposed differences of policy interpretation within the Labor party, and ACAM cabled the prime minister, setting out these disagreements in some detail. It quoted a Labor party official who described Labor as a free trade party.[24]

The confusion over tariff policy within the ALP was taken up briskly by Fraser, who painted his opponents as a low-protection party:

> There is also an absolute contrast between our policy of protecting Australian industry, of protecting Australian jobs, and the Whitlam Labor Party's obsession with reducing protection, with making unemployment a deliberate act of government policy by encouraging imports to undercut Australian manufacturers.[25]

---

[23] H. D. Combe, *Report of ALP National Secretary on the 1977 Federal Election Campaign* (an unpublished report prepared for the internal use of the ALP), p. 4.

[24] Telegram from Australian Confederation of Apparel Manufacturers (ACAM) to the prime minister, Canberra, November 30, 1977. Released to the media as a statement by the National Executive of ACAM. Labor had been, since its inception, a high-tariff party.

[25] J. M. Fraser, Western Australia Press Club Address, December 1, 1977, text, p. 4.

This allowed Fraser to erode the Labor party's emphasis on unemployment by pointing to its ambivalence on industrial protection. In response, Labor spokesmen stressed the benefits that the abolition of payroll tax would give to clothing and footwear manufacturers. This did not mitigate the damaging effects of the party's lack of a clearly defined and consistent position on tariffs. Furthermore, it reinforced popular support for the tax cuts and gave Fraser an opportunity to conduct a positive media campaign on unemployment when, according to the rules, he should have been on the defensive. And it created dismay and discontent in trade unions representing workers in the affected industries, which were normally Labor supporters. The Liberals were quick to mount an extensive campaign within the apparel, textile, and footwear industries to exploit Labor's disunity.

Vietnamese Refugees. The sudden appearance of flotillas of Vietnamese refugees in the coastal waters off Darwin and the Northern Territory created problems for both political parties. It exposed the vulnerability of Australia's northern approaches and vast coastline and it raised subtle questions of race relations. The government stressed the humanitarian aspects of the refugee problem, although its implications for security were raised in Queensland, Western Australia, and the Northern Territory, the states most vulnerable to unauthorized entry of Asian refugees. The minister for defense, Jim Killen, rejected the notion that the refugees were a defense problem and reacted with asperity to questions about the timing of the refugee influx:

> REPORTER: How do you account for the timing of this influx of refugees?
>
> MR. KILLEN: Well now surely you are not suggesting that there has been some secret connivance between what was Saigon and somebody in some political party in Australia...
>
> REPORTER: No, I'm wondering what the Government's attitude is. It does seem strange that around an election time, the influx of refugees is apparently stepped up.
>
> MR. KILLEN: I would see absolutely no connection between the two.[26]

The refugee issue exposed further differences between ALP spokesmen, although here the contradictions were less important in

---

[26] "PM" Broadcast, November 29, 1977, "Mr. Killen Interviewed on Refugees from Vietnam," transcript p. 2.

their impact. A Labor senator, Tony Mulvihill, suggested that some of the refugees should be turned away from Australia, while Whitlam took the realistic view that once the refugees neared Australian shores, they could not be turned back.

Liberal party officials worked hard to coordinate the statements of their spokesmen on an issue whose implications for an election campaign were uncertain. The Australian electorate has become less overtly racist and apparently more tolerant in recent years, but the tradition of "white Australia" remains strong. Some feared that the arrival of the boat people might prompt ill-considered statements and escalate into a damaging election issue. A joint press conference was held in Adelaide by the two government ministers most involved with the refugees, the minister for foreign affairs, Andrew Peacock, and the minister for immigration and ethnic affairs, Michael Mackellar, who made carefully phrased statements designed to contain the issue. In the main, they were successful, and the Vietnamese refugees did not influence the conduct of the campaign or its result.

Uranium. The mining and export of Australian uranium had been an important policy issue in Australian politics during the months that led up to the election. In August 1977, the government had approved the mining of uranium, subject to safeguards ensuring that Australian uranium delivered to other countries would be put to peaceful uses, that environmental protection standards would be met, and that the rights of the Aboriginal people would be respected. In July, the Labor party National Conference had adopted a policy of prohibiting uranium mining and marketing until it was satisfied that nuclear proliferation could be prevented and that safe techniques for waste disposal were available. The party's campaign planners had selected uranium as a principal issue and had come up with the slogan "Uranium—Play it Safe—Vote ALP," as well as television commercials on the issue.

In the period before the elections, surveys showed a dwindling majority in favor of uranium development. The Labor party's planners assumed that Labor's uranium policy was not a proven vote winner and that there might be a need for defensive action in this area. The last polls conducted by the party before the start of the campaign indicated some volatility in popular attitudes to uranium and increasing doubt about uranium mining and marketing, particularly among young married women. This suggested that the Labor party might be rewarded if it campaigned strongly on safe disposal of uranium waste and other hazards of nuclear development.

The Whitlam policy speech included a firm statement of Labor's uranium policy, reinforced in its half-hour television presentation by the inclusion of a strong anti-uranium statement by the South Australian Labor premier, Don Dunstan. This statement was used extensively during the campaign as a television commercial, as was another anti-uranium commercial that depicted the span of life of nuclear waste on a tape divided into units of hundreds of thousands of years. These were effective advertisements, but the Labor party's most powerful anti-uranium commercial, a thirty-second spot showing two babies playing with a grenade, encountered resistance from party officials. It was not cleared for showing until the final days of the electronic media campaign (when it won an extremely favorable response), and the Federation of Australian Commercial Television Stations attempted to prevent it from being shown.

Uranium was given fitful attention throughout the campaign by Whitlam. He developed the themes stated in his policy speech at greater length, most notably in an address to the Adelaide Press Club, where he said: "Labor alone in Australia is genuinely concerned for mothers and for future generations of children in the face of the horrible damage that radiation and nuclear materials can do to our children, and to the children of future generations."[27] Nevertheless, uranium remained very much a subsidiary issue. Whitlam justified playing it down on the grounds that the public was not interested. He pointed to the absence of questions about uranium on his radio talk-back programs and television phone-ins. The Labor party's deputy leader, Tom Uren, who was a principal architect of the party's uranium policy, devoted much of his attention to pushing the issue, but his efforts were inhibited by the meager coverage the media invariably give to all but the party leaders during an election campaign.

The electronic media largely ignored uranium, until two nights before the electronic media blackout[28] when a television program called "Uranium—Time for a Verdict" was shown on the National 9 Network. Uren strongly criticized the program as biased and described its airing as deliberately timed to present the case for uranium mining in a favorable light. "The whole press have been trying to play down the discussion on the nuclear question," he said,

---

[27] E. G. Whitlam, Press Club Luncheon, Adelaide, November 24, 1977, text, p. 7.
[28] Under Commonwealth law, all radio and television stations are prohibited from showing any election material, either advertising or news, from midnight on the Wednesday before an election—always held on Saturday. In 1977, the electronic blackout began at midnight on December 7, 1977.

but to put this on two nights before a television and radio blackout is again showing what the bias of the media [is] and particularly the bias of Channel 9. . . . The Labor Party saw the three major questions in the election as unemployment, inflation and uranium, and they have put their programs on the advertising media as such, but it takes two to tango and the Government members have not come in on the question at all.[29]

The program's producer, Gerald Stone, said that production had begun in late August before there was any suggestion of an election. Part of the shooting had been done in the United States, and the program had not been completed until two days before it was shown. Stone felt that it should be aired before the election "because this was an issue."[30]

The coalition's advertisements disregarded uranium completely, and Fraser was seldom asked about it on television phone-ins and radio talk-backs. Uranium projects were not listed as part of the $6 billion development package that was an important part of his campaign pitch. The prime minister dealt with uranium at any length only when it was revealed that prospecting for uranium in South Australia was continuing even though the Labor state government had banned mining. Aside from that, one of Labor's uranium commercials gave Fraser a chance for a crack. It showed Don Dunstan, premier of South Australia, hoeing bean rows in his garden while intoning a strong anti-uranium message. Fraser's comment (which he used often during the campaign): "We all know what he was digging for!"[31]

Uranium remains an enigmatic factor in postcampaign assessments. If the talk-backs and phone-ins were an accurate indication of the issues that most concerned the electorate, then uranium did not capture the popular interest. The Labor party's research had suggested that opportunity beckoned: there was enough anxiety about uranium among key voting groups, particularly younger women, to justify the Labor party in following the instincts of its researchers and squarely campaigning on uranium. In the circumstances of late 1977, however, caution prevailed and Labor was not prepared to accept the risks of doing so.

---

[29] "AM" Broadcast, December 6, 1977, transcript p. 2.
[30] Ibid., p. 3.
[31] An account of uranium as an election issue is given in Alice Bates, "The Election Issue that Never Was," *New Journalist*, Sydney, April 1978, p. 4ff.

Unexpected Issues. In every election campaign, unexpected issues arise which can be exploited by either side to capture flagging media attention. These issues broke fairly evenly for the two sides in 1977. The Labor party won some momentary gain from conflicting statements by Fraser and the health minister, Ralph Hunt, over whether health insurance costs would rise, then by Fraser and Deputy Prime Minister Anthony over the interpretation of Australia's balance-of-payments figures. Neither issue caused more than fleeting discomfiture to the coalition. Fraser, meanwhile, was able to exploit a telex sent to him by the premier of New South Wales, Neville Wran, calling for a lowering of interest rates:

> I think the main point about Mr. Wran's telex is that he recognizes we have established the pre-conditions which now make it possible to move towards a general reduction in interest rates as it affects the average borrower, the home loan buyer and all the rest. . . . Once the election is over we'll be moving as rapidly as we can consistent with the suggestions that are in Mr. Wran's telex, consistent with our own policies, prudently and sensibly towards a reduction in interest rates.[32]

Even more unpalatable for the Labor party was the leaking during the campaign of the *Report of the Royal Commission on Human Relationships*. The previous Labor government had appointed the commission, and its five-volume report had been in the hands of the government for some months. The report included controversial material on sexual relationships, sexual offenses, homosexuality, and abortion. The leaked material concerned mainly these issues and not the wide range of other social issues investigated by the commission. There is little doubt that selected portions of the report were deliberately leaked in order to damage the Labor party, which had appointed the commission.

In fact the response was extremely mild for Australia, a conservative society where the merest suggestion of any relaxation of codes of sexual behavior has invariably provoked an overreaction from the media. The leaking of the most titillating sections of a vast and complex report produced sensational headlines for a day or so. Fraser disclaimed any knowledge of the unofficial release, but he did not neglect the opportunity to describe parts of the report as horrifying and to state a strong case for orthodoxy in human relationships. Whitlam was advised by party officials to avoid direct comment on

---

[32] ABC TV News, December 5, 1977, transcript, p. 1.

the report, but he could not deny himself some humorous sallies at the prime minister over its subject matter: "Mr. Fraser was a week or so ago referring to dirty politics. He's now, I gather, resorting to the politics of smut. You get the prefect and the fag getting the report, looking at it under the desk and looking for the dirty bits. I want to see the lot before I comment."[33]

The Polls. As in 1975, the opinion polls were a dominating influence on media interpretation of the campaign. Most of the polls published in the first three weeks of November put the Labor party well ahead. The polls on issues also indicated that the Labor party had selected the right strategy by emphasizing unemployment. This early superiority in the polls produced an unwarranted confidence in the Labor party, which expected further rewards as the Lynch affair made its impact. Instead, the polls swung decisively against the Labor party, and the final polls pointed clearly to the ultimate result, though without predicting the extent of Fraser's triumph.

The turnaround in the polls was the principal news story for the latter part of the campaign. Each paper assigned one writer the job of watching the polls and interpreting the findings, especially those of the polls commissioned by the paper. (One of these poll watchers, appropriately, was a drama critic in between elections.) This coverage was broadened to include analysis of a range of polls and comment on state and regional differences. The polls were reflected in newspaper editorials and in the electronic media talkbacks and phone-ins and current affairs programs. Given the sheer volume of polling during the campaign, some of this analysis, inevitably, was incoherent and misleading, and there were obvious rationalizations when commentators hastily reinterpreted their earlier pronouncements as new findings came in.

The polls also distorted the media planning of the Labor party, which accepted at face value their finding that unemployment was by far the most important issue. The discrepancy between what people say are the important issues and what they really regard as the issues that most affect them was pointed out after the election by Len Reason, who directed the Liberal party's advertising campaign:

---

[33] "PM" Broadcast, December 1, 1977, transcript, p. 1. This comment was taped at a Press Club luncheon in Hobart. "Prefect" and "fag" are English public school argot for master and slave; the "prefect" is an older boy with authority to discipline younger boys, in particular the "fag" assigned to act as his servant. In Australian politics the labels have been jocularly applied to Fraser and one of his principal acolytes, Tony Staley. When the Lynch affair was at its height, Fraser described the campaign as the dirtiest he had known.

Political research is like any other research. You can't take everything everyone says at face value. If someone with a clipboard and horn-rimmed glasses knocks at your front door and asks you your favourite pastime, you are more likely to say reading historical novels than having sex. And if someone asks you what the key issue in an election is, you are more likely to attest your virtue by tut-tutting "unemployment" than by confessing your avarice with a vote for tax cuts.[34]

In recent Australian elections the polls have had an overwhelming impact on the course of the campaign and on its media coverage. In the 1972 and 1974 elections, Labor was assisted by the polls. In 1975 and 1977 the polls abetted a decisive movement to the coalition. Because of compulsory voting the Australian polls have achieved a high degree of accuracy in detecting trends during campaigns, and this has assured their continuing influence on campaign strategy and on media coverage of elections.

The polls confirmed the Labor party's research finding that Whitlam was not an electoral asset, although his popularity ratings were not markedly inferior to Fraser's. This dissatisfaction with the national leadership was acknowledged frankly by Whitlam:

> REPORTER: Mr. Whitlam, the opinion polls indicate that the electorate is clearly dissatisfied with the leadership of both you and Mr. Fraser. Do you deserve to be?
>
> MR. WHITLAM: The opinion polls show that they [the voters] would like Mr. Chipp as Prime Minister and Mr. Hayden as Treasurer. That is the overwhelming verdict of all the opinion polls.[35]

Party Strategies

Campaign Openings. In Australian elections each party's campaign is officially opened by the leader, whose "policy speech" summarizes the party platform. Each devotes a substantial part of its free time on ABC television to this ritual campaign launching, and the commercial networks televise it without charge. In 1977, the Liberal and Labor parties allocated half an hour out of their two hours each of free ABC time to the launchings.[36]

---

[34] Len Reason, *The Anatomy of a Political Merchandising Idea* (Melbourne: Masius Australia Pty Ltd., 1977), p. 2.

[35] "AM" Broadcast, December 7, 1977, transcript, p. 3.

[36] Most commercial television stations allocated thirty minutes each to the Liberal and Labor parties and fifteen minutes to the National Country party. Labor offi-

The Liberal party adhered to the traditional format, telecasting live Fraser's opening speech to a political rally in Melbourne. This was done mainly to boost the morale of the Liberal party branch in Victoria, which was concerned about dwindling support for the state government, land scandals, and a pervasive feeling that it must lose seats in a federal election. Liberal campaign officers felt that the evangelistic fervor of a campaign meeting would revive the drooping spirits of the party's members in Victoria. The opening showed this genre at its best: the enthusiasm of the audience was apparently spontaneous, and Fraser performed smoothly in a setting he found congenial. It had the major disadvantage of lack of control, exemplified when an enthusiastic supporter sprinkled Fraser with confetti as he mounted the rostrum. This gave an incongruous touch of frivolity to an otherwise austere presentation and distracted the television audience from the content and style of the opening speech.

The Labor party decided to innovate in its presentation of the campaign opening. It set out unashamedly to produce a show, a television program that would be entertaining, informative, and capable of convincing the swinging voter to vote Labor. The half hour allocated to the policy launching was split into two segments of roughly equal length: a documentary section and an edited version of Whitlam's opening speech, which had been recorded at a lunchtime rally in the Sydney Opera House. The half-hour production was shown on national television networks at 8:30 P.M. that night (November 17, 1977).

The Labor party had developed this format in state election campaigns during the previous year, starting with the Tasmanian elections in December 1976 and evolving through the Western Australia, Northern Territory, and Queensland elections. The national secretary of the Labor party, David Combe, had been sufficiently impressed with the success of the concept to give the producers a free hand in planning and shooting documentary material, in designing the opening meeting, and in editing the videotape of Whitlam's policy speech.

The admixture of documentary and political rally was adopted partly to offset the unfavorable popular response to Whitlam that Labor party research had detected. The campaign organizers consciously attempted to project a Whitlam-Hayden leadership team,

cials protested that there was an imbalance because the government parties got a total of forty-five minutes and the Labor party only thirty minutes. The television stations justified the allocation on the basis that the National Country party was a separate party represented in the Parliament. They did not offer any free time on the same basis to the Australian Democrats.

supported by the Labor party's popular state leaders and a handpicked group of younger federal members. Part of the documentary segment showed Whitlam and Hayden campaigning in the evocative landscape of tropical Queensland. Other interview material was shot as late as possible to prevent it from dating. The documentary segment was scripted and produced to promote recognition of the main figures in a new Labor team, and also to cram in as much policy information as possible without preempting the policy speech. The documentary section was completed on November 16, ready for incorporation with the Opera House segment to be filmed the following day.

Technically, the Labor party's opening production was a fine achievement. It fulfilled the objective of providing a visually attractive and generally entertaining show. The documentary section offered little distraction in the way of new policy, and Whitlam was scaled down to an acceptable political size by the grandeur of the scenery and by the overpowering blandness of his colleagues. The fatal flaw of the exercise lay not in the documentary presentation but in the content of Whitlam's policy speech. The producers of the program were as ill-informed about the nature and possible impact of the ALP's taxation proposals as were the other senior officers. In their postelection analyses, the producers claimed correctly that the policy speech ensured that the election would be fought on the Labor party's chosen issues. It was not their fault that these were issues that could only benefit the government and negate the ingenuity expended on the preparation of the half-hour program.

For its opening media presentation, the National Country party stuck to a conventional studio format, using Deputy Prime Minister Anthony and an unambitious set of studio props. These included a sequence of wall charts which showed, with impressive clarity for a television audience, trend lines of economic performance under the Labor government and under the coalition government. The program was well scripted, well directed, and well performed by Anthony. It was only fifteen minutes long, and this combined with its unpretentiousness to make it in many ways the most effective of the three.

The opening of the Australian Democrats' campaign was not broadcast on the electronic media, and the party received no free time on either television or radio. Its leader, Don Chipp, had sought free time from the ABC on the basis that the Australian Democrats were a formally established party with 150 branches and 7,000 dues-paying members. He also argued that the party's performance in the South Australian and Queensland elections entitled it to some free time in a federal election campaign. This request was rejected by the ABC because the party had not elected a member or polled at least 5 percent of the valid votes cast at the immediately preceding federal election—the two requirements laid down in the ABC's internal guidelines for the allocation of free time. Since the party had not existed at the time of the previous election, it was automatically disqualified.[37]

Apart from the campaign launchings, the major parties had ninety minutes each of free ABC television and radio time. The Labor party devoted its time to a range of television mini-documentaries and equivalent material for radio that included a fifteen-minute segment on rural policy, a five-minute segment on uranium and women, and a five-minute segment amplifying a promise in the policy speech to establish a Federal Children's Department. Other material was supplied by federal party spokesmen and state leaders, again hand-picked. Hayden and Hawke, the ALP president and president of the Australian Council of Trade Unions, each spoke for three five-minute segments. Another ten minutes were devoted to a "campaign closer" broadcast the evening before the electronic blackout was imposed. The Labor party's producers also made a number of special free-time segments for the outlying states of Tasmania and the Northern Territory.

The Liberal party's plans for its ABC free time were revised to take account of the decision to concentrate on the payroll tax issue. The initial plan had been to use the air time to supplement the campaign theme "Doing the Job," but part of it was reallocated to exploit the tax issue. The Liberal party also paid for half an hour of commercial television time for a live telecast of Fraser's final campaign meeting in Melbourne before the electronic blackout. This was designed to bolster the vote in Victoria, which was regarded as uncertain despite the trend shown in the polls. The telecast was considered less than successful by party officials.

Paid Media. The media were not as saturated with political advertising as they had been in 1975 because the principal parties concentrated their advertising at different ends of the campaign. For strategic

---

[37] The Democrats claimed that the wording of the regulations gave the ABC discretionary power to allocate them free time: *"The Commission reserves to itself the right to grant or withhold broadcasts at its discretion to political parties, including those not represented in Parliament, on the basis of its estimate of the measure of significant public support for any party."* (Quoted in Hewat and Wilson, *Don Chipp*, pp. 106-107.) The words "at its discretion" would seem to support the Democrats' case.

reasons, the Labor party chose to schedule the bulk of its advertising in the early part of the campaign, tapering off towards the end. The Liberal party's campaign was five days shorter than the Labor party's and its advertising was much denser in the final days before the poll.[38]

Labor's advertising was influenced by the need to mask its leadership credibility problem. Whitlam was given far less play in the television commercials than in the opening media presentation, where the policy speech necessarily placed him in the spotlight. Labor's paid television advertising, like its free-time material, featured Hayden, Dunstan, Hawke, and Wran. Only one advertisement featured Whitlam—an unemployment commercial which showed the party leader in a schoolyard with a group of high school children—and it was not aired during the campaign.

In August the Labor party's National Campaign Committee had given its advertising agency, Mullins, Clarke, and Ralph, a brief which defined the main issues of a possible election campaign as unemployment, broken promises by the Fraser government, economic competence, the unions, and uranium. In the months that followed, the agency prepared the groundwork for the launching of the Whitlam-Hayden plan, including press advertisements, and the pre-emptive advertising campaign of October. When it came time to prepare advertisements for a certain election, the main focus was on unemployment and uranium, with subsidiary attention to economic problems and a defensive stance on trade unions. The agency was given little policy assistance by the spokesmen of the federal parliamentary Labor party.

These themes were the basis of the advertisements prepared by the agency with the approval of the National Campaign Committee and the Labor party's National Executive. The series of advertisements was imaginative and skillfully executed. One of the television commercials won an international prize. It showed an animated man climbing a trend line of rising unemployment and tumbling down over falling indices in retail sales, car sales, economic growth, home loans, and the value of the Australian dollar. If the election had been fought on the issues these advertisements exploited, they would have been highly effective.

---

[38] The Liberal party found it difficult to understand why Labor had started its campaign so early that it ran out of money and initiatives before the electronic media blackout began. Liberal party spending was weighted very heavily toward the final days of the campaign. There was some feeling among campaign officials that this spending was unwarranted because the battle had already been won; also that these funds should have been allocated to the party machine.

Unfortunately for the Labor party, much of this creative effort was negated: the commercials were not relevant to what became the main issue of the campaign—taxation. A television commercial was prepared using Hayden as Labor party economic spokesman, in which the payroll tax proposal was linked to more jobs and lower inflation. It was used in all of the states, but although of an acceptable technical standard, the Hayden commercial lacked the impact of earlier ones. In the time available, the agency faced insoluble problems in trying to merchandise a complex proposal that could not be explained easily in terms intelligible to the electorate.

Before the campaign opened the Liberal party had prepared a series of advertisements based on commissioned research. The main themes were the record of the Labor government from 1972 to 1975, the success of the coalition government in reducing inflation, and a $6 billion package of national investment projects that would go ahead under a coalition government. The keystone of this prepared material was an advertisement called "Memories." It showed the turning pages of a scrapbook displaying press cuttings of Labor's troubled days in office, while a background voice intoned nostalgically, "Memories, memories." This advertisement was broadcast in the early days of the campaign but was taken off, partly because it was felt that the Lynch affair had undercut its comments on Labor government scandals. When subsequent research showed that "Memories" had achieved a much higher degree of recall among voters than any other commercial, it was restored in an amended form which incorporated the Liberal tax cuts.

Another sequence of twelve advertisements used a "man in the street" format to show that Malcolm Fraser was "doing the job." These were filmed in Melbourne, with a variety of laborers, shop assistants, office workers, and pedestrians offering opinions on inflation, unemployment, and government policy. In one, a laborer commented that Fraser was a "tough bastard" but was doing the job he had set out to do. In each commercial, Fraser made a short comment on the issues discussed.

Once the opportunity offered by Labor's payroll tax policy was grasped, the Liberal party's National Campaign Committee moved quickly to exploit it. The first attempt was fumbled when a commercial showing a short excerpt from the Whitlam policy speech ran into copyright problems. It was withdrawn and the offending material removed and replaced by a still photograph. Despite this setback, television and radio advertising exploiting the payroll tax issue went on the air the weekend of November 20–21, a day before the Fraser policy speech.

This first commercial was followed by hastily produced electronic and press advertisements which pushed a simple message:

> What you [Whitlam] are saying is that the hard-earned wages of Australian working men and women are to be taken away from them and given to large companies....
>
> Mr. Whitlam wants to deny you the tax cuts that are your rights and threaten the future of Australia with yet another wild scheme.
>
> Our tax cuts will be good for you and Australia.

The message was reinforced by relatively simple visual material: a computer print-out listing tax savings in relation to weekly earnings; a ballot box that dissolved into a safe, to represent Labor's cash transfers to big business, and then to a cash register doling out the Liberal tax cuts; a fistful of $5 bills fanned out like a poker hand. The Liberal party's advertising agency, Masius Australia, elected a deliberately unsophisticated approach which conceded nothing to subtlety.

This powerful media campaign was backed by an innovative political merchandising device. Party officials had considered the use of volunteers from the Liberal party to staff a phone-answering service which would inform callers of the size of their tax cuts. This idea was discarded because it was felt that the phone lines could easily be jammed by Labor party supporters. Instead, campaign officers decided to use the facilities of Telecom Australia to provide an automatic answering service which would set out the dimensions of the tax cut. The genesis of the plan was described by the head of Masius Australia, Len Reason:

> The solution came to mind immediately. A recorded Telecom answering service like the weather and time, with different numbers in every state, and machines that wouldn't mind particularly where they were told to shove their tax cuts, so long as the caller had paid his ten cents for the call. So the frenzy of getting that organised commenced and a hundred technical problems were solved by Telecom in order to have the plan operational by 1 December. The equipment was installed in Masius offices in every state, with 40 lines in Melbourne and Sydney each and slightly lesser numbers elsewhere.[39]

---

[39] Reason, *Anatomy*, p. 3. Telecom is a federal government statutory authority which administers Australia's telephone services.

Apart from its direct impact—more than 250,000 calls were made in the first six days—the device generated an immense amount of publicity, particularly on radio. The *Melbourne Herald* featured the service on its billboards: "LIBS SET UP 'DIAL A TAX CUT.'" The telephonic service was coordinated with press advertisements which set out the cuts in simple tables and publicized the phone service: "YOUR LIBERAL TAX CUTS: Dial Melbourne 11562. We'll tell you in a recorded message your tax cut from February 1. As you spend your extra money, you'll be creating more jobs." The phone numbers were also superimposed on television advertising devoted to the taxation issue: "Ring 11562 for Your Liberal Tax Cuts."[40]

The effectiveness of the answering device was described by Reason:

> How much did the "Dial-a-tax-cut" idea contribute to the Liberal cause? It's hard to answer precisely, as with many merchandising ideas, but a number of things are certain. The direct response exceeded all expectations and provided a genuinely useful service to voters who needed this relevant information. It added that magic element to the ads which occurs when you are able to say "do this now" instead of "bear this in mind"; an ad which invites some action is more alive and interesting than one that doesn't. . . . And it livened up the "sales force" (as all good merchandising ideas do) through its originality and its demonstration of vitality back at head office.[41]

The diversion of the Liberal media campaign to taxation had one other ironic consequence. In the early days of the campaign, media commentators expected that the Lynch affair would disadvantage the government. In a campaign hinging on economic issues it was assumed that there would be tactical problems for a government whose treasurer had been forced to stand down. When the acting treasurer, John Howard, performed confidently and competently on two major current affairs programs, Liberal campaign officials decided to use him extensively in the media campaign to sell the government's tax cuts. The move proved successful; a Howard commercial explaining tax cuts showed a high level of unaided recall in a survey on Liberal advertising. Apart from "Memories" it was the most successful television commercial of the Liberal campaign.

---

[40] Ibid., pp. 3-5.
[41] Ibid., p. 4.

The Australian Democrats. The Australian Democrats had been a major news story since the party's formation in May 1977. In its early stages the new party had gained favorable media coverage because of its leader's formidable powers of projection. Don Chipp's resignation from the Liberal party in March was one of the major news stories of 1977, and media coverage swelled with the formation of the Australian Democrats and its entry into national politics. Chipp's public standing and his media skills were the party's principal assets. In addition it won favorable coverage by its record of success in the South Australian and Queensland state elections and in a state by-election in Greensborough, Victoria, where it polled 18 percent of the vote. By the time of the federal elections, the Democrats (or the Chippocrats in media parlance) were well established in the electorate's consciousness.

In the tougher climate of an election campaign, the Democrats could match neither the expenditures nor the exposure of their two established rivals, the Labor party and the Liberal–National Country party coalition. The party lacked an effective national organization and its electoral machinery was improvised hastily. Above all, it lacked the funds to mount even an adequate advertising campaign. The party's policy of publicly disclosing all election donations above a modest ceiling of $600 inhibited corporate donors. The Democrats were very much dependent for campaign funds on their grass-roots support and conducted a "Chipp in for Don" fund-raising campaign. The bulk of the funds raised by the Democrats went to cover the mechanics of electioneering, particularly an intricate how-to-vote card: because the Democrats had decided not to allocate their preference votes systematically to either the Labor party or the coalition, their card had to show the voter how to give a primary vote to the Australian Democrats while making clear that he could give his crucial second-preference vote to either of the two major parties.[42]

With funds for only an extremely modest advertising campaign, the Democrats had to rely for media coverage on their ability to generate news, a burden which rested particularly on Don Chipp. The Democrats got solid coverage in the print media, and Chipp was omnipresent on the electronic media. Even though their overall performance was creditable enough for a minor party, the Democrats fell well below the level of coverage they had established in the months leading up to the election.

Part of the problem was that the Democrats tried to acquaint the electorate with a mass of new policies. These were presented in

---
[42] On how-to-vote cards see Appendix B.

a forty-three-page policy speech and sixty detailed policy statements. Whatever the merits of these policies, they were not saleable in an election campaign, where issues are oversimplified. The only document that got more than passing attention from the media was a rejected draft of a statement on law reform. This contained controversial material on abortion and sexual relationships, including, in the section on bestiality, the recommendation that "controls should be maintained to prevent cruelty to animals." An influential Catholic publicist, Bob Santamaria, commented acidulously: "In this extraordinary confection, it must be regarded as evidence of the [Australian Democrat] party's sensitivity that when a human being engages in what was previously regarded as the unspeakable crime of bestiality, he must at least be kind to the animal."[43] Despite Chipp's rejection of this policy document, it was used against the Democrats in much the same way the Human Relationships Report was used to damage Labor.

The main media stories that emerged from the Australian Democrats during the campaign were not related to the party's policies. The first was the direction of the party's preferences. Although Chipp made it clear early in the campaign that the party would not direct its preferences, this subject aroused speculation until the last few days. The media found it incredible that a party in the position of the Australian Democrats would not do a preference deal with one of the major parties. Chipp noted this aspect of the campaign with some exasperation:

> WARWICK ADDERLEY: Are you saying, Mr. Chipp, that regardless of what happens, you will not declare your preferences publicly before the polls?
>
> Mr. CHIPP: Absolutely. This is funny because people—the media particularly—don't seem to understand that we are not directing preferences and I know it is novel. I think every political party has directed preferences. We are just not. We just think it is wrong in principle because why should we be telling people how to vote? . . . I have said right from the start that our preferences will be decided by the people who vote for us, not by us as a party machine. We think that is quite improper, we think it is the prerogative of the person in the polling booth to put the preferences where they wish.[44]

---

[43] Bob Santamaria, "The Vague Goodwill of Chippocracy," *Australian*, November 25, 1977.

[44] "AM" Broadcast, December 5, 1977, transcript, pp. 1-2.

The Democrats' bold showing in the opinion polls taken during the campaign was the other main news story. The early polls, which showed the Labor party and the coalition running neck and neck, stimulated a wave of speculative stories predicting that the Democrats would control the Senate and, by their preferences, decide the result in many House of Representatives seats.

Campaign Patterns

The media coverage of the 1977 campaign was conducted along much the same lines as that of previous campaigns, although there were some changes of emphasis. The media teams that accompanied Whitlam and Fraser were organized more tightly, adhered more strictly to detailed schedules, and required more media facilities such as bus and baggage services. In addition, the parties appointed special campaign officers to look after the media. The size of the parties traveling with the two leaders was determined by the number of seats available on the aircraft, usually fifteen to twenty. The television networks could cut down on the size of their traveling crews by using local facilities, but some rotation of radio representatives was necessary.

Traditionally, the two leaders have been the focus of Australian election campaigns. Where the leaders are, there also is the campaign covered by the media. This focus has shifted in recent elections to Sydney, Canberra, and Melbourne, where the main offices of the media networks, polling and research organizations, advertising agencies, and political parties are located. It is still necessary for a party leader to visit each state at least once, but more and more this is done with an eye to what is happening in the southeast of Australia, where most of the voters live. If the campaign is to be successful, the media and other support facilities of the Sydney-Canberra-Melbourne axis have to be integrated with the traveling circuses that dramatize the campaign to the electorate. In the 1977 elections, the Liberal party was the most enterprising in resolving these logistical problems. Fraser's campaigning in the outer states was confined to brief swoops, usually of a day's duration. There were slack spots and some miscalculations in the allocation of Fraser's time, but the conflicting objectives described above were met with considerable success.[45]

---

[45] These problems were emphasized in a Liberal party memorandum, "Campaigning: The Leader: The Leader's Itinerary." It outlined the logistical arrangements in these terms: "The danger of losing momentum if away from the Eastern States for too long. It is unwise to be away from the main states for more than a couple of days at a time. A week's absence in South Australia, Western Australia etc. is a grave disadvantage. Despite the extra travelling, it is better to spread the visits to distant states throughout the entire program, so that there is no possibility of any prolonged news blackouts in the Eastern States."

Whitlam concentrated more on Sydney and Melbourne and also fed the electronic media more than he had done in previous campaigns. His campaigning style still favored great sweeps across Australia's vast distances. On one day, Whitlam addressed a morning meeting at Geraldton on the west coast, a fund-raising dinner at Alice Springs in the center, and returned to Sydney on the east coast late at night. The logistics of the stunt were impressive, but it removed Whitlam for twenty-four hours from the vital media networks. By locking the traveling media into an aircraft for much of the time, this approach minimized the effective exposure that a party leader might secure on any given day of the campaign.

The vehicle sought most eagerly by the party leaders was the radio interview show known as the talk-back. The popularity of this unsophisticated combination of phone and radio has remained high, and it has become firmly entrenched as the main morning outlet for politicians.

The talk-backs were adopted enthusiastically by Fraser in 1975 and his use of them was even more extensive in 1977. The structure of the talk-back weights its effect in favor of the answering politician. He can ignore the question if he chooses, or reshape it to suit the answer he wants to give. There is little danger of hostile questions or follow-up questions from the invariably deferential hosts of the programs. Control can be exerted over accuracy of material by reference to written notes and other aids without risk of detection by the vast listening audience. The medium was ideally suited for Fraser's remorseless didacticism, particularly on the tax issue. Whitlam also did more talk-backs than in 1975, although not as many as Fraser.

The talk-backs raised problems for the media traveling with the leaders. They were unsuitable for further media coverage because they consisted only of two people seated in a tiny studio answering questions from listeners. Only a handful of the press party could be admitted with comfort to watch, and mostly there was little to report. The talk-backs catered to Fraser's zest for ceaseless reiteration of basic briefing material, but they frustrated the media, and the talk-back mystique got some rough handling from print journalists in particular:

> Radio, particularly talk-back radio, has become the town meeting of our times, albeit a largely menopausal meeting....
> Now they [politicians] fly hundreds of miles simply to spend a cosy hour in a radio studio, untroubled by the questions of a mindless disc jockey and able to peddle their wares with

unchallenged distortion. Fraser did it, Whitlam did it, and Chipp did it. Who wouldn't?[46]

The ABC television current affairs program "This Day Tonight" used a phone-in format which put Whitlam and Fraser before the cameras to answer questions phoned in by listeners to studio journalists, who read them on camera. The voices of the listeners were not used, so the programs lacked the authentic flavor of the talk-backs. The journalists were confined to reading the questions and were not permitted to ask follow-up questions. Again, it was a framework suited admirably to Fraser's use of the electronic media.

The interest of the electronic media in the election grew increasingly perfunctory as the campaign continued. ABC's television news dropped its election coverage back to the middle of its bulletins. The emphasis on equal time and balanced coverage was inimical to the campaign strategies of the Labor party. Invariably, the networks restricted their coverage to Whitlam and Fraser, and this frustrated Labor's strategy of projecting other spokesmen, particularly Hayden, as a counterpoise to Whitlam. Over a two-day period, the four Sydney television stations filmed eight episodes with Hayden, only one of which was aired on the main television news services. Labor party officials complained that television and radio newscasters often seemed intent on securing from Whitlam material that was irrelevant to the main campaign issues:

> Try as we might to gain blanket TV news coverage for Hayden, Hawke or Dunstan, we were thwarted by the obvious policy of the networks to limit their coverage as far as possible to the leaders . . . finally in order to have Whitlam on the main issues on the electronic media, we had to rely on feeding controlled voice pieces from him to the radio stations each morning.[47]

The work of both the print and the electronic media was facilitated by the basic coverage of Fraser and Whitlam supplied by Australia's only national wire service, Australian Associated Press (AAP). This election service was begun in the 1975 campaign. It meant that the media offices could use AAP material to supplement their own coverage or to suggest possible themes to their correspondents traveling with the leaders. It relieved the traveling media of the tedium of processing basic material such as speech texts and press releases. In theory it gave the political correspondents more time to develop

---

[46] Hewat and Wilson, *Don Chipp*, p. 106.
[47] Combe, *Report*, p. 6.

interpretative reporting. AAP also provided a tape service for radio stations through its head office in Sydney.

Conclusion

Fraser had much the better of the media campaign. He was able to shift quickly from his initial tactical stance to exploit the openings that Labor's proposal to abolish the payroll tax had given him. This got the government's campaign back under control after it showed disturbing signs of running astray under the pressures of the Lynch affair. The government fought the campaign on Labor's chosen ground, taxation and unemployment, and it won the fight convincingly. The Liberal party improvised a campaign that used the full spectrum of the media to depict Labor as the party of high taxes. This was supported by the effective exploitation of subsidiary economic themes, particularly the contradictions among Labor's economic spokesmen and its twitchiness about tariff policy. Potentially embarrassing issues, such as the Vietnamese refugees, and occasional conflicting statements between government spokesmen were kept under control. The government was able to avoid uranium, an issue that might have damaged it, particularly if the Labor party had been less lethargic in pushing its policies.

The way the Liberal party integrated all of its media activity to exploit the taxation issue earned the admiration of its political opponents. According to one ALP internal report, "One outstanding feature of the Liberal campaign was the depth of integration between advertising and other media activity. The consistency the Liberals were able to maintain between their paid advertising and their free media was noticeable to all campaign observers."[48] The Liberal party was able to exercise effective control over the campaign through a small group of senior officials who were based in Melbourne but closely linked to Fraser's traveling party. This enabled Fraser to be given fresher and more pointed political material than Whitlam was able to use. For once his jokes were funnier and more wounding than Whitlam's, a remarkable achievement for a politician with an essentially somber approach to politics, while Whitlam was an acknowledged master of political ridicule. The smooth flow of information and communication between the campaign strategists and the traveling party meant that the basic objectives were met: feeding the Sydney-Canberra-Melbourne media axis, and generating newsworthy

---

[48] ALP, 1977 Election Campaign, *Report on Controlled Media*, p. 3. (A report prepared for the ALP Federal Executive in January 1978.)

material from what the prime minister was doing and saying on the campaign trail.

By contrast, Labor's media campaign was fragmented and ineffectual despite the success of individual components such as the campaign opening and much of the advertising. From the beginning the campaign was divided between concepts developed by the campaign planners, particularly the advertising agency, and the payroll tax formula developed by Whitlam. There was a chasm between the campaign organization and Whitlam's traveling party that was never bridged. This meant that the taxation policy had to be sold by the traveling party without effective support from the campaign organization. The merchandising of the taxation policy foundered on the campaign trail under Fraser's sustained pressure. Whitlam conducted a traditional party leader's campaign, he shot for a distinguished performance on the hustings. The campaign headquarters, meanwhile, tried to coordinate a campaign broadly similar to the Liberals'. It was not possible to reconcile the two conflicting strategies in three short weeks.

In crude merchandising terms, the Liberal party's media strategy was designed to sell to the electorate a policy that appealed to avarice and altruism in roughly equal proportions. The appeal to avarice was the promise of cash in the pocket that would flow from a substantial tax cut. The appeal to altruism was based on the feeling of well-being and self-justification aroused by accepting money to put people back to work. The proposition may not have been completely logical but it was eminently marketable. To quote Reason, "people became franker as they grasped the very acceptable proposition that they could help the unemployed by taking money, an unusual (perhaps unique?) opportunity to be selfish and altruistic simultaneously."[49] In contrast, Labor sought to market a switch in taxation policy that would transfer resources from the individual to the private firm, again with the aim of stimulating employment. It was a policy that mixed idealism with altruism—and that could not be successfully marketed either by advertisers or by unpaid media. These were the conundrums that dominated the media strategies deployed in the 1977 election campaign.

---

[49] Reason, *Anatomy*, p. 2.

9
The Economic Program of the Liberal Party

Ainsley Jolley

On Monday, November 21, 1977, Prime Minister Malcolm Fraser formally opened the Liberal party's campaign for reelection to government. In his policy speech, Fraser emphasized economic matters. He pointed to the achievements of his government in reducing the rate of inflation and providing a favorable climate for the development of new investment projects. He stressed such aspects of the government's economic policies as the restructuring of the personal income tax, new developments in industrial relations policy, and the protection of Australian industry. He also proposed some changes in policy in such areas as training and job assistance, export incentives, support for rural industries, and estate duty.

The economic aspects of the Fraser government's election campaign can be understood most easily in the context of the economic policies developed by this government in its first term of office. Consequently, the first part of this chapter summarizes the development of economic policy by the Fraser government between December 1975 and December 1977. This is followed by a brief discussion of the state of the Australian economy over this two-year period establishing the context in which the economic issues of the election should be seen. The third section summarizes the economic arguments put forward by the Fraser government during the election campaign. The final section of the chapter outlines some of the main influences on the economic policies of the Fraser government.

The Economic Policy of the Fraser Government: December 1975 to December 1977

The development of the economic policies pursued by the Fraser government from December 1975 to December 1977 can be broken into four stages: (1) the anti-inflationary policies pursued until November 1976, (2) the devaluation of November 1976 and the accompanying alteration of other economic policies, (3) the attempted wage/price freeze of April and May 1977, and (4) the economic policies adopted in the second half of 1977.

Anti-inflationary Policies, 1976. For most of 1976, the economic strategy of the Fraser government had as its main objective a reduction in the rate of inflation. Its subsidiary objectives were increasing profits as a percentage of national income to a more normal level and shifting resources back from the public to the private sector.[1]

Fiscal policy, monetary policy, wages policy, and international economic policy all were drawn upon in an attempt to achieve these goals. Economies in government spending and reductions in some taxes were combined in such a way that the budget deficit was reduced, resources were released from the public sector, and demand and cost inflationary pressures were reduced. The rate of growth of the money supply was cut back in order to reduce inflationary expectations. By advocating less than full indexation of wages for past price increases, the government hoped to speed the process of adjustment to a situation of low inflation and higher employment. Pressures for a devaluation of the Australian dollar were resisted and a program of overseas borrowing was instituted in order to maintain the existing exchange rate.

Economies in government spending were achieved in three installments. Savings of approximately $300 million were announced in February and another $1,300 million in May, and further substantial savings were outlined in the 1976-1977 budget presented in August 1976.[2] As a result of these new policies the growth in real Commonwealth outlays (after allowing for inflation) was reduced to zero. Reductions in government revenue through the introduction of new policies were almost as great as the cutbacks in spending. These policies included the indexation of personal income tax to the inflation rate and new allowances for investment and for stock valuation in businesses (to become operative in the fiscal year 1977-1978).

The major initiative in monetary policy was introduced in January 1976. At that time the rate of growth of the money supply was tending towards 23 percent per annum, and reducing the budget

---

[1] Ainsley Jolley, *Macro-Economic Policy in Australia, 1973 to 1976* (London: Croom Helm, 1978), pp. 129, 151-152, 176-177.
[2] Ibid., pp. 130, 152. The first round of expenditure reductions was to be made by the end of June 1976, the second and third installments during 1976-1977.

deficit was one means of curtailing this rapid growth. The other was the introduction of a new government security, the Australian Savings Bond, at an especially attractive interest rate. This reduced the excess liquidity in the economy, and within a few weeks the interest rate on this security was lowered. The rate of growth of the money supply was cut back to an annual equivalent rate of 9 percent in the first half of 1976.[3]

In the quarterly national wage cases held during 1976 the Fraser government argued for less than full indexation of wages for past price increases.[4] It was partially successful: in May and August average award wages were increased by roughly two-thirds of the preceding price increases. However, full indexation was awarded in February and November.

In late 1975 and again in the second half of 1976 the Australian dollar came under strong speculative pressure. In January 1976 the government made it clear that it had no intention of devaluing the dollar, and the subsequent monetary package enabled it to hold the line. In the second half of 1976 a program of overseas borrowing was begun in order to support the Australian dollar, and in early November monetary policy was tightened.[5]

Devaluation. Speculation against the Australian dollar had reached a peak by November 1976. On November 28 the treasurer announced that the Australian dollar would be devalued by 17 percent and that henceforth the exchange rate would be subject to more regular review. The devaluation represented a major setback to the government's economic program. It was realized that the devaluation would put pressure on domestic prices and costs, and therefore some tightening of domestic economic policy would be necessary in order to prevent an acceleration of inflation. The end result of the devaluation was a contraction of the domestic economy rather than an increase in inflation.[6]

The tightening of economic policy was achieved by monetary and fiscal means. Yields on government securities were increased by 0.5 percentage points following the substantial increase in yields on short-term bonds in early November. These measures served to

---

[3] Ibid., pp. 130-139, 152-156, 180-185.

[4] From April 1975, the Commonwealth Arbitration Commission had heard four wage cases a year to decide what level of increase should be granted to all wages determined under federal awards.

[5] Jolley, *Macro-Economic Policy*, pp. 139-142, 156-160, 167-171, 196-199, 202-203.

[6] Ibid., pp. 201-211; also *Commonwealth Record*, vol. 2, no. 8, pp. 212-214.

increase the general level of interest rates. In addition, new savings of $250 million were achieved in government spending.

The devaluation of the Australian dollar was partially reversed in December 1976, and in January 1977 controls on the inflow of funds from overseas were reimposed. This followed a sudden inflow of funds from abroad in December 1976 which threatened to have a destabilizing influence on the monetary situation. The decision in the national wage case in March 1977 provided that 60 percent of price increases would be passed on as wage increases.

The Price Freeze. A further alteration in economic policy occurred in April and May 1977 when a price freeze was introduced.[7] The background to the freeze was concern about a return to increasing inflation following the devaluation of the Australian dollar. At a meeting of the Premiers' Conference on April 14 there was a unanimous call for a three-month pause in price and wage increases.[8] It was agreed that the Commonwealth and state governments should cooperate in implementing such a freeze. Essentially the price freeze was to operate on a voluntary basis. Representatives of every major employer group in Australia gave their support to the freeze and a large number of individual companies publicly pledged their cooperation. The Prices Justification Tribunal was asked to monitor price behavior during the period of the freeze. However, it was quite clear from the outset that the price freeze could not be comprehensive and that the prices of produce sold at auction or of perishable products could not be subject to a freeze.

On April 18 the Australian Council of Trade Unions suggested that there should be a tripartite national conference on the state of the economy at which would be discussed the possibility of trading off a pause in wage increases for a tax cut. This suggestion was not acceptable to the Commonwealth government, which had consistently argued that the fiscal situation would not permit any tax cuts in addition to those already in effect. From here on support for the proposed wage/price freeze began to diminish.

At the national wage case in May 1977 the Commonwealth government argued that there should be no wage increase given the existence of a price freeze. The Arbitration Commission was not

---

[7] The development of the price freeze is documented in newspaper articles from April 15 to April 26, May 4 and 5, May 12, May 20, May 25, and in the *Commonwealth Record*, vol. 2, no. 14, pp. 422-423, 430; vol. 2, no. 16, p. 507; vol. 2, no. 19, p. 585; and vol. 2, no. 20, pp. 616, 637.

[8] The Premiers' Conference is a meeting of state government premiers with leaders of the Commonwealth government. It is held at least once a year.

persuaded that a comprehensive freeze was in effect and awarded substantial increases in wages coming under its jurisdiction.[9] Following this decision the price freeze collapsed.

Economic Policy in the Second Half of 1977. The main principles embodied in the economic policies of 1976 (before devaluation, that is) came into their own again in the second half of 1977. The 1977–1978 budget, introduced in August 1977, was basically cautious; it was followed by a further decline in the rate of growth of the money supply (although interest rates also fell), and the exchange rate remained fairly stable.

The 1977–1978 budget combined a continuation of the current level of real Commonwealth outlays with a further restructuring of taxation. Although personal income tax continued to be indexed to offset the impact of inflation and although a new tax scale was to be introduced in February 1978 which was expected to result in a loss of $400 million in government revenue, it was expected that refunds to taxpayers against past over-payments of tax would fall markedly in 1977–1978 largely as a result of tax changes announced in the 1975–1976 budget. Consequently, revenue from personal income tax was forecast to increase fairly rapidly. The crude oil production levy and the excise duty on petroleum products were both increased to raise an additional $180 million. While the basic corporate tax rate was increased, yielding $200 million in revenue, the previously announced investment allowance and the trading stock valuation adjustment were expected to reduce the government's revenue from corporate tax by some $800 million in 1977–1978.[10] The immediate impact of the budget was seen as contractionary, with the February income tax cuts providing an offsetting expansionary influence later in the fiscal year.

In the 1977 budget speech, the treasurer indicated that the volume of money (M_3) might be expected to increase by 8 to 10 percent over the course of 1977–1978, following an increase of 10.6 percent in 1976–1977. At the time there was doubt that such an objective for money supply, when combined with other economic factors, would permit a reduction in interest rates. However, the combination of capital outflow in the latter part of 1977 with a

---

[9] Award wages of up to $200 per week were increased by 1.9 percent, and higher wages by a flat $3.80; the consumer price index had increased by 2.3 percent in the previous quarter.

[10] Australian Government Publishing Service, *Budget Speech 1977-78 and Statements.*

significant easing in the inflation rate (inflation was lower than had been forecast by most economists) permitted a reduction in yields on government securities. This occurred in three stages: early September, late October, and early November. Yields were reduced by from 0.5 to 0.7 percentage points over this period.

Although there were minor variations in the Australian exchange rate, it was kept fairly stable. Following a significant outflow of private capital in August, the Fraser government announced that an overseas borrowing program of $1,700 million would be commenced. Private capital flows stabilized in October and November. In August the Arbitration Commission announced an increase of 2.0 percent in award wages following an increase of 2.4 percent in the consumer price index in the June quarter.

Two other areas of government economic policy that have particular implications for the structure of employment are worthy of comment: these are protection policies and employment programs. So far as protection policies were concerned, the Liberals' long-term program of tariff review and tariff reduction continued with some delays and modifications. However, temporary assistance (through import quotas) was increased for some industries (notably the textile, clothing, and footwear industries), and a market-sharing scheme was introduced for the motor vehicle industry.

A number of new labor programs were adopted in 1976 and 1977.[11] The relocation assistance scheme (to facilitate people's moving to new localities in order to take up employment or training) and modifications to the national employment and training system had general significance for labor mobility. (These policies were announced in September 1976.) The employability of youth vis-à-vis other sections of the workforce was boosted by a number of specific programs. These included:

- the special youth employment training program, which offered a generous subsidy for employment of young people who had previously encountered employment difficulties, introduced in September 1976 and extended in August 1977
- the community youth support scheme, introduced in October 1976, which provided financial assistance to community groups for supportive programs and services for the young unemployed
- new schemes for apprenticeship training including the new Commonwealth rebate for apprentice full-time training and a program

---

[11] Jolley, *Macro-Economic Policy*, pp. 192-193; *Commonwealth Record*, vol. 2, no. 1, pp. 7-9; vol. 2, no. 5, p. 120; vol. 2, no. 32, pp. 1055-1056.

of pre-apprenticeship and accelerated apprenticeship training, introduced in January 1977
- the educational program for unemployed youth, supporting the development and conduct of courses specially designed for the young unemployed whose educational qualifications were low or inadequate given prevailing labor market conditions, introduced in February 1977.

The State of the Australian Economy, November 1977

By the time of the 1977 election campaign, the Fraser government had been in office for approximately two years. It had been successful in reducing the inflation rate by a significant amount over this period. It had had mixed success in changing the distribution of income between wages and profits and the relative sizes of the public and private sectors. And it had failed to prevent increasing unemployment or strengthen the balance of payments.

The consumer price index had increased by approximately 3.0 to 3.5 percent per quarter during 1975. In the March quarter of 1976 it rose by 3.0 percent, in the June quarter by 2.5 percent, and in subsequent quarters by 2.2 percent, 6.0 percent, 2.3 percent, 2.3 percent, and 2.0 percent, this last in the September quarter of 1977. The underlying trend in inflation is often obscured by temporary variations in prices attributable to seasonal factors or to government decisions on such matters as health insurance arrangements. If the figures are adjusted for these temporary factors, the downward trend in the underlying rate of growth of the consumer price index in 1977 becomes clearer: from an increase of 2.8 percent in the March quarter of 1977 the CPI rate of growth declined to 2.4 percent in the June quarter of 1977 and 2.1 percent in the September quarter of 1977. Overall, inflation dropped from 13.5 percent in 1975 to roughly 8.5 percent by the end of 1977.[12]

The reduction in inflation was largely attributable to four main factors:

- declining expectations of inflation, which in turn reduced actual cost and price increases[13]

---

[12] *National Times*, December 5-10, 1977, p. 67.

[13] An index of inflation forecasts compiled by the Victorian Chamber of Manufactures from data supplied by the main professional economic forecasters in Australia showed that the expected annual inflation rate twelve months in the future had declined from 14.3 percent in the December quarter of 1975 to 13.4 percent in the March quarter of 1976, 12.8 percent in the June quarter of 1976, 12.2 per-

- slow growth in the economy, increasing unemployment, and very competitive market conditions for producers
- the reduction in cost pressures associated with reductions in personal and company income taxes
- the easing of inflationary pressures in the world economy, especially in the second half of 1975 and in 1976 (world inflation tending to stabilize by 1977).

The Fraser government's success in reducing inflation rested on its ability to influence inflation expectations; on its cautious and somewhat contractionary fiscal and monetary policies (which created very competitive conditions in the economy); and on tax policies that had some impact in alleviating cost pressures in the economy. The reduction in inflation expectations was related to the emphasis placed by the Fraser government on getting the inflation rate down and to the trend in monetary policy. It is interesting to note that inflation expectations increased temporarily following the November 1976 devaluation, when confidence in the government's resolve to reduce inflation declined.[14] The subdued levels of economic activity in 1976 and 1977 facilitated the maintenance of partial wage indexation and contributed to an apparent easing of profit margins in 1977. The indexation of personal income tax may have had some influence on wage indexation judgments.[15] The restructuring of corporate tax enabled businesses to more easily absorb cost increases.

While wages as a percentage of national income fell between 1975–1976 and 1976–1977 and the share of company profits in the national income increased over the same period, by the latter part of 1977 both appeared to have stabilized (with a slight reversal in trend). The Fraser government's hope had been that the flow-on from prices into wages would be fairly slight and economic recovery would assist profits. This in turn would facilitate a strong investment and export performance. In practice the degree of indexation of wages for price increases was higher than hoped for, and economic recovery was not firmly established. Consequently, profits were squeezed in 1977.

The Fraser government had hoped that economies in government spending would be more than matched by increased spending in the private sector. While this happened to some extent in 1976, the trend

---

cent in the September quarter of 1976, 9.7 percent in the December quarter of 1976, 12.2 percent in the March quarter of 1977, 10.8 percent in the June quarter of 1977, 9.5 percent in the September quarter of 1977, and 8.0 percent in December quarter of 1977.

[14] Jolley, *Macro-Economic Policy*, pp. 212-214.

[15] Ibid., pp. 150-152, 156-160.

was reversed again in 1977. Although significant economies were made in Commonwealth government spending, strong growth continued in state and local government spending. In addition, spending by the private sector was sluggish in 1977.

Conditions in the labor market continued to deteriorate in 1976 and 1977 following the recession of 1974–1975. Statistics compiled by the Commonwealth Employment Service indicated that the actual unemployment rate had increased from 2.5 percent in October 1974 to 4.1 percent in October 1975, 4.3 percent in October 1976, and 6.0 percent in October 1977. Variations in the growth of the labor force (slower growth in 1975–1976 and more rapid growth in 1976–1977) helped to account for the different trends in unemployment in 1976 and 1977. Nevertheless, it remained true that the creation of new job opportunities was proceeding at a fairly slow rate through 1976 and 1977. The government believed that high real wages and low profits were inhibiting the creation of new jobs. However, it was also clear that the rate of economic growth was too low to support a reduction in unemployment.[16]

Production levels had begun to recover in 1976 but slumped again in 1977. Following the recession of 1974–1975, gross nonfarm product grew by 2 percent in 1975–1976 (after allowing for inflation), 3.7 percent in 1976–1977, and 1.9 percent between the September quarters of 1976 and 1977. The recovery in 1976–1977 was led by housing, private investment in plant and equipment, and stock accumulation. Nondwelling building and construction and international trade were tending to retard recovery, however. By 1977, the housing industry had entered a deep recession, and private consumption and business investment were sluggish.

One of the major barriers to the recovery of the Australian economy was the international situation. Sluggishness in the world economy in 1976–1977 and the weak demand for Australia's principal exports (primary products and minerals) combined with high costs in Australia to damage the country's trade performance. This factor, in addition to the government's cautious monetary and fiscal policies, dampened economic recovery.

Australia's balance of payments remained weak through 1976 and 1977. The balance of payments on current account (comprising trade in goods and services) was running at an annual deficit of

---

[16] Statistics quoted in this chapter are taken from official sources available at the time of the 1977 election; in some cases these statistics were revised in 1978. However, if we are to paint an accurate picture of the economic scene as viewed in late 1977, it is appropriate to use statistics available at that time.

approximately $1 billion in 1977. Although the November 1976 devaluation had begun to reduce the volume of imports by mid-1977, exports were very sluggish in 1977. Significant outflows of private capital occurred in December 1975, April 1976, the second half of 1976, and the latter part of 1977. Pending a more consistent revival of private capital inflow, the government embarked upon a strong overseas borrowing program to finance the balance-of-payments deficit on goods and services.

The 1977 Election Campaign

During the 1977 election campaign the Fraser government naturally gave major emphasis to the positive side of its economic policies. The reduction in the inflation rate to approximately 8 percent per annum was emphasized, and Prime Minister Fraser predicted that inflation would be down to between 6 and 8 percent per annum by mid-1978.[17] Fraser also argued that the economy was gearing up for a strong performance in the period ahead, stimulated by lower inflation and falling interest rates, and he described $6 billion worth of investment projects that were likely to be undertaken over the coming years.[18] For these and other reasons, Fraser said that unemployment would begin to fall after the seasonal peak of January 1978.[19]

In outlining the existing economic policies of the government, Fraser gave a great deal of emphasis to personal income tax and tariff policies. The restructuring of the personal income tax in February 1978, a measure included in the 1977–1978 budget, was highlighted as a means of stimulating consumer spending in 1978. Fraser went on to argue:

> The February tax cuts are an integral part of the government's plan for continual steady economic recovery. The reform not only greatly simplifies the tax rate scale, it does not only assist two hundred and twenty five thousand low income earners—including tens of thousands of pensioners—by relieving them of tax; it not only provides a new incentive for work, by putting 90 percent of taxpayers on the same

---

[17] *Commonwealth Record*, vol. 2, no. 46, p. 1744.

[18] This list of major investment projects was referred to in most of Fraser's speeches given during the election campaign; see *Commonwealth Record*, vol. 2, no. 47, pp. 1809-1813.

[19] *Commonwealth Record*, vol. 2, no. 46, p. 1736. While there was a general expectation that the inflation rate would fall further in the future, a significant number of economists believed that increases in seasonally adjusted unemployment were likely.

marginal tax rate, and allowing them to increase their earnings up to sixteen thousand dollars a year before moving beyond this standard rate; it also provides for a responsible stimulus to the economy which will add to spending and activity, leading to higher employment.[20]

Fraser also gave strong emphasis to the government's tariff policies:

> The Liberal government is giving Australian industry the protection it needs. We have shown that it is possible simultaneously to give effective protection to industries and to reduce inflation. And we appointed an inquiry under Sir John Crawford to find the best ways of achieving long term structural adjustment of industry without unacceptable social costs. But to talk of rapid structural change for industry now, when many factories are operating below capacity, when unemployment needs to be reduced, is in practical terms sheer nonsense. Yet this is precisely the kind of unreal, impractical theory to which all but a minority in the Labor Party are firmly wedded, the type of gross generalisation reflected in Mr. Whitlam's speech to the Press Club in July. . . . The Liberal Government has taken firm action where necessary to protect industries under threat. We have increased protection for industries with a total employment of over a quarter of a million Australians in major industries such as motor vehicles, clothing, footwear, textiles, plywood and many others. We rejected out of hand the disastrous I.A.C. draft report on textiles, clothing and footwear. We have taken decisions to protect those industries for at least three years. . . . As a consequence of that draft report, we decided to change the law governing the I.A.C. We have introduced legislation into Parliament to require the I.A.C. to report on: the assistance necessary to maintain present levels of activity in the industries they examine, how each industry's structure might be improved, the employment consequences of its recommendations, and their impact on decentralised industry.[21]

The Fraser government basically campaigned for reelection in 1977 on economic policies that had been announced well before the

---

[20] Prime Minister's Press Release, address at Hobart campaign luncheon, November 28, 1977, p. 4.

[21] Prime Minister's Press Release, address at Western Australian Press Club luncheon, December 1, 1977, p. 5. The Industries Assistance Commission (IAC) is an independent statutory commission advising the government on tariff and other industry assistance policies.

election. The new commitments offered in the election policy speech were of limited importance to the overall macroeconomic environment. Fraser estimated in his policy speech that the total cost of the new programs would be an additional $20 million in 1977–1978 and $250 million in 1978–1979.[22] These new commitments included some widening of existing labor market programs (the N.E.A.T. Scheme, the relocation assistance scheme, and the education program for young unemployed people), a new export incentives program, new rural policies, a deposit insurance scheme covering building societies (financial institutions that specialize in borrowing through short-term deposits from the public and lending through housing mortgages), and the phased abolition of Commonwealth estate duty.

The one new economic commitment of major importance for the macroeconomic framework concerned interest rates. We have already seen that in the months preceding the election, yields on government securities were reduced by between 0.5 and 0.7 percentage points. However, certain critical interest rates (such as those on housing mortgages and bank overdrafts) had not changed over this period. On November 29, Fraser commented: "We have brought about the first consistent downward movement in government interest rates in more than four years, and I am confident—with present government policies continuing—that interest rates could fall up to 2 percent within the next twelve months. This will have a significant effect on the housing industry."[23] On December 5, Fraser made it quite clear that this comment applied to interest rates on housing mortgages: "Interest rates are coming down. In the next twelve months they could be reduced by as much as 2 percent. This will save the average young couple buying a new home ten dollars a week."[24] These comments were to create major problems for the implementation of government policy in 1978, since reductions of this order of magnitude could only be sustained, given continuing reductions in inflation, if the budget deficit were also cut back and the balance of payments improved.

Naturally, Fraser was severe in his criticism of the Labor party's economic policies. The central criticism was that Labor's total policy program would be very costly to implement and that a clear explanation of how it was to be financed had not been forthcoming.[25] Fraser

---

[22] *Commonwealth Record*, vol. 2, no. 46, p. 1737.
[23] Prime Minister's Press Release, Sydney campaign rally, St. Mary's, November 29, 1977, p. 1.
[24] *Commonwealth Record*, vol. 2, no. 8, p. 1863.
[25] Ibid., no. 47, p. 1814.

said that Labor's promises would cost more than $3 billion, which would have to be met through either increased taxation or an increased budget deficit. In addition, he argued that increased government spending and new job schemes would increase inflation rather than reduce unemployment.[26] Fraser was strong in his attack on the apparent confusion about Labor's taxation policies.[27] The Labor party's proposal to abolish payroll taxes was also criticized for its alleged ineffectiveness in stimulating employment and for its cost to the private citizen, forced to forgo his income tax reduction.[28]

Main Influences on the Fraser Government's Economic Policy

What were the main influences on the economic policies pursued by the Fraser government in 1976 and 1977? To what extent did these policies reflect the Liberal party's general outlook on economic policies? Or did they arise out of the circumstances of the time or from technical economic advice emanating from the public service?

Ideology. Political commentators have frequently suggested that the Liberal party has a less positive ideology than the Labor party and that Liberal governments are essentially pragmatic. Yet Liberal attitudes on economic matters over the period 1973 to 1977 seem to have had quite a high ideological content. Thus, they placed higher priority on reducing inflation than on reducing unemployment, stressed the need to reduce the relative size of the public sector, advocated redistributing income from wages to profits, and proposed to shift the balance of taxation from direct to indirect taxes.

At the core of Liberal ideology is support for private enterprise, the private accumulation of wealth, and the profit motive. There is a belief that the unfettered exercise of private initiative is important to the maximization of community welfare. From this central belief flow such conclusions as the need for careful control over the size of the public sector, the minimization of government regulation of the economy, the need for some differential in income to provide an incentive for enterprising behavior (which can provide support for a restructuring of taxes away from direct taxes and towards indirect taxes), and the need to ensure that the distribution of income between wages and profits reflects the real productivity of labor and capital in the economy and thereby provides an incentive for economic efficiency.

---

[26] Ibid., no. 46, p. 1741.
[27] Ibid., p. 1744.
[28] Ibid., and vol. 2, no. 47, p. 1814.

During the 1960s the Liberals' economic policies did not appear to be much affected by these ideological considerations. The public sector was allowed to grow relative to the private sector, and direct taxation was increased relative to indirect taxation. The Liberal party adopted a firmer ideological position during its period out of power, from 1973 to 1975. It can be argued that the experience of being in opposition tends to strengthen the ideological basis of party policies. The leader of the opposition in 1973 and 1974, Bill Snedden, led this process in the area of macroeconomic policy by stressing the need to restrain the growth of public spending and the importance of wage restraint and adequate profits. His successor as leader of the parliamentary Liberal party, Malcolm Fraser, developed this theme further. The resurgence of Liberal ideology was strengthened by the review of the overall performance of the party undertaken over this period. By the time the Liberals had regained power, they were committed to policies that would result in sharp cutbacks in government spending, encourage a return to more normal profitability of private enterprise, and introduce changes in taxation that would control the drift towards increasing reliance on direct taxes as a source of revenue. These policies found sufficient support within the bureaucracy and the community at large to be continued in 1976 and 1977.

The thesis that Liberal ideology was an important determinant of the basic economic policies of the Fraser government in 1976 and 1977 is attractive, but it must be qualified at a number of points. To begin with, it does not explain the party's preoccupation with reducing inflation as the prime objective of economic policy. Second, the Liberal party's basic ideological position on economic issues is difficult to define. The above summary could be criticized as an oversimplification; certainly it would be possible to find divergent opinions within the Liberal party on such subjects as the optimum size of the public sector vis-à-vis the private sector, the best tax structure, and the desirable distribution of income between wages and profits. Third, policy decisions by government are usually complex responses to a variety of influences rather than direct responses to a single influence.

While critics of the Liberal party have sometimes sought to portray it as a proponent of high unemployment/low inflation policies, there is no consistent thread in Liberal ideology that would support this view. For most of the postwar period it seemed clear that the private enterprise economy thrived on a situation of low unemployment and that some inflation (2 or 3 percent per annum) was an acceptable accompaniment to full employment. The Liberals in government were basically committed to full employment, and policies adopted by Liberal governments that temporarily increased unemployment were generally the result of either miscalculations or the need to resolve short-term balance-of-payments problems. The movement towards policies that emphasized inflation control to a greater extent than employment creation should not be seen as an ideological one. A complex set of factors, including judgments on technical economic questions, the prevailing views expressed in the media or the community as a whole, advice tendered by economists within and outside the bureaucracy, the historical setting of the period, the policies of the Whitlam government, and the personal position of Fraser on this issue, has determined the anti-inflationary emphasis of the Fraser government's policies.

The Ministries, the Public Service, and the Reserve Bank. But what about the comparative importance of each of these influences in explaining the government's decisions? The members of the cabinet who bear responsibility for overall macroeconomic policy will normally seek to obtain information and opinions from a wide range of sources and try not to become too dependent on any one source.[29] Often the course a minister chooses is one that has been recommended by a number of sources. Only the politician himself can explain precisely why the decision was made, and even he is not necessarily aware of the process by which his advisers formed their views.

The cabinet is the key decision maker in the area of macroeconomic policy in Australia. However, many important decisions affecting the economy are made by a few senior ministers rather than by the full cabinet.[30] Obviously, the prime minister's role is crucial. A Liberal prime minister often has greater personal power than a Labor prime minister, who must continually answer to his party's caucus.[31] When Fraser became prime minister in December 1975 his leadership of the coalition parties was unchallenged, and he sought to control general policy development as well as the timing of decision making. His extensive contacts in, and knowledge of, the bureaucracy gave him greater influence over the shape of the advisory network than most other prime ministers, while his interest in detailed questions of policy and his great capacity for work enabled him to exercise strong personal control over economic policy.

---

[29] Jolley, *Macro-Economic Policy*, pp. 12-17.
[30] Ibid., pp. 14-16.
[31] Ibid., pp. 17-18.

In the area of economic policy, the treasurer holds a key position in the cabinet. His department had control over the main budget processes until 1978,[32] as well as the main authority for monetary policy and substantial authority for policies concerning the exchange rate and international capital movements. He also receives detailed briefings from his department on wages, prices, trade, and industry policy. However, the extent to which this potential power becomes actual power depends in part on the leadership style of the prime minister and on the way the treasurer operates in cabinet and in other political discussions.

Phillip Lynch was treasurer for the whole of 1976 and most of 1977. He brought to his office considerable experience as a spokesman on economic matters, and he had a reputation for being a strong advocate in cabinet discussions. During 1976 and 1977 Lynch worked very closely with his department, was sympathetic to the Treasury's approach to economic policy, and tended to argue the Treasury line in general policy discussions. However, his experience as opposition spokesman on economic matters from 1973 to 1975 meant that he had been closely involved in the formulation of opposition economic policy, and he regarded the 1975 election commitments as very important. He also played an important part in 1976 in developing and broadening the bases of consultation between the government and the private sector on economic matters.[33] Other ministers with responsibilities in the economic area—Tony Street, Doug Anthony, Ian Sinclair, John Howard, Peter Nixon, and Robert Cotton—figured prominently in the economic debate on particular issues. Within the cabinet there were no fundamental divisions on economic policy of the sort that had divided the Liberal and Country parties in 1971.[34]

Major decisions on macroeconomics, while formally made by the cabinet, usually reflect technical advice tendered by the Commonwealth public service, the Reserve Bank of Australia, or the ministerial staffs. The Liberal party developed a tradition of close partnership between the cabinet and the public service during its twenty-three years in power from 1949 to 1972. Indeed, the public service was often the principal source of policy advice, and while political factors were important in determining the Fraser government's economic

---

[32] By 1978 ministerial responsibility for detailed spending policies belonged to the minister for finance, Eric Robinson, rather than the treasurer.

[33] Jolley, *Macro-Economic Policy*, pp. 217-218.

[34] Laurie Oakes and David Solomon, *The Making of an Australian Prime Minister* (Melbourne: Cheshire, 1973), pp. 43, 83.

policy in 1976 and 1977, the public service retained its dominance in the advisory network.

While the Treasury has traditionally been the most influential department in economic policy, other departments have made significant contributions. The Department of the Prime Minister and Cabinet provides advice on macroeconomic policy to the prime minister. In 1976 the department had a comparatively small staff of economists, but its resources were upgraded at the end of 1976. The department's major role has been to tender advice on the broad thrust of macroeconomic policy and to work on some specific task force projects. It was quite influential in 1976 and 1977, although its advice differed from that of the Treasury only in degree; in fact, the two senior economists in the department were former Treasury officials. The Department of Employment and Industrial Relations played an important role in manpower and wages policy, the Department of Business and Consumer Affairs administered prices policy, the Department of Immigration and Ethnic Affairs was responsible for immigration policy. Industry and resource allocation policies were administered by the Departments of Industry and Commerce, Primary Industry, National Resources, and Transport, while trade matters were affected by the Departments of Overseas Trade, Foreign Affairs, Business and Consumer Affairs, Industry and Commerce, and Primary Industry.

The Treasury is the main source of advice on macroeconomic policy.[35] It was the principal adviser on fiscal, monetary, exchange rate, and foreign investment policies for much of 1976 and 1977 and an important adviser on wages policy. The Reserve Bank of Australia is the principal monetary authority in the country. In the event of a disagreement between the bank and the treasurer, the legislation under which the Bank operates provides that the treasurer's view will prevail, and in recent years the Treasury has been more influential than the Reserve Bank in determining the main features of monetary policy (the exchange rate, administered interest rates, and the management of government debt). The bank, meanwhile, exercises its influence primarily in the day-to-day conduct of monetary policy, through intervention in the money markets, control over foreign exchange markets, and monitoring of the activity of various financial institutions. It should be added that the prime minister and treasurer both employ

---

[35] Jolley, *Macro-Economic Policy*, pp. 20-21. Note that the Department of Finance was created in November 1976 and absorbed some of the functions previously held by the Treasury, in particular the control of government outlays. However, Lynch was both treasurer and minister for finance for most of 1977, so the distinction between the Treasury and Finance Departments was blurred over that period.

professional economists on their staffs, and consultative committees provide economic advice.[36]

Political Factors. Probably the most important of the political factors to influence the government's macroeconomic policy was the election mandate, that is, the housing commitment made in the process of winning the election.

Campaign commitments have generally been an important factor in Australian political life, and in 1975 they influenced such policies as the introduction of the investment allowance, the indexation of the personal income tax, the restructuring of corporate tax, and, to some extent, the program of cutbacks in government spending. These election commitments arose as a result of the opposition experience of the Liberal party in the years 1973 to 1975.[37] While the opposition's policies were strongly influenced by Fraser's personal approach to economic issues,[38] other factors were also important. These included:

- The economic circumstances of the times, including the dramatic spiral of prices and costs in 1973–1974. This was reinforced by evidence of the public's great concern on this issue.[39]
- The need to oppose the Labor party, which had implemented a program of big increases in government spending and had initially emphasized employment creation rather than inflation reduction.
- Traditional Liberal party attitudes on such questions as wage policy.
- Snedden's personal position on economic matters. Of particular importance were his emphasis on the relationship between wage claims and tax levels (dating back to the time when he was minister for labor in 1970 and 1971), his experience in administering spending economies and tax cuts as treasurer in 1971 and 1972, and the priority he placed on the reduction of interest rates, which implied the need for anti-inflationary policies to emphasize fiscal restraint and the control of budget deficits rather than overreliance on monetary policy).
- The beliefs of Snedden's staff economist, Richard Sheppard, and certain academic economists. Their monetarist approach to the

---

[36] Ibid., pp. 218-219.
[37] Ibid., pp. 22, 36-38, 41-42, 44-47, 49-52, 55-61, 73-74, 76, 80-81, 86-87, 89-93, 98-99, 104-107, 109-110, 115-118, 220-226.
[38] Ibid., pp. 231-238.
[39] Ibid., p. 57.

reduction of inflation featured in Liberal policy pronouncements from early 1975.
- Advice tendered from sources within industry and by some academic economists in favor of the investment allowance and other tax reforms.

In addition, interest groups and the media may have influenced the details of particular economic policies, especially by reinforcing other influences.[40] And the public's concern about high inflation and high tax burdens had its effect.

The Treasury and the Fraser Government. The Treasury sees inflation as the number one economic problem.[41] Its recipe for a successful anti-inflationary policy is maximum restraint over public spending, the preservation of the Commonwealth government's revenue base, reduction of the budget deficit, slower growth in the money supply, preservation of a fixed exchange rate, a phased reduction in tariffs on imports, and reduction of the rate of growth of wages through hard-line submissions to the Conciliation and Arbitration Commission in wage cases advocating minimal or zero wage increases. Some of the subsidiary objectives of the Treasury are reduction in government interference with market mechanisms and in the size of the public sector relative to the private sector. The Treasury is skeptical of the efficacy of prices and incomes policies and is more tolerant of proposals to reduce taxation than of proposals to increase government outlays. It resists policies that imply an acceptance of, and accommodation with, inflation (for example, floating exchange rates in the current economic context and all forms of indexation).

The analytical basis of the Treasury's anti-inflation policy can be described in the following terms. Average wages in the economy are determined in part by Arbitration Commission decisions, in part by market forces, the most important of which are the level of demand and the growth of world prices as expressed in Australian dollars. Expectations about future inflation are largely determined by actual inflation in the past and public perceptions about the strength of the government's anti-inflationary policies. The exchange rate will influence the level of world prices as expressed in Australian dollars.

---

[40] Ibid., pp. 24-25.

[41] The extent of the Treasury's influence over the economic policies adopted by the Fraser government in 1976 is summarized in Jolley, *Macro-Economic Policy*, pp. 226-230. The Treasury was perhaps less influential in 1977, although the overall thrust of fiscal and monetary policy was not too far out of line with Treasury thinking.

The pursuit of contractionary monetary and fiscal policies in the short run will increase unemployment but decrease inflation and reduce expectations about future inflation. Control over the exchange rate and advocacy of minimal increases in award wages before wage-fixing authorities will help to reinforce these anti-inflationary policies. In addition (because the Treasury emphasizes the importance of labor costs as a factor in influencing the level of employment) the reduction in real wages will facilitate increased employment at some stage. Once inflation and expectations about future inflation have been moderated, an easing of contractionary policies will be permitted and a return to high employment will be more likely.

To achieve the second objective of its economic policy—the reduction in the relative size of the public sector—the Treasury advocates a contractionary fiscal policy to take the weight off monetary policy and restraint in government spending as a means of achieving a contractionary fiscal policy. This combination implies low government spending and avoidance of increases in taxation or interest rates that would discourage the private sector. The Treasury argues that containing the public sector will increase economic efficiency in the long run (assuming that the public sector is less efficient in the use of economic resources than the private sector) and will establish a more competitive environment, which will discourage excessive increases in wages and prices. It also permits lower taxation, which increases incentives in the private sector. The Treasury suggests that reliance on monetary rather than fiscal policy as a means of restraint is also undesirable because it necessitates an increase in the proportion of government debt to other assets held in the private sector, and this can only be secured by continuing increases in interest rates on government securities. This process not only causes "crowding out" effects so far as the private sector is concerned, but also causes uncertainty and instability in financial markets.

Inflation is regarded as the most important of the current economic problems. It is argued that high inflation causes eventual unemployment and a poor growth performance. High inflation has an adverse impact on private consumption because would-be consumers cut spending and increase savings in order to preserve or restore the real equivalent of money balances and to guard against the adverse economic conditions that have become associated with high inflation. Private investment is also adversely affected by inflation. High inflation causes increased uncertainty about the likely future relationship between costs and prices, thereby increasing the risks associated with long-term investment. It has also been associated with a business profit squeeze which has reduced expectations about the profitability of future investment and reduced the real internal cash flows available for financing investment. The reduction in real cash flows has increased reliance on the capital market for financing investment. However, increasing inflation has reduced the supply of funds available for financing long-term projects as lenders opt for short-term assets (a rational response when economic uncertainty is increasing). Finally, where the local inflation rate is higher than the world inflation rate and the exchange rate is fixed, high domestic inflation causes a deterioration in the current account of the balance of payments, with adverse consequences for local production and employment.

Fraser's Personal Views. In recent years Fraser has been a supporter of low government spending, low taxation, reduction of the budget deficit, government control over the money supply, and low interest rates. He favors government control over the exchange rate and government intervention in wages cases.[42] Fraser sees the basic objectives of economic policy as price stability, full employment, a high rate of national development, the minimization of the public sector, and the attainment of a strong position in the economy for the primary, mining, and manufacturing sectors. He has always realized the possible inconsistency between what he regards as the two primary economic objectives: price stability and national development. During the early part of his political career he was inclined to the view that progress in national development should take precedence over inflation control where the two objectives were incompatible. However, he recognized that balance of payments constraints would occasionally force the government into taking stronger action against inflation. Fraser became particularly concerned about accelerating inflation during 1973, and by 1974 he had come to accept the need for tough policies to reduce inflation. However, there were times during the 1975 election campaign and in 1976 when Fraser appeared to be giving greater emphasis to the problems of economic development than to restraining inflation (the November devaluation being the foremost example). By 1977 Fraser was once again emphasizing anti-inflationary policies.

The prime minister has suggested that the underlying cause of the current high inflation is that expectations have outstripped national resources. This has occurred because (1) there has, at times, been excess demand in the economy, (2) governments have over-committed

---

[42] Ibid., pp. 231-238.

themselves and increased expectations in the community, and (3) the trade unions were exerting stronger pressure than in the past as their assumptions about employment opportunities changed and their bargaining position improved. In order to reduce these unrealistic expectations tough policies are required, of which the most important is restraint in government spending.

Fraser believes that the key to national development is progress in the primary, mining, and manufacturing industries and in investment-led (rather than consumption-led) expansion. A strong rate of development requires not only restraint in the growth of the public sector and low taxation but also the provision of specific incentives through the tax or tariff systems. Low interest rates and the setting of the exchange rate can help to achieve rapid development.

Conclusions

The main objective of the Fraser government's economic strategy has been the reduction of the inflation rate. Its subsidiary objectives have been to increase the share of profits in the national income to a more normal level and to shift resources from the public to the private sector. In order to achieve these policy objectives, the Fraser government economized on public spending, reduced some taxes, reduced the growth of the money supply, and argued before the Arbitration Commission for minimal (or no) wage increases.

By the time of the 1977 election campaign, the government had managed to reduce inflation but had not had a major effect on the distribution of income between wages and profits or the relative sizes of the public and private sectors. Unemployment was still increasing and the balance-of-payments situation remained weak. During the 1977 election campaign, the Fraser government emphasized the positive features of its existing economic policies. However, it did suggest that a considerable reduction in interest rates would be possible in the period following the election.

While the economic policies adopted by the Fraser government in 1976 and 1977 were influenced by Liberal party ideology, this could not be regarded as the dominant influence on policy development. Policy responded to the economic events of the period and to the community's apprehensions about high inflation. Reactions to Labor policies, the personal influence of Snedden in 1973 and 1976 and Fraser thereafter, and the advice of public servants and economists outside the public service and industry have all been important influences on the development of economic policy by the Fraser government.

10
The Economic Program of the Labor Party

Duncan Ironmonger

From an economist's viewpoint, the economic program of the Labor party, indeed of any party, could be assessed under three broad headings: macroeconomic management, structural development policy, and provision for social equity.

For the first—macroeconomic management—the major issues are inflation, unemployment, and the balance of payments, while the major instruments of policy are tax rates, interest rates, and exchange rates. Day-to-day and week-to-week, decisions must be made about how to use them. Equally continuous are the associated problems of supervising monetary and fiscal policies and establishing a climate for income restraint.

The second—structural development policy—involves the whole structure of agricultural, mineral, industrial, and commercial development, which determines the climate and directions of economic growth. It also includes the provision of economic infrastructure through public works and through institutional controls and incentives such as tariffs, subsidies, and the running of government enterprises.

The third—social equity—involves income maintenance and the provision of social welfare, health, and education services through cooperative arrangements between federal, state, and local governments and voluntary bodies and agencies.

The Platform

What are the intentions of the Australian Labor party in regard to the economy? The answer is to be found in the statements made by the leaders of the party inside and outside Parliament or in pamphlets or paperback books like *Towards a New Australia*, edited by John

McLaren and published by the Victorian Fabian Society in 1972. The principal up-to-date statement of economic policy intentions is to be found in the policy speech made by the leader of the party at the opening of the last election campaign.

However, for the Labor party in 1977 we have, in addition, the statement published by the national secretary of the party, David Combe, following the Thirty-Second National Conference in Perth in July 1977. This statement, the *Australian Labor Party Platform, Constitution and Rules*, is in fact a 140 page book known as the platform. At each biennial national conference the platform, which represents the "official" or "endorsed" views of the party, is brought up to date and reissued.

In 1977 a great effort was made to make the platform readable. Most of the items are presented under the heading "Proposals for Reform." Compared with the earlier platforms (which followed a Ten Commandments approach, listing tenets the wording of which had obviously been argued at length by the biennial conference) the 1977 platform is full of explanatory passages and references to recent events. Proposals for the economy are given a high priority, coming immediately after the passages on constitutional and legal reform and citizens' rights with which the platform begins.

The introduction to Labor's proposals on the economy is worth quoting to give the flavor of the document:

> We no longer live in the relatively calm and quiescent economic world of the 1950's and 1960's. New forces are at work, both in Australia and elsewhere, generating more difficult economic problems, particularly with regard to unemployment and inflation.
>
> Recent levels of unemployment reflect more than a cyclical recession. Changes in technology, increasing concentration in ownership and control of industry, changes in the international, regional and industrial placement of investment, evolving trade patterns, and populations trends, are disturbing the routine of the past. A Labor Government will accept responsibility for achieving full employment and stable prices, but these will not be achieved simply or as a matter of course.
>
> Broad-brush approaches, through monetary and fiscal measures alone, are not adequate in a situation where economic problems are becoming more complex and severe.
>
> We need detailed sectoral and regional consideration and planning of our economy. We cannot allow, as has happened all too often in the past, industries to be massacred—just

because perhaps some overall restraint on activity is required. We need to look at the parts as well as the whole.

Planning must be conducted in a democratic fashion, not merely because that is the political philosophy to which we subscribe, but because planning is unlikely to be effective unless those whose lives are being influenced are genuinely consulted and become part of the decision-making process. Genuine democratic economic planning of this kind is not an easy task, but it is vital for our future.

Ultimately the primary concern of economic policy is the satisfaction of the needs and desires of people. In this sense, population policies are an integral part of economic and social planning.

The proposals for the economy indicate that the Labor party learned a lot from its brief experience of federal government. Whereas platforms produced prior to its three years in office could be said to concentrate heavily on the second of my three broad headings, structural development policies, the post-government platform shows numerous indications that the party now has views and proposals for the reform of macroeconomic management.

The section of the platform on "Complementary Short Term Policy" is indicative of the new emphasis:

14. complement planning with stabilisation policies designed to minimise economic fluctuations;
15. provide a more stable policy framework for economic activity, because abrupt changes in policy, especially those related to levels of monetary liquidity, bring disruptive economic consequences;
16. nevertheless, use all the tools of economic policy, including variations in taxation, government spending, exchange rates, and money supply, to maintain growth as stable as possible; and
17. keep an appropriate relationship between growth in the money supply and the prospective increase in prices and output because too rapid an increase in the money supply may bring unacceptable inflation, and too slight an increase may result in reduced output in general and severe damage to the prospects of particular industries.

Unfortunately for the Labor party, although its leaders are aware of the need to develop ideas and capabilities for macroeconomic management, and this concern has found expression in the platform, the public has not yet fully realized how much the Labor party has developed. At the time of the 1977 election the electorate obviously believed that the Liberal-National Country party coalition had the better macroeconomic management team, or at least that it ought to be given a further period in office to prove itself.

Herein lies one of the real problems of the Labor party in gaining acceptance as a viable alternative government: it is easier for Liberal and National Country party leaders to present themselves as successful economic managers since, as the leaders of the conservative parties, they are the natural allies of business. Business is to do with management, with employing others, with making business decisions. The public tends to credit the Liberal and National Country parties with the ability to manage the economy, which, it assumes, is somehow akin to running a large business or even a large farm. Both the 1977 campaign and Labor's experience in office illustrate its problems.

The Campaign

In the 1977 election campaign there was little that the Labor party could offer as an alternative economic management strategy because, no matter what recipe it came up with as a means of escape from the twin evils of unemployment and inflation, the Liberals could point to two simple facts that were only too well known and accepted: under Gough Whitlam's Labor government of December 1972 to November 1975 (1) unemployment had doubled, from 2.2 percent of the labor force to 4.4 percent, and (2) the rate of inflation had almost trebled, from 5.9 percent to 16.7 percent.

Although the Fraser government had no success with reducing unemployment in its two years in office (on the contrary, the rate rose to over 5 percent of the labor force) it had modest success with inflation, which fell to around 10 percent. Moreover, the Fraser government had stuck to the line that inflation had to be brought down *before* anything could be done about jobs. Indeed, in Labor's last year in office the treasurer, Frank Crean, had endorsed the view that "One man's pay rise was another man's job." Since it is widely believed that there is an inverse correlation between wage rises and inflation on the one hand and jobs on the other, the Labor party had some difficulty persuading the voters that it had the formula to swim against the tide and simultaneously improve both inflation and jobs. Nevertheless Labor proposed just such a program.

The Payroll Tax Proposal. The ALP's main variation on the Lynch budget of August 1977 was the proposal to eliminate both the payroll tax and the government's personal income tax cut due to come into operation on February 1, 1978. During the campaign it emerged clearly that the leaders of the Labor party had done little to think out the details of this major proposal. Indeed, there was considerable opposition at a high level within the party to the particular form of the proposal announced in the policy speech. Nevertheless there was, and is, much merit in the idea of cutting indirect taxes as a means of simultaneously bringing down inflation and encouraging expansion and the creation of jobs. What is doubtful is whether abolishing the payroll tax is the most efficient means to that end.

The payroll tax, levied on employers, was first instituted in Australia as a means of financing child endowment (the family allowance paid regularly to mothers by the government for the "maintenance, training and advancement" of children). It was introduced in May 1941 as a federal tax at the low rate of 2.5 percent of the total wages and salaries paid by an employer; collected monthly, it formed the basis of Australian monthly employment statistics. Employers with annual payrolls of less than $20,800 (approximately four employees) were exempt. In 1971 the Liberal prime minister, William McMahon, who was under some pressure to give the state premiers access to a "growth" tax (one with potential for expansion as the economy grows), handed the payroll tax over to the states, which promptly raised the rate to 3.5 percent; by the end of 1974 it had reached 5 percent.

The trade-off proposed by Labor was quickly seized upon by the Liberals as taking money out of the pockets of wage earners and giving it to their employers. The Liberals presented the Labor proposal as a reversal of Labor's usual concern for the little man. In fact, however, any serious economic assessment of the relative merits of the two parties' proposals is necessarily complex. The coalition's tax cut could be criticized on the grounds that it was very heavily biased towards the upper end of the income spectrum, so that an unusually high proportion of the increase in disposable income was likely to be absorbed in higher savings. Neither was the income tax cut part of any wage-tax trade-off, and the skewed distribution of the benefits made it unlikely that the trade unions would accept it as such. Thus the coalition's measure could be faulted as an inefficient means either of stimulating the economy or of slowing inflation. On the other hand, the elimination of the payroll tax would initially be reflected in higher business incomes, and its effect on prices, household incomes, and employment would depend on subsequent business decisions that could not be foreseen with certainty. Thus a prima facie case could be made that the payroll tax measure was a less efficient means of stimulating the economy and reducing inflation than cuts in excise or sales taxes or reductions in charges for public transport, gas, and electricity, which directly affect prices and household incomes, or a wage-tax deal, where again the consequences are fairly direct and predictable.

A reasonably complex chain of reasoning is required to show that an indirect tax cut such as the elimination of the payroll tax would be more beneficial to the economy than a personal tax cut like that proposed by the government. Selling the idea to the public, therefore, was a delicate business that needed to be carefully thought out in advance. But the Labor party did not adequately prepare the ground in 1977. Another tactical mistake may have been to propose the renunciation of the personal tax cut as a means of paying for the elimination of the payroll tax—an attempt at fiscal "responsibility." The ALP may well have needed to show the electorate that it was responsible. The question is whether this was the way to do it.

In 1977 Labor attempted to take away from the taxpayer a break on which he was already counting. Liberal campaign offices soon established telephone services in the capital cities where people could phone in to find out how much tax they would save starting February 1, 1978, under the Liberal scheme. Labor found it almost impossible to sell the idea of giving up such apparently concrete benefits for the prospect of the faster decline in inflation and the faster rise in employment it claimed would follow as payroll tax savings were passed on to the consumer in lower prices or to the labor force in more jobs. To the electorate these prospects were unproven. One is reminded of the Australian television quiz game where the contestant has the option of accepting the money he has already won or asking for another box to be opened and taking a chance on winning a bigger prize. The audience always barracked for "the box" but many contestants opted for "the money."

In 1977 the Australian electorate opted for the money—and its preference for immediate financial returns proved to be misplaced: In August 1978 when the Liberal government found it could no longer afford to finance the February 1, 1978, tax cut, it not only did not revert to the previous tax scale but it imposed a 1.5 percentage point *increase* in tax rates across the board (an average increase in taxes of about 5 percent in 1978–1979). The longer run and probably more beneficial option of abolishing the payroll tax, with its strong cost-push effects on employment and inflation, was thus passed over.

Echoes of 1975. Labor had missed out by presenting a "responsible" image once before, on the occasion of its last budget, the Hayden budget of August 1975. In November 1974, in one of his rare interventions in economic policy, Labor Prime Minister Gough Whitlam had established a Committee of Inquiry into Inflation and Taxation. This committee was to report by May 1975 on two vital issues that had been raised in relation to inflation and taxation: (1) the advantages and methods of indexing personal income tax and (2) the advantages and methods of applying inflation accounting to the assessment of company profits for taxation.

The committee, under Professor Russell Mathews, reported on schedule in May 1975 that both proposals had merit and urged that they be introduced immediately in the August budget. The economic and equity arguments in favor of both measures were strong, and personal tax indexation was a relatively simple matter that could be introduced at once. Company tax inflation accounting was more complicated, involving all sorts of measurement problems and conceptual difficulties that have plagued the accounting profession for decades; still Mathews claimed to have found a way through the maze and suggested its gradual implementation over a period of three years.

Of course in bureaucratic eyes such reforms would be a "cost" to the government of perhaps $1,000 million a year. As more indexation arrangements came into force (wages were to be indexed quarterly on movements of the consumer price index, pensions half-yearly on movements in average weekly earnings) the Treasury saw that more and more people could learn to live with inflation.

One might be excused for seeing bureaucratic politics at work in subsequent developments. The day after the Mathews report appeared, another report on the taxation system was released, that of the Asprey Committee, which had been appointed years earlier to make a wide ranging review of the structure of the tax system, and which had filed its final report with the Treasury some time before. The Asprey Committee, although it had scarcely made any inquiry into the effects of taxation on inflation, was unconvinced of the case for automatic statutory indexation of personal income tax. This provided a counterweight to the Mathews proposals.

At the same time another inquiry into taxation was set up by the Treasury—a secret inquiry under Professor Trevor Swan of the Australian National University. In May or June 1975 and unannounced to the public, Swan apparently was asked to devise a simplified rate structure for the personal tax system for immediate introduction in the August 1975 budget.

By August 1975 inflation was running at an annual rate of around 15 percent and the officials of the cabinet's Expenditure Review Committee were trying hard to cut some $2,000 million from the "first bids" of the departments. This would prevent the domestic deficit's increasing from an estimated $1,740 million in 1974–1975 to a "roughly" estimated $3,650 million in 1975–1976. Consequently, Treasury officials exerted strong pressure on the new treasurer, Bill Hayden, to prevent the adoption of the Mathews Committee proposals, and on August 19, 1975, Hayden introduced a budget with a new simplified personal income tax rate scale divided into seven steps instead of fourteen. For dependents of taxpayers the regressive system of deductions from taxable income was replaced by a more equitable tax rebate system. Hayden argued that this was a major reform of the tax system, and the Mathews reforms were put aside with a vague promise that they would be looked at in "next year's" budget. But there was to be no second Hayden budget. In fact it was this "responsible" budget that eventually was deferred by the Senate, leading to the dismissal of the Labor government on November 11, 1975.

In the subsequent election campaign the Liberal-National Country party platform put forward really only one major economic policy: the implementation of the Mathews report. Fraser promised that this would be done over the course of three years, and in the meantime, since the company profits position seemed desperate, tax concessions in the form of a 40 percent investment allowance on new plant and equipment would be given to stimulate recovery. Thus the Mathews Tax Reform banner that Labor had left lying by the roadside was eagerly seized by the Liberals, who carried it at the head of their caretaker government. Although other issues obviously dominated the 1975 election, this banner, in my view, at least gave the Liberals a credible economic policy.

The Problem of Tax Indexation. In the 1977 campaign tax indexation came up again. Between 1975 and 1977 Malcolm Fraser had forced through, against the protests of an unwilling Treasury, the promised indexation of personal income tax and some of the inflation accounting recommendations for corporate taxation. These measures were accompanied by a severe pruning of government expenditure which naturally had depressing effects on economic activity. The August 1977 budget of Liberal Treasurer Phillip Lynch simplified the personal tax scales still further. The seven-rate structure introduced by Hayden in August 1975 would be replaced by a three-rate structure as of February 1, 1978. Since this simplified structure also reduced the average rates of tax, particularly for high incomes, the promised indexation adjustment due on July 1, 1978, would be reduced to only 50 percent of the appropriate increase in the consumer price index. With this measure, the Treasury both reduced the net cost to the revenue and managed to moderate the movement towards indexation.

When Labor proposed to cancel the Lynch tax cuts due on February 1, 1978, to help pay for the proposed elimination of the payroll tax, the question of what would happen to the 50 percent tax indexation due on July 1, 1978, was left up in the air. During the campaign it became clear from Whitlam's statements that Labor's tax indexation policy had not been clearly thought out. Whitlam first said that tax indexation would be postponed. When pressed for an elaboration he then said that he expected Labor would bring in full, not half, indexation in 1978–1979 and that Chris Hurford, Labor's economic spokesman, would issue a statement clarifying the issue. The Hurford statement promised less than expected and indicated only that the aim of the next Labor government would be to "adopt full tax indexation as soon as responsibly possible."[1] In the meantime Whitlam, Hayden, and Hurford had conferred, and although Hurford was confident that full indexation could be introduced in 1978–1979, Hayden was more skeptical about its desirability and believed Labor would be very unwise to "lock itself in" on the revenue side. Clearly the equity and economic management arguments sustained in the Mathews report had not been accepted by Hayden or were outweighed in his mind by other factors, such as the constraints on future economic initiatives posed by the budget deficit.

Labor and Economic Management

Obviously in an election campaign, when reporters are more than ordinarily eager to probe the statements of political leaders, occasional contradictions and confusions will surface. But this incident shows, in addition, that the Labor party has concentrated too much of its intellectual effort on structural issues and too little on the fine points of macroeconomic management. It will be interesting to

---

[1] This quote and the next are from Paul Kelly, Andrew Clark, and Peter Freeman, "Labour: Back From the Dead? A Special Report," *National Times*, no. 356 (November 28, 1978), p. 22.

see whether in its post-mortem on the 1977 campaign the Labor party itself comes to similar conclusions.

One of the main weapons used by the Liberal party in the 1977 campaign was to present the ALP as the party of poor economic managers, the "spendthrift" party that allowed, if not caused, inflation and unemployment to soar to heights unprecedented in postwar Australia. That the economy got into deep trouble during the Labor government's term of office is undeniable. It happened.

The question of what went wrong and who was to blame has not to my mind been properly answered. Professor Fred Gruen, economic adviser to Gough Whitlam when he was prime minister, has published his assessment of what went wrong.[2] According to Gruen, the rise in inflation in 1973 and 1974 can be traced to several causes, including policies of the previous Liberal government under William McMahon; the stimulus to wages initiated by the Labor government's minister for labor, Clyde Cameron; the cost-push effects during 1973 and 1974 of the progressive tax system; and external influences such as the sharp rise in the price of meat and of imported goods flowing from movements in world commodity prices.

The rise in unemployment is more difficult to trace. The timing is clear: the rise was very sharp in 1974 and coincided with a sharp fall in seasonally adjusted job vacancies (from 88,000 in April to under 40,000 in October). All through 1973 job vacancies had been well in excess of 40,000. The rise in unemployment resulted from a very sharp cutback by private employers over a period of six months. Why did it happen? It is clear that the government, whether willingly or unwillingly, administered the "short, sharp shock" that the Treasury had been advocating as a means of curbing inflation. Before 1976, it did not get very far with its plans to administer this shock through fiscal policy, but it succeeded in its monetary policy.

The central bank, the Reserve Bank of Australia, is not an independent body like the Federal Reserve Board or even the Bank of England. It is very much an arm of the government and follows the interest, credit, money supply, and exchange rate policies established in Canberra. High interest rates were anathema to the Labor party, yet in September 1973 the Labor treasurer called for a substantial rise in bond rates. This rise in the official rates was

---

[2] Fred H. Gruen, "What Went Wrong? Some Personal Reflections on Economic Policy under Labor," *Australian Quarterly*, vol. 48, no. 4, pp. 15-32.

dwarfed by the rise in private rates that was to ensue in 1974, as official policy gradually brought on a monetary squeeze.

In 1974 two months, May and June, were taken up with the election that followed the dissolution of both House and Senate. Returned to office on May 18, 1974, Labor was concerned with all the drama and excitement of a joint sitting of the houses of Parliament to pass the legislation that had previously been rejected by the Senate. By then it was too late. Credit had been squeezed. The shock had been administered. Short-term interest rates for bank certificates of deposit rose sharply to 21 percent; the money supply had a negative real rate of growth and several large finance companies collapsed.

In the wake of these shocks the building and manufacturing industries cut back production. After inventories in the private nonfarm sector ran down in 1972 and 1973 there was a sudden and excessive buildup of inventories in the first half of 1974. At the same time the 28 percent tariff cuts of July 1973 were at last producing the intended effect of introducing more imports into the Australian economy. This competition was at last restraining domestic price rises, but combined with the credit squeeze it produced a very hard market environment. In addition, Labor's new Prices Justification Tribunal was in operation, requiring large companies to notify the tribunal of price rises before putting them into effect and retaining the option of delaying any price rise while it held an inquiry.

The combined effect was a strain too great for the economy to stand, and employment snapped. The Labor cabinet no doubt thought that the policies of tight money, prices justification, and tariff cuts would only affect prices. One wonders whether the cabinet was ever warned by the Treasury that this combination of policies would have a catastrophic effect on jobs.

The lessons to be learned seem clear. If the Labor party really wants to live up to its platform promise to provide a stable economy, it will have to work very hard at economic management when next it achieves office. The structural development of the economy and the provision of social equity are important; but management is critical. But then managing inflation and unemployment is a far from perfect art—as the Fraser government in turn is gradually learning.

11
The Case of the Arrested Pendulum

Colin A. Hughes

In predicting election results or the weather, "no change" is the safest forecast: tomorrow's weather will be like today's, and the party in office will win. On the other hand, there are times when a prediction of "no change" appears to fly in the face of all the evidence. The December 1977 election was one of these. For one thing, it followed a redistribution of electoral boundaries, which was bound to introduce an element of uncertainty. For another, the previous election, in December 1975, had brought a massive swing to the Liberal-National Country party coalition that had reduced the Australian Labor party to one of its lowest points in both seats and votes since the two-party system was established in 1910; such a landslide was unlikely to be repeated. Moreover, it was generally agreed that the prime minister had decided to go to the country a year earlier than he needed to for the House of Representatives and six months earlier for half the Senate because economic conditions were expected to deteriorate still further in 1978 and because the Labor party might choose a more effective leader in the meantime; the voters might take a dim view of being conned in this fashion, particularly by a government that had turned out its predecessors for economic mismanagement, only to find the economy unresponsive to its own tough strategy. It was the coalition's turn for scandal, too, most dramatically when the Liberal deputy leader and treasurer was forced to resign in the middle of the 1977 election campaign. Finally, the atmosphere of constitutional crisis surrounding the 1975 poll had been dissipated by two years of political stability.

The ALP had gone to the bottom in 1975. Now there appeared to be nowhere for it to go but up. Opinion polls provided signs of a recovery, and this seemed to accelerate once the campaign began in earnest. In May 1976 the ALP had regained government in the largest state, New South Wales (admittedly by the narrowest of majorities in the lower house), after eleven years out of office. In 1977 there was a healthy swing to Labor in Queensland at the state election, insufficient to seriously threaten the entrenched coalition government of Johannes Bjelke-Petersen in Brisbane but enough to suggest that the anti-Labor mood that had cost the party two-thirds of its seats in the state parliament in 1974 and all but one of its House of Representatives seats in 1975 had dissipated. The swing to Labor in the 1977 Greensborough by-election for the state lower house in Victoria showed a recovery in the sort of outer suburban constituency that had contributed disproportionately to the party's federal gains in 1969 and 1972.

Any cautious prophet, at this point, would have had to say that Labor was bound to win back some votes and some seats. On the other hand, it would have required a faith vouchsafed to few to believe that the ALP's recovery could be on the scale experienced after the last political crash in 1966. This had allowed the party to reach a level in 1969 from which a further push in 1972 could put it into federal office for the first time since 1949. The present writer expressed skepticism about a repeat of the 1966–1969 swing following 1975[1] but, like his colleagues in academia and journalism, expected that there would be a swing in votes sufficient to restore the opposition to something like the fifty House of Representatives seats it had averaged in the two lean decades between 1949 and 1972.

By election night 1977 it was clear that whatever wave of enthusiasm for Labor there had been had crested and receded, but as the results were posted an extraordinary picture emerged: At the national level the swing in votes was barely measurable, a mere 1.1 percentage points to the ALP.[2] The Fraser government had defied all the omens and retained 54.6 percent of the two-party-preferred vote, although it suffered a small loss of seats. In 1975 in a House

---

[1] Colin A. Hughes, "The Electorate Speaks—And After," in Howard R. Penniman, ed., *Australia at the Polls: The National Elections of 1975* (Washington, D. C.: American Enterprise Institute, 1976), pp. 303-305.

[2] Because preferential voting is used in Australian elections it is possible to calculate a national "two-party-preferred" vote for each constituency, for each state or federal territory, and for the country as a whole. Such calculations for recent federal elections are supplied in three works by Malcolm Mackerras: *Elections 1975* (Sydney: Angus and Robertson, 1975), "Double Dissolution Election, December 13, 1975," Department of Government, Faculty of Military Studies, University of New South Wales, 1976, mimeographed, and "Australian General Election and Senate Election: December 10, 1977," Department of Government, Faculty of Military Studies, University of New South Wales, 1978, mimeographed.

of 127 members it had held 91, to Labor's 36; in 1977 in a House of 124 members it held 86, to Labor's 38. Before counting had finished for the evening, Gough Whitlam announced that he would not be a candidate for his party's leadership again. This was the only significant change recorded on December 10.

A quick conspectus of the distribution of seats among the parties is provided by Table 11–1, which traces the waxing and waning of ALP fortunes since the party's previous trough in 1966. The Liberals had fielded a new leader, Harold Holt, in 1966, against an old Labor leader, Arthur Calwell; popular support for the war in Vietnam had still been strong; and the postwar economic boom had not yet run its course.

In the two largest states, New South Wales and Victoria, the rout of 1975 was confirmed in 1977, leaving the ALP very much where it had been in 1966. But in the rest of the country, especially in the three outlying states, Queensland, Western Australia, and Tasmania, the results were noticeably worse. As I have noted,

TABLE 11–1

PARTY DISTRIBUTION OF HOUSE SEATS FROM NEW SOUTH WALES, VICTORIA, AND THE SMALL STATES, 1966–1977

Election	New South Wales			Victoria			Small States[a]		
	ALP	Liberal	Country party[b]	ALP	Liberal	Country party[b]	ALP	Liberal	Country party[b]
1966	17	20	9	8[c]	19	5	16	22	6
1969	22	15	8	11	18	5	26	13	7
1972	28	10	7	14	14	6	25	14	7
1974	25	11	9	16	12	6	25	17	6
1975	17	19	9	10	19	5	9	30	9
1977	17	18	8	10	20	3	11	29	8

[a] Includes the four smallest states (Queensland, South Australia, Western Australia, and Tasmania), the Australian Capital Territory, and, from 1969 onwards, the Northern Territory.

[b] The National Country party since 1975. In some states its candidates run under other labels.

[c] Plus one Independent Labor.

SOURCE: Colin A. Hughes, *A Handbook of Australian Government and Politics 1965-1974* (Canberra: Australian National University Press, 1976); Malcolm Mackerras, "Australian General Election and Senate Election: December 10, 1977," Department of Government, Faculty of Military Studies, University of New South Wales, 1978, mimeographed.

recent elections have shown a tendency for Labor's support to be concentrated in a southeastern heartland composed of New South Wales, Victoria, and South Australia, and effectively in the three metropolitan centers of those states—Sydney plus Newcastle and Wollongong, Melbourne plus Geelong, and Adelaide.[3]

At the 1975 election the ALP retained only five seats outside those three metropolitan areas: one each on the edge of Brisbane and Perth, one in South Australia based on three industrial towns around Spencer Gulf, one in New South Wales based on the mining town of Broken Hill, and one in the public service community of Canberra. In 1977 it retained those five (two by the narrowest of margins because of boundary changes which brought in more agricultural and pastoral areas) and picked up two more, both in Queensland. One comprised the inner city area of Brisbane, the other the provincial centers of Rockhampton and Gladstone. Following the 1972 and 1974 elections 68 percent of Labor members in the House represented metropolitan districts. In 1975 the figure became 92 percent, and in 1977 it was still 89 percent. (Labor's dependence on the metropolitan areas is illustrated in Figure 11–1; see also Figure 11–2).[4] Moreover, as Malcolm Mackerras shows, examination of the swings between 1975 and 1977 indicates that in each of the six states Labor's performance in 1977 was less satisfactory in rural electorates than in urban ones. (See Table 11–2. It should be added that the author's use of "metropolitan" and "non-metropolitan" differs slightly from Mackerras's use of "urban" and "rural," though the difference affects only one seat—the urban but nonmetropolitan electorate of Fraser in the Australian Capital Territory, which does not appear in Table 11–2.) The long-term concentration of Labor in the capital cities accelerated in 1975 and showed no sign of reversing in 1977. For some years the Labor party had been concerned that the electoral weight given to areas outside the capital cities placed it at a disadvantage;[5] thus the consequences of the redistribution conducted by the Fraser government must figure in any account of the 1977 election.

---

[3] Hughes, "The Electorate Speaks," pp. 283–284.

[4] This map continues a series for Australian national elections since 1955. For the earlier maps see: Colin A. Hughes and E. E. Savage, "The 1955 Federal Redistribution," *Australian Journal of Politics and History*, vol. 13 (April 1967), pp. 8–20; Colin A. Hughes, "The 1972 Australian Federal Election," *Australian Journal of Politics and History*, vol. 19 (April 1973), pp. 11–27; and Hughes, "The Electorate Speaks," pp. 288–289.

[5] Hughes, "The Electorate Speaks," pp. 286-291.

Figure 11-1
Australian Electoral Map,
House of Representatives Election, 1977

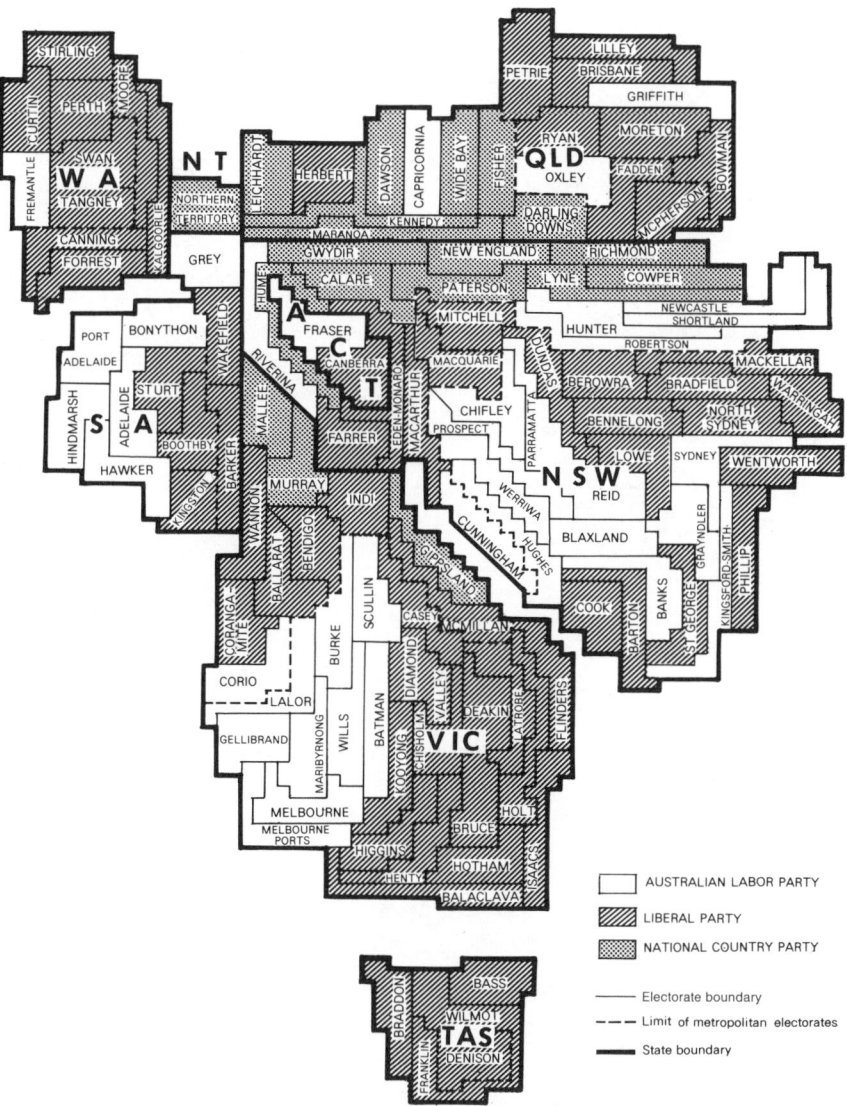

NOTE: For this figure the Australian electoral map has been redrawn to compensate for the extreme diversity in size of the electorates. Each electorate here occupies the same area, just as all have equal respresentation in the House of Representatives. Contiguity has been preserved; each electorate has its actual neighbors, though not necessarily for the actual proportion of boundary length.
SOURCE: Author.

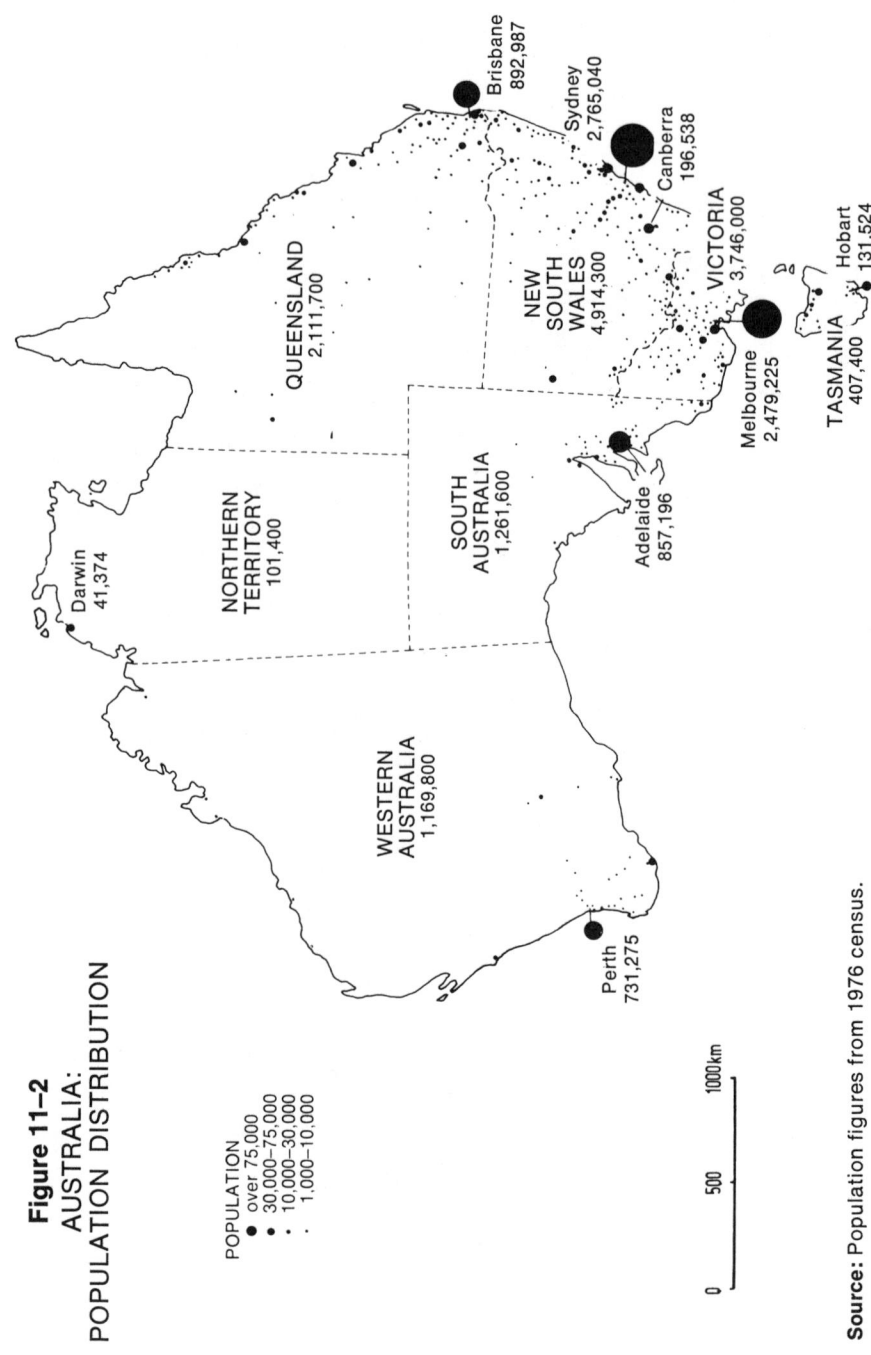

Figure 11–2
AUSTRALIA:
POPULATION DISTRIBUTION

Source: Population figures from 1976 census.

TABLE 11-2

Mean Urban and Rural Swings to Labor, 1975–1977
(swing in percentage points)

	Urban		Rural	
State	Mean swing	Number of seats	Mean swing	Number of seats
New South Wales	1.1	31	−0.1	12
Victoria	1.0	24	0.1	9
Queensland	3.3	10	0.5	9
South Australia	4.1	8	3.4	3
Western Australia	−1.0	6	−1.6	4
Tasmania	1.1	3	−2.4	2

Source: Mackerras, "Australian General Election, 1977," pp. 52, 55.

The 1977 Redistribution

One of the unusual features of elections in Australia is that electoral boundaries are drawn, not by the government of the day, but by nonpartisan distribution commissioners whose proposals require approval by both houses of Parliament but cannot be altered or amended. This practice began in the colony of New South Wales in the 1890s, and after the formation of the federal Commonwealth of Australia on January 1, 1901, it was promptly adopted for the national House of Representatives. Initially one commissioner was appointed for each state, then three commissioners became the rule—the federal electoral officer for the state, the state government's surveyor-general, and one other, usually a senior federal official whose departmental duties gave him familiarity with the state's geographic and economic characteristics.

As the Constitution provides that seats in the House of Representatives are shared among the states in proportion to their population, each national census raised the possibility of a redistribution, but the government of the day had no constitutional or even statutory obligation to activate the redistribution machinery. When the government did initiate a redistribution, the commissioners were supplied by the chief federal electoral officer with the "quota" or average enrollment (voter registration) for the districts in their state and had then to devise constituencies whose enrollments were no more than 20 percent above or below that quota. They were also directed to give due consideration to community or diversity of interest, means of communication, physical features, and existing boundaries. Although the population of Australia grew steadily up to the Second World War and enrollment expanded from just under 1 million in 1901 to 4.2 million in 1940, change in the electoral map was slow. Occasionally a constituency had to be abolished in a rural area or in the center of one of the larger state capitals to provide for a new constituency in the spreading suburbs, and occasionally a seat was transferred from one state to another, but most redistributions were a matter of fine tuning rather than drastic reorganization. That of 1977 was the eighth full federal redistribution to be accepted.[6]

In 1948 the Chifley government decided on a substantial enlargement of the federal Parliament. The membership of the House of Representatives was increased from 74 to 121 and of the Senate from 36 to 60, 10 senators from each state in place of the original 6. The Constitution had provided that each of the six original states would be guaranteed a minimum of 5 members of the House of Representatives. This, together with the guarantee of equality of representation in a Senate with substantial powers, had helped induce the smaller colonies to join the federation despite the fear that they would be swamped by populous New South Wales and Victoria. Up to 1933 the constitutional provision overrepresented the two smallest states, Western Australia and Tasmania; since then only Tasmania has been overrepresented, with one seat more than strict adherence to population would provide. In the 1960s the two federal territories, the Australian Capital Territory and the Northern Territory, secured full voting rights for their representatives in the House; in 1974 the A.C.T. acquired a second member, in keeping with its population growth, and the territories were given two senators apiece. After World War II population growth accelerated, fed partly by immigration, partly by a recovery in the birth rate after the depression, and the outward explosion of the suburbs speeded up the redistribution process. The 1949 redistribution was drastic: the number of constituencies (technically known as divisions) almost doubled. There was another redistribution in 1955 and another in 1962, though the latter was dropped by the Menzies government

---

[6] In the first federal election, in 1901, four states used constituency boundaries drawn up by the state legislatures and the other two states voted at large. In 1903 commissioners drew constituency boundaries for these two states. The first complete federal redistribution to become effective was in 1906. Of the seven since then, one came in two stages (1934-1937) when on the first round the existing boundaries for some states were allowed to stand temporarily and new ones were accepted for others. In addition, several redistributions have been totally rejected, including two since World War II, in 1962 and 1974-1975.

when its junior coalition partner, the Country party, threatened to vote with the Labor party to defeat it. The Country party sought to maintain the rural representation that would be sacrificed to the bulging capital cities if the redistribution went through, and it secured important concessions from the Liberals; these included a small change in the formula by which seats were allocated among the states which preserved the number of seats in Western Australia where the Country party was threatened by Liberal encroachment, and the provision that the distribution commissioners must consider disabilities arising out of remoteness or distance, density or sparseness of population, and area. The next redistribution, by then long overdue, took place in 1968.

The Labor party opposed any attempt to overrepresent areas outside the cities. Once in office after the 1972 election, it sought to delete from the electoral law the new criteria favoring rural electorates and to restrict the permissible variation in enrollments to 10 percent above or below the quota. In practice past commissioners had seldom used their power to deviate as much as 20 percent,[7] but when they had, it had been in favor of constituencies held or contested by the Country party. The coalition-controlled Senate rejected the amendments, but they were eventually passed at the joint sitting of the Commonwealth Parliament held after the 1974 double-dissolution election. The Whitlam government then directed a redistribution on the new rules, but the coalition still controlled the Senate and rejected the boundaries once they had been drawn. (By a savage irony the Liberal leader in the Senate, Senator Reg Withers, who had led the fight to defeat the boundaries drawn on the Labor legislation, was forced out of office in the Fraser government after he was found by a Royal Commission in 1978 to have committed an "impropriety" in the course of the Liberals' own redistribution in 1977: Withers had induced the national electoral officer to ask the distribution commissioners at work in Queensland to change the name of a proposed electorate in that state—quite unnecessarily since there would be ample opportunity to change the constituency's name when the proposals came before Parliament. Moreover, the 1977 redistribution itself was largely unnecessary.)

Following the 1975 election the National Country party, as it was now known, sought to restore the 20 percent tolerance. Its ministers were defeated in the cabinet on this point, but they did

---

[7] Hughes and Savage, "1955 Federal Redistribution," p. 12.

secure a novel provision that no division with an area of 5,000 square kilometers or more should have an enrollment larger than any division with an area less than 5,000 square kilometers. This ensured that within the plus or minus 10 percent range, rural constituencies would all have smaller enrollments than urban constituencies. It also restricted the commissioners' ability to assign relatively low enrollments to the areas that would experience the fastest growth in population and enrollment during the period that the new boundaries would operate. An unanticipated consequence was the need for great exactness in the commissioners' calculations. Special validating legislation had to be passed for one state, New South Wales, when it was discovered that an arithmetical error had put one division, smaller than 5,000 square kilometers but with anticipated rapid enrollment growth, below the enrollments of the divisions above the 5,000 square kilometer line.

A further refinement in the redistribution process was introduced in 1968. Previously commissioners had published provisional versions of their proposed boundary changes and then considered any objections interested persons might lodge before making their final proposals to Parliament. Under the 1968 legislation the procedures were opened up for more extensive public participation. As a first step after their appointment the commissioners advertise for "suggestions" for boundaries; these suggestions are public documents which may be consulted, and members of the public may lodge "comments" on them before the commissioners start their own work. After provisional maps have been published, there is still the opportunity to lodge "objections" before the commissioners finalize their proposals. All documents submitted to the commissioners are then tabled in Parliament (and printed in a limited edition) with the commissioners' proposals. By convention the commissioners no longer justify their proposals: their reports to Parliament are the bare bones, sets of figures and maps showing the old and new boundaries.

To judge from the three redistributions conducted under these rules—1968, 1974, and 1977—most of the participation at the first two stages, in the form of suggestions and comments, comes from the political parties, which seek to shape the proposed boundaries to their own advantage. At the third stage, members of the public as well as local party officials and members of Parliament intervene to try to prevent changes that might disrupt existing political networks or tip the scales in favor of their opponents, and local government authorities file objections to electoral boundaries dividing their territory.[8]

The 1977 redistribution was bound to introduce substantial alterations to the existing boundaries, which (except in Western Australia) were almost ten years old. In addition to the normal movement of population from the older city-centers into the suburbs and the growth of the metropolitan areas relative to the rest of the country, a High Court decision had found unconstitutional the provision passed in 1964 whereby each state received an additional seat for any fraction of its quota left over after its total population was divided by the assigned quota. The High Court had also ruled that only the sixty senators elected from the states, and not the additional four from the territories, could be counted to determine the size of the House of Representatives, which the Constitution fixed at "as nearly as practicable" twice the number of senators. Finally, there had been a relative decline in the population of New South Wales. As a result of these factors, the 1977 redistribution gave four states altered representation: New South Wales lost two seats and Victoria and South Australia each lost one, while Queensland gained a seat, thereby reducing the House of Representatives from 127 members to 124.

In terms of party support the pattern is more complicated and can best be examined state by state. In New South Wales three constituencies vanished from the map: two safe Labor seats, Darling and Lang, and one marginal Liberal seat, Evans, while a new seat, Dundas, was created, safe for the Liberals. Four other seats were significantly changed: Calare and Riverina moved from safe NCP to marginal NCP, Parramatta from marginal Liberal to marginal Labor, and Robertson from marginal Labor to marginal Liberal. In Victoria the consequences were more limited. One safe National seat (the NCP uses the label National party in Victoria) was abolished, Wimmera. Two reasonably safe Liberal seats, Hotham and Isaacs, became more marginal; one marginal Liberal seat, Holt, became somewhat safer; and one marginal Labor seat, Maribyrnong, became even more marginal. In Queensland a new division was created: Fadden, safe for the coalition with the Liberals more likely to win it than the Nationals (as the NCP is known in Queensland). Also in

---

[8] Colin A. Hughes and Don Aitkin, "The Federal Redistribution of 1968: A Case Study in Australian Political Conflict," *Journal of Commonwealth Political Studies*, vol. 8 (March 1970), pp. 18-39; Colin A. Hughes, "Electoral Planning," in John S. Western and Paul R. Wilson, eds., *Planning in Turbulent Environments* (St. Lucia: University of Queensland Press, 1977), pp. 183-197.

Queensland, one Liberal seat, Griffith, safe in 1975 at least, became marginal, and a marginal Liberal seat, Brisbane, became fairly safe. In South Australia a safe Liberal seat, Angas, was abolished, and two marginal Labor seats, Grey and Hawker, became marginal Liberal seats. In Western Australia a marginal Liberal seat, Perth, became safe Liberal, and another, Swan, became marginal Labor. In Tasmania the boundary changes were slight and had little political impact.[9]

Thus, although the 1977 redistribution amounted to a massive reorganization of the national electorate, its consequences for party politics were limited and would be significant only in the event of a very close result. Only the NCP could fairly claim to have been disadvantaged: the abolition of Wimmera and the merger of most of Riverina with Darling seemed likely to cost it two seats, and Calare was now at risk.

Competitiveness

Analyzing the results of the 1975 election, I pointed out that at each election from 1955 to 1975, between one-fifth and one-quarter of the seats in the House of Representatives had been "ultra-marginal," with the winner's lead in the two-party-preferred vote no more than ten percentage points.[10] Table 11-3 classifies the results of the Australian national elections of 1966 through 1977 according to the "safeness" of seats on a two-party-preferred vote at each election. The categories employed are: ultra-safe, the winning party received 70 percent of the vote or better; safe, 60.0–69.9 percent; marginal, 55.0–59.9 percent; and ultra-marginal, 50.0–54.9 percent. The proportion of House of Representatives seats in each category at each election is shown in the table.

Compared with the ebb and flow of party strength between earlier pairs of elections, the change between 1975 and 1977 was minimal. Labor with barely 30 percent of the seats had more than half in the marginal and ultra-marginal categories, but so did the coalition, which held 70 percent of the seats. Just over half the seats in the House could be classed as marginal or ultra-marginal. After 1975 I wrote, "If one supposes that no member of Parliament sleeps well at night unless he had 60 percent of the vote at the previous election, then between 45 and 60 percent of the members of the House of Representatives are constantly sniffing the political

---

[9] Mackerras, "Australian General Election," pp. 6-11.
[10] Hughes, "The Electorate Speaks," p. 281.

TABLE 11-3
Safeness of House Seats, 1966–1977
(in percentages)

Safeness Rating	Election					
	1966	1969	1972	1974	1975	1977
Ultra-safe, Labor	0.8	4.0	4.0	7.1	0.8	0.8
Safe, Labor	8.2	19.2	20.8	17.3	10.4	14.5
Marginal, Labor	14.8	12.0	14.4	10.4	8.7	6.5
Ultra-marginal, Labor	9.9	12.8	13.6	17.3	8.7	8.9
Ultra-marginal, Coalition	9.9	14.4	22.4	17.3	15.7	13.7
Marginal, Coalition	11.5	16.8	11.2	10.4	20.4	23.4
Safe, Coalition	33.5	19.2	13.6	18.1	28.4	27.4
Ultra-safe, Coalition	11.5	1.6	0	2.4	7.1	4.8

NOTE: For explanation of method, see text, p. 310. Figures may not add to 100 percent because of rounding.
SOURCE: Hughes, "The Electorate Speaks," p. 282; Mackerras, "Australian General Election, 1977."

wind."[11] The 1975 landslide, which demolished the Labor men who had built up the winning majority of 1972, also brought in a large contingent of coalition supporters, mainly Liberals. On the assumption that the political pendulum had swung as far as it ever would and must inevitably begin to swing back, many of them could look forward to a place in parliamentary history as "oncers," single-term M.P.s who are unceremoniously returned either to private life or to three years in the electoral wilderness trying to get back to Canberra.

Seniority comes to those with safe seats, and ministerial office tends to come with seniority.[12] Prime Minister Fraser has been quicker than his Liberal predecessors to advance bright new members to the ministry and even to the cabinet—witness the meteoric rise of John Howard, who became treasurer in the middle of the 1977 election campaign. But of the twenty-two M.P.s in the ministry he formed on December 20 after the 1977 election, only four held marginal seats: one member of the cabinet, Ian Viner (Stirling), and

---

[11] Ibid.
[12] Since Robert Menzies introduced the British practice in 1956, coalition ministries have been divided into an inner group, who attend all meetings of the cabinet, and the remainder, or outer ministry, who attend only when required by a particular item of business. Meetings of the full ministry are held, but not often.

three members of the outer ministry, Tony Staley (Chisholm), Kevin Newman (Bass), and Ray Groom (Braddon). No member with an ultra-marginal seat was given office, but seventeen ministers held safe seats and one, Peter Nixon of the NCP, the ultra-safe constituency of Gippsland. Similarly, any senator who is included in the ministry is virtually guaranteed a safe place—number one or number two—on the party ticket; indeed, he is unlikely to have achieved office without it. Thus the inner circle of policy making is insulated from the temporary shocks of electoral pressure.

Ultra-safe seats are exceptional. In 1977 Labor had only one, the constituency of Sydney, and the coalition only six: two Liberal strongholds in the upper-middle-class North Shore of Sydney, and four NCP bastions, three of them in Victoria, one in Queensland. The government's safe seats are spread around the country—thirteen in New South Wales, half of which are rural; eight in Victoria, including three rural; six in Queensland, including three rural; three in South Australia, including two rural; and four in Western Australia, of which one is entirely rural and one partly so. These figures show the weight that the NCP and the rural wing of the Liberal party can bring to bear within the coalition. In sharp contrast, eleven of the ALP's safe seats are concentrated in New South Wales, while Victoria has four and South Australia three. All are to be found in the Newcastle-Sydney-Wollongong, Melbourne, and Adelaide metropolitan areas. Of the four seats Labor carried in 1978 in the three outlying states, three (Capricornia, Griffith, and Fremantle) were ultra-marginal and the fourth, Bill Hayden's electorate of Oxley in Queensland, ultra-marginal in 1975, had become marginal.

For more than thirty years Australia has been tipped electorally in favor of the coalition. Labor's support peaked with John Curtin's triumph over the disunited anti-Labor parties in 1943, and once it drifted away to Robert Menzies's refurbished Liberals, the best Labor could manage was a finger tip grip on power. Twice, in 1954 and 1961, it managed to win more than 50 percent of the two-party-preferred vote but missed office because of the vagaries of the electoral system. Twice, in 1972 and 1974, it managed a razor-thin majority in the House of Representatives but failed to control the Senate. Since the coalition usually polls more votes than the ALP, it is not surprising that it usually has more safe and ultra-safe seats. These have provided a ballast of experienced and unflappable M.P.s who have maintained the aura of stability that Menzies's sixteen years in office first spread over the coalition's political image.

Fairness

Single-member constituencies generally disadvantage the losing party—give it less than a share of the seats proportionate to its share of the total vote.[13] In Australia the ALP has usually been the losing party in federal elections, and its representation in the lower house has suffered. The worse its performance in the total vote, the larger has been the shortfall of seats. In 1975 that shortfall amounted to twenty seats on the two-party-preferred vote or, under the "cube rule" formula to make allowance for the effect of single-member constituencies,[14] seven seats—which suggests that about one-third of the shortfall might be explained by boundary factors and larger enrollments in Labor-won constituencies and two-thirds by the single-member-constituency factor. In 1977 the results were much the same. Had its share of seats been proportionate to its share of the two-party-preferred national vote, the ALP would have carried an additional eighteen seats, or, under the cube rule, an additional seven.

However, it is unrealistic to speculate about the country as if it were a single constituency. Under the federal Constitution (which has proved extremely difficult to amend) the members of the federal Parliament must come from the several states. Table 11-4 provides the calculations for the six states and then for Australia as a whole. (The two federal territories can be omitted because the results in the Australian Capital Territory, with two seats, one of which went to Labor, and the Northern Territory with only one seat, would not have been different under a different system of determining the results.) This breakdown by state reduces the ALP shortfall against a proportionate distribution of seats to seventeen; against a cube rule distribution the shortfall remains seven. Any explanation of that shortfall of seven seats can only be speculative, but it may be significant that the Pearson's product moment correlation coefficient of the ALP's two-party-preferred vote and enrollment in each constituency is .242. Labor does better in the more populous constituencies, and this must operate as a drag on its electoral performance. Even though the 10 percent limit on variation from the quota ensured a high degree of equality in constituency size in the 1977 election, the effect

---

[13] See Colin A. Hughes, "Fair and Equal Constituencies: Australia, Jamaica and the United Kingdom," *Journal of Commonwealth and Comparative Politics*, vol. 16 (November 1978), pp. 256-271.

[14] See Hughes, "The Electorate Speaks," p. 286. The cube rule states that when there are two parties, if the ratio of votes is $A:B$, the ratio of seats will be $A^3:B^3$.

TABLE 11-4
Two-Party-Preferred Votes and Seats, by State, House Election, 1977

State	Estimated Two-Party Vote		Seats					
			Proportionate		Cube Rule		Actual	
	L–NCP	ALP	L–NCP	ALP	L–NCP	ALP	L–NCP	ALP
New South Wales	52.4	47.6	23	20	25	18	26	17
Victoria	55.5	44.5	18	15	22	11	23	10
Queensland	58.0	42.0	11	8	14	5	16	3
South Australia	51.3	48.7	6	5	6	5	5	6
Western Australia	60.1	39.9	6	4	8	2	9	1
Tasmania	56.2	43.8	3	2	3	2	5	0
Australia	54.6	45.4	68	56	79	45	86	38

NOTE: For an explanation of method see text. The two territories have been included in the national totals.
SOURCE: Mackerras, "Australian General Election, 1977."

of the 5,000 square kilometer qualification was a bias against Labor that almost certainly would have contributed to the shortfall of seven seats on a cube rule calculation.

Proportional representation has its advocates in Australia, and the president and vice-president of the New South Wales Proportional Representation Society have conducted an analysis of the 1977 results. If the electoral map were redrawn to produce ten 7-member constituencies, one 6-member constituency, and nine 5-member constituencies, returning a total of 121 members under proportional representation, they claim, the 1977 results would have produced the following distribution of seats: Liberals 50, NCP 15, ALP 49, Australian Democrats 10.[15] The government would have retained its majority but with a much smaller margin, while the ALP would have picked up another 11 seats and the Australian Democrats would have become a significant presence in the House of Representatives.

For the first half of the twentieth century in Australia, proportional representation was an exotic phenomenon confined to the lower house of the Tasmanian Parliament (which used the five federal constituencies as multimember constituencies returning six, later

[15] J. F. H. Wright and E. W. Haber, "Equal Electorates, Unequal Votes—1977 House of Representatives Election Aftermath," *Australian Quarterly*, vol. 50, no. 2 (June 1978), pp. 93-103.

seven, members each) and a brief experiment in New South Wales in the 1920s. Because Tasmania's House of Assembly was small in membership and, still worse, for much of the period contained an even number of seats, an evenly divided House was a frequent threat to the stability of government. Although the Tasmanians appeared happy with their system and used it with great effect to pick and choose among their preferred party's candidates,[16] in the mainland states there was little enthusiasm for adopting its benefits. The Chifley government introduced proportional representation for Senate elections beginning in 1949. Previously each state had elected three senators at each election on a winner-take-all basis and, because of the national uniformity of electoral swings, two successive poor performances could virtually wipe out the losing party. In the 1940s the coalition had been reduced to three seats in a Senate of thirty-six for the life of one Parliament. After 1949 effective representation for both major parties was assured (including such representation as the Country party could extract in joint-ticket negotiations with the Liberals) but the door was opened for minor parties and the occasional independent to win Senate seats, and the coalition governments after Menzies as well as the Whitlam Labor government were beset by a rebellious Senate. Thus the third quarter of the century did little to encourage either the Liberal party or the ALP to look kindly on PR and its form of "electoral justice."

Nevertheless, Labor governments in South Australia and New South Wales have recently chosen to introduce proportional representation for Legislative Councils, the state upper houses. In South Australia a combination of massive weighting in favor of rural areas in the drawing of Legislative Council boundaries and until recently a restricted franchise left the state ALP with only token representation in the upper house, even when it was able to win comfortable majorities in the lower house. In New South Wales the upper house had never been directly elected; nomination on the advice of the government of the day was followed by a system of indirect election, using PR, by an electoral college comprising the members of the lower house and the three-quarters of the members of the upper house not retiring at the current election. In 1976 the incoming Labor government of New South Wales, faced with the prospect of a hostile upper house for several more elections, used a popular referendum (a device originally introduced to preserve the upper house from abolition by a radical government) to eject a majority of the sitting

---

[16] See W. A. Townsley, *The Government of Tasmania* (St. Lucia: University of Queensland Press, 1976), p. 27.

members and introduce PR. In both states the whole state will constitute a single electorate, returning one-half (South Australia) or one-third (New South Wales) of the members of the upper house at each election.

It may be that the adoption of proportional representation for the election of two venerable chambers never previously noted for moving with the times will generate more interest in PR for the federal lower house. One or two political scientists have tentatively floated the idea of a "West German solution," with half the members elected from large single-member constituencies, which would preserve the link between members and the localities they represented, and half from statewide party tickets, filling out each party's state delegation until it was proportionate to the total vote cast for that party. Given the huge areas and diversity of interests of at least three of the states (New South Wales, Queensland, and Western Australia) and the remoteness of Canberra, this appears to be a more attractive solution than either turning each state into a single constituency for the House of Representatives or creating the huge five- or seven-member constituencies that would be required for proportional representation to work effectively. However, if recent British experience is any guide, converting one of the major contestants—much less both—to a change that might deny them an absolute majority in the lower house and certainly would encourage minor parties to come forward, will be a long and difficult business.

Preferential Voting

The adoption of proportional representation is no more than a remote possibility. The alternative vote, meanwhile, has been a distinctive feature of House of Representatives elections for almost sixty years. Known to Australians as preferential voting, it requires the voters to express their "preferences" by rank ordering each and every candidate on the ballot. The alternative vote was introduced by an anti-Labor government to prevent the splitting of the anti-Labor vote between the Liberals (at that time the Nationalists) and the new Country party. Labor was officially committed to its abolition until the 1974 election, when Whitlam advocated making the expression of preferential voting, but any commitment to changing a rule with which demise of the DLP had removed the principal threat to the ALP from preferential voting but any commitment to changing a rule with which even the most venerable voters had grown up left the ALP open to the accusation (made in quite extravagant terms) that it was planning to rig elections. In a landslide like 1975, the counting of preferences could have no influence on the overall result, and the whole issue dropped out of sight. The coalition parties, which needed each other's preference votes when both parties were in the field and which had reaped most of the benefits from the system, certainly would not want to make preferential voting optional. The leading advocates of electoral reform within the ALP had been the veteran Fred Daly and Whitlam himself; the former retired in 1975, the latter reduced somewhat the range of his interests in Parliament after his government's defeat.

Table 11-5 shows the consequences of preferential voting over the last six elections. The advent of the Australian Democrats in 1977 brought the number of electorates in which preferences were counted back up to the level that prevailed when the DLP was still active and the overall result was close—as it was in 1969 and 1972. However, the fact that the Australian Democrats apparently draw their support fairly equally from the coalition and the ALP meant that preferences determined the result in far fewer electorates. One would have to go back to 1955, when the DLP had just appeared and ran candidates in only three of the six states, to find an election when preferences changed fewer results.

In eleven of the forty-six electorates where preferences had to be counted, candidates from both coalition parties ran. Eight of these were safe or fairly safe for the government to begin with: Indi and Mallee in Victoria, Fadden and Herbert in Queensland, Canning, Forrest, Kalgoorlie, and Moore in Western Australia. Calare in New South Wales had been rendered marginal by redistribution. Most of these seats were ones over which the partners had squabbled in previous elections. The remaining two were marginal seats, won by Labor; in 1977 the Liberals and the NCP both ran candidates in the hope that a close transfer of preferences could save the seat. In Griffith, Queensland, the elimination of three other candidates (Independent, Progress party, and Australian Democrat) gave the Labor candidate an absolute majority over the two coalition candidates. In Grey, South Australia, only 87.6 percent of NCP preferences went to the Liberal, perhaps because the NCP had the "donkey vote" cast by apathetic or ill-informed voters who number their ballot-paper straight down from the top, and the Labor incumbent retained the seat with 50.05 percent on the final count.

In twenty-six electorates the presence of an Australian Democrat candidate was the principal reason for the need to count preferences. Only four of these were three-way contests between coalition, Labor,

TABLE 11-5
Seats Affected by the Distribution of Preferences, House Elections, 1966–1977

Election	Total Seats		Seats Won by the ALP	
	Preferences were counted	Preferences changed the result	Preferences were counted	Preferences changed the result
1966	31	5	6	0
1969	40	12	5	0
1972	49	14	12	0
1974	33	10	9	1
1975	24	7	6	0
1977	46	4	11	0

NOTE: The entries under "Preferences were counted" are total numbers of electorates where no candidate won a majority on the first count and thus voters' preferences came into play in subsequent counts. The entries under "Preferences changed the result" are total numbers of electorates where the winner after preferences had been counted was not the candidate who had received the largest number of first preferences.
SOURCE: Hughes, "The Electorate Speaks," p. 292.

and Australian Democrat candidates: Banks and Robertson in New South Wales, both retained by Labor, and Leichhardt in Queensland and Kingston in South Australia, both retained by the coalition. In the other twenty-two, additional candidates further complicated the count: five in New South Wales, all held narrowly by the coalition (Barton, Macarthur, Macquarie, Phillip, and St. George); ten in Victoria—where the rump of the DLP polled 5.3 percent of the state vote—of which three (Batman, Corio, and Maribyrnong) were saved for the ALP and the other seven (Deakin, Henty, Holt, Hotham, Isaacs, La Trobe, and McMillan) were held by the Liberals; two in Queensland, where the Progress party was the additional factor—Brisbane held by the Liberal incumbent and Capricornia retaken by the former Labor member; Hawker in South Australia held by Labor; two in Western Australia, where again the Progress party intervened—Fremantle held by Labor and Swan held by the Liberals despite the redistribution which had made it a likely prospect for Labor; and two territorial seats retained by the coalition, Canberra and the Northern Territory.

In eight seats the coalition vote was strong enough that the elimination of other candidates gave coalition candidates absolute majorities while the Australian Democrat and Labor candidates were still left in the count: Ballarat, Bendigo, Casey, Chisholm, and Diamond Valley in Victoria, where the DLP preferences still went solidly to the Liberals; and Bowman and Lilley in Queensland and Tangney in Western Australia, where the Progress party gave its support to the Liberals. The forty-sixth contest where preferences were counted was Riverina in New South Wales where an independent was eliminated to give the seat narrowly to Labor.

The pattern of the distribution of preferences is shown in Tables 11–6, 11–7, and 11–8 for the three minor parties. The allocation of Progress party preferences was quite erratic. With a small national vote, only 0.67 percent of the total and an average of 1.9 percent in the forty-four electorates it contested, its vote may well have been swollen by those electors who apparently mark their

TABLE 11–6

DISTRIBUTION OF PROGRESS PARTY PREFERENCES, HOUSE ELECTIONS, 1977

	Percentage of Progress Party Preferences Going To:			
Electorate	Coalition	Labor	Australian Democrats	Independent
Macarthur	58.9	13.7	27.4	—
Macquarie	25.3	27.1	6.8	40.7
St. George	26.1	19.0	54.9	—
Bowman	26.7	8.8	64.5	—
Brisbane	71.4	11.9	16.7	—
Capricornia	58.5[a]	15.9	25.6	—
Fadden	53.9[a]	19.4	14.6	12.1
Griffith	70.8[a]	8.6	14.4	6.2
Herbert	55.2[a]	11.8	27.1	5.9
Lilley	29.3	10.6	36.3	23.8
Canning	58.1[a]	30.0	11.9	—
Forrest	43.6[a]	48.2	8.2	—
Fremantle	50.3	17.2	27.5	5.0[b]
Kalgoorlie	74.0[a]	11.0	15.0	—
Moore	79.9[a]	6.4	13.8	—
Swan	61.9	12.1	15.8	10.2[c]
Tangney	59.8	26.1	14.1	—
Northern Territory	42.2	28.4	29.4	—

[a] Includes preferences given to both coalition parties.
[b] Communist.
[c] Socialist.
SOURCE: Mackerras, "Australian General Election, 1977," pp. 43-47.

TABLE 11–7

DISTRIBUTION OF DLP PREFERENCES, HOUSE ELECTIONS, 1977

Electorate	Percentage of DLP Preferences Going To:		
	Coalition	Labor	Australian Democrats
Ballarat	85.5	5.8	8.7
Batman	83.2	9.0	7.8
Bendigo	82.7	10.1	7.2
Casey	80.7	15.0	4.3
Chisholm	84.4	7.5	8.1
Corio	86.0	7.5	6.6
Deakin	60.4	33.9	5.7
Diamond Valley	84.0	8.2	7.8
Henty	82.9	8.5	8.6
Holt	72.2	14.8	13.0
Hotham	74.9	8.8	16.3
Indi	89.1[a]	6.7	4.2
Isaacs	79.4	6.7	13.9
La Trobe	82.5	6.2	11.3
McMillan	78.8	11.8	9.4
Mallee	59.7[a]	40.3	—
Maribyrnong	87.8	5.2	7.0

[a] Includes preferences given to both coalition parties.
SOURCE: Mackerras, "Australian General Election, 1977," pp. 26–29.

ballot-papers at random and thereby ensure that the most lunatic of independents or fringe parties will poll something.[17] However, the Progress party collected the donkey vote in very few races. Generally its preferences went to non-Labor candidates; the ALP received more than a quarter in only five cases, and in Forrest, where it received most, the donkey vote moved down to the Labor candidate. In two-thirds of the electorates the coalition received more than half the Progress party preferences.

The supporters of the other two minor parties were more disciplined. The DLP voters were the rump of a once deadly phalanx that had moved solidly up or down the ballot-paper, determined to keep the ALP out of office. The 5.3 percent of the total vote the DLP took in Victoria in 1977 was on a par with its performance at the two

---

[17] The Progress party took 1.7 percent of the vote in New South Wales, where it contested sixteen electorates; 1.5 percent in Queensland with seventeen electorates; 2.8 percent in Westrn Australia with ten electorates; and 2.8 percent in the Northern Territory.

TABLE 11-8
Distribution of Australian Democrat Preferences, House Elections, 1977

Electorate	Percentage of Australian Democrat Preferences Going To:		Electorate	Percentage of Australian Democrat Preferences Going To:	
	Coalition	Labor		Coalition	Labor
Banks	59.0	41.0	Maribyrnong	42.0	58.0
Barton	45.8	54.2	Brisbane	48.1	51.9
Calare	59.2[a]	40.8	Capricornia	56.0[a]	44.0
Macarthur	47.5	52.5	Fadden	53.3[a]	46.7
Macquarie	48.8	51.2	Griffith	51.8[a]	48.2
Phillip	47.8	52.2	Herbert	53.2[a]	46.7
Robertson	45.2	54.8	Leichhardt	56.0	44.0
St. George	58.7	41.3	Grey	59.1[a]	40.9
Batman	46.2	53.8	Hawker	47.2	52.8
Corio	43.6	56.4	Kingston	50.8	49.2
Deakin	49.1	50.9	Canning	55.1[a]	44.9
Henty	47.6	52.4	Forrest	56.8[a]	43.1
Holt	44.4	55.6	Fremantle	49.8	50.2
Hotham	47.7	52.3	Moore	56.6[a]	43.4
Indi	58.4[a]	41.6	Swan	48.9	51.1
Isaacs	55.6	44.4	Canberra	48.2	51.8
La Trobe	42.8	57.2	Northern Territory	49.5	50.5
McMillan	40.7	59.3			

[a] Includes preferences going to both coalition parties.
SOURCE: Mackerras, "Australian General Election, 1977," pp. 34-41.

previous elections (5.2 percent in 1974 and 4.8 percent in 1975), and its anti-ALP determination was as firm as ever. The two electorates that stand out as exceptions, Deakin and Mallee, were the two where the DLP had the donkey vote and passed it on to the Labor candidate.

The Australian Democrats were an unknown quantity in 1977. Their national vote was large enough (9.4 percent of the total) that it cannot be accounted for by random voting and the donkey vote, which the Democrats had in only 20 of the 115 electorates they contested. Their performance in Labor-won seats (9.4 percent on average) was much the same as in the constituencies won by the coalition (10.2 percent).[18] Australian Democrat preferences were

---
[18] Mackerras, "Australian General Election, 1977," p. 33.

counted in thirty-five contests: in eleven the coalition received between 55 and 60 percent, in four between 50 and 55 percent, in fifteen between 45 and 50 percent, and in five between 40 and 45 percent. Nowhere did either of the major contestants receive more than 60 percent of the Democrats' preferences.

The distribution of preferences changed election outcomes in only four electorates in 1977, in each case when a coalition candidate overtook the front-running Labor candidate with the preferences of his coalition partner. DLP preferences may have once been critical to coalition success, but Australian Democrat preferences were irrelevant in 1977. As Paul Reynolds points out in Chapter 5, this was partly because the party chose not to try to direct them to either of the major contestants. It left the choice to party supporters, who divided almost equally between Labor and the coalition. Had Chipp and the other Democrat leaders attempted to direct preferences, two consequences must have followed: their total vote would have been substantially reduced by the withdrawal of those who favored the party against which the decision had gone, and there would have been a substantial leakage of preferences contrary to the party's instructions. Neither loss nor leakage can be estimated with any accuracy, but it is doubtful whether more than half a dozen seats would have gone differently and certainly not enough to overturn the Fraser government's great victory. Discretion proved to have been the better part of valor. The Australian Democrats polled a handsome total, offended none of their supporters, and retained the possibility of living to fight another day.

The Senate Count

Analyzing the Senate vote after the 1975 election, I pointed to the reversal of the long-term trend in favor of minor party candidates for the upper house at the double-dissolution elections of 1974 and 1975 and unwisely went on to predict:

> Should Prime Minister Fraser avail himself of the opportunity to dissolve the House six months or so earlier than he need in 1978 and keep House and Senate elections in step thereafter, one might expect [the minor party vote to return to about 5 percent, where it had been before the appearance of the DLP]. If he does not and Senate elections return to the "by-election atmosphere" of the 1964–70 period, then maverick candidates might get a larger share of the poll, though it is difficult to imagine who would get

the necessary one-sixth of the votes to win a seat in the Senate when only five are at stake from each state.[19]

This prediction failed to anticipate the mushroom growth of the Australian Democrats, and the prime minister did indeed have to move the election forward to avoid the "by-election atmosphere." The major parties (including a separate NCP team in Western Australia) polled only 82.3 percent of the total vote, the lowest proportion at any Senate election since proportional representation came into operation in 1949, with the exception of 1970 when only the Senate was being elected and the figure dropped to 80.4 percent. At the two recent double-dissolution elections the figures had been 91.2 percent (1974) and 92.6 percent (1975) respectively. One might hazard the guess that, had Don Chipp stayed with the Liberals, the major parties would again have been in the 91–92 percent range—that is, the 6.5 percent of the vote that went to minor party and independent candidates other than the Australian Democrats would have been augmented by some of the anti-major-party votes attracted by the Australian Democrat alternative.

In elections conducted under proportional representation, interest usually focuses on the last seat to be allocated—in Australian Senate elections, the fifth seat in each state. The major contestants carry off the first four, then there is a real race. In 1977 there were some variations on this pattern. The strong vote for the coalition and the poor showing of ALP candidates in Western Australia, for example, meant that the first ALP candidate's surplus was insufficient to elect the second member of the team immediately. In the other states there was the usual tight distribution of surpluses down the party ticket to determine the first four places, upwards of 98.5 percent of each candidate's surplus going to the next candidate on the ticket except in Tasmania, where only 92.3 percent of the Liberal surplus and 93.1 percent of the ALP surplus went to the second candidate after the first had been elected. Table 11–9 shows the position at the beginning of the interesting stage of the Senate count in each state.

In New South Wales the elimination of the twenty-five "other" candidates had little impact. Slightly fewer than half their preferences went to the two major party candidates, with the ALP doing better than the coalition (in this case the NCP). Next out was the Reverend Fred Nile of the Call to Australia, a minor party that sternly opposed the permissive society; three-quarters of his preferences went

---

[19] Hughes, "The Electorate Speaks," pp. 300-301.

TABLE 11-9
The Count after the Election of the Fourth Senator in Each State, 1977

NEW SOUTH WALES Quota: 436,875			VICTORIA Quota: 331,740		
Coalition	no. 3	259,360	Democrat	no. 1	321,921
Democrat	no. 1	212,006	Coalition	no. 3	168,436
ALP	no. 3	174,761	DLP	no. 1	117,258
Progress	no. 1	56,674	ALP	no. 3	16,154
Wentworth	no. 1	56,159	Marijuana	no. 1	14,507
Call to Australia	no. 1	46,089	20 others		23,306
25 others		68,700			

QUEENSLAND Quota: 183,146			SOUTH AUSTRALIA Quota: 117,037		
Coalition	no. 3	193,745	Liberal	no. 3	108,683
Democrat	no. 1	97,298	Democrat	no. 1	77,603
Socialist	no. 1	27,845	ALP	no. 3	23,981
ALP	no. 3	13,781	12 others		23,803
15 others		33,619			

WESTERN AUSTRALIA Quota: 100,027			TASMANIA Quota: 39,238		
ALP	no. 2	94,043	Liberal	no. 3	37,033
Liberal	no. 3	76,245	Townley	no. 1	14,332
Democrat	no. 1	72,756	Democrat	no. 1	12,602
NCP	no. 1	36,324	ALP	no. 3	9,420
12 others		20,709	2 others		4,877
			Deferred surplus from ALP		211

NOTE: In every state except Western Australia, the first four Senate seats went swiftly to the two major groups; for these states the count after the election of the fourth senator is given in the table. For Western Australia, where the ALP did poorly, the count after the election of the third senator is given since it was at this stage that the race became close. The quota is the number of votes required for election in the state; the candidate's number refers to his place on his party's list. In Queensland the third candidate on the coalition's list has more votes than the quota and thus is elected. In all of the other states, since no candidate has more votes than the quota, the next step is the distribution of preferences, a complicated procedure described in detail in Appendix A.

In Tasmania the distribution of preferences—in this case a "deferred surplus"—is combined with the elimination of the bottom runner. When the surplus of the candidate just elected is smaller than the difference between the votes for the two bottom candidates, it is not distributed immediately since distributing it could not affect which candidate would be eliminated next. Instead, the count proceeds with the exclusion of the bottom runner and the distribution of the deferred surplus in one combined step.

SOURCE: *The Senate Election 1977: Result of Count of First Preference Votes and Distribution of Surplus Votes and Preferences* (Canberra: Australian Government Publishing Service, 1978).

to the coalition and the ex-Liberal W. C. Wentworth. However, when the Progress party candidate was eliminated, 89 percent of his preferences went to the next remaining candidate on the ballot-paper, the Australian Democrat, although on ideological grounds one might have thought the coalition and Wentworth much more acceptable to a militant free-enterprise group. The explanation is that the Progress party headed the ballot-paper in New South Wales and thus benefited from the donkey vote. The share of preferences going from the Progress party to the Democrats was swollen, if not almost wholly accounted for, by donkey votes. The elimination of Wentworth saw about half his preferences go to the coalition, with the Democrats getting the larger share of the remainder, to produce a penultimate count of L-NCP 338,788, AD 319,820, and ALP 215,141. Almost 92 percent of ALP preferences went to the Australian Democrat, the author Colin Mason, who won the fifth seat from New South Wales with a lead of more than 160,000 votes over the third member of the coalition team. Given his substantial lead over the third ALP candidate at the beginning of the later stages of the count, the likelihood that he would do better than the ALP in pulling in preferences from eliminated candidates, and the certainty that the ALP preferences would be quite solid, Mason's election was assured once the count of first preferences was known.

The success of his leader, Don Chipp, in Victoria was even more likely. After the first four senators had been elected, two from the Liberals and two from the ALP, Chipp was only 10,000 short of a quota. The elimination of the first candidate of the Marijuana party put him just past the required number: AD 333,602, coalition (again the unlucky National party was in third place on the ticket) 173,002, DLP 127,308, and ALP 29,564.

Despite the Australian Democrats' good showing—admittedly only in a limited number of electorates—at the state election a few weeks earlier, the coalition's massive support in Queensland gave it a third quota at once. The Socialist party of Australia had a substantial vote in this most right-wing of states only through the luck of the draw for places on the ballot-paper, which put it at the top and thus gave it the donkey vote. (The even more minuscule Nazi party of Australia once managed the trick at a Senate election in Queensland and startled a few innocent observers.)

There was every reason to expect a good Australian Democrat vote in South Australia, despite the return of Steele Hall to the Liberal fold, and after the first four places were filled their candidate had a plausible chance of taking the fifth. However, she did not secure quite as many preferences from the twelve minor candidates as her Liberal opponent and was left requiring an impossible 98 percent of ALP preferences to overtake him. Although 94.3 percent of ALP voters gave her their preferences, the final count was Liberal 118,208, Democrat 115,862.

In Western Australia the poor ALP vote, as already noted, prevented the immediate filling of the fourth place. None of the three front-runners gained much advantage from the twelve minor contestants, but the elimination of the NCP candidate (incidentally, completing the rout of that party in federal politics in Western Australia, where it had lost its two House of Representatives seats to the Liberals in 1974) ensured the election of both the third Liberal candidate and the second ALP candidate: Liberal 115,178, ALP 102,380, AD 82,519.

Tasmania showed its usual susceptibility to an independent, retaining the sometime Liberal Rudge Townley in the count up to the last round. First the third ALP candidate was eliminated, with half the Labor preferences going to the Democrat, then the Democrat went out with 60 percent going to Townley. The final count was Liberal 46,362, Townley 31,902.

The Australian Democrats, then, secured the fifth Senate place in only two states, albeit the two largest. They missed the fifth place very narrowly in South Australia, and in Western Australia they were within striking distance of the fifth seat though it would have been at the expense of the ALP which would have been reduced to a single seat. In a "by-election atmosphere" they might well have managed both seats, and Townley might have been returned in Tasmania. In that event the composition of the Senate after July 1, 1978, when the new senators took their places, would have been coalition 33, ALP 25, Australian Democrats 4, independents 2. The Fraser government would have controlled the Senate with a majority of one after providing the president. In such a situation Townley might well have reverted to the Liberal party, or at least regularly supported the government with his vote, so the threat was not as serious as it might appear, but the possibilities certainly vindicate the prime minister's judgment in going to the polls early. At the next Senate election the fifth seats at risk in five states will be held by the coalition, and in the sixth, Tasmania, by the independent Brian Harradine. If the Democrats were able to retain something like their present strength they might collect the fifth seat in three states— New South Wales, Victoria, and South Australia. Alternatively a Labor revival might give that party the fifth seat in New South Wales and South Australia. In either case it is difficult to see how the coalition could lose its absolute majority in the upper house at the next election.

The "Informal" Vote

The existence of compulsory voting in Australia combined with preferential voting for the House of Representatives and proportional representation for the Senate leads to a significant proportion of ballot-papers' being spoiled, deliberately or accidentally, by voters who will not be bothered with or cannot master the complexities of the voting system, those who object to compulsion, or those who dislike all the alternatives available on the ballot-paper.[20] These spoiled ballots are known as informal votes; Table 11–10 shows the proportion of informal votes cast at recent elections.

In 1977 the level of informal voting for the House of Representatives was up slightly in comparison with the two preceding elections. This might reflect dissatisfaction with the recent frequency of elections and possibly irritation with the political and economic troubles of the last few years, but there is no hard evidence on the subject, and either explanation is difficult to reconcile with the slight decline in informal voting for the Senate. As in previous elections the proportion of informal votes was higher in Labor-held seats than in others, which presumably reflects the lower levels of formal education in these districts and the presence of greater numbers of immigrant voters who have not found the local party system to their liking or are baffled by the intricacies of the voting system. This disparity does not seem to have been large enough to affect the results in any contest, though one might wonder about the two most marginal coalition victories, La Trobe and Swan.

Campaign Expenditures

The regulation of party finances and campaign expenditures is a subject that has been ignored by Australian political scientists, mainly because the sources available to the public are geographically scattered and expensive to inspect.[21] The records for each state are kept in the federal electoral office in the state capital and are made available only for a period of six months after the election. Moreover,

---
[20] Ibid., pp. 294-296.
[21] For a treatment of these topics in relation to the ALP see D. W. Rawson, "The Labor Campaign," in Penniman, ed., *Australia at the Polls, 1975*, pp. 98-102.

TABLE 11–10

Informal Voting, 1966–1977

(in percentages of ballots cast)

Election	House	Senate
1966	3.10	—
1967	—	6.10
1969	2.54	—
1970	—	9.41
1972	2.17	—
1974	1.92	10.77
1975	1.89	9.10
1977	2.52	9.00

NOTE: Figures are entered in only one column when only one house was up for election. Informal ballots are those spoiled or left blank by the voters.
SOURCE: Hughes, "The Electorate Speaks," p. 295.

they are notoriously defective in what they purport to disclose.[22] The real figures have been secrets closely guarded by the parties and candidates. While estimates of the global cost of given campaigns occasionally appeared in the newspapers, little could be said with any certainty beyond the obvious—that the coalition parties usually outspent the ALP by a handsome margin and that the cost of television advertising was placing an increasing burden on all the parties.

The rules laid down by the federal Electoral Act of 1946 are simple enough. A maximum expenditure of $500 is set for candidates for the House of Representatives, $1,000 for candidates for the Senate. Such limits are nonsense considering the size of the constituencies: for the House they average more than 60,000 electors and can exceed 100,000 when a redistribution is due, and three states have more than a million voters for Senate contests. A conscientious candidate would do well to pay the printing costs for his how-to-vote cards; given to voters as they enter the polling station, these cards are essential, first because the ballot-paper does not indicate the candidate's party and second because the party wants to ensure that its supporters assign their preferences to maximum advantage.[23] Once

---

[22] Colin A. Hughes, "Australia," in Richard Rose and Arnold J. Heidenheimer, eds., *Comparative Political Finance: A Symposium* (reprinted from the *Journal of Politics*, vol. 25 [1963], for the International Study Group on Political Finance), pp. 646-663; Colin A. Hughes, "The Cost of the 1963 Election," *A.P.S.A. News*, vol. 9 (1964), pp. 2-5; Colin A. Hughes, "Control of Electoral Expenses: Australia," *The Parliamentarian*, vol. 50 (1969), pp. 285-292.

[23] On how-to-vote cards see Appendix B.

he had paid for his how-to-vote cards, the law-abiding candidate would have no funds left for advertising in the local press, radio, and television or for leaflets to be delivered by hand to voters at home or out shopping on Saturday mornings. Meanwhile no limit is imposed on expenditures not directly attributable to a particular candidate, so the parties cheerfully spend hundreds of thousands of dollars on statewide or national advertising which sets out policies, extolls the party's leaders, and (coming close to a breach of the act) sometimes lists all the party's candidates in that state. The Electoral Act requires that all candidates and all persons who have incurred campaign expenditures lodge returns in the prescribed form within eight weeks of polling day showing a broad breakdown of how the sums were expended. A stiff fine or imprisonment is prescribed for failure to comply with the act, though initiative for prosecutions under the act lies with federal electoral officials, and by long-standing custom none are ever brought, presumably because the requirements are regularly disregarded by both sides.

During the Whitlam government's term of office consideration was given to a realistic set of campaign expenditure controls coupled with disclosure of the sources of contributions, but instead of launching yet another public inquiry (one that might have educated the public to the extent of the problem), Labor allowed the situation to drift. After the 1975 election Whitlam's attempt to borrow funds from Iraqi sources prompted some to suggest that legislation to regulate fund raising was long overdue.[24] Then in March 1976 a Liberal federal minister and a former Liberal senator were prosecuted for a breach of the Electoral Act after a report had appeared in the *Canberra Times* alleging that an independent candidate for the Senate from the Australian Capital Territory was given financial assistance in return for directing his preferences to the Liberal candidate. The magistrate found that a prima facie case had been established but held that a jury properly directed would not convict and discharged the accused. As a consequence of the prosecution, the minister resigned his portfolio and did not return to the ministry for fifteen months. The two incidents so close together stirred up momentary interest in the enforcement of the Electoral Act, which quickly died away.[25]

---

[24] E. g. John Jost, "Fund Flow Needs Checking," Melbourne *Age*, March 3, 1976. On the Iraqi affair, see Rawson, "The Labor Campaign," pp. 99-102.

[25] Hobart, *Mercury*, March 27, 1976. It was discovered, for example, that only eight of the twenty-eight candidates standing for the Senate and the House from Tasmania had filed the required returns, including none of the five who were successful for the House and only three of the ten elected to the Senate.

The 1977 election passed off without any particular excitement on the campaign expenditure front. Nevertheless, several months after the election it was disclosed that the coalition parties were investigating the possibility of government financing of parties as practiced in several overseas countries.[26] The idea of government support was promptly endorsed by the federal secretary of the ALP, David Combe, who stated that his party had spent $2 million at each of the two previous elections, in 1975 and 1977, and estimated that the coalition had spent $4 million in 1977.[27] When the *Canberra Times* checked 1977 returns in four states and the two territories it found, among other things, that only four of the twenty-one senators and House members elected in South Australia had lodged returns and none of the twenty from Western Australia, while one of the South Australians showed an expenditure of $2,600, more than five times the permitted maximum for a House contest. This report quoted the former prime minister, Sir William McMahon (whose own return added up to $488.55), as describing the Act as "foolish and leading to deceit."[28]

Occasionally a scrap of worthwhile information floats to the surface, for example the fact that during two weeks of the campaign in Melbourne the ALP and the Liberals spent about $50,000 each on television spot commercials.[29] Expenditures on the electronic media are reported to the Australian Broadcasting Tribunal and eventually appear in its annual reports. Expenditures on the press, still a substantial part of the total, and all other forms of expenditure remain subject only to the Electoral Act disclosure rules, and these as we have seen are treated with contempt. Any hope of discovering either the total for each party or its allocation among the various types of campaign expenditure in any future Australian election must depend on the federal government's amending the law so that it becomes workable. That might well have to await the return of a Labor government with a majority in the Senate.

Results

The two most remarkable features of the 1977 election—the performance of the Australian Democrats, who secured almost 10 percent of the total House of Representatives vote within a few months

---

[26] Melbourne *Age*, February 23, 1978.
[27] Ibid., February 24, 1978.
[28] *Canberra Times*, June 4, 1978.
[29] *Media Information Australia*, no. 8 (May 1978), pp. 72-73.

of the formation of their party, and the unexpected absence of any real swing to the ALP[30]—are both difficult to explain. Australia has seen third parties rise before, and by coincidence both the Country party after World War I and the DLP in the mid-1950s took about the same share of the vote in their first national contests (9.3 percent and 9.4 percent). But both those parties converted existing political networks to their own use, whereas the Australian Democrats started from scratch and sprang up in a much shorter period of time. Moreover each of the two earlier parties drew its support predominantly from one sector of the political continuum, the Country party from the rural wing of the old Liberals (then recently renamed Nationalists), the DLP from the right wing of the ALP. The Australian Democrats came up the middle of the political road, with approximately half their electoral following switching from the coalition, a third from the ALP, and the remainder from various small groups contesting the 1975 election.[31] Paul Reynolds's detailed analysis in this volume shows that the Australian Democrats' performance varied somewhat with the type of constituency, but except in Tasmania, where they did poorly, its uniformity was more impressive than the variations. The New South Wales state election of October 1978 provided the first test of whether that vote could hold firm. Amid a strong swing to the ALP (almost ten percentage points), the Australian Democrats' vote plummeted to just above 2.5 percent for the upper house and just below for the Legislative Assembly—less than one-third of their federal votes of the previous year. The next test will be the state election due in Victoria before the middle of 1979, after which it should be possible to say whether the party has struck root or whether it will prove to have been only a brief aberration after the ferment of the Whitlam years that died away when calm was restored.

As to the second feature, the absence of a significant swing to the ALP, it takes us back to the metaphor of the pendulum. Once a party wins office, so the argument goes, it starts losing support. It is forced by circumstances to take decisions that are unpopular, to offend powerful interests and injure voters. All that an opposition need do, an Australian journalist once explained, is run after the bus

---

[30] E. G. Malcolm Mackerras, "No Change: Analysis of the 1977 Election," *Politics*, vol. 13 (May 1978), p. 131.

[31] This conjecture is based on the actual swings between 1975 and 1977 recorded in *General Election for the House of Representatives 1977: Result of Count of First Preference Votes and Distribution of Preferences* (Canberra: Australian Government Publishing Service, 1978), p. 1.

of government policy, picking up and comforting the passengers as they fall out when it hits bumps in the road and takes corners too tightly. In practice things are not quite as simple as that. The electoral cycle is usually longer than a single interelection period. After nearly losing the 1961 election, the coalition improved its economic performance and picked up support in 1963 and 1966. Labor touched bottom in 1966, then recovered in 1969 and scored further gains in 1972. Further, the periods of coalition ascendancy last longer than those when the tide is running in favor of Labor. Considering that the ALP was on the upgrade from the Senate election of 1967 to the House election of 1972 and maybe the joint election of 1974, the new phase of coalition ascendancy could last fifteen or twenty years.

On so grand a time scale, the absence of movement in the first two years would not be surprising. In many respects the 1977 election was a rerun of 1975. The alternative prime ministers, Fraser and Whitlam, were the same. Memories of the disastrous last months of the Labor government were still fresh in the voters' minds and were revivified by the Liberals' campaign and the evidence of division, at least on economic questions, among the ALP's leaders. Inflation was still enough of a worry to remind the voters of how it had galloped a year or two earlier when alarmists had begun to talk of Weimar Germany; unemployment, meanwhile, was widely attributed to Labor's mismanagement of the economy, the excessive wage demands of trade unions, or the irresponsibility of the unemployed. Some voters changed allegiance, but they moved in almost equal numbers in opposite directions. There was a net increase in enrollment of more than 300,000, and David Kemp has pointed to the ALP's better performance among the young, but this factor would have been insufficient by itself to produce the tiny swing to Labor that shows up in the national two-party-preferred vote. Instead of a tide of electoral change, such as usually occurs, there were only eddies in 1977. It remains to be seen whether the ALP's new leadership will combine with a further deterioration in the economy to start the tide flowing again.

APPENDIX A
The Vote and the Count

Senate Elections. The scrutiny of ballot-papers, culminating in the filling of vacancies in the Senate election, is effected under a system of *Proportional Representation*, based on preferential marking of the ballot-papers for all the candidates. Under this system where there are two or more vacancies to be filled, it is not necessary for a candidate to obtain more than half of the votes to be elected—a candidate is elected when he receives a number of votes equal to the quota. The quota is determined by dividing the total number of first preference votes in the count by one more than the number of candidates required to be elected and by increasing the quotient so obtained (disregarding any remainder) by one. For example, where there are five candidates to be elected, the quota is one-sixth of the total first preference votes, plus one.

When all the Senate ballot-papers recorded at all polling booths in any Division have been returned to the respective Divisional Returning Officer, he will open the parcels and make a fresh scrutiny of the ballot-papers, thus carrying out a complete recheck of the counting which was done at the counting centres.

The total number of all first preference votes recorded for each candidate will then be tabulated and the results transmitted to the Australian Electoral Officer for the State. When final figures have been received from each Divisional Returning Officer, the Australian Electoral Officer will determine the quota for election in the manner previously described.

This appendix consists of excerpts from Frank L. Ley, *Commonwealth Electoral Procedures*, Australian Electoral Office (Canberra: Australian Government Publishing Service, 1976), pp. 34-36 and 71-79. The 1977 ballots, which have been substituted for the 1974 ballots reproduced in Ley's booklet, were kindly provided by K. W. Pearson, who succeeded Ley as chief Australian electoral officer.

Any candidate who has then received a number of first preference votes equal to or greater than the quota is deemed to be elected. Where an elected candidate has received a number of votes in excess of the quota, a number of votes equal to the surplus will be transferred to the other candidates remaining in the count in the manner described in the next paragraph.

All of the ballot-papers of the first elected candidate are then sorted into parcels according to each voter's next preference indicated thereon to determine the proportion in which the surplus votes are to be transferred. The surplus votes are then transferred in their correct proportion to the continuing candidates (the actual ballot-papers being taken at random), and the remainder (i.e. the number of ballot-papers of the elected candidate equal to the quota) are set aside as finally dealt with. After the surplus votes have been distributed, any candidate who has reached the quota is deemed to be elected and his surplus votes (i.e. that portion he received from the previously elected candidate over and above the number which was required to reach the quota) are distributed to the remaining candidates in the order of the voters' preferences. If, after the distribution of the surplus votes of all elected candidates, fewer candidates than the number of vacancies to be filled have been elected, the candidate with the least number of votes in the count at that stage is excluded and the ballot-papers which have been sorted to him are transferred, in accordance with the next preferences thereon, to the candidates still remaining in the count (i.e. to those candidates who have not been elected or excluded up to that stage).

If no candidate is then elected, or fewer than the required number have been elected, the process of excluding candidates is continued until a further candidate is elected, in which case (unless all vacancies have been filled) the surplus votes of that elected candidate are then transferred. If necessary, the process of excluding candidates one by one is continued until all the vacancies have been filled.

If on any count two or more candidates have an equal number of votes, the Australian Electoral Officer decides which shall be excluded or the order of their election, as the case may be. If in the final count for filling the last vacancy two candidates have an equal number of votes, the Australian Electoral Officer exercises his casting vote but, except in these circumstances, he does not vote at the election.

House of Representatives Elections. The *Alternative Vote* system used for a House of Representatives election also relies upon the preferential marking of the ballot-papers by the voters to indicate their order of preference for all the candidates. This method of marking the ballot-papers affords the voter an alternative choice of candidates or indeed several alternatives should his earlier choices become ineffective due to the exclusion of candidates at various stages of the count.

In a House of Representatives election, if the number of first preference votes recorded in favour of a candidate is greater than one-half of the total number of formal votes in the election (i.e. an absolute majority of the formal votes), that candidate is elected. If no candidate has received an absolute majority of the votes, the candidate who has received the fewest first preference votes is excluded from the count and each ballot-paper counted to him is transferred to the candidate next in order of the voter's preference. This process of excluding candidates one by one is continued until a candidate receives more than half the number of votes in the count, when he is elected.

If on any count two or more candidates have an equal number of votes and one of them has to be excluded, the Divisional Returning Officer decides which shall be excluded, or, if in the final count two candidates have an equal number of votes, the Divisional Returning Officer will record his casting vote to decide the result of the election but otherwise he does not vote in the election.

Recount of Ballot-Papers. At any time before the declaration of the result of an election, the officer conducting the election may, if he thinks fit, at the written request of a candidate, or of his own volition, recount the ballot-papers. A recount is generally undertaken only where the closeness of the final result makes it desirable.

Declaration of the Poll. As soon as possible after the scrutiny of the ballot-papers has been completed the result of the election will be declared. This is called the "Declaration of the Poll." In the case of a Senate election, the poll is declared at the office of the Australian Electoral Officer and, in the case of House of Representatives elections, the declaration of the poll is made at the offices of the respective Divisional Returning Officers.

Court of Disputed Returns. A candidate at an election or a person who was qualified to vote thereat may dispute the validity of the election by addressing a petition to the High Court sitting as the Court of Disputed Returns.

Example Showing the Application of Proportional Representation
(As used in Senate elections)

Say, 4 candidates to be elected; 610 votes recorded of which 15 are informal, i.e. there are 595 formal votes:

$$\text{Quota for election} = \left(\frac{595}{5}\right) + 1 = 120$$

Candidates ....

	A	B	C	D	E	F	G	H	I	J	Total votes in count
First preference votes	30	10	20	320	5	150	40	..	10	10	= 595

D 1st elected with a surplus of 200 votes
F 2nd elected with a surplus of 30 votes

D's first preference votes are now sorted to continuing candidates, according to next available preference thereon (this is to ascertain the proportion in which surplus votes are to be transferred). Say they go:

A	B	C	E	G	H	I	J
..	300	16	..	..	..	..	4

Transfer value of D's surplus votes = $\frac{200}{320}$ (i.e. surplus ÷ 1st preferences) ∴ actual votes to be taken at random and transferred =

$$\left. \begin{array}{l} \text{to B } \frac{200}{320} \text{ of } 300 = 187 \\ \text{to C } \frac{200}{320} \text{ of } 16 = 10 \\ \text{to J } \frac{200}{320} \text{ of } 4 = 3 \end{array} \right\} = 200$$

F's 150 1st preference votes sorted to continuing candidates according to the next available preferences thereon. Say they go:

A	B	C	E	G	H	I	J
100	15	10	15	6	1	1	3

Transfer value of F's surplus votes $\frac{30}{150}$ (i.e., surplus ÷ 1st preferences)

∴ actual votes to be transferred:

$$\left.\begin{array}{l} \text{to A } \frac{30}{150} \text{ of } 100 = 20 \\ \text{to B } \frac{30}{150} \text{ of } 15 = 3 \\ \text{to C } \frac{30}{150} \text{ of } 10 = 2 \\ \text{to E } \frac{30}{150} \text{ of } 15 = 3 \\ \text{to G } \frac{30}{150} \text{ of } 6 = 1 \\ \text{to H } \frac{30}{150} \text{ of } 1 = 0 \\ \text{to J } \frac{30}{150} \text{ of } 3 = 1 \end{array}\right\} = 30$$

Tally sheet now reads:

Candidates	A	B	C	D	E	F	G	H	I	J	Total votes in count	Number of elected candidates' votes set aside
First preference votes	30	10	20	320	5	150	40	..	10	10	= 595	
D's 200 surplus votes transferred	..	187	10		..	2nd Elected	..	..	..	3	..	120 } i.e.
F's 30 surplus votes transferred	20	3	2	1st Elected	3		1	..	..	1	..	120 } 2 quotas
Progress totals	**50**	**200**	**32**		**8**		**41**	..	**10**	**14**	**= 355**	

B 3rd elected with a surplus of 80 votes.

The 190 votes received by B from D and F now sorted to continuing candidates. Say they go:

A	C	E	G	H	I	J
..	..	..	..	187	3	..

Transfer value of B's surplus votes $= \dfrac{80}{190}$ (i.e. surplus votes ÷ votes received by B at the previous stage of the count)

∴ actual votes to be transferred:

$$\left.\begin{array}{l} \text{to H } \dfrac{80}{190} \text{ of } 187 = 79 \\ \text{to I } \dfrac{80}{190} \text{ of } 3 = 1 \end{array}\right\} = 80$$

338

Tally sheet now reads:

Candidates	A	B	C	E	G	H	I	J	Total votes in count	Number of elected candidates' votes set aside
Progress totals, brought forward	50	200	32	8	41	..	10	14	= 355	120 (i.e. 1 quota)
B's surplus votes transferred	..	3rd Elected	..	..	..	79	1	..	.	
Progress totals	50		32	8	41	79	11	14	= 235	

No further candidate now having a quota, E with the fewest votes, is excluded and his 8 votes are transferred. Say they go:

	A	C	G	H	I	J		
	2	..	..	..	5	1		
Progress totals	52	32	41	79	16	15	= 235	

J with the fewest votes, is now excluded and his 15 votes are transferred. Say they go:

	A	C	G	H	I			
	..	..	..	12	3			
Progress totals	52	32	41	91	19	= 235		

I with the fewest votes, is now excluded and his 19 votes are transferred. Say they go:

	A	C	G	H				
	..	..	9	10				
Progress totals	52	32	50	101	= 235			

C with the fewest votes, is now excluded and his 32 votes are transferred. Say they go:

$$\frac{A}{12} \quad \frac{G}{10} \quad \frac{H}{10}$$

Progress totals .... 64 60 111 = 235

G with the fewest votes, is now excluded and his 60 votes are transferred. Say they go:

$$\frac{A}{55} \quad \frac{H}{5}$$

Progress totals .... 119 116 = 235

A 4th elected.

Complete tally sheet would read:

Candidates	A	B	C	D	E	F	G	H	I	J	Total votes in count	Number of elected candidates' votes set aside
First preference votes	30	10	20	320	5	150	40	..	10	10	= 595	
				1st Elected		2nd Elected						
D elected, 200 surplus votes transferred	..	187	10		..	..	..	..	..	3	.	120
F elected, 30 surplus votes transferred	20	3	2		3		1	..	..	1	.	120
Progress totals	**50**	**200**	**32**		**8**		**41**	..	**10**	**14**	**= 355**	
		3rd Elected									
B elected, 80 surplus votes transferred	..		..		..		..	79	1	..		120
Progress totals	**50**		**32**		**8**		**41**	**79**	**11**	**14**	**= 235**	

340

E excluded, 8 votes transferred	2	:	:	:	:	5	1			
Progress totals	52	32	52	32	52	16	15 Excluded			= 235
J excluded, 15 votes transferred	:	:	:	:	:	3				
Progress totals	52	32	52	32	52	19 Excluded				= 235
I excluded, 19 votes transferred	:	:	:	9	10					
Progress totals	52	32	52	50	101	Excluded				= 235
C excluded, 32 votes transferred	12	:	10	10						
Progress totals	64	32 Excluded	60 Excluded	111						= 235
G excluded, 60 votes transferred	55			5						
Progress totals	119 4th Elected			116						= 235

Example Showing the Application of the Alternative Vote
(As used in House of Representatives elections)

Let it be assumed that there are 5 candidates for which 610 votes were recorded and of these 10 are informal, i.e. there are 600 formal votes. For election a candidate must receive an absolute majority of the formal votes—i.e. 301 votes.

Candidates	Adams	Brown	Grey	Jones	White	Total
First preference votes	150	200	70	100	80	600

No candidate having received an absolute majority of the votes, candidate GREY, with the least number of votes, is excluded. His 70 ballot-papers are now sorted to continuing candidates according to the next available preference thereon. Say they go:

	Adams	Brown	Jones	White	
	10	..	40	20	

Tally sheet now reads:

	Adams	Brown	Grey	Jones	White	Total
First preference votes	150	200	70	100	80	600
Grey excluded—70 ballot-papers transferred	10	..	Excl.	40	20	
Progressive totals	160	200	..	140	100	600

No candidate yet having received an absolute majority of the votes, candidate WHITE with the fewest votes is now excluded and the 100 ballot-papers which were previously sorted to him are transferred to the next continuing candidates. Say they go:

Adams	Brown	Jones
15	30	55

342

This will give ADAMS (160 + 15) 175 votes, BROWN (200 + 30) 230 votes and JONES (140 + 55) 195 votes. ADAMS is now excluded and his 175 ballot-papers are transferred. Say they go:

	Brown 60	Jones 115				
	Adams	Brown	Grey	Jones	White	Total
Tally sheet now reads:						
First preference votes................	150	200	70	100	80	600
GREY excluded—70 ballot-papers transferred................	10	..	Excl.	40	20	
Progressive totals................	160	200	..	140	100	600
WHITE excluded—100 ballot-papers transferred................	15	30	..	55	Excl.	
Progressive totals................	175	230	..	195	..	600
ADAMS excluded—175 ballot-papers transferred................	Excl.	60	..	115	..	
Progressive totals................	..	290	..	310	..	600

Candidate JONES having received an absolute majority of the votes in the count is elected with 310 votes.

Examples of Ballots

Form F (To be initialed on back by Presiding Officer before issue.)

BALLOT-PAPER

COMMONWEALTH OF AUSTRALIA

STATE OF VICTORIA

Electoral Division of MELBOURNE

Election of One Member of the House of Representatives

DIRECTIONS:—Mark your vote on this ballot-paper by placing the numbers **1, 2, 3, 4** and **5** in the squares respectively opposite the names of the candidates so as to indicate the order of your preference for them.

CANDIDATES

☐ **BURKE, Desmond John**

☐ **FALLSHAW, Robert**

☐ **INNES, Urquhart Edward**

☐ **SCHWARZ, Veronica**

☐ **WILSON, Roger Michael**

C11819/77   F D Atkinson Government Printer Melbourne

Form E

BALLOT-PAPER

(To be initialed on back by Presiding Officer before issue)

COMMONWEALTH OF AUSTRALIA

STATE OF VICTORIA

ELECTION OF FIVE SENATORS

DIRECTIONS.— Mark your vote on this ballot-paper by placing the numbers, 1, 2, 3, 4, 5, 6, 7, 8, 9, 10, 11, 12, 13, 14, 15, 16, 17, 18, 19, 20, 21, 22, 23, 24, 25, 26, 27, 28 and 29 in the squares immediately to the left of the names of the respective candidates so as to indicate the order of your preference for them.

CANDIDATES

A	☐ **BROSNAM,** James Daniel	B	☐ **INGVARSON,** Carolyn Elizabeth	C	☐ **CHIPP,** Donald Leslie	D	☐ **MISSEN,** Alan Joseph	E	☐ **HEARN,** Ronald	F	☐ **EVANS,** Gareth John	G	☐ **McROACH,** Jay Jenidene	H	☐ **KRUSE,** Derek Johann		☐ **WATSON,** Shane Andrew Clarke
A	☐ **HILTON,** Leslie Randle	B	☐ **MORTON,** Elizabeth Alma	C	☐ **SIDDONS,** John Royston	D	☐ **HAMER,** David John	E	☐ **McCANDLESS,** Trevor	F	☐ **BUTTON,** John Norman	G	☐ **McKENZIE,** Peter Neal	H	☐ **HEATH,** David		☐ **BATEY,** Ronald Francis
A	☐ **McMANUS,** Richard Paul	B	☐ **QUINN,** Marie Anne	C	☐ **BATEMAN,** Janice Gwendoline	D	☐ **TEHAN,** Thomas Joseph	E	☐ **KOKKINOS,** Hariklia	F	☐ **BROWN,** William Walter Charles			H	☐ **FARRELL,** Gaii		☐ **KAVANAGH,** Peter Damian
				C	☐ **JEFFREY,** Harold Hugh												☐ **VINE,** Terence Reginald William
				C	☐ **SLEEP,** Neil Reginald												

NOTE.—The letter "A" or "B" or "C" or "D" or "E" or "F" or "G" or "H" appearing before the square immediately to the left of a candidate's surname indicates that that candidate and each other candidate who has the same letter appearing before the square immediately to the left of his surname have been grouped by mutual consent. The fact that no letter appears before the square immediately to the left of a candidate's surname indicates that the name of that candidate has not been included in any group.

Actual ballot size is 16¾" x 5".

APPENDIX B
How-To-Vote Cards

How-to-vote cards and advertisements are a crucial form of campaign publicity in Australia, where the ballot carries no party labels and a vote is invalid if all the candidates (of whom there may be scores for the Senate) are not numbered in order of the voter's preference. Essentially pre-marked mock ballots, they show the voter exactly how to fill in his real ballot in order to give his first-preference vote to the stated party and to distribute his lower-order preferences according to that party's electoral strategy. Under the Australian preferential voting system, second preferences in particular can be decisive, and the parties try to maximize their vote and minimize the vote of their principal opponents through the order of preference they endorse.

Most voters follow their party's instructions closely, copying directly onto the ballot from how-to-vote cards posted inside the voting booths, handed out by party workers at the polling places, or clipped from the newspaper. Even so, the number of "informal" ballots (invalid ballots, including both those that are deliberately spoiled and those that are incorrectly marked) is high, reaching more than 10 percent in many Senate elections.

Reproduced here are three newspaper advertisements from the 1977 election: the Labor party's from the *Sydney Morning Herald*, which shows voters in New South Wales how to vote for the ALP; the Liberals' full-page spread in the *Age*, showing how to cast a vote for the coalition in the state of Victoria; and the Senate portion of the Australian Democrats' advertisement in the *Sydney Morning Herald*, showing how to give a first-preference vote to the Democrats and a second preference to either Labor or the coalition in New South Wales. The cartoon, also from the *Herald*, comments on the plight of a large minor party under this voting arrangement and on the Australian Democrats' unprecedented decision not to direct their supporters' second preferences.

Here's how to get Australia working:

How to vote ALP for the House of Representatives.

BANKS
- [2] GREENE, M. B.
- [3] HINTON, P. R.
- [1] MARTIN, V. J.

BARTON
- [3] BELLCHAMBERS, E. C.
- [4] BRADFIELD, J. M.
- [1] CUNNINGHAM, Ron
- [2] WHITE, P. J.

BENNELONG
- [4] HOWARD, J. W.
- [2] IRWIN, B. M.
- [3] RENNIE, D. M.
- [1] WELSMAN, N. O.

BEROWRA
- [4] EDWARDS, H. R.
- [1] JONES, M. C. H.
- [3] SIMPSON, G. M.
- [2] VAN AGGELE, J. C.

BLAXLAND
- [4] HAGGERTY, W. J.
- [1] KEATING, P. J.
- [3] NAPOLI, S.
- [2] SULI, S. S.

BRADFIELD
- [3] BROWN, C. T.
- [4] CONNOLLY, D. M.
- [1] KIBBLE, P. M.
- [2] MARRABLE, D. D.

CALARE
- [3] ASHTON, J. W.
- [2] BAIRD, D. L.
- [4] MACKENZIE, A. J.
- [1] SIMMONS, D. W.

CHIFLEY
- [1] ARMITAGE, J. L.
- [4] MUNDEY, J.
- [3] TAYLOR, R. J.
- [2] TOZER, A. K.

COOK
- [2] DAY, W. A. R.
- [3] DOBIE, J. D. M.
- [4] SOPER, H. L.
- [1] THORBURN, R. W.

COWPER
- [1] CLAGUE, C.
- [2] ROBINSON, I. L.

CUNNINGHAM
- [6] DENNETT, O. L.
- [5] DEZELIN, R.
- [4] GRIFFIN, T. J.
- [3] NIXON, M. F.
- [2] SAMPSON, R. W.
- [1] WEST, S. J.

DUNDAS
- [3] McKINNON, M. G.
- [2] MOHIDE, B. A.
- [1] ROLLASON, R. G.
- [4] RUDDOCK, P. M.

EDEN-MONARO
- [2] HELMERS, N. L.
- [3] LEGRAND, M. G.
- [1] MAGUIRE, B. R.
- [4] SAINSBURY, M. E.

FARRER
- [5] FIFE, W. C.
- [1] FLEMING, D.
- [2] GUY, T. E.
- [3] HEALEY, M. N.
- [4] NATHAN, M. E.

GRAYNDLER
- [1] STEWART, F. E.
- [2] TOWNEND, C. E.
- [3] VASSELEOU, B.
- [4] VOUROS, F.

GWYDIR
- [5] ALLEN, B. R.
- [1] FISH, F.
- [2] HOWE, H. B.
- [4] HUNT, R. J. D.
- [3] MUNRO, L. J.

HUGHES
- [6] BOOTH, J. E.
- [3] HALLIWELL, H.
- [2] JOHNSON, K.
- [1] JOHNSON, L.

HUME
- [1] BRENNER, G.
- [3] LUSHER, S. A.
- [2] RICHARD, M.

HUNTER
- [3] FENNELL, O. R.
- [1] JAMES, A. W.
- [2] KIRKBY, E.

KINGSFORD-SMITH
- [1] BOWEN, L. F.
- [3] O'NEILL, C. V.
- [2] WARD, E. J.

LOWE
- [3] BINGLE, C. F. S.
- [1] HALL, R. V.
- [4] McMAHON, W.
- [2] TROSS, F. H.

LYNE
- [2] EDWARDS, A. B.
- [3] LUCOCK, P. E.
- [1] UNICOMB, N. V.

MACARTHUR
- [4] BAUME, M. E.
- [1] KERIN, J. C.
- [2] SPEIRS, W. O. M.
- [3] THOMAS, V. P.

MACKELLAR
- [1] BARCLAY, J. C.
- [7] CARLTON, J. J.
- [5] DAVIS, R. R.
- [4] GEYLE, B. J.
- [3] MELLOR, T.
- [2] WILLIAMS, R. C.

MACQUARIE
- [3] BARRATT, M. M.
- [4] FOSTER, A. N.
- [1] FREE, R. V.
- [5] GILLARD, R.
- [2] MONAGHAN, P. J.

MITCHELL
- [2] ALLAN, R. A.
- [4] CADMAN, K. G.
- [3] HARTNELL, M.
- [5] MIKULASEV, D.
- [1] THOMPSON, Ellen

NEWCASTLE
- [3] DAWSON, D. E.
- [2] HAY, I. T.
- [1] JONES, C. K.
- [4] SAMUELS, E. V.

NEW ENGLAND
- [1] DEAN, S. V.
- [2] MULLIGAN, B. J.
- [3] SINCLAIR, I. M.

NORTH SYDNEY
- [3] CORRIE, P. G.
- [1] GRAHAM, B. W.
- [4] MAHER, J. F.
- [2] PIERCE, J. W.

PARRAMATTA
- [1] BROWN, J. J.
- [3] COX, D. A.
- [2] LUKUNIC, P.

PATERSON
- [2] BAKER, P.
- [3] O'DONNELL, W. I.
- [4] O'KEEFE, F. L.
- [1] SCOTT, K. D.

PHILLIP
- [4] BIRNEY, R. J.
- [3] ELLIOTT, B. N.
- [2] NEEDHAM, A. D.
- [1] RIORDAN, J.

PROSPECT
- [2] BOURKE, L. W.
- [3] BYERS, A. E.
- [1] KLUGMAN, R. E.

REID
- [2] BLUCK, F. P.
- [3] SHANAHAN, T. P.
- [1] UREN, T.

RICHMOND
- [1] ANTHONY, J. D.
- [4] MALLETT, J. M.
- [2] MAXWELL, J. H.
- [3] WALRUT, V. J.

RIVERINA
- [1] FITZPATRICK, J.
- [2] LAWRENCE, R. B.
- [3] SULLIVAN, J. W.

ROBERTSON
- [3] BROOKS, M. H.
- [1] COHEN, B.
- [2] WILLSHER, T. L.

SHORTLAND
- [3] BEVAN, R. A.
- [2] LAMBKIN, L. J.
- [1] MORRIS, P. F.

ST. GEORGE
- [2] KIRWOOD, R. C.
- [3] KRISS, D.
- [4] NEIL, M. J.
- [1] WHITLAM, A. P.

SYDNEY
- [6] BEAVER, A. W.
- [5] BLACK, H. B.
- [4] MAYERS, N. R.
- [3] McMAHON, J. L.
- [2] MORRISON, A. S.
- [1] ROBERTS, J. A.

WARRINGAH
- [4] KELIHER, S. R.
- [2] MACKELLAR, M. J. R.
- [1] OSBORNE, C. R.
- [3] STILLER, A. J.

WENTWORTH
- [4] CURVERS, J. W. A.
- [3] ELLICOTT, R. J.
- [2] KERSEY, J. S.
- [1] WINTERS, M. J.

WERRIWA
- [4] ABROMAS, J.
- [2] MAY, R.
- [3] OLSON, C. K.
- [1] WHITLAM, E. G.

For the Senate.

A	B	C	D	E	F	G	H	I	J
[9] BRACKEN	[4] MASON	[12] Chan	[14] NOTARY	[17] SMITH	[21] NILE	[24] WENTWORTH	[1] MULVIHILL James Anthony	[26] BILLINGTON	[32] WOODBURY
[10] HOWARD	[5] McLEAN	[13] CHAN	[15] WILLARD	[18] MILES	[22] SCARF	[25] YOUNG		[27] FULLER	[33] CLANCY
[11] SCHOLLBACH	[6] HILBERY		[16] JONES	[19] PATTEN	[23] JUDGE		[2] GIETZELT Arthur Thomas	[28] LIVESEY	[34] HARDING
	[7] MALLETT			[20] ROUMELIOTIS					[35] ESPOSITO
	[8] CLARK						[3] SIBRAA Kerry Walter		
								[29] BAUME	
								[30] LAJOVIC	
								[31] ROSS	

Australian Labor Party.

[ADVERTISEMENT]

HOW TO VOTE LIBERAL FOR VICTORIAN ELECTORATES ON SATURDAY DECEMBER 10.

SENATE. Liberal-National Party Team. (White Ballot Paper.)

Copy the numbers from left to right.
You must number every square.
Voting is compulsory.

GROUP A	GROUP B	GROUP C	GROUP D LIB./NAT.	GROUP E	GROUP F	GROUP G	GROUP H	UNGROUPED
4 BROSNAN J. D.	7 INGVARSON C. E.	10 CHIPP D. L.	1 MISSEN A. J.	15 HEARN R.	18 EVANS G. J.	21 McROACH J. J.	23 KRUSE D. J.	26 WATSON S. A.
5 HILTON L. R.	8 MORTON E. A.	11 BIDDONS J. R.	2 HAMER D. J.	16 McCANDLESS T.	19 BUTTON J. N.	22 McKENZIE P. N.	24 HEATH E.	27 BATEY R. F.
6 McMANUS R. P.	9 QUINN M. A.	12 BATEMAN J. G.	3 TEHAN T. J.	17 KOKKINOS H.	20 BROWN W. W. C.		25 FARRELL G.	28 KAVANAGH P.
		13 JEFFREY H. H.						29 VINE T. R. W.
		14 SLEEP N. R.						

HOUSE OF REPRESENTATIVES. (Green Ballot Paper.)

BALACLAVA
3 FUREY Z. V.
2 LAWLOR P. J.
1 MACPHEE I. M.
4 STEELE R. G.

BALLARAT
4 BAKER N. J.
3 GOUGH G. J.
2 GRIFFIN W. C.
1 SHORT J. R.

BATMAN
1 BROWN G. E. L.
4 HOWE B. L.
2 LORENZ P. P.
3 PIRAINO M. C.

BENDIGO
1 BOURCHIER J. W.
2 BRENNAN P. G.
4 MULDOON D. P.
3 PRICE I. H.

BRUCE
4 BURKE T. P.
2 MULHOLLAND J. V.
1 SNEDDEN B. M.
3 SUTCLIFFE J. P. D.

BURKE
3 JOHNSON L. K.
1 LENGYEL M.
4 SPENCER E. J.
2 WALSH C. W.

CASEY
1 FALCONER P. D.
2 FELTHAM F. T.
3 HEATHERICH M. H.
5 HILLMAN S. G.
6 LEGGETT H. G.
4 WATSON P. R.
3 WHITTLE M. R.

CHISHOLM
5 CAULFIELD R. C.
1 MAYER D. H.
3 STALEY A. A.
2 STANLEY J. A.

CORANGAMITE
5 AMBROSE S. E.
4 MAY K. F.
2 McDONALD N. G.
3 O'BRIEN F. J.
1 STREET A. A.

CORIO
1 BUBB C.
2 JORDAN J. J.
3 SAHR G.
4 SCHOLES G. G. D.

DEAKIN
2 CONDON D. G.
4 GAY N. C.
1 JARMAN A. W.
3 TEED A. D.

DIAMOND VALLEY
1 BROWN N. A.
2 CURTIS C. D.
4 DOWNING J. O.
3 GOLDMAN R. J.

FLINDERS
2 CASS J. L.
5 EASTWOOD G. D.
3 FRASER H. A.
4 HOLLOW R. F. M.
1 LYNCH P. R.

GELLIBRAND
2 BAILEY A. J.
3 SMITH J.
4 WILLIS R.
1 ZAJC A.

GIPPSLAND
3 INGLE B. F. H.
2 McMAHON R. J.
1 NIXON P. J.
4 REID T. A.
5 SWITZER W. N.

HENTY
1 ALDRED K. J.
5 CHILD J.
2 DEART M.
4 FARRELL T. F.
3 INGAMELLS F. H.

HIGGINS
2 CAHILL M. P.
3 JACKSON A.
1 SHIPTON R. F.
4 THORNLEY J.

HOLT
4 DUFFY M. J.
2 LEYDON K. J.
3 STOCKTON B. G.
1 YATES W.

HOTHAM
1 JOHNSTON J. R.
4 ROSS A. B.
3 WEAVER K. L.
2 WOODS E. J.

INDI
1 CAMERON E. C.
3 CODY C. C.
5 DENNIS J. G.
2 HOLTEN R. M.
4 SAVAGE N. V.

ISAACS
1 BURNS W. G.
2 CLEARY R. J.
3 McLEOD F. B.
4 WILLIAMS K.

KOOYONG
2 GAYNOR B. W.
3 McBRIDE M. P.
1 PEACOCK A. S.
4 WILKINSON J. W.

LALOR
2 BILSTON D. W.
4 DAY J. G.
1 DICKINSON H. R.
6 JONES B. O.
3 SKIDMORE O. D.
5 VICARI R.

LA TROBE
1 BALLIEU M.
3 HELLEMA C. A. J.
5 LAMB A. H.
4 McCANN A. J.
2 PENNA J. A. V.

McMILLAN
3 DENT R. W.
5 ELKINGTON R. L.
2 HAND J. EY B. G.
4 HOLYOAK N. F.
1 SIMON B. D.

MALLEE
3 COTTER J. F.
4 FERNS G. K.
2 FISHER P. S.
1 HINCKSMAN W. J. H.

MARIBYRNONG
3 BRASS A.
4 CASS M. H.
1 FITZHERBERT P. J.
2 TAIT A. J.

MELBOURNE
2 BURKE D. J.
1 FALLSHAW R.
4 INNES U. E.
3 SCHWARTZ V.
5 WILSON R. M.

MELBOURNE PORTS
2 HABERMAN G. J.
1 HILL D. J.
4 HOLDING A. C.
3 RAINEY V.

MURRAY
4 HUNTER G. M.
2 LLOYD B. T.
5 MACARTNEY G. W.
3 PAYNE J. B.

SCULLIN
1 CLARKE G. S.
4 JENKINS H. A.
2 McGRATH B. J.
3 SAMARGIS G.

WANNON
2 CASANOVA J. L.
1 FRASER J. M.
4 FROST A. W.
3 TRAYLING T. G.

WILLS
4 BRYANT G. M.
1 BURROWES T. J.
2 FLINT J.
3 WEAVER V. E.

You must put a number in every square. Voting is compulsory.

This is a serious appeal to every Victorian Elector to carefully consider your Senate vote. The balance of power in minority hands will create uncertainty and instability in Government. Do not waste your Senate Vote on Saturday.

Joy Mein
State President

For all information phone 654 2866.

LIBERAL. DOING THE JOB.

Authorised by N. R. Hughes, 104 Exhibition St., Melbourne.

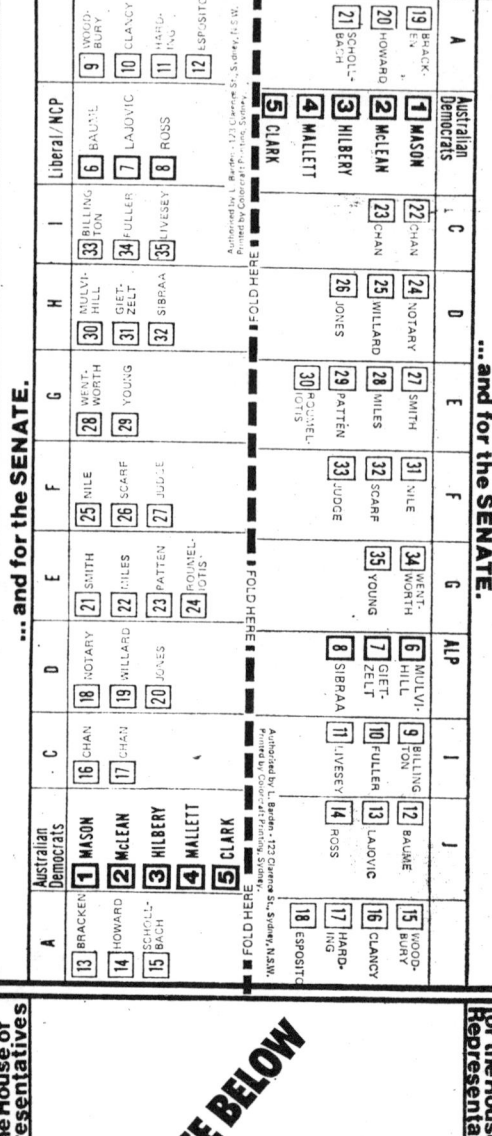

"Cripes! Do you realise our second preference is more important than our first?"

APPENDIX C

Australian National Election Results, 1977

Compiled by Richard M. Scammon

1977 ELECTION RESULTS, AUSTRALIAN HOUSE OF REPRESENTATIVES

State	Total	Labor	Liberal	Country/National	Democrat[a]	Other[b]
New South Wales	2,833,785	1,201,560	1,018,257	320,051	239,808	54,109
% of state vote		42.4	35.9	11.3	8.5	1.9
Seats	43	17	18	8	—	—
Queensland	1,175,663	443,221	326,135	305,275	77,169	23,863
% of state vote		37.7	27.7	26.0	6.6	2.0
Seats	19	3	9	7	—	—
South Australia	757,208	322,883	340,383	6,065	85,578	2,299
% of state vote		42.6	45.0	.8	11.3	.3
Seats	11	6	5	—	—	—
Tasmania	246,819	103,877	134,687	—	8,255	—
% of state vote		42.1	54.6	—	3.3	—
Seats	5	—	5	—	—	—
Victoria	2,127,526	791,083	842,545	120,032	250,943	122,923
% of state vote		37.2	39.6	5.6	11.8	5.8
Seats	33	10	20	3	—	—
Western Australia	632,024	205,793	307,699	25,559	70,590	22,383
% of state vote		32.6	48.7	4.0	11.2	3.5
Seats	10	1	9	—	—	—
Australian Capital Territory	115,091	57,823	48,190	—	8,544	534
% of territory vote		50.2	41.9	—	7.4	.5
Seats	2	1	1	—	—	—

353

1977 ELECTION RESULTS, AUSTRALIAN HOUSE OF REPRESENTATIVES

State	Total	Labor	Liberal	Country/National	Democrat[a]	Other[b]
Northern Territory	34,738	14,811	—	16,462	2,478	987
percentage of territory vote		42.6	—	47.4	7.1	2.8
Seats	1	—	—	1	—	—
Total, Australia	7,922,854	3,141,051	3,017,896	793,444	743,365	227,098
% of total vote		39.6	38.1	10.0	9.4	2.9
Seats	124	38	67	19	—	—

NOTE: The party labels used here are those employed by the Australian Electoral Office in its official returns for 1979.

[a] In New South Wales, South Australia, and Western Australia, the National Country party; in Queensland and Victoria, the National party; in the Northern Territory, the Country Liberal party.

[b] Democratic Labor, 113,271; Progress party, 52,767; Communist party, 14,098; Socialist party, 1,895; miscellaneous, 45,067.

SOURCE: Australian Electoral Office.

1977 ELECTION RESULTS, AUSTRALIAN SENATE

State	Total	Labor	Liberal/ National[a]	Liberal	National Country/ Country Liberal[b]	Democrat	Other[c]
New South Wales	2,621,249	1,050,672	1,136,215	—	—	218,364	215,998
% of state vote		40.1	43.4	—	—	8.3	8.2
Seats	5	2	2	—	—	1	—
Queensland	1,098,872	380,418	564,190	—	—	98,165	56,099
% of state vote		34.6	51.3	—	—	8.9	5.1
Seats	5	2	3	—	—	—	—
South Australia	702,218	258,643	—	344,351	—	78,496	20,728
% of state vote		36.8	—	49.0	—	11.2	3.0
Seats	5	2	—	3	—	—	—
Tasmania	235,427	88,722	—	117,217	—	13,793	15,695
% of state vote		37.7	—	49.8	—	5.9	6.7
Seats	5	2	—	3	—	—	—
Victoria	1,990,436	680,673	833,477	—	—	322,493	153,793
% of state vote		34.2	41.9	—	—	16.2	7.7
Seats	5	2	2	—	—	1	—
Western Australia	600,158	196,781	—	278,413	36,619	74,912	13,433
% of state vote		32.8	—	46.4	6.1	12.5	2.2
Seats	5	2	—	3	—	—	—

1977 Election Results, Australian Senate

State	Total	Labor	Liberal/ National[a]	Liberal	National Country/ Country Liberal[b]	Democrat	Other[c]
Australian Capital Territory	114,200	49,374	—	43,897	—	14,561	6,368
% of territory vote		43.2	—	38.4	—	12.8	5.6
Seats		1	—	1	—	—	—
Northern Territory	33,647	13,593	—	—	15,463	2,766	1,825
% of territory vote		40.4	—	—	46.0	8.2	5.4
Seats		1	—	—	1	—	—
Total, Australia	7,396,207	2,718,876	2,533,882	783,878	52,082	823,550	483,939
% of total vote		36.8	34.3	10.6	.7	11.1	6.5
Seats		14	7	10	1	2	—

NOTE: The party labels used here are those employed by the Australian Electoral Office in its official returns for 1979.

[a] In New South Wales, Liberal/National Country; in Victoria and Queensland, Liberal/National.

[b] In Western Australia, National Country; in the Northern Territory, Country Liberal.

[c] Democratic Labor, 123,192; Progress party, 85,170; Call to Australia, 49,395; Australian Marijuana party, 44,276; Socialist party, 42,740; Australia party, 8,283; Workers' party, 3,033; miscellaneous, 127,850.

SOURCE: Australian Electoral Office.

CONTRIBUTORS

TERENCE W. BEED is founding director of the University of Sydney Sample Survey Centre, which was set up in 1975. Prior to this he was managing director of Australian Nationwide Opinion Polls from its inception in 1970. He is coauthor of *Australian Opinion Polls, 1941-1977*.

DAVID BUTLER, a fellow of Nuffield College, Oxford, since 1951, has studied and lectured widely in the United States. He has written extensively on British politics and elections and is the author of *The Canberra Model*, coauthor of *Political Change in Britain*, and coeditor of *Referendums*.

MURRAY GOOT is a senior lecturer in politics at Macquarie University in Sydney. He is the author of *Policies and Partisans* and coauthor of *Women and Voting Studies* and *Australian Opinion Polls, 1941-1977*.

JEAN HOLMES is a senior lecturer in Australian politics at Melbourne University and a regular media commentator on Australian elections. Her recent publications are on state government in Victoria and Australian federalism, and her current research concerns social values, patterns of political behavior, and party loyalty in Australia.

COLIN A. HUGHES is a professorial fellow in political science at the Australian National University. He is joint editor of half a dozen volumes of Australian electoral statistics and editor of a series on Australian state government. His most recent book is *A Handbook of Australian Government and Politics 1965-1974*.

DUNCAN IRONMONGER is reader in applied economic research at the University of Melbourne and deputy director of its Institute of Applied Economic and Social Research. He was editor of the *Australian Economic Review* from 1968 to 1975 and writes and broadcasts widely on the Australian economy.

AINSLEY JOLLEY is general manager of the Economic Affairs Division of the Victorian Chamber of Manufactures and was economic adviser to Treasurer Phillip Lynch in 1975 and 1976. He is a member of the Australian government's economic panel, the Federal Liberal party's economic advisory committee, and the economic advisory panel to the premier of Victoria.

DAVID KEMP is professor of politics at Monash University. He is the author of *Society and Electoral Behaviour in Australia*. In 1978 he was a visiting fellow at the Center of International Studies at Princeton University.

C. J. LLOYD is a Canberra journalist and a former visiting fellow in the urban research unit at the Australian National University. He is the coauthor of three books on recent Australian political history and public administration and has completed a study of the National Press Gallery in Canberra. He is now engaged in a study of Australia's governor generals and a history of the economic policies of the Labor government of 1972 to 1975.

PAUL REYNOLDS is a senior lecturer in Australian politics and political sociology at the University of Queensland. He is the author of *The Democratic Labor Party* and articles on Australian and New Zealand politics.

RICHARD M. SCAMMON, coauthor of *This U.S.A.* and *The Real Majority*, is director of the Elections Research Center in Washington, D.C. He has edited the biennial series *America Votes* since 1956.

PATRICK WELLER is a research fellow in the department of political science at the Australian National University. He is the editor of *Caucus Minutes 1901-1949* and *Federal Executive Minutes 1915-1955* and coauthor of *Treasury Control in Australia* and *Politics and Policy in Australia*. In 1978-1979 he was director of research at the Commonwealth Public Service Board.

INDEX

Abortion, ALP position: 76
AD: see Australian Democrats
Adderley, Warwick: 260
Advertising, paid: see Mass media
Age poll: see Opinion polls
ALP: see Australian Labor party
Alternative vote: see Preferential voting
Anderson, Sir Kenneth: 191n
ANOP (Australian Nationwide Opinion Poll): see Opinion polls
Anthony, Doug: 99, 103, 107, 115–116, 249, 281
    surveys, campaign use of: 221–223
AP: see Australia party
APOP (Australian Public Opinion Poll): see Opinion polls
Asprey Committee: 294
Australia party (AP): 23, 125–126, 140
Australian: 242
Australian Associated Press (AAP): 263–264
Australian Broadcasting Commission (ABC): 251–254, 263
Australian Confederation of Apparel Manufacturers (ACAM): 244
Australian Council of Trade Unions: 269
Australian Democrats: 23, 31, 125, 126
    constituency: 11–12, 122, 128–129, 133, 146, 331
    denial of free broadcast time to: 253–254
    election results, national: 134–138, 325–326, 330
    election results, state: 131–134
    future prospects: 138–140
    ideology: 8, 130
    media coverage of: 259–261
    opinion poll ratings: 145–147, 160–161
    organizations: 130–131
    preference distribution, 1977 House elections, tables: 139, 321
    refusal to direct preferences: 138, 260, 322
    surveys, campaign use of: 187, 223–228
    uranium mining, position on: 213–215
Australian Labor party (ALP):
    1977 election results, impact: 9–10
    abortion, policy on: 76
    anticipation of early election: 77–78, 202–204, 232–233
    blockage of supply crisis, 1975: 4–5, 16
    budget, 1975: 294–295
    campaign expenditures: 330
    campaign mismanagement: 78–80, 82–85, 242–244, 265
    campaign strategy: 251–254
    candidate selection: 89
    Catholic voters' support, decline in: 38
    constituency: 64
    cube rule, impact of: 313–314
    demoralization, 1975–1977: 65–66
    economic policies: 12–13, 78, 217, 233, 288–291
    failures in office: 291, 296–298, 329
    financial problems: 79–80
    future prospects: 88–91, 140
    history and practices: 67–69
    ideology: 49, 67, 96

immigrant groups, support from: 41–43
Iraqi proposed campaign donations: 73, 143, 329
leadership, opinion polls on: 205, 217–220
leadership conflicts: 69–71, 85–86, 204–205
media advertising by: 255–256
opinion poll ratings: 143–147, 155–161, 191–192
payroll tax, proposed abolition: 291–293
platform revision: 74–77
policies, 1960s: 126
policies, 1970s: 128
pollsters, regard for: 204–205
preference distribution, Senate elections: 325
redistribution, attitude towards: 307
redistribution, effects of: 111, 309–310
strength of party identification: 30–32
strengths at state level: 87–88
surveys, campaign use of: 78–79, 186–187, 204–211
surveys, expenditures for: 229
tariff policy: 244–245
tax indexation: 243–244, 295–296
unemployment, use of polls on: 215–217
union affiliation: 24, 86–88
uranium policy: 77, 211–215, 246–248
Vietnamese refugees, policy toward: 245–246
young voters, support from: 43–44
see also: Whitlam, Gough E.
Australian Nationwide Opinion Poll (ANOP): see Opinion polls
Australian Public Opinion Poll (APOP): see Opinion polls

Balance of payments: 15, 249, 274–275
Ballots:
  recounts: 335
  valid and invalid: 327, 328
  samples: 344–345
Beazley, Kim: 66
Bjelke-Petersen, Johannes: 9, 115, 300
Bland, Sir Henry: 143–144
Bolte, Sir Henry: 13, 114
Bowen, Lionel: 72, 85
Brachen, Barry: 228
Broadcasting: see Mass media

Broadcasting and Television Act: 154
"Broadcasting blackout": 154n, 247n
Budget:
  as campaign issue: 197, 206, 207
  Liberal budget, August 1977: 144–145, 240, 270–271
Bury, Leslie: 105
Business and Consumer Affairs Department: 282
Button, John: 86

Cabinet, economic responsibilities of: 280–281
Cairns, Jim: 65, 66
Cairns Post: 243
Call to Australia party: 323
Calwell, Arthur A.: 71, 126, 301
Cameron, Clyde: 65, 85, 297
Campaign advertising: see Mass media
Campaign expenditures:
  ALP: 330
  controls, suggested: 329, 330
  legal allowances: 328–329
  Liberal party: 330
  records, inaccessibility of: 327–328
  surveys, expenditures for: 229–230
Campaign issues:
  August 1977 budget: 197, 206, 207
  balance of payments: 15, 249
  constitutional crisis of 1975: 15–16
  criteria for: 12, 167–168
  distinctiveness of party policy on, importance of: 172–178
  economic policies: 249, 275–278
  foreign affairs: 15
  health insurance costs: 249
  inflation: 168, 171, 199
  labor relations: 206–210
  "Lynch affair": 13, 82, 113–114, 195–196, 234–239
  Medibank: 143, 168
  as not indicative of voter's party choice: 181–182
  parties' handling of: 119–124
  party leadership: 14
  public ratings of, table: 169–170
  report on sexual behavior: 249–250
  tariff policy: 244–245
  taxation: 12–13, 168, 172, 179–181, 199–201, 239–244
  tax indexation: 243–244, 295–296
  unemployment: 12, 215–217
  union strikes: 197–199, 206–210
  uranium: 15, 83, 143, 145, 246–248
  Vietnamese refugees: 245–246
  see also: Opinion polls

360

Campaign strategies: 17–18
  ALP: 251–254, 262–265
  Country party: 115–117, 253
  Liberal party: 111–115, 117–118, 251–252, 254, 261–265
Canberra Times: 329, 330
Candidate selection, ALP: 89
Carige, Colin: 221
Cassell, Barry: 221
Cattlemen's Union: 134
Chifley, Ben: 13n, 306, 315
Chipp, Don: 8, 11, 16, 135, 253, 322
  election to Senate: 134, 325
  media coverage of: 138, 259
  personal and political background: 109, 127–128, 232
  surveys, campaign use of: 223–224, 226–228
  uranium mining, opposition to: 215
  see also: Australian Democrats
Civil service: *see* Public service
Coalition government: *see* Fraser coalition government
Combe, David: 78–80, 143, 330
  analyses of ALP position: 217, 218, 244
  anticipation of early election: 77, 202–204
  campaign planning: 212, 213, 252
Commonwealth Electoral Act: 20
Commonwealth Employees (Employment Provisions) Act: 198, 206, 209
Communist party: 125
Compton Advertising agency: 221
Compulsory voting: 2, 251
Connor, R.F.X.: 192
Constituencies: *see* Electorates
Constitutional crisis: 4, 15–16
Corporations, affiliation with Liberal party: 24–25
Cotton, Robert: 281
Country party (NCP):
  campaign issues and techniques: 115–117, 253
  constituency: 40–41, 103–104
  expenditures for surveys: 229
  ideology: 96, 97, 99–100
  redistribution, effects of: 103, 111, 118
  strength of party identification, table: 31
  structure: 103
  surveys, campaign use of: 187, 220–223
Court of Disputed Returns: 335
Crean, Frank: 66, 72, 291

"Cube rule": 313–314
Curtin, John: 312

Daly, Fred: 317
Dart, Bill: 224, 226
"Declaration of the Poll": 335
Democratic Labor party (DLP): 8, 11, 31, 125, 140
  constituency: 39, 139
  ideology: 126
  preference distribution, 1977 House elections, table: 320
Department of: *see specific department names*
Devaluation policy: 268–269
DLP: *see* Democratic Labor party
Dunstan, Don:
  abortion, position on: 76
  popularity: 9, 215, 219
  uranium policy: 214, 247, 248

Economic policy:
  ALP platform: 288–291
  anti-inflationary policies, 1976: 267–268
  budget, August 1977: 144–145, 240, 270–271
  cabinet influences on: 280–283
  as campaign issue: 249, 275–278
  devaluation: 268–269
  exchange rate: 271
  interest rates: 277
  Liberal ideology: 278–280
  national economy, state of, November 1977: 272–275
  political factors affecting: 283–284
  price freeze: 269–270
  public service influence on: 281–282
  Reserve Bank influence on: 281, 282
  structural aspects of: 288
  tariffs: 271
  tax cuts versus payroll tax abolition: 291–293
  tax indexation: 295–296
  youth employment: 271–272
Eggleton, Tony: 107, 187–188, 191, 193, 196, 202
Election procedures:
  compulsory voting: 2, 251
  cube rule: 313–314
  declaration of the poll: 335
  disputed returns: 335
  how-to-vote cards: 328, 347–351
  and informal voting: 327, 328

361

proportional representation: 2, 313–316, 323, 333
recount of ballots: 335
single transferable vote: 2
two-party-preferred vote: 10n
weighting of votes: 20
see also: Preferential voting
Election results:
   analyses: 7–8, 10–11, 330–332
   informal voting, level in 1977 elections: 327, 328
   state elections, AD party gains: 131–134
   see also: House elections; Senate elections
Elections, early:
   opinion polls on: 147–149
   opposition to: 191
Electoral Act of 1946: 328–330
Electoral districts: see Electorates
Electoral system: 2–3
Electorate:
   American and British electorates compared: 28–29, 51–52
   attitude toward roles of political leaders: 22–24
   consensus in: 61–63
   dissatisfaction with political system: 24–25
   ideology: 48–52
   immigrant groups' preferences: 41–43
   interest in politics: 20–22
   national characteristics: 19, 26–28
   party loyalty: 28–33
   preference changes: 44–48
   religious affiliation and partisanship: 38–40
   rising level of education: 25–26
   rural/urban cleavage: 39–41
   social class perceptions: 34–38
   values and partisanship: 52–61, 63–64
   young voters' preferences: 43–44
Electorates:
   House results in, map: 303
   NCP organization in: 103
   range of swing in: 11
   see also: Redistribution
"Electronic blackout": 154n, 247n
Electronic media: see Mass media
Employment and Industrial Relations Department: 282
Evans, Huw: 236
Evatt, H.V.: 71
Exchange rate: 271

Fadden, Arthur: 100
Federal elections: see Election results; House elections; Senate elections
Foreign Affairs Department: 282
Foreign policy:
   as campaign issue: 15
   Fraser policies: 109–110
Fraser coalition government:
   ALP tariff policy, campaign issue of: 244–245
   budget of August 1977: 144–145, 240, 270–271
   campaign financing proposal: 330
   economic policies: 12–13, 109, 266–272, 275–278, 295–296
   foreign policies: 109–110
   "Lynch affair": 9, 13, 82, 113–114, 195–196, 234–239
   opinion poll ratings: 143–147, 155–161, 192
   policies, factors influencing: 280–284, 287
   tax cut proposals: 239–243
   tax indexation: 295–296
   uranium policy: 197, 215, 248
   Victoria strike, impact: 197–199, 210
   see also: Fraser, Malcolm; Liberal party
Fraser, Malcolm:
   campaign patterns: 261–263
   "caretaker" prime minister, appointment as: 4, 5, 65
   economic views: 286–287
   media management by: 110–111, 233, 262
   opinion poll ratings: 182–184, 192, 200–202, 217–218
   overseas trips: 143, 144
   personal financial assets: 238
   policy speech: 266
   political style: 8, 14, 280, 311
   rise to power: 6–7, 108
   sexual behavior report, comments on: 249
   synchronization of House and Senate elections, attempt: 5–7, 231–232
   see also: Fraser coalition government; Liberal party

Gair, Vince: 71
Gallup, George: 195
Gallup polls: see Opinion polls
Garland, Vic: 203
Gorton, John: 6, 102, 107, 110
Groom, Ray: 312

Half-Senate elections: *see* Senate elections
Hall, Steele: 325–326
Harradine, Brian: 326
Hartley, Bill: 143
Hawke, Bob: 72, 82, 83, 210, 219
Hay, Andrew: 235–236
Hayden, Bill: 82, 83, 90, 312
 abortion, position on: 76
 as ALP leader, support for: 7, 72, 73, 85–86, 204, 205
 economic policies and responsibilities: 13, 75, 78, 233, 242–244
 media coverage of: 263
 personal financial assets: 239
 popularity: 219–220
 tax system reform: 85, 295, 296
Headey, Bruce: 54
Health insurance: 249
Herald survey: *see* Opinion polls
Holt, Harold: 105, 107, 126, 301
Holten, R.M.: 221
House elections:
 1977 results, by state tables: 353–354
 analyses of: 118–120, 124, 299–305
 Australian Democrats' impact on: 134–139
 cube rule, impact on seats won: 313–314
 forecast errors, table: 163
 party distribution by state, tables: 119, 301
 preferential voting system: 2–3, 316–322, 334–335
 proportionate and cube-rule election systems, impact on seats won: 313–316
 results by district, map: 303
 swing to ALP, 1975–1977, table: 305
 see also: Senate elections
House of Representatives:
 as "people's house": 19
 representation in: 20
 safeness of seats: 310–312
 seat distribution: 305, 306
 Tasmania, overrepresentation of: 306
How-to-vote cards:
 necessity: 328
 samples: 347–350
Howard, John: 258, 281, 311
Hunt, Ralph: 249
Hurford, Chris: 13, 78, 220, 243, 296

Immigrants, partisanship of: 41–43
Immigration and Ethnic Affairs Department: 282
Indexation: *see* Taxation
Industry and Commerce Department: 282
Inflation:
 adverse impacts of: 285–286
 as campaign issue: 168, 199
 Fraser anti-inflationary policies, 1976: 267–268
 opinion polls on: 149–152, 171
 reduction in: 272–273, 291
 rise, 1973–1974, reasons for: 297
Informal voting: 327, 328
Interest rates: 277
International affairs: 15, 109–110
Iraqi loans affair: 73, 143, 329

Kemp, David: 190, 198
Kerr, Sir John: 9, 15, 144
 dismissal of Whitlam: 4, 65
 opinion polls on: 188n
Killen, Jim: 245

Labor party: *see* Australian Labor party
Labor relations, as campaign issue: 206–210
Landeryou, Bill: 235
Lang Labor party: 125
Leadership: *see* Party leadership
Leake, Peter: 234
Liberal Movement: 125, 126
Liberal-National Country party (L-NCP):
 economic policy: 295
 internal friction: 104–106, 126–127
 see also: Fraser coalition government
Liberal party:
 1972 defeat, impact: 106–107
 campaign expenditures: 330
 campaign strategy: 111–115, 117–118, 251–252, 254, 261–265
 constituency: 102–103
 corporations affiliation: 24–25
 "dial-a-tax-cut" plan: 113, 257–258
 economic ideology: 278–280
 ideology: 49, 96–100
 leadership struggles: 107–108
 media advertising by: 256–258
 Menzies's role: 108
 ongoing surveys: 187–188
 pre-campaign surveys: 188–191
 redistribution, attitude toward: 307
 redistribution, effects of: 309–310
 return to power, 1975: 108–109

Snedden leadership and defeat: 107–108
strength of party identification, table: 31
structure and organization: 100–103
surveys, campaign use of: 186, 191–202
surveys, expenditures for: 229
Vietnamese refugees, policy toward: 246
see also: Fraser coalition government; Fraser, Malcolm
Liberal Reform Group: 125–126
Little, Graham: 190
Lynch, Phillip R.:
administrative role: 144, 281
illness: 13, 235–236, 239
personal financial affairs, investigation into: 113–114, 234–237
resignation: 9, 13, 82, 195–196, 237–238
Lyons, Joseph: 101

Mackeller, Michael: 246
Macroeconomic policy: *see* Economic policy
Marijuana party: 325
Masius, Wynne-Williams agency: 188–189
Mason, Colin: 134, 325
Mass media:
AD coverage by: 259-261
"broadcasting blackout": 154n, 247n
campaign coverage: 17–18, 231–234, 261–264
campaign strategy and: 117–118, 251–254
Fraser use of: 110–111, 233, 262
"Lynch affair" investigations: 113–114, 234–239
opinion polls, media coverage: 152–154, 250–251
paid campaign advertising in: 254–258
radio talk-back shows: 262–263
sexual behavior report, publication of: 249–250
tax proposals, presentation of: 242–244
uranium issue, coverage: 247–248
Mathews, Russell: 294
McClelland, Doug: 203
McEwen, Sir John: 105, 107
McMahon, William: 105, 107, 292, 297, 330

McNair Gallup poll: *see* Opinion polls
Media: *see* Mass media
Medibank: 143, 168
Menzies, Sir Robert: 6, 8, 97, 100, 101, 107, 108, 306
Millhouse, Robin: 131, 133
Ministers, economic responsibility of: 280–281
Minor parties:
as ideological alternatives: 125–127
underrepresentation in House: 20
Morgan, Gary: 157, 179, 189, 193
Morgan Gallup poll: *see* Opinion polls
Morgan Research Center: 187–189
Mullins, Clark, and Ralph agency: 206
Mulvihill, Tony: 246
Murdoch, Rupert: 242

National Alliance: 125
National Country party (NCP): *see* Country party
National elections: *see* Election results; House elections; Senate elections
National party: 100–101
National Resources Department: 282
National Times: 212
Nazi party: 325
NCP (National Country party): *see* Country party
Negus, George: 196
New Liberal Movement: 125, 126, 131
Newman, Kevin: 312
Newspapers: *see* Mass media
Nile, Fred: 323
Nixon, Peter: 281, 312
Non-Labor coalition: *see* Fraser coalition government; Liberal-National Country party

Oakes, Laurie: 197
Opinion polls:
1977 election predictions: 141–142
analysis of forecasting errors: 163–167
on association between class self-placement and party identification: 35–38
on attitudes toward early election: 147–149
and compulsory voting: 251
data analysis methods: 187
on distribution of power and influence: 25
election forecasts, October–December 1977: 161–163

on electorate's support of political parties: 21
expenditures for: 229–230
on extent of power of unions and corporations: 24–25
forecast errors: 161–163
on Fraser and government: 143–147, 155–161, 182–184, 192, 200–202, 217–218
on identification with social class: 34–35
on inflation: 149–152, 171
on Kerr: 188n
media coverage of data: 152–154, 250–251
organizations conducting polls in 1977: 141–142
on party identification: 29–33
political parties' use of: 186–187
polling patterns: 142–143, 152–154
questions asked: 148n, 154–155
on relationship of religion and party identification: 38–40
role in election campaigns: 16–17, 185–186, 229–230
on role of political leaders: 22–24
showing trends in party support: 143–147, 155–161, 191–192
survey methods: 192–195
types of: 142
on unemployment: 149–152, 168, 171, 189–191, 197
on uranium: 168, 172, 173, 197, 211–215
on voter intentions, tables: 45, 156, 160, 161
voters' economic assessments, tables: 176–178, 180
on Whitlam: 182–184, 192, 200–202, 205, 217–220, 251
see also: Campaign issues
Overseas Trade Department: 282

Parliament: see House of Representatives; Senate
Party identification: see Electorate
Party leadership:
ALP struggles: 69–71, 85–86, 204–205
as campaign issue: 14
Liberal party: 107–108
as linked to party power: 22–23
opinion polls on: 205, 217–220
Party system:
historical development: 94–96
overview: 92–96

state party organizations, role of: 93
ties with unions and corporations: 24–25
Payroll tax: see Taxation
Peacock, Andrew: 127, 246
Perth conference, July 1977: 74–77
Polls: see Opinion polls
Preferential voting: 2–3, 316–317
in House elections: 317–322
procedures: 333–335
in Senate elections: 323–327
Premiers' Conference, April 1977: 269
Press: see Mass media
Price and wage freeze: 269–270
Primary Industry Department: 282
Prime Minister and Cabinet, Department of: 282
Prime minister, authority of: 280
Progress party: 125, 126, 134
preference distribution, 1977 elections: 319, 325
surveys, campaign use of: 187, 228–229
Proportional representation: 2, 313–316, 323, 333
Protection policy: see Tariff policy
Public opinion polls: see Opinion polls
Public service:
advisory position on economic policy: 281–282
penalties for strikes by: 206–208

Queensland Labor party: 125

Radio broadcasting: see Mass media
Rawlinson, Martin: 187, 188, 193
Reason, Len: 179, 180, 188, 191, 250–251, 257, 258, 265
Recount of ballot: 335
Redistribution: 11, 203
background and rules for: 305–309
effects on parties' prospects: 103, 111, 118, 221, 309–310
Redistricting: see Redistribution
Religion, and party identification: 38–40
Report of the Royal Commission on Human Relationships: 249
Reserve Bank of Australia: 281, 282, 297
Robinson, Claude: 195
Rural/urban cleavage in electorate: 39–41

365

Santamaria, Bob: 260
Saulwick *Age* poll: see Opinion polls
Senate:
:   blockage of supply crisis, 1975: 4–5, 16
:   membership: 306
Senate elections:
:   1977 results, by state, table: 355–356
:   analysis of: 322–327
:   preferential voting system: 2, 323–327, 333–334
:   proportional representation: 2, 323
:   synchronization with House elections, attempt by Fraser: 5–7, 231–232
:   see also: House elections
Senate Vacancies Amendment: 9
Sheppard, Richard: 283
Sinclair, Ian: 281
Single transferable vote: 2
Singleton, John: 228
Socialist party: 325
Snedden, Bill: 105, 110
:   economic policy: 279, 283
:   leadership and defeat: 6, 107–108
Spectrum Research: 221
Staley, Tony: 312
State elections: see Election results; House elections; Senate elections
Stone, Gerald: 248
Street, Tony: 189, 281
Strikes, as campaign issue: 197–199, 206–210
Surveys: see Opinion polls
Swan, Trevor: 294
Sydney Morning Herald: 191–192

Tariff policy:
:   as campaign issue: 244–245
:   Liberal policies: 271, 276
Taxation:
:   as campaign issue: 12–13, 168, 172, 179–181, 199–201
:   indexation: 243–244, 295–296
:   media campaign coverage: 242–244
:   payroll tax abolition versus tax cuts: 239–244, 291–293
:   tax cuts: 275–276
Television broadcasting: see Mass media
Townley, Rudge: 326
Trade unions: see Unions
Transport Department: 282
Treasury Department:
:   economic policy: 284–286
:   influence on economic policy formation: 282–283
:   treasurer's authority: 281
Two-party-preferred vote: 10n

Unemployment:
:   as campaign issue: 12, 215–217
:   increases in: 274, 291
:   opinion polls on: 149–152, 168, 171, 189–191, 197
:   rise in 1974, reasons for: 297–298
Unions:
:   affiliation with ALP: 24, 86–88
:   labor relations as campaign issue: 206–210
:   Victoria strike, impact on election: 197–199, 210
United Australia party: 101, 119
Uranium:
:   ALP policy: 77, 211–215, 246–248
:   as campaign issue: 15, 83, 143, 145, 246–248
:   opinion polls on: 168, 172, 173, 197, 211–215
Urban/rural cleavage in electorate: 39–41
Uren, Tom: 72, 85, 86, 214, 247

Victoria:
:   land deals: 196, 234–235
:   maintenance workers' strike, impact on election: 197–198, 210
Vietnamese refugees, as campaign issue: 245–246
Viner, Ian: 311
Voting: see Election procedures; Preferential voting

Wage and price freeze: 269–270
Weighting of votes: 20
Wentworth, W.C.: 325
Whitlam, Gough E.: 16, 23, 77
:   campaign patterns: 262–263
:   defense of Labor platform: 75
:   dismissal by Kerr: 4, 5, 65
:   leadership criticized and challenged: 7, 14, 65–66, 71–74
:   "Lynch affair," campaign use of: 235, 238–239
:   opinion poll ratings: 182–184, 192, 200–202, 251
:   payroll tax, proposed abolition: 217, 240–242
:   personal financial assets: 238–239
:   policy speech, 1977: 80–82
:   preferential voting, attitude toward: 316–317

resignation of party leadership: 8, 85, 301
sexual behavior report, comments on: 249–250
style of governing: 6, 71
see also: Australian Labor party
Willis, Ralph: 82, 217

Willis, Sir Eric: 191n
Withers, Reg: 307
Workers' party: 125, 126, 228
Wran, Neville: 76, 219, 249
Wriedt, Ken: 86

Young, Mick: 203, 218, 230

REFERENDUMS

A Comparative Study of Practice and Theory

Edited by David Butler and Austin Ranney

This study has come at a time when the use of popular referendums to express dissatisfaction with the responsiveness and sagacity of elected representatives is increasing in several nations around the world. The "taxpayers' revolt" in America has been waged largely through referendums, like the one California held on Proposition 13. Scotland and Wales voted not to increase their autonomy, and Quebec and Puerto Rico announced their intention to hold referendums on home rule.

The editors assembled studies of referendums in Australia, California, France, Ireland, Scandinavia, Switzerland, the United Kingdom, and the United States. On the basis of these studies they offer conclusions about why referendums are held, whether they tend to produce conservative or liberal policies, and how they affect the institutions and health of representative democracy. The contributors, besides Butler and Ranney, are Jean-François Aubert, Eugene C. Lee, Don Aitkin, Vincent Wright, Sten Sparre Nilson, and Maurice Manning.

1979/250 pp./$4.75

Contents of

Australia at the Polls:
The National Elections of 1975

Edited by Howard R. Penniman

Published by the American Enterprise Institute

Price: $5.00

PREFACE

---

1 THE AUSTRALIAN POLITICAL SYSTEM Leon D. Epstein

The National Setting/Federalism and the Constitution/The National Government/Parties/Elections/Constitutional Crisis

---

2 THE RISE AND FALL OF WHITLAM LABOR: THE POLITICAL CONTEXT OF THE 1975 ELECTIONS Patrick Weller and R. F. I. Smith

Changing Political Patterns/Liberal-Country Party Government in the 1960s/The Rise of Whitlam Labor/June 1974 to June 1975:/The Beginning of the End/June to November 1975: The Decline and Fall of the Labor Government

---

3 THE LABOR CAMPAIGN D. W. Rawson

The ALP: Traditions and Innovations/The Course of the Campaign/The Trade Unions/Finances—Before and After

---

4 THE LIBERAL PARTY Michelle Grattan

The Background/The Liberals in Opposition/The Liberal Campaign/Victory and Its Aftermath

---

5 THE COUNTRY PARTY Margaret Bridson Cribb

Organization/The Country Party between 1970 and 1975/The Campaign/Conclusion

---

6 THE ROLE OF THE MINOR PARTIES Paul Reynolds

Minor-Party Formation/Minor-Party Survival/1975: A Watershed

7 **THE MEDIA AND THE ELECTIONS** *C. J. Lloyd*
The Australian Mass Media/The Buildup to the 1975 Campaign/Bias and the Journalists' Strike/The Media and the Campaign/Some Final Thoughts

8 **OPINION POLLING AND THE ELECTIONS**
Terence W. Beed
A Concentrated Press and a Concentrated Population/The Record of Australian Opinion Polls/The 1975 Election/Conclusion

9 **AUSTRALIA'S FOREIGN POLICY AND THE ELECTIONS OF 1972 AND 1975** *Owen Harries*
Background to 1972/The Whitlam Years/The Return of the Coalition/Conclusion

10 **THE ELECTORATE SPEAKS—AND AFTER**
Colin A. Hughes
Long-Term Electoral Patterns/Electoral Patterns in 1975/Labor's Prospects/The Broad Implications of 1975

APPENDIX A Politics and the Constitution: Twenty Questions Left by Remembrance Day *David Butler*

APPENDIX B The Vote and the Count

APPENDIX C A Summary of Australian National Election Results, 1972–75 *Richard M. Scammon*

CONTRIBUTORS

INDEX

AEI's *At the Polls* Studies

In addition to this volume, the following titles have been published by the American Enterprise Institute as part of the *At the Polls* series, a collection of studies dealing with national elections in selected democratic countries.

Australia at the Polls: The National Elections of 1975, Howard R. Penniman, ed. (373 pp., $5)

Britain at the Polls: The Parliamentary Elections of 1974, Howard R. Penniman, ed. (256 pp., $3)

Britain Says Yes: The 1975 Referendum on the Common Market, Anthony King (153 pp., $3.75)

Canada at the Polls: The General Elections of 1974, Howard R. Penniman, ed. (310 pp., $4.50)

France at the Polls: The Presidential Elections of 1974, Howard R. Penniman, ed. (324 pp., $4.50)

Germany at the Polls: The Bundestag Election of 1976, Karl H. Cerny, ed. (251 pp., $4.75)

India at the Polls: The Parliamentary Elections of 1977, Myron Weiner (150 pp., $3.75)

Ireland at the Polls: The Dáil Elections of 1977, Howard R. Penniman, ed. (199 pp., $4.75)

Israel at the Polls: The Knesset Elections of 1977, Howard R. Penniman, ed. (333 pp., $6.75)

Italy at the Polls: The Parliamentary Elections of 1976, Howard R. Penniman, ed. (386 pp., $5.75)

Japan at the Polls: The House of Councillors Election of 1974, Michael K. Blaker, ed. (157 pp., $3)

A Season of Voting: The Japanese Elections of 1976 and 1977, Herbert Passin, ed. (199 pp., $5.75)

Scandinavia at the Polls: Recent Political Trends in Denmark, Norway, and Sweden, Karl H. Cerny, ed. (304 pp., $5.75)

Studies are forthcoming on 1977 elections in Greece; 1978 elections in Colombia, France, New Zealand, and Venezuela; 1979 elections in Canada, Britain, Italy, and Sweden; the 1977 and 1979 elections in Spain; and the elections to the European Parliament in 1979.

LIBRARY OF DAVIDSON COLLEGE

Books on regular loan may be checked out for **two weeks**. Books must be presented at the Circulation Desk in order to be renewed.

A fine is charged after date due.

Special books are subject to special regulations at the discretion of the library staff.